Robert Ellis Thompson

**Elements of Political Economy**

With Especial Reference to the Industrial History of Nations

Robert Ellis Thompson

**Elements of Political Economy**
*With Especial Reference to the Industrial History of Nations*

ISBN/EAN: 9783744645102

Printed in Europe, USA, Canada, Australia, Japan

Cover: Foto ©Suzi / pixelio.de

More available books at **www.hansebooks.com**

# ELEMENTS

OF

# POLITICAL ECONOMY

WITH SPECIAL REFERENCE TO THE

# INDUSTRIAL HISTORY OF NATIONS.

BY

ROBERT ELLIS THOMPSON, M.A.,

PROFESSOR OF SOCIAL SCIENCE IN THE UNIVERSITY OF PENNSYLVANIA,
AND MEMBER OF THE AMERICAN PHILOSOPHICAL SOCIETY.

---

"The true greatness of kingdoms and estates, and the means thereof, is an argument fit for great and mighty princes to have in their hand; to the end that neither by overmeasuring their forces, they lose themselves in vain enterprises, nor on the other side, by undervaluing them, they descend to fearful and pusillanimous counsels."—*Lord Bacon.*

PHILADELPHIA:
PORTER & COATES.

Copyright by PORTER & COATES, 1875.

Copyright by PORTER & COATES, 1882.

# PREFACE.

This work forms a third and revised edition of the author's "Social Science and National Economy," published in 1875, and in a revised edition in the following year. The author retains his preference for the earlier title, but the general use of the term Political Economy to designate this science renders it desirable to make this change.

The author of this book has had a twofold purpose in its preparation,—*first*, to furnish a readable discussion of the subject for the use of those who wish to get some knowledge of it, but have neither the time nor the inclination to study elaborate or voluminous works; *secondly*, and more especially, to provide a text-book for those teachers—in colleges and elsewhere—who approve of our national policy as in the main the right one, and who wish to teach the principles on which it rests and the facts by which it is justified. Of course the book is not exactly what it would have been had either of these purposes been kept singly in view. Some explanations are given, which are here only because this is meant to be a text-book; there are discussions of a political kind, for instance, in the second chapter, whose presence is necessitated by the fact that no specific instruction in political philosophy is ordinarily given in our college courses, and the teacher of

National Economy cannot always assume that his classes are already familiar with the conception of *the state* in its full significance. On the other hand, in the closing chapters, what the theological controversialists used to call "the present truth" has been stated and defended with a fulness which would ordinarily be needless in a text-book, and it is suggested that in the use of those chapters a selection be made, and the rest omitted. But it is believed that nothing has been inserted, and it is hoped that nothing has been omitted, whose insertion or omission will interfere with either purpose of the book.

The form of the book is entirely different from the ordinary arrangement under the three rubrics, "Production, Distribution and Consumption." The method pursued of itself excludes that artificial and symmetrical distribution of its parts which—the author believes—sacrifices life and reality to system. Whatever interest or other merits the book possesses it owes to the method which underlies its construction. In so far as the author has succeeded in being faithful to that method, he must have succeeded also in showing that this science is not one that is "up in the clouds," but one that touches on human life and the world's history at all points.

The author has had access to the library of the late Stephen Colwell, Esq., now in possession of the University, and only regrets that he has not been able to use its treasures more freely. It contains some eight thousand books and pamphlets, whose collection occupied Mr. Colwell's leisure till his death in 1869, and it embraces nearly every important book, periodical or pamphlet on the subject, that had appeared in the English, French or Italian languages, besides a large number in German and Spanish.

Of the books that the author has drawn upon, the writings of Mr. Henry C. Carey hold the first place. Then come those of his school—Dr. Wm. Elder, Hon. E. Peshine Smith (especially in chapter III.), Dr. E. Dühring (chapter I.) and Stephen Colwell (chapter VIII.). Free use has also been made of the writings of Sir Henry S. Maine and Rev. E. Mulford (chapter II.), W. R. Greg (chapter IV.), Cliffe Leslie, Maine, and E. Laveleye (chapter V.), W. T. Thornton (chapter VII.), R. H. Patterson (chapter VIII,), J. Noble (chapter IX.), and Edward Young (chapter XII.). Other authorities are specified in the notes appended to various paragraphs.

For the correction of many small and some large errors, and for suggestions which have contributed to whatever completeness of discussion or other merits the book possesses, the author is greatly indebted to the kindness of Cyrus Elder, Esq., of Johnstown, to Joseph Wharton, Esq., and especially to his friend Wharton Barker, Esq., to whose encouragement this book owes its existence.

*University of Pennsylvania.*

# CONTENTS.

### CHAPTER I.
DEFINITION AND HISTORY OF THE SCIENCE.................. 11

### CHAPTER II.
THE DEVELOPMENT OF SOCIETY.—THE NATION............. 32

### CHAPTER III.
WEALTH AND NATURE............................................. 41

### CHAPTER IV.
THE SCIENCE AND ECONOMY OF POPULATION................ 49

### CHAPTER V.
THE NATIONAL ECONOMY OF LAND............................ 70

### CHAPTER VI.
THE NATIONAL ECONOMY OF LAND (*continued*).—HOW THE EARTH WAS OCCUPIED.................................... 101

### CHAPTER VII.
THE NATIONAL ECONOMY OF LABOR............................ 115

### CHAPTER VIII.
THE SCIENCE AND ECONOMY OF MONEY........................ 142

## CHAPTER IX.

NATIONAL ECONOMY OF FINANCE AND TAXATION ......... 179

## CHAPTER X.

THE SCIENCE AND ECONOMY OF COMMERCE ................... 197

## CHAPTER XI.

THE SCIENCE AND ECONOMY OF MANUFACTURES.—THE THEORY ....................................................................... 219

## CHAPTER XII.

THE SCIENCE AND ECONOMY OF MANUFACTURES.—THE PRACTICE ..................................................................... 267

## CHAPTER XIII.

THE SCIENCE AND ECONOMY OF INTELLIGENCE AND EDUCATION ................................................................... 365

# POLITICAL ECONOMY.

## CHAPTER FIRST.

### Definition and History of the Science.

§ 1. Political or National Economy is that branch of the science of man which treats of man as existing in society, and in relation to his material wants and welfare. It is therefore a subdivision of the science of Sociology, or the science of social relations, which itself is a subdivision of the greater science of Anthropology, or the science of man.

§ 2. It has been objected by some that there can be no such thing as a science of man. "Science," they say, "deals only with things whose actions and reactions can be foretold, after we have mastered the general laws by which they are governed. The test of science, as Comte says, is the power of prediction. There is a science of Chemistry, because there is a possibility of foretelling what compound will be produced by the union of any two elements or known compounds. But man is not governed by laws of that sort; he is a being possessed of affections and a will, which often act in the most arbitrary way,—in a way that no one can foresee or predict."

This objection expresses a truth which can never be left out of sight. If we ignore it we shall miss the conditions under which man's material welfare is to be achieved. Men can never be put to a good use of any sort, while they are regarded or treated as *things*. To do so will be to keep them poor, as well as to degrade them morally; for the best work and the wisest economy can be got out of them, only by bringing their free will into play in the desirable direction.

But the possibility of constructing a science of man does not rest upon the power to foresee the line of action that each individual man will pursue. Man lives in a world which his will did not create, and whose "constitution and course of nature" he cannot change. If he act in violation of its laws, he must take the penalty. Thus if he indulge in habits that contravene the constitution of his moral nature, then moral degradation, unhappiness and remorse will be the necessary results. Because there is such a moral "constitution and course of nature," there is a science of ethics, which enables us to predict, not the conduct of each individual man, but the consequences of such conduct, whatever it may be. And there exists equally for society an economic "constitution and course of nature;" the nation that complies with its laws attains to material well-being or wealth, and the nation that disobeys them inflicts poverty upon itself as a whole, or upon the mass of its people. To learn what those laws are, is the business of the student of social science; to govern a nation according to them is the business of the statesman, and is the *art* of national economy.

While men are beings possessed of a will, they ordinarily act from motives. This is especially true of their conduct in regard to their material welfare; in this connection the same motives act with great uniformity upon almost all men. The same wants exist for all; the same welfare is desired by all; so that in this department of the science of man there is so little caprice, that there is nearly as much power to foresee and foretell what men will do, as in some of the sciences to foresee the actions of things. Nearly, but not quite so much; for while men are agreed as to the *end* here, there is room for difference of opinion as to the *means*, and consequently for variety of action—for wise and unwise ways of procedure.

§ 3. What the science of man and of society lacks in certainty, as compared with the sciences of nature, it more than makes up in the higher interest that it excites. Whatever science deals with our own species and its fortunes, comes very close to each one of us. Whatever it can tell us of the probable future of our nation, or our race, concerns us more than predicted eclipses or chemical discoveries. The most brilliant chemical or astronomical certainty could not move an Englishman so deeply as that bare conjecture of Macaulay, that the time may come "when some traveller from New Zealand shall take his seat on a broken arch of Westminster bridge to sketch the ruins of St. Paul's." The other sciences have an independent value; but they interest us most when we see that they have a bearing upon this, when they open still larger utilities of nature to human possession, and add to the welfare of mankind. We ask the chemist: "Shall the time ever come when we shall no longer be dependent upon our coal deposits for light and warmth, but shall be able to produce both from the decomposition of water?" We ask the physicist: "Shall we soon be able to use this subtle, omnipresent electric force as a motive power? Shall we ever be able to move through the air in manageable balloons, with speed and safety?" These are not the greatest problems that science has to solve, but they have an interest for us all that more abstract questions can never possess.

§ 4. Our Science considers man as existing *in society;* we find him, indeed, nowhere else. The old lawyers and political philosophers talked of a state of nature, a condition of savage isolation, out of which men emerged by the social contract, through which society was first constituted. But no one else has any news from that country; everywhere men exist in more or less perfectly organized society;—they are born into the society of the family without any choice of their own; and they grow up as members of tribes or nations, that grew out of families. All their material welfare rests upon this fact, and must be considered in connection with it. The coöperation by which they emerge from the most utter poverty to wealth, is possible only within society and under its protection. Upon the wise management of its general policy, and the efficiency of its government, the welfare and the security of the individual depend. The natural right to property, by which that welfare is perpetuated from day to day, is realized only in society. The transmission of the things that contribute to material welfare from one generation to another—of real and personal property, of knowledge, skill and methods of industry—would be impossible but for the existence of bodies that outlive the single life, and aim at their own perpetuation. *Vita brevis, ars longa*, or else each new generation would have to begin at the foundation. Hence it is that this science begins with the conception of social state; not with the study of wealth in the abstract, nor of the individual man and his desires.

> At the fall of the civilized societies that made up the ancient world, the useful arts and sciences would have perished in Western Europe with the politics under which they were developed, had not the great Benedictine order gathered both into their monasteries. These were at once schools of learning and industrial establishments, and the only places safe from the barbarous intrusions of half-Christianized barbarians.

§ 5. Political economy is an art as well as a science. The term economy, or house-thrift, does not mean here wise saving, any more than it means wise spending. It is borrowed from the management of the first and simplest of all human societies, the unit out of which all other societies have grown—the family. The adjective *political* prefixed indicates the transfer of the conception of thrift to the society which exists that justice may be done and natural rights be realized, and which for that purpose is put in trust with the lives and the material possessions of the whole people.

§ 6. The *art* of political economy is much older than the *science*. The former came into existence with the first nation, the latter began to be studied about the time of the discovery of America, and first gained a place as a recognised science a century ago. There is nothing unusual in this, for nearly every science lags for a time behind its related art. Themistocles knew "how to make a small city great" long before Plato and Aristotle founded the science of politics. Dyeing, cooking, and a thousand other applications of chemistry were in use from the earliest historic periods; but the first centennial of Dr. Priestley's discovery of oxygen, that laid the foundation of that science, has been celebrated in our own time. Sometimes the two—the science and the art—exist together, with little or no influence upon each other, for a long period. Thus there was for centuries a science of music, taught and studied by men who were not practical musicians; while those that were, pursued their art without giving the slightest heed to the science.

All human experience shows that science can be of the greatest service to its related art. As chemistry has improved and simplified the industrial methods that existed before Priestley and Lavoisier, so the discovery of the economic laws that govern the advance of society in wealth, has greatly changed for the better the economic methods of the nations. Some of the older empirical rules it has vindicated as right; others it has condemned and set aside as wrong; it has suggested new and extended the applications of others that were old. It runs the risk, indeed, of rejecting some methods that were clearly right; and it must guard against this, by making the most careful and thorough survey of all the facts of the case.

In the first stages of a science, which we may call the mechanical, empirical *rules* predominate among the doctrines; but gradually the simpler and far less numerous scientific *principles* that underlie these rules are perceived. When these are once grasped, the process of submitting rules to the test of principles is an easy and safe one. The science has then passed into its dynamical stage.

The ancients knew no science of political or national economy. Commonplace remarks and moralizing reflections on the subject are found scattered here and there through their literatures. Single facts that could hardly escape their notice, such as the advantage of the division of labor, and of the transition from barter to the use of money, and the difference between value and utility, were remarked upon, especially by Aristotle. In these hints lay the possible germs of social science, but they were not followed up, nor the underlying laws investigated.

§ 7. The rivalry excited in other parts of Europe, by the prosperity of Venice and Genoa, first led men to study the subject, and we find it occupying a place in the literatures of Italy and Spain, France and England, from the sixteenth century. The circumstances of the times gave shape to these studies. This was the nationalist period of history. Europe had revolted against all the schemes of a universal monarchy; and independent sovereign kingdoms, with national languages and literatures, and even churches, divided its area among them. That a thing was Spanish or was English, was praise enough in the ears of Spaniard or Englishman. How to aggrandize to the utmost their own country, at whatever expense to others, was the great problem of statesmanship, especially after the religious heats, that had divided Europe into two hostile camps, cooled off somewhat. And of all means to that end, the possession of an abundance of money seemed the best and readiest. After a money-famine that had begun with the Christian era, and had grown in intensity for fifteen centuries, the discovery of America and the East Indies had brought in a vast and sudden supply, which had given Spain for a time an undue preponderance in European politics, and had everywhere bettered the condition of the people. How to acquire it by a foreign trade that would give a balance in favor of our own country,—how to keep it here at home for general circulation and national uses in case of need, was the question. The Mercantile school of writers, as they are now called, set themselves to find methods. As a rule their books were corrective of common errors; they showed that the best way was the indirect way,—to stimulate home industry and have plenty of commodities to sell, not to put a premium on foreign coins and prohibit the export of gold. Theirs was a real science, but in the mechanical stage.

Among the notable writers of this school are Antonio Serra (1613, a Neapolitan); Thomas Munn (*England's Treasure by Foreign Trade*, 1664); Andrew Yarranton (*England's Improvement by Land and Sea*, 1677–81); John Locke (*On the Interest and Value of Money*, 1691 and 1698); Sir

Wm. Petty (*Essays in Political Arithmetic* 1691). The systematic writers are the Abbé Genovesi (*Lezzioni di Commercio e di Economico Civile,* 1765) and Sir James Steuart (*Principles of Political Economy,* 1767). Contemporary opponents are Sir Josiah Child (*Brief Observations concerning Trade,* 1668); le Sieur de Boisguillebert (*Factum de France,* 1712, &c.); Marshal Vauban (*Projet d'une Dîme Royale,* 1707); and J. F. Melon (*Essai Politique sur le Commerce,* 1734.) The opinions of the Mercantile school are wretchedly caricatured by many modern writers.

The new science was as yet a very subordinate branch of the larger subject of politics, and political aims predominated in its treatment of the subject. As we have seen, the questions that it proposed to solve were not of its own suggestion, but were propounded by political leaders. It was not yet strong enough to take the initiative, or to insist on the benefit of an economic policy to the well-being of the people. The final end held in view, both in theory and in practice, was the abundant supply of money for royal coffers, and the practice was far behind the theory. The most absurd financial methods were kept intact if they seemed to subserve this end. Monopolies were created *ad libitum,* and sold to foreigners; the trade between provinces of the same kingdom was burdened with customs-duties, as if between separate kingdoms; the export of grain, as well as of gold, was prohibited, that its price might be kept down; the industry created and fostered with one hand, was crushed under excessive taxation and arbitrary regulations with the other. Even the great Colbert, whose policy was the grandest and most successful illustration of all of the best and some of the worst teachings of the school, died broken-hearted with the ruin of his plans through the royal ambition that wasted the nation's resources in war, and the royal superstition that was robbing France of millions of her best and most industrious citizens.

§ 8. The second school is that of the *Economistes* or *Physiocrates,* founded by Quesnay, the physician and "thinker" of Louis XV. If the mercantile school unduly subordinated the science to the art, the *Economistes* went to the other extreme and made a complete divorce between them. Starting from a few simple ideas as the postulates of the science, they built up a fantastic structure of deductions and theories, that stood in no vital relation to the actual life of society. Their professed aim was to attain a *natural* line of thought, and in that age the "natural" was conceived as the antithesis of civilization, as then existing.

In Quesnay's view nature,—by which he meant the productive powers of the soil,—is the sole source of a nation's wealth; agricultural labor is therefore the only productive industry, all others being sterile. That this labor produces more than the farmer and his household consume, is the origin of all wealth,—which is merely the net-product of his tillage. The values produced by all other labor are measured by the cost of the raw materials and of the workman's food. The web of cotton cloth is but so much raw cotton and so much corn turned into another form, but retaining the same value. The utility of the new form is greater; the amount of wealth the same. From this he inferred that national policy should do nothing to develop such sterile industries as commerce and manufactures, but merely remove all restrictions from agriculture, from the trade in grain, &c. As agriculture alone produces wealth, it alone must, in the last resort, bear all the national burdens, however these may be imposed. Turgot, his chief disciple, divests the theory of much that is fantastic, and in his policy as minister of finance applied for the most part merely its just rejection of the system of monopolies, close corporations, duties on exports, &c.

Quesnay's first book (*Tableau Economique*, 1758) was preceded by articles (on *Fermiers* and *Grains*) in the famous *Encyclopédie* (1756-7). The elder Mirabeau, "the oldest son of the doctrine," wrote much, of which *L'Ami des Hommes* (6 vols., 1755-60) is the best known. His greater son furnished the theoretic part of Mauvillon's voluminous statistical work on *La Monarchie Prussienne* (See § 285). Turgot's chief book is *Réflexions sur la Formation et la Distribution des Richesses* (1766 and 1778). Of the many other writers, none add either to the substance or the clearness of the doctrine. Dr. Franklin, whose visit to France occurred at a time when these opinions were in fashion, became a disciple of Quesnay.

§ 9. The third or Industrial school of economists was founded by Adam Smith, a Scotch professor, and a friend of Quesnay's.

His great work (*An Inquiry into the Nature and Causes of the Wealth of Nations*, 1776, 1778, 1784 and 1788) occupied him for five years. It shows that he was influenced by the *Physiocrates*, yet it is a decided advance upon their teachings. He finds the source of wealth in all the three forms of industry, but gives the first place in point of productiveness to agriculture, the last to foreign commerce; while he classes as unproductive all those forms of human activity that are not directed to the production or exchange of commodities. Tracing the natural growth of the three great industries, through whose association men advance from the poverty of the savage life to material welfare, he pronounces against all efforts of the state to direct and foster any one of the three, as most likely to turn capital out of more into less productive channels. He, like the *Economistes*, would have the State adopt ordinarily a purely passive policy as regards the industrial life of the people. By leaving every man to do what he will with his own, and to use it in whatever way will secure the largest possible returns to himself, society will receive the largest possible benefit. In the principle of free competition he discerns the tap-root of all national industrial life and growth; the enlightened and active selfishness of the individuals who make up society, is the source of general well-being. That which is good for the individual, is good for society also. If there are inequalities of profits or of wages, capital or labor will shift from one channel to another, till things find their natural level.

The chief fault in the book is its failure to fulfil the promise of the title. Promising to discuss "the wealth of *nations*," it practically ignores their existence, and treats the whole question as if there were no such bodies. Smith writes as if the world were all under one government, with no boundary lines to restrain the movement of labor and capital,—no inequalities of national civilization and industrial status, to affect the competition of producer with producer. He ignores, therefore, many of the most important elements of the problem that he undertook to solve. Sharing in the reaction of the Physiocratists against the excessively political drift of the Mercantile school, he also goes to the other extreme, and gives us, not a science of national or political economy, but of cosmopolitical economy, which is not adapted to the actual historical state of the world, but only to a state of things which has not, nor ever will have, any existence.

This way of thinking was the popular one at that period; Europe was in a state of reaction against the nationalist drift of the previous centuries, and did not recover from it until the French Revolution had carried many very pretty theories to their logical consequences, and had shown what they were worth. To be "a citizen of the world" was the ambition of educated men, and many of the foremost minds of Europe—Lessing and Goethe, for instance—formally repudiated the sentiment of patriotism as unworthy of an enlightened civilization.

§ 10. In spite of the great nationalist reaction that began with Burke and Fichte, the cosmopolitan way of thinking has not yet lost its attractions for men. The existence of the cosmopolitical school of economists for nearly a century, and the adhesion given to it by a majority of English, and a great number of Continental and American writers, are a proof of this.

In *France* Jean Baptiste Say reduced the teachings of Smith to a more systematic shape, giving them that clearness of expression and perfection of form for which French literature is famous. In his hands, the cosmopolitanism of the system is complete; his very first title-page dropped the awkward words "of nations," and from this time the abstract conception of wealth, its production, distribution and consumption, became the themes of what was still called "*political* economy." He enlarged the conception of wealth, however, to embrace immaterial as well as material products. Since the passive policy was especially assailed as leading to a foreign trade in which the balance may be unfavorable, he devoted especial attention to the theory of commerce. He was the first to announce that commodities are always paid for in commodities, and that therefore to check the amount of imports is to limit in equal measure the power of export. Later writers of the same nation have, like Say, generally spent their pains in the elaboration of the English theories, without adding much to their substance. Not a single recognised doctrine of the cosmopolitical economists can be traced to a French author since Say, while the French literature, in which those doctrines are defended and enforced, is even larger than the English.

> Chevalier, Rossi, Blanqui and Molinari are the chief French representatives of this school. Bastiat belongs to it in his general tendencies, but his system is a mixture of its doctrines with those of Carey.

In *England* Rev. T. R. Malthus furnished a discussion of the other side of the picture—the poverty of nations (*Essay on Population*, 1798, 1803, 1807, 1817 and 1826). At a time of great political disturbances, when the impoverished classes of Europe were calling the governments to account for the bad policy or no policy that had led to so much misery, this gentleman, a member of the Conservative party, was led to a study of the economic conditions in which that misery originated, that he might close the mouths of agitators by showing that governments had nothing to do with it,—that it was the effect of a cause beyond the control of the ruling classes. He found that cause in the excessive growth of population, which led to the pressure of numbers upon subsistence, and could only be permanently controlled by the self-restraint of the lower classes themselves. This discovery was a godsend to the cosmopolitical school, as it enabled it to tide over a dangerous period of popular agitation, when a thousand circumstances seemed to conspire to enforce upon economists as well as rulers the lesson that governments are put in trust with the national welfare, as well as the national honor and safety, and that no mere passivity of industrial policy could be a sufficient discharge of the trust.

In the view of Mr. Malthus, the condition of the mass of the people oscillates between ease and misery; as soon as any sudden advance in their welfare takes place, there is a rapid increase of numbers through the increase of recklessness as to the future, and then years of scarcity follow hard upon the years of plenty. It was an easy inference that there is a natural rate of wages, a medium between these two oscillations, above which and below which the rate was unstable and could not be permanent. Also that, calling the amount of capital in the country that was available for the wages of labor the wage-fund, the only way to increase the rate of wages was to increase that fund or diminish the number between whom it was to be divided.

Somewhat later, David Ricardo carried the investigation of the subject a step farther, desiring to show the first cause of the inequality of condition that distinguishes different classes of society. Looking through Whig spectacles, as Malthus had looked through Tory ones, he found that inequality to result not from the operation of a natural and unavoidable cause, but from the effects of an artificial monopoly, the tenure of land. The few who have been lucky enough to possess themselves of the best soils at the first settlement of a country, form a privileged class that can live in idleness upon the labor of others, through exacting payment for the use of the natural powers of those soils. This theory—though so different in its motive—was accepted by the school as supplementary to that of Malthus. Both—as they came to be taught—had the merit of showing how the apparent anomalies of society grew out of circumstances either natural or generally accepted as natural; in the last analysis the principle of competition was shown to be the tap-root of industrial phenomena in both cases; both vindicated the passive policy as the only wise one, and argued all national interference to be a fighting against invincible facts.

Mr. Ricardo (following Say and Torrens) also elaborated the theory of international exchanges, in connection with the notion that money is a purely passive instrument of exchanges, changing its purchasing power according to the amount of it that a country possesses. From this it was an easy inference that a drain of money from a country would either have no effect, or would correct itself by so increasing the purchasing power of money in comparison with commodities, as to make the country a bad place to sell in, but a good place to buy in.

With him the constructive period of the English school ends, and, after a time in which the writers are chiefly commentators on the traditional body of doctrines, a critical period begins.

> Ricardo's theory of rent has a great many aspects, according to the side from which it is studied. Did he, like the earliest writers who followed his lead, accept the landlord's monopoly as natural and inevitable, or look upon it as a mischief that society would be well rid of? His dry method of discussion makes it hard to say. Later writers draw from the theory the inference that landed property, as differing from all other property in that its utility is not the product of labor, is especially subject to national control. This is probably more in accord with Ricardo's own motive, as may be inferred from his hostility to the legislation by which the landowner was secured against foreign competition in the grain market. His *Principles of Political Economy and Taxation* (1817) is the last piece of *positive* work of the school,—the crowning of the edifice. McCulloch, James Mill, Chalmers, De Quincey, and many others are his commentators; the later writers, from Senior to Thornton, his critics.

§ 11. About the year 1833 English thinking, and its expression English literature, took a new departure, becoming less dry and mechanical, more fresh, vigorous and genial. Economic literature shared in the impulse. N. W. Senior led off (1835) with a vigorous criticism of both Malthus and Ricardo. He especially emphasized the fact that as political economy considered wealth in the abstract, and excluded all political considerations, it had no right to intrude into the political sphere with its conclusions, and insist on statesmen acting in accordance with them. At the utmost, they could be but one of many considerations that should influence them. The divorce of the science from the art in the English school—a divorce like that which once existed between the science and the art of music—was thus candidly confessed. But this nice distinction, as is commonly the case, was not kept in view by most writers or by the statesmen who took lessons from them.

Thomas Tooke (*History of Prices*, 6 vols., 1838–58) gave a refutation of the theory that money plays a mere passive part in industry, prices rising in proportion to its increase, and falling in proportion to its decrease. He thus indirectly brought into question the theory that an unfavorable balance of trade can be of no injury to the nation.

W. T. Thornton showed that the theory of a natural and necessary rate of wages was not borne out by the facts,—that there is no uniformity but rather the most arbitrary difference in their rate,—that capital can unnaturally depress it below what is right and natural when the workmen stand alone,—and that workmen in combination can raise and have raised it. Consequently the theory of a wage-fund, changing in amount with the growth of capital, and divided *pro rata* among the workmen of a country, is a fiction. He especially exhibited the disastrous effects of English theories upon English agriculture, in separating the mass of the people from the soil and breaking up the small farms to make large ones.

Herbert Spencer (partly anticipated by N. W. Senior and Poulett Scrope, and followed by W. R. Greg) refuted the Malthusian theory by the evidence of facts. He showed that there has been a pressure of population on subsistence in the earliest stages of society and those only, and that with every advance in numbers and the closeness of association, the pressure naturally diminishes.

German and English students of the history of land tenure (*i. e.* Von Maurer, Nasse, Maine and Laveleye) showed that Ricardo's theory of the origin and nature of rent was not sustained by history. In the earliest times contracts for land were unknown, and all payments were determined by custom, not by competition. They showed that the transition from customary status to free contract is the great industrial drift of progressive society; but that the transition is by no means perfect, and that the assumption that it is, whether as made by jurists or by economists, has been a fertile source of wrong to the poorer classes of society.

John Stuart Mill, besides emphasizing Senior's separation of the science from the art, called in question the whole system of the distribution of the products of labor and capital, as an artificial and perhaps dispensable one. Accepting the theories of Malthus and Ricardo, and seeing no augury of a better future for the working classes from the present workings of the wages system, he declared it doomed, unless it proved capable of better things, to pass away. In this he partly followed those socialists, who demand a reconstruction of society and the extension of the sphere of government so as to embrace the direction of industry.

More moderate men, equally convinced of the failure of the system of competition, contract and wages under the existing conditions, hope for a change through the voluntary association of masses of the people, so that they may become their own employers and their own providers.

All these writers have departed from the spirit and the method, as well as the teachings, of the recognised masters of the school. They have reached the conclusions embodied in these criticisms by an inductive study of the actual facts of industrial life, instead of coming at them by a series of deductive inferences from premises assumed at the outset. Prof. J. E. Cairnes undertakes to vindicate both the method and the conclusions (with some unavoidable modifications and extensions) of the older authorities, and to refute the unhappy concessions of these later writers.

§ 12. In America the cosmopolitical school has had many adherents, who have written largely in defence of its doctrines, but none of them are of any importance in a scientific point of view. They have rendered less service, even, than its adherents in France, for while they have added nothing to the substance of the teaching, they have, at the least, not surpassed their English masters in vigor of presentation and artistic form.

<small>Deserving of mention are Condy Raguet, Prof. Thomas Cooper of South Carolina, W. B. Lawrence, Dr. Wayland, the poet Bryant, Prof. A. Walker, Prof. A. L. Perry, and David A. Wells.</small>

§ 13. Within the present generation there has arisen in Europe and America a school whose controlling motive seems to be a reaction against the excesses of the English or cosmopolitical school They are called sometimes the school of the *Kathedersocialisten*, and sometimes the Historical School. To this last title they have no proper right, as, while they reproduce in their books a great number of historical facts, they do not start from the consideration of national life, which is the unit of history. They are cosmopolitan, like the economists they criticise, and, in the absence of any stable principle of economic science, they often carry their destructive criticisms of the older doctrines to an unwarrantable length, assigning to law, custom, and individual idiosyncrasy a reach of influence which leaves no room for any genuine economic science. Yet this new school has been of great service in its criticisms of the unscientific methods of the older economists, and in disputing their claims to have placed their teachings upon a truly scientific footing. It has helped to recall men from the world of theories to that of reality.

> The best known representatives of this school are Prof. Roscher in Germany, Prof. Laveleye in Belgium, Profs. Cliffe Leslie and Ingram in the United Kingdom, and Profs. F. A. Walker, Dunbar, and Bolles in the United States. It has representatives among the economists of every European country.

§ 14. The nationalist school of economists may be traced to later writers and statesmen of America and Germany. Yet we might even claim Adam Smith himself as its founder, for in his happy inconsistencies he gives his sanction to nearly all its principles. A still earlier writer, the great Bishop Berkeley of Cloyne (in his *Querist*, 1735 and 1752), gives suggestions of a line of national policy, and of the economic reasons for it, that give him a clearer as well as a prior claim to the honor. The form of his work, a series of nearly 600 leading questions, has caused it to be neglected; but many of the bishop's notions, especially as to the nature and functions of money, are ahead of current ideas in our age as well as his own. The wretched condition of his native Ireland, its lack of money and of manufactures, furnished the motive to these investigations, while his travels on the Continent and his knowledge of England furnished him with materials for comparison.

Passing by statesmen and state-papers (though Alexander

Hamilton and his famous *Treasury Report* of 1791 deserve mention), we find an early literary champion of the Nationalist school in the great philosopher Fichte. His book (*Der geschlossene Handelsstaat*, 1801), however, is not in strictness an economic treatise, but as its title page tells us, an appendix to his treatise on jurisprudence, and a specimen of a larger treatise on politics. He finds the wealth of the nation in the equilibrium of the three great industries, and regards it as the function of the government to produce and perpetuate it by sufficient legislation. Regarding the interchange of national productions, save of those that cannot be produced in all latitudes, as a remnant of the barbarism and free trade that reigned in Europe before the existing nations had taken shape, he would at once put a stop to it by substituting paper money, current only within national bounds, for the gold and silver that pass current between the nations. As to cosmopolitanism and the possibility of a world-state, it will be time enough to talk of that, when we have really become nations and peoples. In striving to be everything and at home everywhere, we become nothing and are at home nowhere.

Other German philosophers,—Franz Baader (as early as 1790), J. J. Wagner, K. C. F. Krause, K. A. Eschenmayer;—political writers,—Adam Müller, Robert von Mohl;—and economists,—C. A. Struensee, C. F. Nebenius, F. B. G. Herrmann, J. G. Büsch,—with many others, opposed the passivity theory in their writings.

Samuel Taylor Coleridge, the illustrious English poet, critic and philosopher (in his *Lay sermon on the existing Distresses and Discontents*, 1817), without entering into details or proposing any definite economic remedies, deplored the over-balance of the trade spirit in English politics—theoretical and practical; and declared his belief that that spirit is "capable of being at once counteracted and enlightened by the spirit of the state, to the advantage of both." He called in question the maxims received as fundamental by the school, seeing "in them much that needs winnowing. Thus instead of the position that all things find, it would be less equivocal and far more descriptive of the fact, to say that things are always finding, their level;

which might be taken as the paraphrase or ironical definition of a storm. But persons are not things—but man does not find his level." Quite in his spirit, his chief disciple F. D. Maurice speaks (*National Education*, 1839) of "the mass of doctrines going under that name" of political economy, " part of them statements of undoubted facts; part of them useful or curious observations about facts; part of them more or less successful attempts to eliminate laws from facts; part of them crude and heartless apophthegms of morality."

§ 15. It was the sufferings inflicted on Germany by persistence in the policy of passivity after the peace of 1815, that led to a general study of the question, and in Frederick List the German people found one who could state and explain their needs as a nation, and defend a more national policy on scientific grounds. After a course of successful agitation, that laid the foundation of the Zollverein, he came to the United States in 1825, leaving all his books behind him, to study the laws of social growth in the practical examples offered by the new world. As the country was then making rapid advances in wealth, under the protection of a nationalist policy, he had a large field for study, and repaid what he learnt with his *Outlines of American Political Economy* (1827), a brief pamphlet that contains the germ of his larger work, *The National System of Political Economy*, (*Das Nationale System der politischen Œconomie*, 1841; English transl. 1856), which he prepared after his final return to Germany in 1832. The title well describes the book, and List's line of thought. In his view nations are industrial as well as political wholes, characterized by an internal equality of industrial capacity, and destined to advance in wealth and prosperity, when they remove all obstacles to the mutual interchange of services between their own people. If all nations stood on the same ground of equality in numbers, capital and industrial development, no such obstacle would be presented by the freest trade with all other nations; but in the actual historical state, a few possess in their enormous wealth both the power and the will to bring the rest into a state of industrial subordination by the tyrannous power of capital. If, therefore, a poorer nation wishes to have free trade at home, she cannot remain passive as to the direction of the national industry.

§ 16. Of native American writers, a very considerable number defended the nationalist theory of economy, from the beginning of our union into one people, and some even earlier. Of these Alexander Hamilton, Tench Coxe, Matthew Carey and Charles J. Ingersoll deserve mention. But their aim was not to furnish a scientific basis for a national economy, but rather to urge a certain economic policy from reasons of direct and evident utility.

The former work was accomplished by Mr. Henry C. Carey, in whose writings, as we believe, the science of national economy passes out of the mechanical into the dynamical stage, i. e. becomes a true science. Instead of giving us a mass of empirical rules and maxims such as we find in the writings of the mercantile school,—or a mass of fine-spun speculations that stand in no vital relation to the practice and life of nations, as is done by the school of the *Economistes,* and (in a less degree) by that of Adam Smith,—he presents a body of economic teaching, that rests on a few great and simple principles or conceptions, drawn by actual observation from life itself, yet nowhere incapable of direct application to any practical question. These principles are the laws that govern the constitution and course of nature in things economical. They are at once the laws of human nature, and of that external nature, in harmony with which man was created.

Their discovery involves a searching criticism of the very premises of the so-called Industrial School, and of those conclusions that fairly earned the name of "the dismal science." For it shows that these natural laws are laws of progress towards wealth and the equality of wealth. Where they are allowed to act freely and fully, men rise from poverty, isolation and lawlessness, to wealth, association and national order. The history of human economy is the story of man's transition from the savage's subjection to nature, to the citizen's mastery of her forces; and with every advance the greater advantage is reaped by the most numerous class, that is, the poorest. It thus "vindicates the ways of God to men," and vindicates also the existing framework of our civilization against the destructive criticisms of socialists and communists.

And wherever the wretchedness of the savage perpetuates itself or reappears within the sphere of civilization, there is to be seen, not the effects of natural law, but of its violation. There some class—at home or abroad,—through some vicious legislation or defect of legislation, has interfered for selfish ends to hinder the natural progress toward wealth, equality and the harmony of interests in the national equilibrium of industries. To remove such obstacles is the sole function of the state, as regards the active direction of industry.

> Of Mr. Carey's books the chief are *Essay on the Rate of Wages* (1835); *The Past, the Present, and the Future* (1848); *The Harmony of Interests* (1851); *The Slave Trade, Domestic and Foreign* (1853); *Principles of Social Science* (3 vols. 1858); and *The Unity of Law* (1872). Of these and others of his works, translations of one or more have appeared in eight of the principal languages of Europe.
>
> Other members of this school: in America, the late Stephen Colwell (*The Ways and Means of Payment*, 1859), the late Hon. Horace Greeley (*Essays designed to elucidate the Science [Art?] of Political Economy*, 1870); Hon. E. Peshine Smith (*Principles of Political Economy*, 1853 and 1872); and Dr. William Elder (*Questions of the Day, Economical and Social*, 1870). In France, M. Fontenay, Benjamin Rampal and A. Clapier (*De l'Ecole Anglaise et de l'Ecole Américaine en Economie Politique*, 1871). Fred. Bastiat borrowed some of Mr. Carey's ideas (*Harmonies Economiques*, 1850 and 1851) to fight the socialists, and made a curious mixture of these with those of the cosmopolitical school. In Italy the statesman and economist Ferrara gives his adherence to Mr. Carey's first principles, and censures Bastiat for his half discipleship. He has translated the *Principles* into Italian. In Germany Dr. Dühring of the University of Berlin (*Carey's Umwälzung der Volkswirthschaftslehre und Socialwissenschaft*, 1865; *Capital und Arbeit, neue Antworten auf alte Fragen*, 1865; *Die Verkleinerer Carey's, und die Krisis der Nationalökonomie*, 1867; *Kritische Geschichte der Nationalökonomie und Socialismus*, 1871; *Cursus der National- und Socialökonomie*, 1873); and Schultze-Delitzsch, the great antagonist of socialism, and promoter of co-operation (*Capitel zu einem Deutschen Arbeiter-Katechismus*, 1863; *Die Abschaffung des geschäftlichen Risico durch Herrn Lassalle; ein neues Kapitel zum Deutschen Arbeiter-Katechismus*, 1866; besides many smaller works. French trans-

lation of these two by Rampal, 1873.) In England, Judge Byles (*Sophisms of Free Trade*, 1st edition 1849; 9th edition 1870; American edition 1872.)

§ 17. The differences that exist between the two schools is not merely in regard to the details; it is a difference about foundations and first principles. Neither can concede to the teaching of the other the name and rank of a *science*, without giving up its own claim to that name and rank.

The difference is one of *method* also. The English school adopt the deductive method of the mathematical sciences, and reason down from assumed first principles to the specific facts. They claim that the necessary data for this are already at hand, in the known characteristics and tendencies of human nature, the avarice and the desire of progress, which control and direct the economic conduct of great masses of men. They leave all other elements out of account as inconstant, while they regard these as constant. Theirs is therefore "a science based upon assumptions" (*Saturday Review*); it "necessarily reasons from assumptions, and not from facts" (J. S. Mill).

The American and German school apply the inductive method of observation and generalization, which has produced such brilliant results in the natural sciences. They begin with a wide study of the actual working of economical forces, and endeavor to reason upward from the mass of complicated facts to the general laws that underlie and govern all. They begin by recognising the existence of an actual constitution and course of nature, instead of seeking to devise an artificial one on assumed principles.

These differences will be exemplified in the following chapters

## CHAPTER SECOND.

### The Development of Society.—The Nation.

**§ 18.** "Man is a political animal," Aristotle tells us. His nature has not attained its perfection until he is associated with his fellows in an organized body politic. Whatever may be the historical *occasion* of the origin of the state, this fact of man's nature is the sufficient *cause*.

The first type of society is the *family*. This, like the state, is a natural form. It is a relationship not constituted by a reflective act of its constituent parts. No man has a choice as to whether he will or will not be born into a family, though he may by his own act cease to belong to it. Like the state, the family has a moral personality and a distinct life. It is a whole which contains more than is contained in the parts as such; that is, it is an organism, not an accretion.

**§ 19.** The family expanded into the *tribe*. Related or neighboring families held or drawn together by natural affection or neighborly good feeling, or a sense of the need of union for the common defence, but chiefly by the political needs and instincts of their nature, formed an organic whole. By the legal fiction of adoption, all were regarded as members of one family and children of the common patriarch, living or dead. The reverence for the common father whose name they bore became a hero-worship, and bound them together by religious ties. Their living head or chief was regarded as inspired with judgment to pronounce upon disputed cases, which gradually gave rise to a body of judicial rules or laws revered as of divine authority.

**§ 20.** The tribe became—though not always—a city. A hill-fort thrown up for defence against some sudden attack became the rallying-point and then the residence of its people. The conquest or adoption of other tribes added to their numbers and strength, and their home was enclosed by a wall capable of defence. The tribal gods of the first citizens obtained general recognition as the defenders of the city, but those of the newcomers were still worshipped by the clans. The first and the adopted tribes took the place of power, claiming to be "the people," and forming an aristocracy who possessed exclusive knowledge of the laws and religion of the city. Only after prolonged struggle were these published in a code, and places of responsibility opened to the new citizens or *plebs*.

§ 21. By the conquest of other cities, the city in some cases attained an imperial rank. In other cases a number of cities freely united in a league of offence and defence, and ceded their power to make war to a central congress, and established a common treasury. Both movements are in the direction of the nation, the complete form of the state, as the tribe and the city are incomplete forms. The nation is scarcely found in ancient history, save perhaps among the Jews and the Egyptians, and even among them the tribal divisions perpetuated themselves within the national unity.

§ 22. The nation in its true form first appears in the kingdoms founded in Western Europe by the Teutonic tribes, after the destruction of the Roman Empire. The Teuton hated cities and loved the open country. When he spared a city he generally left it to its old occupants and made them his tributaries. He divided the open country into *marks* or communes, whose occupants were actually or by adoption members of one family-clan and bore the same name. Several of these were gathered by force of the political instinct into "hundreds," hundreds into "shires," and shires into kingdoms. Over each of these subdivisions an elder, alderman or chief presided. In this way the race passed from the tribal to the national constitution, without developing the vigorous municipal life that had previously thwarted all attempts at establishing any larger body politic than the city, except a military, imperial despotism.

Within the Teutonic mark towns grew up by the same process as in the ancient world, and the antipathy of the race to the town life wore off. But before these new municipalities were powerful enough to hinder the national growth, the nation had become an established fact. A second enemy of the national unity was the feudal system, which conferred large powers upon the local barons, in countries that had been conquered rather than occupied. Everywhere save in Germany itself the joint efforts of the king and the people overthrew this local power, and made the central government supreme. Thus the national consciousness superseded all other political attachments.

§ 23. The nation is the normal type of the modern state, as the city was that of ancient society, and the tribe that of the prehistoric times. Besides many inaccurate definitions of its nature, several that deserve our notice have been given from different stand-points.

(1) Geographically the nation is a people speaking one language, living under one government, and occupying a continuous area. This area is a district whose natural boundaries designate it as intended for the site of an independent people.

No one point of this definition is essential, save the second.

(2) Politically the nation is an organization of the whole people for the purposes of mutual defence from outside interference and of doing justice among themselves. It is a people who "will to be one" in a body politic, for the purpose of realizing and making positive those natural rights which inhere in man's nature.

(3) Ethically the nation is a moral personality vested with responsibility and authority, and endowed with a life peculiar to itself, i. e., not possessed by the parts as individuals.

§ 24. All these notions, and others besides, are elements of the historical conception of the nation. The historical nation is an organism, a political body animated by a life of its own. It embraces not one generation but many, the dead and the unborn as well as the living. It contemplates its own perpetuity, making self-preservation the first law, and being incapable of providing for its own death or dissolution. There is in its own nature no reason why it should ever cease to exist, and the analogies often drawn from the life and death of the individual man are fallacious. The end of the nation is its own perfection; towards that it tends by a continual progress to a larger and freer life. Thus in its laws it continually aims to make political rights more and more the realization of natural right. In its gradual or sudden modifications of the form of government, it tends to make it more and more the exponent of the wants and the powers of the governed. Industrially it continually aims to develop the resources of its soil and the activities of its people, until they become in all necessary things independent and self-sufficient.

§ 25. The nation as a moral personality must have had the same ultimate origin as other moral personalities, whether we conceive of it as the direct creation of God or as the work of His creatures. The traditions of all ancient cities with which we are acquainted, point to the first of these alternatives, that is, to a divine origin of their unity and their laws; and no one who believes in the continual government of the world by the Divine Will can doubt that nations exist in consequence of that will. "He setteth the solitary in families. . . . He fixeth the bounds of the nations." Then national laws are authoritative because they set forth that Will, though its agency be concealed by reason of its working through and by the will of man. Hence the right of the nation over the lives and persons, as well as the possessions of its members. It has a delegated authority from the Giver of life.

§ 26. The state is either the creature of God, with authority limited because delegated, or is an uncreated entity with authority unlimited because original. In the latter case it can confess none of its acts to be wrongful, since it owns no law or morality above or beyond its own will. It must punish all appeals to "the higher law" as treasonable. The atheistic theory of the state thus necessarily leads to the despot's construction of its powers. Those who hold it have generally been in modern times, by a happy inconsistency, on the liberal side in politics, but when they attain to power, the logic of their position must lead them on to despotic measures. The only lasting and inviolable guarantee of personal freedom is in the doctrine of the state's divine origin and authority, though even this doctrine may be abused to serve the purpose of despots, when the state is conceived as constructed *ab extra* by the imposition of a government by a divine authority from without. But the doctrine of the Old Testament is that the state is constituted through the people themselves being drawn into national unity, and that the government is the result and exponent of this fact. The governor, as the word originally signified, is the steersman of the vessel, giving direction to its course. But it is not his function to furnish the moving force of the ship of state. That is furnished by the vital force of the whole body politic.

§ 27. As God made the state, he had a purpose in making it, a purpose which includes some elements common to all states and others that are peculiar to the particular state. Each state, like each man, has a calling, a vocation. Every nation is an elect or chosen people. It has a peculiar part to play in the moral order of the world. When it recognises this purpose, it is, in Hebrew phrase, a people in covenant with God. The leading purpose of the Old Testament is to set forth the manner of such a national life, and the moral laws that govern it. It gives the essential features of such a life, in connection with some that are peculiar to the Jewish nation.

§ 28. The universal element in the vocation of a state is expressed in the statement that it is the institution of rights. This differentiates it from the family, which is the institution of the affections; also from mankind at large, as rights are realized and made positive through the existence of the state. Justice or Righteousness, Plato discovered, is of the essence of the state. It can therefore attain to the purpose of its vocation only by complying with the ideal of justice as apprehended by the national conscience,—an ideal ever advancing in clearness and completeness as the nation tries to realize it. At the first this ideal requires only the righteous treatment of its own citizens as alone invested with the rights it recognises. Afterwards men are brought by analogy to feel that as the state judges between man and man, God is judging between nation and nation. Hence originates a body of law between the nations.

If justice be of the essence of the state, any wilful and conscious violation of it, i. e., any national unrighteousness that does not spring from and find its palliation in a low ideal of righteousness, must be a blow at the national life and existence. It must weaken the bonds which bind men to one another. Hence to plead the necessity of the national life as the excuse for such acts, is to plead that the state can only be saved by being destroyed. A state that has ceased to aim at righteousness has given up its *raison d'être*, and is a practical contradiction. It has ceased to be a body politic, and has become a band of pirates.

§ 29. Justice has two aspects. (1) It is the state's function to do justice upon evil-doers within (and sometimes without) its own boundaries, by punishing them for past and deterring them from future invasions of the rights of others. (2) It is also called upon to *do itself justice;* that is, to secure the fullest and freest development of the national life in all worthy directions. As self-preservation is its first duty, there is involved in that duty this obligation—to progress in national life. "The end of the state is not only to live, but to live nobly."

§ 30. In the order of nature, progress is attained through the differentiation of the parts of a living organism from each other and from the whole. "The higher a living being stands in the order of nature, the greater the difference between its parts, and between each part and the whole organism. The lower the organism, the less the difference between the parts, and between each part and the whole" (Goethe).

"The investigations of Wolff, Goethe, and Von Baer, have established the truth that the series of changes gone through during the development of a seed into a tree, or an ovum into an animal, constitute an advance from homogeneity of structure to heterogeneity of structure. . . . The first step is the appearance of a difference between two parts of its substance. . . . This law of organic progress is the law of all progress. Whether it be in the development of the earth, in the development of life upon its surface, in the development of Society, of

Government, of Manufactures, of Commerce, of Language, Literature, Science, Art—this same evolution of the single into the complex, through successive differentiations, holds throughout. From the earliest traceable cosmical changes down to the latest results of civilization [it] is that in which progress essentially consists. . . . As we see in existing barbarous tribes, society in its first and lowest forms is a homogeneous aggregation of individuals having like powers and like functions, the only marked difference of functions being that which accompanies difference of sex. Every man is warrior, hunter, fisherman, tool-maker, builder; every woman performs the same drudgeries; every family is self-sufficing, and, save for purposes of aggression and defence, might as well live apart from the rest" (Herbert Spencer).

See also Coleridge's *Idea of Life*. (Works, Vol. I., esp. p. 388.)

This is true less of the spiritual than of the material side of the national life. It applies especially to those relations to nature, which are the theme of social science in the sense that we take it,—relations which come very directly under the action and control of natural laws (See § 2). As regards the higher or spiritual side of that life, each member of the perfect state is in some sense a reproduction of the whole body politic,—like it a free moral personality.

> Yet the Apostle Paul applies this analogy of difference and interdependence to the most purely spiritual form of society. "The body is not one member but many, and all members have not the same office. . . . The eye cannot say to the hand, I have no need of thee."

§ 31. Every fully developed state is a complex form of life, whose elements may be distinguished as three. There is the industrial state, the jural state, and the culture-state. The second embraces the state's political life, the people's advance in freedom and social morality, and its development in legislation; the third is the sphere of intellectual movement, progress in the fine arts, in literature and the sciences. The first is the sphere of the material well-being of the people. The full development of each of the three is essential to the highest well-being of the whole body politic.

§ 32. In seeking the full and free development of the national life on all its sides as its chief end, the state cannot be charged with selfishness. The affections and the attachments of finite beings are of necessity circumscribed, that they may be intense, vigorous and healthy. In the family life we should count the man immoral who loved other men's wives as he loved his own: unnatural if he had no more affection for his own children than for those of other men. To "provide for his own, especially for them that are of his own house," is one of the first duties of the head or the member of a nation as well as of a household.

While acting first of all for the interest of his own nation, he is not bound to seek to injure or cramp the natural development of other nations. He can quite consistently cherish the warmest desires for the welfare of every other national household, and scrupulously avoid any act that would interfere with it. The more strong and hearty and pure the attachment he feels towards his own nation, the more likely he is to sympathize with the patriotic citizens of other nations. The late F. D. Maurice well says: "If I being an Englishman desire to be thoroughly an Englishman, I must respect every Frenchman who desires to be thoroughly a Frenchman, every German who strives to be thoroughly a German. I must learn more of the grandeur and worth of his position, the more I estimate the worth and grandeur of my own. . . Parting with our distinctive characteristics, we become useless to each other,—we run in each other's way; neither brings in his quota to the common treasure of humanity."

> Those who cherish the enthusiasm that men feel for their own nation, as ethically right, do not necessarily repudiate "the enthusiasm of humanity." They may very well recognise its value and dignity, while feeling that it belongs to another sphere than either the jural or industrial state. There is another kingdom, "not of this world" or order, in which "there is neither Jew nor Greek," founded by him who awakened the sense of human brotherhood in the hearts of men.

§ 33. The industrial state contains three great fundamental classes,—the agricultural, the commercial and the manufacturing. A nation takes high rank industrially in proportion as all the three are fully developed and exist in equilibrium. If any one of the three is depressed or hindered in its development, the whole body politic suffers accordingly. The others may seem to prosper at its expense, but because the state is a living organism and not a dead aggregate of individuals, one member cannot suffer, but all the members must suffer with it.

§ 34. The individuality of the parts of an organism has its end in their interdependence and mutual helpfulness. A flock of animals, though "a collection of individuals," is not a whole made up of differentiated parts. It is only "a numerical extension of a single specimen." A mob of men is equally deficient in true organic unity. It is united only by the existence of the same overmastering rage or lawlessness in each single individual, as animates the entire mob. A state is a body in which men have different functions as well as different personalities; in which each has his place of service to the whole body. The greater and more marked the variety of the parts, the more closely the whole body is bound in an effective unity. The nation takes a low rank industrially whose members are not employed chiefly in serving one another, but in serving the members of other nationalities.

§ 35. All history illustrates the principle that the chief growth of the state is from within. Nations have often imparted to each other wholesome and stimulating impulses, but beyond a certain limit foreign influence has always been a hindrance, and has been jealously resented by the wise instincts of the people. We see this in the history of art, literature, language, law and political institutions, and every other side of the national life.

Any plan of human life, any project for human improvement, which, either in the interest of imperial ambition or of cosmopolitan philanthropy, ignores the existence of the nations as parts of the world's providential order, can work only mischief and confusion.

## CHAPTER THIRD.

### Wealth and Nature.

§ 36. We are engaged in "an inquiry into the nature and causes of the *wealth* of nations." The word wealth is used in two senses; as meaning either the aggregate of possessions that minister to man's necessities and tastes, or the possession of an abundance of such objects. . In the former or popular sense wealth is the measure of man's power over nature; in the latter or scientific sense it is the power itself developed to more than the average degree.

Closely connected with the term *wealth* is the term *value*. The one is the antithesis of the other. If wealth is the measure of man's power over nature, value is the measure of nature's power over man,—of the resistance that she offers to his efforts to master her. Some of the natural substances are to be had everywhere, always and in the form needed for man's consumption. These have no value, though the very highest utility. Others, such as the water for the supply of a great city, need to be changed in place, and have a value proportional to the cost of their transfer. Others need to be changed in form by manufacture as well as changed in place before their use, and have a still higher value. In other instances the resistance takes the form of scarcity, and is therefore in some degree insuperable, and the degree of the value is still higher.

§ 37. Man stands in close relation to nature, as the possessor of a body which forms part of the physical world. He therefore needs the services of nature continually. His body is undergoing incessant decays and renewals. Motion, respiration, sensation, digestion, circulation of the blood, even thought itself wear away its tissues, and unless this waste be replaced the man must die literally of exhaustion.

Furthermore, these vital processes can be carried on only in the presence of a certain amount of animal heat, which must be supplied from within, and (in most climates) shielded from without to prevent its excessive radiation.

> The chemical substances that form the bodily frame are chiefly Oxygen, Hydrogen, Carbon and Nitrogen. The two first in the form of water make 75 per cent. of the whole body, and 83 per cent. of the most common foods. Berzelius says that the living organism is to be regarded as a mass diffused in water, and another chemist has humorously defined man as fifty pounds of nitrogen and carbon suspended in six buckets-full of water.
>
> The starch which forms so large an element in the ordinary foods enters into the composition of none of the tissues. It is consumed in the lungs to furnish the vital heat, and breathed off as carbonic acid.

§ 38. Hence man's two great material necessities are food and clothing. The desires for these furnish the motive to the vastest activities of the race. As his brain expands, indeed, and as society develops, other desires grow into life and become motives to action; but these two are universal. Others are voluntary; these are enforced by the sensations of hunger and cold. Others are directed to comforts or luxuries; these to things necessary and indispensable.

The productions of the three kingdoms of nature do not equally satisfy these desires. Though there are apparent exceptions, it may be laid down as a rule that he obtains food and clothing from the animal and vegetable kingdoms only. The animal kingdom as a whole is supported by the vegetable, which in its turn depends upon the abundance and fitness of the great mixtures of vegetable and mineral substances which we call soil. Only the lowest type of vegetation can support its life upon mineral food alone.

§ 39. We can trace the story of the earth's development back to a period when vegetation, and therefore soil, did not yet exist upon its surface. Some of the natural agents already at work were indeed preparing for the formation of soil. Glacial corrosion and other violent forms of action were grinding masses of rock into fine sand, and the frosts were chipping away the edges and faces of the rocks by sudden expansion of the water that they had absorbed.

Vegetation began with the lichens and the mosses, which

secured a foothold on the surface of the rocks, and slowly crumbled down a few grains of sand from the hard mass (by the action of the oxalic acid which they secrete), and dying, mingled therewith the ashes of their own decay. This furnished the first soil for the next highest order of vegetable life, and thus through successive orders of vegetable life the soil was deepened and enriched.

> As illustrating Goethe's law of progress by differentiation of the parts from the whole and from each other (see § 30), it is worth while to notice the stages of this development as given in the great classification of Oken. First come the *acotyledons* (lichens, mosses, &c.), which have neither root nor stem, neither bark nor wood, neither leaves nor seeds. Then the *monocotyledons* (grasses, lilies and palms), which have no branches nor true leaves, but may have either woody stems, or venous *liber*, or bark—never the three united. The third are the *dicotyledons* (fruit and forest trees, &c.), which unite all these parts in one organism.

This process of the formation of soil on a rocky surface by successive vegetable growths, still takes place with some modifications in the coral islands of the Pacific. When the coral polyp has raised its rocky fortress above the sea level, the surface is soon strewed with fragments that the waves break off and grind into sand, which is mixed with the remains of the coral polyp. A cocoanut carried safely in its rough husk on a long voyage is washed ashore and takes root. The decay of its leaves forms a new soil, and the birds that rest on its branches bring the seeds of other vegetation in their crops, so that a multifarious growth rapidly covers the barren rock.

§ 40. The sustenance which the growing plant derives from the mineral kingdom is not taken solely nor even mainly from the soil through its roots, but from the air through its leaves. Were it otherwise, the growth of the soil must stop as soon as its depth became as great as that to which the plants thrust down their roots. But six feet of soil is not uncommonly found on the prairies of the West, and even that depth still increasing. The chief food of plants is carbonic acid, one of the elements of the air, which in the early geological ages was so abundant that only vegetable life could have existed on the earth's surface. The first luxuriant vegetable growths, the mosses and the ferns absorbed it in vast quantities, growing with marvellous rapidity, and forming the deposits of decayed vegetation, now known to us as coal, after having been subjected to vast pressure for unnumbered ages. By burning this as fuel we give back to the atmosphere a small part of the carbonic acid that once saturated it, and thus furnish food for new vegetation from the substance of those which flourished ages ago. Nothing that is consumed or that decays upon the earth's surface is wasted;—nothing is wasted but what goes into the sea. "Atmospheric air is the grand receptacle from which all things spring and to which they will return. It is the cradle of vegetable and the coffin of animal life" (Dr. Jno. W. Draper).

> Carbonic acid forms but a thousandth part of the chemical mixture that we call air.

§ 41. The foliage of the plant is a vegetable substitute for mouth and lungs. It presents a vast absorptive surface to the air through which it drinks in carbonic acid and transmutes it into woody fibre. To pluck all the leaves of a tree in the early summer would be to kill it by suffocation and starvation. From the vast storehouse of the air the plant draws its food, and the atmospheric supply is kept up by the decay of other plants, by the respiration of animals, and by the consumption of wood and coal as fuel. When the plant dies, a small percentage escapes back to the air again, but the great mass is added to the wealth of the soil, from which so little was taken.

The proportion of sustenance that a plant takes from the air has been ascertained by experiment to be about nine parts in ten. In one case a willow tree weighing five pounds was planted in a box, in two hundred pounds of soil that had been carefully dried and weighed. To prevent the settlement of dust in any appreciable quantity, the soil was covered with a metal plate pierced with very fine holes to allow the free passage of the air; and it was moistened with rain-water only. After a few years the tree was removed, and the soil was carefully collected and dried. On weighing them it was found that the tree had gained sixty-seven pounds and the soil had lost eight ounces.

> The late Prof. J. F. Frazer told me that while engaged in the geological survey of Pennsylvania he found a willow tree growing in the cleft of a rock where there was absolutely no soil whatever, but a continual ooze of water was keeping the cleft moist.

§ 42. The fertility of the earth is therefore not an accomplished fact, but a vast process that is still going on. Nature is preparing for the time when man will make still larger demands upon her resources than at present. Even when the fertility of a piece of ground has been exhausted by continual abuse, she brings her restorative energies into play. Thus the abandoned tobacco plantations of Eastern Virginia have been covered by a growth of pines, whose long taproots reach down below the exhausted surface, and bring up mineral substances, which after the fall of the leaves and the decay of the stems enrich the soil. A similar instrument of recuperation nature furnishes to the farmer in the clover plant, whose peculiarity it is to thrust down its roots to the mineral subsoil and feed only upon that.

§ 43. The soil, it has been already said, is a *mixture* of mineral and vegetable matter. The former, even when less in amount, is by no means inferior in importance. It predominates in the *subsoil*, and in the best soils appears mainly as silicious sand and clay. The first use of the former is to keep the soil porous and make it ready to receive,—of the latter to keep it compact and able to retain. An excess of either substance imparts to the soil a corresponding defect.

In the plant the silex or flint of the sand reappears as the skeleton. The slight and fragile stalks of our grains and grasses are kept upright under their load of seed by a thin coating or varnish of silica. Every acre of wheat requires from 93 to 150 pounds. This mineral element is but slightly present in the fruits and seeds which man carries from the soil; somewhat more largely in the stems and trunks of trees, but most of all in the leaves which return to the soil at once, or after having served as food for cattle. The leaves of trees contain fifteen times as much as the trunks.

§ 44. Persistent human stupidity can bring to nought the most beneficent arrangements of nature. The fertility of the soil may be destroyed in spite of tendencies to perpetuate and extend itself, and that in more ways than one.

(1) By the absence of any system of rotation of crops. Year after year men will take the same elements from the soil by growing the same crop upon it, wheat or tobacco, or some other. There is land around Albany where forty-five bushels to the acre was once no excessive yield in wheat, but where at present not more than fifteen can be grown. Much of the country in which the last battles of the late civil war were fought is made up of exhausted tobacco plantations. The whole system of Southern agriculture under the slaveholding regime tended to the same result.

§ 45. (2) By continually taking away from the soil and never making any return. The absence of a single element that enters into the composition of a plant will as much prevent its growth as would the absence of all. "For every fourteen tons of fodder carried off from the soil there are carried away two casks of potash, two of lime, one of soda, a carboy of vitriol, a large demijohn of phosphoric acid, and other essential ingredients" (Prof. Johnston).

Substances that have served as food for birds and animals are worth most to keep up the fertility of the soil. In passing through the digestive organs they are reduced in size to their finest particles, and enriched with organic elements, which the animal derives from the atmosphere. They are especially much richer in nitrogen than the food itself. In some districts of England cattle are stall-fed with oil-cake and other expensive foods, simply for the sake of the manure, and by this system one district of moorland in Lancashire has been reclaimed and brought up to a high degree of fertility.

Whenever, therefore, the products of the soil are consumed in the vicinity of the farm, the farmer will have at hand the means of making such a return to the soil as will keep up and even increase its fertility. But whenever they are transported to a considerable distance for consumption the power to make an adequate return to the soil is seriously diminished, if not absolutely destroyed. The richest soil cannot long sustain such a process of exhaustion, if its proprietors are engaged in sending its natural wealth over land and sea to a distant market.

§ 46. The existence of the means and the power to make adequate returns to the soil is no guarantee that these will be fully employed. Through the sewers of our great cities, and the rivers into which they empty, immense quantities of fertilizing matter are poured into the sea, and are thus utterly lost. The soil around the city of Chicago, for instance, is naturally sterile; in the refuse of her slaughtering-houses the city has the means of raising it to a very high degree of fertility. At a great expense provision has been made to carry off the whole mass and pour it through the Illinois and the Mississippi rivers into the Gulf of Mexico; on all hands the measure is applauded as a bold and wise piece of engineering. Belgium is the only civilized nation that is fully awake to the importance of this subject, but England bids fair to emulate her.

§ 47. (3) The fertility of a country may be destroyed by stripping it of its trees, which seem to affect very greatly the amount of rain that falls on its surface. In some parts of upper India the trees have been cut away, the wells have sunk, the rain-fall has ceased, and the country threatens to become a wilderness. The Punjaub seemed likely to meet the same fate; when the British conquered it not a single tree was observed in its vast area, and the country was rapidly becoming a desert, when its plantation was begun and the waste was arrested. Numidia, the Plain of Babylon, and Judea are instances of countries once proverbially fertile, and now barren (it is believed) through denudation. When Europeans occupied the Cape Verde and Canary Islands, and St. Helena, they found them well wooded and fertile. As the trees have been recklessly cut down, droughts have become common, and the capacity of the islands to support a large population has disappeared. The increasing sterility of parts of France, of Lombardy, and of large districts of Spain, is ascribed to the same cause. In Lombardy it has been found that the denudation of the country contributes to the rapidity and the volume in which its light and friable soil is washed into the Adriatic by the Po and its tributaries. Great injury has thus been done to the agricultural capacity of the country, and still greater is feared. And as a rule, the absence of trees seems to lead to the concentration of the rain-fall in great storms, and the disappearance of better distributed and more moderate showers. The streams alternate between the destructive violence of torrents and the desolation of drought. The tribes of Arabia perceived the connection between drought and the absence of trees ;.the oldest law recognised as binding on the whole peninsula is one for their protection, and it was repeated in the injunctions given by the Prophet and the Caliphs to the captains whom they sent forth to subdue the world.

§ 48. All these ruinous results are matters for control and correction by the action of the state. Individual selfishness is always shortsighted; the nation as the supreme owner of the national domain has the fullest right to guard against its reckless exhaustion. The state is owner of the national domain in a sense that is not true of individual proprietors. Much or all of it that is incapable of individual appropriation, is national property,—such as rivers and other inland waters, harbors and fisheries.

Especially is it a question of national policy, because insoluble to individual effort, to bring the farmer and artisan into neighborhood, and secure the consumption of the crops within reasonable distance of the farm.

# CHAPTER FOURTH.

## THE SCIENCE AND ECONOMY OF POPULATION.

§ 49. THE evolution of life upon our planet, after passing through the vegetable and the merely animal stages, was crowned in the advent of man, the especial theme of social science. All the great processes of nature's development that preceded his coming, were but preparations to fit the earth to be his home, and to gratify the capacities and bring into action the powers with which he was endowed. The earth was given into his hands, and he was commanded to "multiply and replenish the earth and subdue it."

§ 50. To "subdue the earth," to become master over nature, is, as we have seen, only another way of stating the transition from poverty to wealth. And, as the command implies, that transition has gone hand in hand with the increase of numbers. In the earlier stages of society man lives in comparative isolation from his fellows, weak in the presence of nature's vast powers and therefore poor in the command of her resources. The scattered families, the isolated tribes, are unequal to helpful coöperation; for the most part they are confined to the use of such of nature's provisions as are easily accessible to their ineffectual and wasteful labor. First the wild beasts and birds and fruits of the forest are brought into use; then the peaceful flocks whose skins furnish ready-woven clothing, and whose milk and flesh supply food. The wealth of the mine, of the grain-field, of the cotton plantation, are utterly beyond their reach.

§ 51. But with the growth of numbers too great to be fed by the mere pasturage of the land, comes the transition to agricultural industry. New powers of nature, forces that lay unused so long as the scantiness of men forbade efficient coöperation for their mastery, are made to serve man; cattle that ran wild and were slain for food, are tamed to the labors of plough and cart;

plants that grow wild on the hillside are brought under culture, and by improvement and the selection of seed, produce an ever-increasing quantity of food and clothing. The waterfall that fell idly over the rocks, or the wind that blew unburdened as it listed, turns the mill; the peat and coal that lay neglected are made into fuel. A *division of labor* separates the functions of the human members of society, and each species of work is done more effectively and productively for employing the whole time and attention of the men employed in it. Better tools and implements are invented; and last of all, machinery, and the giant forces that actuate it, come into play in man's service, taking the place of muscular strength, and at every advance lowering the value of articles of utility, and making them obtainable in larger quantities and by a larger number of persons.

§ 52. At every step in this great past of man's industrial development, the growth of numbers and of wealth has gone on with equal strides. In the earlier stages the pressure of population upon the means of subsistence is marked and painful; yet beneficent, as thrusting men into closer and more helpful association, and forcing them to adopt wiser and better methods. But every advance has been richly rewarded, for with each acceleration in the rapidity of social movement, the resistance to be overcome has diminished. Each generation has worked not for itself only, but for all that were to come; and the result of all wisely directed work has been to make easier and more effective the task of those who came later. "Other men labored; ye have entered into their labors."

§ 53. It is, therefore, apart from all merely ethical considerations, a wise economic policy for a nation to guard the lives and the health of its people, and to remove all artificial obstructions to the natural growth of population. It is indeed the *duty* correlative to its right to command their lives and persons in its own defence; but it is also the best policy, in view of both the military strength and the industrial welfare and contentment of its people. For the more people there are productively employed in any well-managed country, the greater the share of food and clothing, of necessaries and comforts, that will fall to each one of them. Whatever tends to diminish their numbers,—or, what comes to much the same thing, to lower their bodily health and strength—has also the tendency to impoverish them by diminishing their power of coöperation and association. Every retrogression to the sparse numbers of earlier times, is also a retrogression to their poverty.

§ 54. "But," it will be said, "what need is there of state interference in the matter? In every man's breast is implanted the instinct of self-preservation, to lead him to take care of himself. Surely we can leave this matter to individual action, and to the voluntary coöperation of individuals." The instinct in question is exceedingly effective as a motive in the presence of visible and well-understood danger. But where the peril is more recondite, though not less real, the instinct is good for nothing. Only reflection and forethought, accompanied with a large and exact knowledge of the scientific conditions of life and health, and a readiness, by no means universal, to act upon these, is sufficient in this case. The state can command the services and opinions of the best judges; it can carry out wholesale measures, and override the mulish opposition of wrongheaded people, in cases where only general action is of any avail. In so doing, it is not overriding "the judgments of individuals respecting their own interests, but giving effect to that judgment; they being unable to give effect to it except by concert, which concert again cannot be effectual unless it receives validity and sanction from the law" (J. S. Mill). Thus in England the law recently passed to limit the hours of work in mills and factories for married women, received the support of nearly all that class of mill-hands. They were free to make such private contract with the mill-owner as they pleased, but in fact their freedom amounted to nothing whatever until the law required them to refuse excessive work.

In other cases the right of state interference rests on the same ground as the laws that forbid and furnish attempts at self-murder. The man who persists in maintaining a dunghill or a cesspool under his windows, or in living in a house sordid with filth or imperfectly ventilated, may have the excuse of ignorance, but society has not. The officers of the state have as much right to force him to reform these things, as they would have to dash a dose of poison out of his hand. In some cases there is not even this excuse. Certain trades, such as cutlery-grinding in Sheffield, are paid at a high rate because they prove fatal in ten or fifteen years to those who engage in them; but the workmen have been known to resist stoutly any provision that was meant to diminish the risk (or rather to postpone the certainty) of death, as tending to lower wages. "A short life and a merry one!" is the reckless saying with which such people take their lives in their hands.

§ 55. The state, then, is the steward of the life and the health of its individual members. There are many measures by which it naturally and fitly discharges this trust; such as (1) requiring local governments and municipalities to enforce public cleanliness and to provide thorough drainage, and good roads for safe travel; (2) by quarantining vessels and persons who come from places where infectious diseases are raging; (3) by enjoining the adoption of preventive measures (disinfectants, vaccination, &c.), in times of epidemics; (4) by chartering and endowing colleges competent to give medical instruction and to grant medical degrees, and by requiring that a doctor so qualified shall sign a certificate of death and of its cause, before legal interment shall take place; (5) by forbidding the sale of unripe, overripe, diseased or adulterated articles of food; (6) by forbidding women and minors from engaging in excessive work or in night-work in factories; (7) by requiring that dangerous employments shall only be carried on, and explosive machines used, with all possible precautions for the safety of the workmen and the public, and by enforcing this by general state inspection.

Besides these negative checks on the waste of human life and health, there are many positive measures that contribute to the same end. Such are the public instruction of the young in the first principles of practical hygiene; the establishment of public baths, parks and gymnasia; the requiring of cities to furnish an abundance of pure water, and to see that it is introduced into every house.

> It is questionable whether the sale of what are called patent medicines should be allowed by the state. Most of these substances, I believe, are compounds that would be useful in some cases of disease, but are exceedingly dangerous when used indiscriminatingly, as they must be in the absence of competent advice. Others are simply fraudulent, and contain nothing that could have any effect, either good or bad.

§ 56. But all this is open to a general objection, that has occupied a very large space in the discussion of this subject. It will be said that measures to hinder the action of those destructive agencies, and more especially such as tend to promote and foster the increase of a nation's population, will do a very great deal of mischief instead of good. For unless something check it, the number of people in a country will double every twenty-five years, and go on increasing in a geometrical ratio, while subsistence increases only by an arithmetical increment. Thus in two centuries, "taking the whole earth and supposing the present population equal to a thousand millions, the human species would," if the growth were thus unchecked, "increase as the numbers 1, 2, 4, 8, 16, 32, 64, 128, 256; and subsistence as 1, 2, 3, 4, 5, 6, 7, 8. In two centuries the population would be to the means of subsistence as 256 is to 9; in three centuries as 4096 is to 13; and in two thousand years the difference would be incalculable" (Rev. T. R. Malthus).

> Mr. Malthus's *Essay on Population* appeared in 1798. Its main position was anticipated by Herrenschwand (*Discours fondamental sur la Population*, 1786), but the theory obtained its wide currency through the English writer. It was eloquently opposed by Godwin, the author of *Political Justice*; then in detail by Sadler, Allison, Doubleday, N. W. Senior and Quetelet. Its latest English opponents are Herbert Spencer and W. R. Greg. The latter says: "The doctrine has been accepted by every writer of repute on economical subjects. . . None of the many authors who have questioned or assailed it, . . . have been able to shake in any degree its hold upon the public mind. . . It has remained the fixed, axiomatic belief of the educated world." (*The Enigmas of Life.*)

§ 57. If this view be correct, it is not the growth of population, but the efficiency of the "checks" upon it, that best contributes to the well-being of the nation. These checks are of two kinds: (1) positive, such as war, famine, pestilence, &c.; (2) preventive, such as sexual immorality and voluntary celibacy. The practical inferences drawn by Mr. Malthus and his school from this theory were that wherever the state can discourage the increase of the population without interfering with personal liberty, it should do so. Regarding pauperism as the result of over-population, they were in general opposed to any provision for the poor, either public or private; regarding that as a premium upon recklessness and self-indulgence, and as a useless interference between the violators of a divine law and their divinely-appointed punishment. Or if provision must be made for the poor, they would have it managed in such a way as to discourage and prevent "the propagation of a race of paupers." They especially labored to create a strong public opinion on the subject, and to diffuse this through all classes. J. S. Mill would have "the producing large families" "regarded with the same feeling as drunkenness or any other physical excess."

One inference drawn from the theory was that a high rate of wages is exceedingly undesirable. For when working people are paid abundantly they naturally become reckless as regards the future; the rate of increase is accelerated, the labor-market overstocked, and the workmen must suffer a fall of wages to or even below "the natural rate" again. Any high rate must therefore be merely temporary, and add to the misery and discontent of the working classes, by accustoming them to enjoyments, which they afterwards lose the power to command.

§ 58. The theory obtained general currency in England and some other countries as an easy and not unsatisfactory explanation of the misery that existed in the closely settled countries of Europe. It was an explanation that involved no censure of the leaders in social policy, and that gave full sanction to their disposition to give themselves as little trouble as need be about the suffering classes. But it had such a plausibility in it, that men of quite another stamp adopted it heartily,—men like Chalmers and the younger Mill, who really longed and labored for the social elevation and welfare of their countrymen.

§ 59. The earlier disciples of Malthus, and their master, treated this alleged tendency of population to outrun subsistence as an insurmountable obstacle to the permanent welfare of the mass of mankind. In the several editions of the *Essay on Population*, his statements of this opinion are somewhat toned down in concession to hostile criticism; but even the last remains open to the same interpretation. Or if he has any hope, it is from the progress of society in education and knowledge, until all men shall be able to "read, mark, learn and inwardly digest" his pleas for voluntary restraint in this matter. (He himself had only eleven children, as M. de Sismondi tells us.) Mr. McCulloch also lays it down as a "principle that the power of increase in the human species must always, in the long run, prove an overmatch for the increase of the means of subsistence." James Mill says: "The general misery of mankind is a fact which can be accounted for upon one only of two positions, either that there is a tendency in population to increase faster than capital, or that capital has by some means been prevented from increasing so fast as it has a tendency to increase." Rejecting the latter of the two suppositions, he accepts the former as the fact. And he declares that "however slow the increase of population, provided that of capital is still slower, wages will be reduced so low that a portion of the population will regularly die of want."

§ 60. The later writers of this school seem inclined to lay more stress upon the counteracting forces, viz.: the growth of subsistence and the checks to population. Archbishop Whately even assigns to these the rank of a counter-tendency, comparing the two to the centrifugal and the centripetal forces that keep the earth for ever moving in the same orbit, and emphasizing the fact that "much as our population has increased within the last five centuries, it yet bears a far less ratio to subsistence than it did five hundred years ago." N. W. Senior offering a mass of evidence to the same purpose, says: "I believe in the actual power of population to increase so as to press upon the means of subsistence. I deny the habitual tendency. I believe the tendency to be just the reverse." Yet he also says that "there are few portions of Europe the inhabitants of which would not be richer if their numbers were fewer, and would not be richer hereafter if they were now to retard the rate at which their population is increasing."

§ **61.** Mr. John Stuart Mill better represents the great mass of English writers on this topic. He holds that the tendency pointed out by Malthus is the constant element in the problem, and all others are inconstant and variable. Not that there is any need to despair in view of this fact. If the mass of society were really and generally enlightened, the preventive check of abstinence would be quite sufficient to overmaster this unhappy and dangerous tendency. All the progress of human civilization has been through the growing ascendancy of man's higher over his lower nature. The race of men have their future in their own hands in this matter, and as they awake to the realization of the fact, they will govern themselves more wisely. The social moralist might fairly object here that this constant victory of the higher nature of man has been won through men entering into those relationships from which Mr. Mill would have them abstain, and from their being drawn out of their sordidness and selfishness thereby. Some of the social regulations and institutions on the Continent, which Mr. Mill unhappily chose for eulogy, show us by their effects that whatever discipline the self-contained philosopher may find in this solitary life, it is to the mass of men the road to degradation and debasement.

But we need not go out of the strictly economic sphere, nor even outside of Mr. Mill's concessions, to find arguments. Since the law was enunciated, whatever its acceptance by the intellectual classes, the mass of men have neither believed nor acted on it. Yet, as Mr. Mill admits, the actual state of society, as compared with what it was, does not bear out the theory. "This does not prove that the law does not exist, but only that some antagonistic principle is at work which is capable for a time of making headway against the law." This exceptional and antagonistical principle he finds in the progress of material civilization; that is, in the growth of man's power over nature and her utilities. He specifies the improvements in agriculture and in machinery, better roads and means of communication, and the spread of education. Very right, save in regarding civilization and its progress as exceptional, whereas it is the law; and in accepting misery as the law, whereas it is the needless exception. In this point lies the deepest ground of distinction between the English view of the subject and that here advocated. The latter looks to the future hopefully, tracing there with prophetic foresight all the great ascending lines of human progress as carried forward without stop or limit. The other regards that future with despondency, or at least a gloomy uncertainty, being most impressed with the existence of forces and tendencies that have wrought misery and promise ruin.

§ 62. The theory is discredited by the experience of the past in this matter. The pressure of population upon subsistence is characteristic of the periods and the places where population is most sparse,—not of those where it is densest. "Let any one," says Mr. McCulloch, whom we quoted above, "compare the state of this or of any other European country five hundred or a thousand years ago, and he will be satisfied that prodigious advances have been made, that the means of subsistence has increased much more rapidly than population, and that the laboring classes are now generally in possession of conveniences and luxuries that once were not enjoyed by the richest lord."

Take the extreme case of Belgium, whose Flemish provinces, though naturally poor in soil, are the most densely peopled district in the world. In spite of the absence of large manufactures and a too general dependence on agriculture, the standard of comfort is high, and continues to rise. Switzerland rivals these provinces in density of population and in the general diffusion of comfort among her people. Were the population of

Europe to be doubled, there is no reason to suppose the soil would furnish them insufficient support. Deducting one-third of her soil as not arable, and assigning two acres per head to her possible population, she would easily support 800 millions, or three times her present population. Yet Zurich has one person to every one and a quarter acres.

>Belgium has 440 people to the square mile; one of her Flemish provinces has 1800. Four cantons of Switzerland approach her average; Basle 420; Argovie 398; Thurgovie 368; Zurich 365. Lombardy has 370; England and Wales 350; Holland 300; Italy 225; France, Germany and Ireland 180; Austria 164; Switzerland 157; Spain 90; Turkey in Europe 76; Russia 30; Sweden 22.

Asia is generally regarded as the cradle of the human race. Here then we must find —if anywhere—the sad effects of a prolonged multiplication of the race. Yet Asia is only one-third as densely peopled as Europe, and the part of Asia in which population is densest, Hindoostan, is capable of supporting a much greater number.

>The stories told of the density of the population in China, like many other details about that empire that have come down from last century, are apocryphal. China, according to the census of 1864, has about 260 to the square mile; but Chinese statistics are not very trustworthy. The census of 1812 put the density at 283 to the square mile.

America, Africa and Australasia are but very thinly settled, and it is hardly possible to estimate the greatness of the population which they are capable of supporting.

§ 63. Of the soil actually under cultivation, not more than a very small part is cultivated as it might be, even in the existing stage of agricultural science. The average yield of wheat in England, for instance, is 26 bushels to the acre. But the fact that 57 and even 60 bushels have been grown is enough to show that England is under no necessity to import one-fourth of her breadstuffs. Only a very small part of her soil is farmed scientifically, and official returns made in 1873 show that she has seven and a half million acres, more than half of them in the most fertile part of the island, not under cultivation. In the opinion of N. W. Senior the yield of food would be quadrupled during the century then beginning (1835), and might possibly be multiplied tenfold. Even soil that is held too poor to repay cultivation, may be made fertile by the skill of the agricultural chemist. Thus Mr. Huxtable on an acre of chalk down—generally given up to the sheep—raised twenty-five tons of turnips, two years running, at a less expense than is usually required for a scantier crop on good soil.

But these better methods are the product of an age when population is dense, coöperation easy, and the human mind is in high activity.

> Great Britain contains 56,815,353 acres, of which only 31,102,600 acres are cultivated, and 2,187,078 acres are returned as woods and plantations for the growth of timber or the protection of game; leaving 23,525,675 acres in a state of nature. Of this Wales has nearly 2,000,000; England about 7,500,000, and the rest is in Scotland. Most of this is in the mountainous counties, northern and south-western; but over 18 per cent. of the most fertile parts of the kingdom are still uncultivated. Outside of the Scandinavian kingdoms, which may be compared to Scotland, no European country of which we have trustworthy statistics, allows so much of its domain to lie idle. Austria proper has eight per cent. uncultivated; Bavaria less than six and a half; Wurtemburg not five.

§ 64. The earlier records of all civilized countries, and the existing state of savage nations, disclose to us habitual poverty, frequent famines and consequent pestilences. In the *Saxon Chronicle* and the earlier mediæval historians, there is a sad and monotonous record of famines, year after year; and England is no exception among European nations. Since the populations have trebled and quadrupled, they are rarely heard of, save in thinly-settled countries like Sweden and Persia. If they occur elsewhere, they are owing to drought or some other unforeseen calamity, and owe much of their desolating force to the bad economic management that has kept the whole people to a single occupation, or made them dependent upon a single crop; for a failure or a series of failures of that crop must produce dreadful misery. But that is the condition of an undeveloped and imperfect society, not of one whose industrial growth has been allowed to keep pace with its growth of numbers. "But even Ireland, poor and populous as she is, suffers less from want with her eight millions of people [1829] than when her only inhabitants were a few septs of hunters and fishers." So again in our own country, a large proportion of the early colonists from Europe died of hunger and privation, and colonies were broken up, because their lack of numbers and of the power of mutual help made them unable to cope with the resistances of nature. Their successors struggled long with the hardships of their life. As numbers grew, famines disappeared; a century ago two or three millions were abundantly fed on the soil that had hardly supported forty thousand Indians before the coming of the white man. A much vaster number is now still more abundantly provided for, from the food grown in the same area.

"Whatever tends to develop the natural resources of a country, to call forth a spirit of enterprise among its inhabitants, to render each part less dependent upon itself, and to bind up the commonwealth by the ties of mutual assistance and common interest, tends to mitigate the actual pressure of a famine. The whole list may be expressed in four words—enlightened government and modern civilization. These are the specifics for famine. Where they exist, scarcity will never result in depopulation. Where they do not, the utmost endeavors of government may mitigate, but they cannot avert."—Hunter's *Annals of Rural Bengal*, p. 55.

§ 65. History shows us also that a vast decrease in the population of a country, through the sweeping operation of Mr. Malthus's positive and preventive checks, is a dangerous possibility. The investigations of Dureau de la Malle and Zumpt have established the fact—now accepted by scholars generally—that the vast decline in its population was a chief cause, if not *the* cause, of the overthrow of the Roman Empire by the barbarians. Greece declined steadily, in this respect, from the time of the Persian wars; Italy from that of the struggle with Carthage. The free population of Italy—not including Cisalpine Gaul—at that period was about three millions; the decrease was so marked and rapid that the *jus trium liberorum* was created to make marriage a profitable investment, and discourage celibacy. The speech of the Censor Metellus, in praise of marriage as a duty though an unpleasant one, was revived and read in the senate by Augustus Cæsar, and a multitude of laws passed, but to no lasting purpose. The great famines and pestilences of the times of the Antonines made the ruin of the Empire only a question of time. The benefits that might have been expected from the diffusion of Christianity and the restoration of public morality and the sanctities of the family life, were frustrated by the extravagant estimate put upon celibacy as a religious virtue. At last " Rome fell for want of men."

See Seeley's *Roman Imperialism*, First Essay. The name *proletariat*, given to the lower classes of the Roman population, means that the state supported them in idleness simply that by the growth of their offspring (*proles*) the state might be strengthened.

" The process of depopulation in many provinces of the Roman dominions, since the times of the Antonines, has been excessive, and unaccountable on any of Malthus's hypotheses. We may instance especially the north of Africa, so populous in the palmy days of Rome, and Asia Minor and Syria. According to Merivale, Asia Minor once supported 27,000,000 of people. According to McCulloch, they do not now contain more than one-fourth of those numbers. Yet we do not find that they have become either unhealthy or unfertile" (Greg).

It may be said that all this but illustrates the potent efficacy of the preventive checks. It does more; it shows that it is from those checks to the growth of population, rather than from the growth itself, that we are to fear the most deadly injuries to society.

§ 66. In modern nations the growth of numbers—as officially ascertained—varies so greatly as to set at nought all attempts to fix a general rate of increase. Nor can the difference be traced to the operation of preventive checks. In England the population doubles about once in 47 years, while the annual death-rate is one in 44. In France, with the same death-rate, there is hardly any increase, if not an actual decline. In Prussia the increase is as great as in England, though the death-rate is one in 32. In the United States and Lower Canada—immigration being deducted—the population doubles in about 40 years. In some parts of Mexico much more rapidly.

The population of Gaul in Roman times was about ten and a third millions; in the fourteenth century after Christ the kingdom of France, about a third of the present area, contained two and a half millions of hearths, or between ten and eleven millions of people, being 32 to the kilometre (something over three-eighths of a square mile). In 1515 the population was actually less dense—30 to the kilometre; in 1599, 34; in 1698, 39; in 1772, 45; in 1850, 67; in 1867, 71.4; in 1872, 67.3. The greatest rapidity was in the decade 1816–25, just after the Napoleonic wars, when the annual increment was 7½ to the thousand. By 1848 it fell to about a third of that number, and by 1870 it had as good as ceased.

In England the population is said to have been almost stationary under the Tudors. In six censuses taken during the present century beginning with 1811, the rate of increase was found to be 14, 18, 16, 14, 13 and 12 per cent. for each decade. This shows a diminution during and a great increase following the Napoleonic wars, as in France. After that the rate fell steadily, and should it not cease to do so, the time will come when England, like France, will cease to add to her population.

Ireland is often quoted by the Malthusians. It is alleged that under the great impulse given to Irish prosperity during the last quarter of the eighteenth century, her population rose from 2,690,556 in 1777 to 5,395,456 in 1805. These figures do not rest upon any official census, and may therefore be questioned. The first is an estimate based on the returns of the house-tax; the second is the computation of an individual statist. If it be true, then the population increased but fifty-one per cent. in the next thirty-six years, rising to 8,175,141 in 1841. The failure of the potato crop under the blight of a single night, August 5, 1846, broke the one staff of life upon which the Irish people leaned, and the famine of 1847 followed.

But even at that period Ireland was not as closely populated as England. There was no necessary pressure of population on subsistence, for large amounts of grain were raised for exportation to England, and there had been no great want of food at home. By the year 1874, population had fallen—chiefly through emigration to America—to 5,301,336, a decrease of $37\frac{1}{2}$ per cent.; such a removal of "the pressure on subsistence" ought to have produced the happiest effects, if Malthus be right. But Professor Cairnes, of Galway, wrote in 1865: "We fail to perceive any solid improvement, scarcely any sensible improvement, in the present race of daily laborers in Ireland, as compared with their predecessors twenty years ago." Wages have risen, but food has risen equally; as clothing is cheaper their "condition is probably somewhat better physically."

§ 67. There are *reasons* why the Malthusian theory cannot be true, as well as *facts* to show that it is not.

It is an ascertained law of nature that the lower any form of life stands in the scale of existence, the greater the rate of its propagation and multiplication; the higher it stands the less its rate of increase. Vegetables, as a whole, therefore surpass the animal kingdom as a whole. A potato sprout multiplies twenty fold in a single year; a grain of wheat even two hundred fold under favoring circumstances. The gardener who would make a plant propagate freely, starves it; but he knows that when by care and attention he has doubled its petals and brought it to an artificial perfection, it becomes sterile. The wild rose of the open fields brings its seeds to perfection; the rose of the garden cannot be raised from the seeds of its like.

So in the animal kingdom. The *Clio borealis*, of which vast shoals furnish a mouthful to the whale, multiplies by millions; the whales themselves almost as slowly as man. The progeny of a pair of rabbits in a few years will be reckoned by thousands; that of a pair of wild elephants not by dozens, while tame elephants, though well fed and cared for, and living under their native skies, and allowed a large degree of freedom, cease to breed.

**§ 68.** Does not this natural law continue in force when we compare the highest of animals with the rest? Why should the whole order of nature be reversed in man's case? The things that serve him as food, stand below him in the order of nature; their multiplication must therefore be more rapid than his.

Not only does the law hold good as to man in comparison with the animals; it is equally true of man as compared with man. The higher the form of life, the slower the rate of its increase. Whenever any nation, or class within a nation, have attained to a high degree of development and culture, there is a reduction of its rate of propagation, and in many cases its extinction begins. It is proverbial that men of genius leave no posterity. In ancient *Greece* and *Italy* the extinction of rich and privileged families went on constantly. Augustus had to reconstruct the Roman Senate from among the plebeians, as only fifty families of senatorial rank were left. In *France* De Tocqueville could specify two hundred old families in one district alone that had become extinct from various causes within a century. Mr. Greg ascribes the markedly Gallic character of the French nation to the extinction of the superior Frankish race who gave their name to the country and constituted its feudal aristocracy. In *England* few of the Barons who took part in the Wars of the Roses are still represented in the English aristocracy, and genuine pedigrees rarely extend farther back than the times of the Tudors. Of the Norman aristocracy who came in with the Conqueror, and who were one in forty-two of the whole population, only a single descendant was known in David Hume's time. In spite of new creations, the ratio had fallen to one in eighty-eight at the beginning of the fifteenth century, and to one in 12,500 at the beginning of the present century. A multitude of peerages are extinct for want of heirs, and of 1400 baronets created between 1611 and 1819, the families of 783 are now extinct. In the *United States*, although the rate of increase is very high, yet it is by no means universally so. In the New England States, the native population, which in two centuries grew from 45,000 to

4,000,000 souls, is now increasing very slowly indeed. This might be ascribed to the great emigration to other parts of the country, but the observations founded upon the number of births to marriages shows this reason to be not sufficient. The most cautious estimate makes the number in the earlier periods to have been six children to a marriage; in the later, about four. [Franklin (1751) says: "Marriages in America are more general, and more generally early, than in Europe. And if it is reckoned there that there is but one marriage per annum among one hundred persons, perhaps we may here reckon two; and if in Europe they have but four births to a marriage (many of their marriages being late), we may here reckon eight."] On the other hand, the foreign population is growing rapidly, and doubtless will continue to do so, until it rises to the level of the native in education and general culture. In New York the census of 1865 showed that in nearly one-fourth of the families of that state no children had been born, and that in more than three-fourths the average was little over one child to each family.

> It is of course extremely probable that prudential considerations have much to do in these cases with the avoidance and the postponement of marriage, and consequently with diminishing the increase of the population. As society grows in wealth and in an exaggerated respect for wealth as an element of social standing, young people are less and less disposed to "begin life where their parents began; they must begin where their elders left off." The only point of objection that we would raise to Mr. Malthus's view of this "moral check on population" is that such artificial and exaggerated prudence is not a beneficent check to a wrong tendency, but itself a wrong and lamentable habit,—which detracts from the health, the happiness and the morality of the community.

§ 69. As of classes, so of nations. A high degree of civilization and mental culture imposes an immediate and natural check upon the growth of numbers. The growth of mind and the growth of numbers are two balancing forces, two tendencies that counteract each other.

But the growth of mind is a natural result of the growth of numbers, unless the constitution and course of nature have been wilfully or thoughtlessly interfered with by a bad social economy. There is implanted in the nature of the race a tendency to rise from poverty and barbarism to wealth and civilization. But this tendency has scope for its exercise only when man can rely upon the help and coöperation of a sufficiently large body of his fellow-men, in the work of subduing nature, and when association and coöperation are not artificially hindered or checked. The more people there are in a well-managed country—up to any number that ever has been reached or is likely to be—the better each man will be fed and clothed, if their industry be wisely directed. The more the numbers, in that case, the greater that people's mastery over nature, and the larger the share of the good things that will fall to each individual.

Thus we find that population is self-regulative. Its multiplication brings the civilization, that is the one effectual and all-efficient check to all undue multiplication. "The excess of fertility has rendered the process of civilization necessary; and the process of civilization must inevitably diminish fertility, and at last destroy its excess" (Herbert Spencer).

§ 70. Mr. Doubleday was the first who argued that a physiological reason or several of them lay at the root of these facts. He suggested that ample and sufficient food had directly the effect of lowering the fecundity of the race. There may be truth in the suggestion, but it is more probable that cerebral development has that tendency. This seems to be true even of the higher animals, as is seen in the case of the tame elephants of India. As man's brain expands, the objects of his desire multiply, and the natural desires common to the whole race lose their prominence and despotic strength. For a time they continue to exist in an excessive and unnatural force, the fruit of long ages of unrestrained indulgence,—the survivals of the period of barbarism. The passion for alcoholic liquors, for instance, may be fairly traced back to ages when drunkenness formed the only escape from a sordid, uncultured life, which admitted of no less material exhilaration.

in this particular instance, the distribution of the chemical elements of the human frame—phosphorus especially—seems to be closely connected with the question. But we may well hold with Mr. Greg "that other physiological causes of antifecund tendency are yet to be discovered; and that races, nations and families would not so often die out were it not so."

§ 71. By another compensatory law of nature, the less the rate of the reproduction of any form of life, the greater the prolongation of the life of the individual specimen. What nature produces with difficulty, she guards with care.

This law also holds good between different classes of men. Steadily for centuries past there have been added days, months, years to the average length of human life,—partly from occult natural causes, partly from the growth of medical science and the adoption of wiser sanitary and hygienic methods. Thus, as Macaulay notes, the death-rate in London in any ordinary year of the seventeenth century was greater than in a bad cholera year of the nineteenth; and the poorest woman in our times can command better medical attendance than the queens of that era could have obtained. The death-rate fell between 1655 and 1845 from one in twenty-three to one in forty. French and German statistics show that the wealthy and educated classes live at least a third longer than the poor and uncultured classes.

So again it is a mark of the great advance of Christendom, as compared with other groups of nations, that the great epidemics no longer originate within its borders. And since Christian governments have taken measures to put under sanitary regulations, the vast Mohammedan and Pagan pilgrimages and festivals, which still breed pestilences, it is to be hoped they soon will cease.

§ 72. Supposing that a bad social economy should check a people or a large mass of it in its natural growth in civilization and intelligence, what would be the effect on their numbers? That would depend upon the vitality and elasticity of the stock to which the people belonged.

(1) In some cases, as in the provinces under Mohammedan rule, oppression seems to produce a depression of spirits or of

nervous energy, and thereby to exercise a singularly sterilizing influence. The population of a besieged city is notably sterile.

(2) More ordinarily, however, the removal of the true preventive checks, the growth of intellect and the access of comfort, tends to cause a rapid and abnormal increase of numbers. The starved man, like the starved plant, propagates freely. Reduce the people to the level of the beasts and they will multiply like the beasts. And so their numbers may become really excessive, and the mass of a community sink ever deeper in poverty and misery. Such a result may be expected when the wealth of a nation tends to concentrate in the hands of a few, instead of being disseminated throughout the whole people in something like equality. Overpopulation in such a case is not the consequence of natural laws, but of man's wilful interference with them.

§ 73. Man's history as a producer of food may be described as ordinarily passing through three stages. In the first he is a hunter depending upon the voluntary, and therefore the scantiest, productions of the earth that were fitted for his use. In the second he is a shepherd, who has mastered the services of that division of nature which meets his wants with most directness and least labor; but he is compelled to migrate with his tribe when they seek new pastures, and he has no rights and no safety save as a member of it. In the third he is a tiller of the soil, a member of a body politic, possessed of a fixed home. He makes an acre produce as much food as hundreds did in the first stage, or tens in the second. He is able to act in greater independence of other men; able also to associate more closely with them. The societary circulation moves more rapidly and consequently more forcefully. The resistance of nature diminishing, the pressure of population upon the means of subsistence, which was very great in the first stage, and great still in the second, in large measure disappears. It was that very pressure that overcame the natural inertia of man and forced him to press forward. "For his sake" the earth was accursed to be the home of briers, thorns and thistles, that difficulties might develop his power as the earth's appointed master.

**§ 74.** Man's "power over nature" continues to grow with every advance in the compactness of society. Men obtain the use of more iron and coal, houses and ships, wool and cotton, in return for less labor, as society advances. When the density of population made it worth while to carry the water in pipes through the streets of our city, it was obtained with far less outlay of labor than when every man carried his bucket to the river's bank, or even to the pump, whose erection also marked a stage in social development. So when through the growth of population it becomes "worth while" to sink a shaft to the coalbed, it is no longer necessary to waste wood as fuel and spend labor in chopping it, and the time saved can be spent in turning the trees into lumber or some other profitable work. Till the grist-mill is erected the labor of a thousand arms is expended in grinding grain; the work then becomes the business of a few persons, and the rest have the more time for better work than turning hand-mills or pounding the wheat in *querns*. And these are but specimen facts that represent the whole movement of society.

"From the beginning," says Herbert Spencer, "the pressure of population has been the proximate cause of progress. It produced the original diffusion of the race. It compelled men to abandon predatory habits and take to agriculture. It led to the clearing of the earth's surface. It forced men into the social state; made social organization inevitable; and has developed the social sentiments. It has stimulated to progressive improvements in production, and to increased skill and intelligence. It is daily thrusting us into closer contact and more mutually dependent relationships. After having caused, as it ultimately must, the due peopling of the globe, and the raising of all its habitable parts into the highest state of culture; after having brought all processes for the satisfaction of human wants to perfection; after having at the same time developed the intellect into complete competency for its work and the feelings into complete fitness for social life,—the pressure of population must gradually bring itself to an end."

## CHAPTER FIFTH.

### The National Economy of Land.

§ 75. We have defined a nation as a people occupying a continuous area, and owning this in a more eminent sense than any part of it is owned by any of its citizens. Its stewardship of the economic interests of its people extends to the general oversight of their rural economy, and calls for the careful removal of all obstacles—especially those of a legal kind—to its improvement and that of the people engaged in it; and also for the adoption of such measures of improvement as are not easily attainable by individual action. It may justly be said that this is true of the duty of the state towards any form of industry; but from the peculiar relation of agriculture to the very existence of the nation, the state stands in a relation of far greater responsibility here. Many of those who most incline to exclude the state from all activity in the sphere of industrial interests, are quite ready to admit that where motives of public policy call for interference, the landowner may fairly be treated as the trustee or steward of the national property, not in any absolute sense the owner.

§ 76. What was said in the preceding chapter of the general advance of industrial methods through the growth of numbers and of the resulting power of coöperation, is eminently true of agriculture. As time advances, larger crops are reaped at a less cost upon lands that were early occupied, and those that were previously inaccessible to tillage, are cleared or drained. A larger amount of labor and capital becomes available, and can be expended with perfect safety upon the same field, as the crops are increased in still greater ratio. Especially the division of labor contributes to this. The early agriculturist was "Jack of all trades and master of none." His house, his clothing, his rude tools, everything that he had, was his own workmanship. But when these are produced for him by skilled artisans, who set him at leisure to do his farm-work better, he obtains all these things at a less outlay of labor, and of much improved quality.

§ **77.** Early agriculture was *extensive* in its method; that is, it expended a small capital upon a large surface. Just as the hunter required a larger area than the shepherd, and the shepherd more than the farmer, so the bad and imperfect agriculture of a poor half-savage age, required a larger area than when methods of tillage are highly improved and the capital at the command of the farmer has increased. Thus we find half-barbarous peoples in earlier times driven by famine from lands that now sustain a dense population.

English agriculture in the middle ages is a case in point. As much of the land as is now under wheat was taken up in raising as much food as would now suffice for a million and a half of persons. The population was something between that number and two and a half millions; yet nearly the whole people were employed in producing food; even the townsmen poured out into the country to help to gather in the harvest, and the Long Vacation at the Universities was established that their thirty thousand students might go home to assist. As much seed was sown to the acre as at present, but the average yield was only above one-fourth what it is now. Yet the climate of England, as of all Northern Europe, was warmer than it now is. Grapes grew plentifully in the open air, and wine was made that compared with those of France. "The land was imperfectly drained; the working of the soil was shallow; the manures employed were limited" to such as were ready at hand, at a time when the Flemish farmers imported English marl. "Scanty as the crop was, it seems to have been very exhausting, for half the land, in ordinary cases, lay fallow. . . Such crops as were obtained, were not procured without large relative expenditure." The agricultural implements were of the poorest; the plough was a ponderous structure of wood and iron, which it took four horses to drag over, rather than through, the soil. Metal was so scarce, being mostly imported from Normandy, that the wear and tear of plough-iron in a dry season was a large item in the farm budget.

As little hay and no green crops were raised, the sheep were mostly killed at Martinmas; and such as were left, with the oxen, starved through the winter, so that improvement of stock was impossible. As late as 1547, bullocks bought for the navy weighed less than 400 pounds. Few garden-vegetables were cultivated, and down to the reign of Elizabeth, they were imported for the tables of the rich from the Continent. This want and the general use of salt food spread scurvy and even leprosy among the people.

 See Prof. Thorold Rogers's *History of Agriculture and Prices in England*, vol. i.

§ 78. Later agriculture is *intensive;* that is, it expends a large capital upon a small surface. It finds at its hand sources of wealth that tax all its resources for their mastery, but more than repay the larger outlay. It goes down to the sub-soil, instead of spreading over the top-soil of new fields; it finds a new farm under the old one. It gives up methods of rotation in which the land lay fallow, and adopts a new one, in which, through generous returns to the soil, it yields two crops a year. It multiplies the number of live-stock on a farm, and feeds them generously and under shelter, that it may obtain the means to overcome the natural barrenness of the soil or multiply its fertility. It masters the coldness and heaviness of clayey or low-lying soils by artificial drainage, so that the crop in harvest is advanced by weeks and the peril of the autumnal rains avoided. It offers the highest premium for improvements in live-stock, seeds and implements. "Many of these agricultural practices are only possible where there is a large agricultural population; for which, on the other hand, work is found by these very practices" (Laveleye).

§ 79. While the finest results in agriculture are achieved (as in parts of Saxony) by the outlay of a large capital, directed by large intelligence, upon a considerable area of land,—yet, with the actual human material engaged in farming, and in the existing state of its intelligence, the best results, on the whole, are had where the farms are small and especially where they are owned by the actual cultivators. Progress towards the subdivision of the land—up to a certain limit—is a gain to agriculture. The opposite is a retrogression.

This fact was known even to the ancients. Solomon seems to refer to it when he says: "Much food is in the tillage of the poor;" and the Mosaic law forbade the permanent alienation of lands after their distribution among the people. But the law was evaded or ignored in the eagerness to form great estates; and Isaiah denounces a woe upon "them that join house to house and field to field, till there be no place, that they may be placed alone in the midst of the land," and the woe is the desolation of the land and the reduction of its average yield of food for man (V. 8–10).

Under Roman rule in Italy the small holdings were swallowed up in the great estates of the aristocracy, in spite of the efforts of the Gracchi to preserve the patrimony of the poor. The first step seems to have been the enclosure (*possessio*) of the common lands (*ager publicus*) upon which the common people depended for grazing, and which were absolutely necessary to their methods of agriculture. (The same process was arrested in Attica by the laws of Solon, but was carried out in Lacedæmon.) Pliny tells us the result: "Large estates have been the ruin of Italy (*Latifundia perdidere Italiam*)." The peninsula declined steadily in all the elements of wealth and production. The emperors had to obtain from Africa and Egypt the wheat that fed the Roman populace. The incursions of the barbarians led to the breaking up and redistribution of these monstrous estates, and Italy was able to feed her own children again.

§ 80. In the kingdoms of Western Europe only England and Spain have repeated the experience of ancient Italy, and only the former persists in the policy that led to it.

In these kingdoms (as in most, perhaps in all, countries in the earliest stage of society), the land was at first held, not by individual owners "in severall," but by bodies of freemen associated in a village community. Their land or *mark* lay, as it were, in two concentric circles around the village or *thorp*. The outer and broader was the *folk-land* or common on which their cattle mostly grazed. The inner circle of lands that lay next the thorp was divided into three *fields*, in each of which every *marksman* had a share, but the whole was cultivated in common by customary methods and under a rotation of crops that left one field fallow and under pasture each year. In the thorp itself every man's house and courtyard were his personal possessions; here community gives way to immunity.

Gradually the equality of the marksmen in possession and dignity gave way to a more aristocratic constitution of society. A manor-house, often a castle, rose above its humbler neighbors, and a lion's share of the mark fell to the lord of the manor, while upon the inferior marksmen devolved the duty of cultivating these demesne lands as well as their own. A social revolution, like the Norman Conquest of England, brought in a new lord of the manor, but added to, instead of removing the burdens of the people. The bulk of them latterly became *villeins*, as tenants who paid for their lands in the form of customary services in tilling the lands of their lord a certain part of their time. The value of this labor was so trifling that the lord was quite willing to commute the service for a money-payment, so that villeins became copyhold tenants at a fixed rent. With the progress of society, labor rose in value and produce fell, through the former becoming more productive. The people grew richer; the lords of the manors poorer. From tenants the farmers became freeholders, for if the lord wanted money, the price of broad acres would be readily forthcoming from some old stocking hid away in the thatch-roof. " There can be no doubt that the lands of the feudal lords were largely alienated in small parcels. Many causes contributed to this result" (Thorold Rogers). The masters now sought—especially after the enormous reduction in the labor-supply by the black death,—to cancel these contracts and reduce their tenants to villeinage, requiring at their hands the old services. Fortunately for the latter, the principle of custom or usage was all-powerful in that early age. In the absence of large intelligence and intellectual freedom, every established usage was treated as having the strongest prescriptive right.

The custom that fixed the form and amount of the tenant's rent was as valid as that by which the lord held his estates. The people rose in Wat Tyler's insurrection against the innovation, and the aristocracy, although successful in putting them down, relinquished their claim rather than provoke another such rebellion on conservative principles.

§ 81. An indirect way of stopping this reconquest of the land by the people was found in the enclosure acts, of which the first was the famous Statute of Merton (temp. Henry III). By the provisions of these the aristocracy were authorized to enclose such parts of the outlying folk-land as were not necessary for the use of the tenants and freeholders of the manor. By others passed at a later date the enclosure of demesne lands lying in the fields of the mark itself, and consequently the breaking up of the old system of tillage, was allowed. This last measure, which involved a complete revolution in the rural economy of the country, was consummated by the sixteenth century. It was one that must have been adopted sooner or later. The old system of communistic land tenure imposed burdensome checks upon industry and enterprise; it held back the farmer from adopting any but customary or traditional methods of tillage; it took away some of the strongest incentives to industry. After its abolition, although the large landowners turned a large part of their enclosed lands into pasturage, to avoid paying what seemed to them the extravagant wages then asked, yet such was the improvement in methods of tillage that there was an increase in the entire production of wheat.

But this " dissolution of the ancient copartnership in the use of the soil, and the establishment of separate and independent farms in its stead," called for the most scrupulous and careful adjustment of rival claims both in the laws and in their interpretations. Instead of this we have loosely worded statutes, passed by Parliaments in which the landed interest was supreme, and interpreted by subservient and corrupt judges. Sir Thomas More, an exception that did honor to the bench, tells us of "husbandmen thrust out of their own; or else by covin and fraud, or violent oppression, put beside it; or by wrongs and injuries so wearied that they be compelled to sell all." Vastly disproportionate shares of the common grazing lands were enclosed; parts of the three fields to which the lord had no claim were taken in with his demesne lands. Even when the farmer was not dispossessed of his plough-land by force or fraud, he was often broken in spirit and in fortune by the enclosure of the commons, and sank into the rank of a day-laborer. "The peasantry lost not only the benefits derived from the right of common over the greater part of England, but that loss involved in numerous cases the loss of their separate fields. They had lived upon the produce of the two, and their husbandry was based on it."

§ 82. The dissolution of the monasteries, and the distribution of the church lands among the new aristocracy created by the Tudors, added to the misery of the people. The new owners treated tenants and freeholders as possessed of no rights in the land. The outcry of the people could not be stifled; it forced the Protector Somerset to appoint a commission of inquiry, which reported that the charge of wholesale and general injustice was fully substantiated by the evidence; but they could suggest no remedy. From this period we begin to hear of a "dangerous class" in the alleys and back streets of English cities, where disbanded monks and broken agriculturists congregated. The yeoman class, which had been and still was the strength of the nation, in peace and war, at home and abroad, in church and state, was greatly reduced in numbers and weight, and oppressed by rack-rents. "My father," says Bishop Hugh Latimer, "was a yeoman and had no lands of his own; only he had a farm of three or four pounds by the year at the uttermost, and hereupon he tilled so much as kept half a dozen men. He had walk for a hundred sheep, and my mother milked thirty kine. He was able and did find the King a harness with himself and his horse while he came to the place where he should receive the King's wages. I can remember that I buckled his harness when he went unto Blackheath field [in 1497]. He kept me to school, or else I had not been able to have preached before the King's majesty now [in 1549]. He married my [six] sisters with five pounds (or twenty nobles) apiece, so [besides] that he brought them up in the fear of God. . . . He kept hospitality for his poor neighbors. And some alms he gave to the poor. And all this did he off the said farm, where he that now hath it payeth sixteen pound by the year or more, and is not able to do anything for his Prince, nor for his children, or give up a cup of drink to the poor."

§ 83. Under the kings of the house of Stuart and under the Commonwealth, the yeoman class rallied as to numbers and weight in the nation. We find patriotic writers boasting of them as the glory of England and the terror of France. Lord Chancellor Coke speaks of one-third of England as held in copyhold, i. e., at rents incapable of being raised above the rates specified in the copy or roll of the manor. "Now copyholders," he says, "stand upon sure ground; now they weigh not their lord's displeasure; they shake not at every blast of wind; only having an especial care of the main chance, namely, to perform exactly what services their tenure doth exact,—then let the lord frown, the copyholder cares not, knowing himself safe." Lord Macaulay estimates the landowners in 1660 at 160,000, and as forming with their families one-seventh of the population. At that time all copyhold and similar tenures were converted into soccage tenures by being placed under the jurisdiction of the king's courts. Down to the middle of the eighteenth century the distribution of the land among small holders and owners was going on without interruption, but at that date it ceased, the tendency to concentration took its place. The subsequent history of English land tenure is a record of the enclosure of the commons without regard to the rights of the poor,—of the absorption of small holdings in great farms without regard to customary tenure, and of the extinction of the yeoman class without regard to the nation's higher interests. Between 1701 and 1867 one-third of the farmed and pasture lands of England were enclosed by the rich, often by means of money loaned them by the state for the purpose.

Leases are become exceptional, being rarer for nine years than in the Middle Ages for ninety. Much of the land is held at rack-rent; that is, the highest price that can be got in the open market. The great mass of it is gathered into large estates, which grow in bulk, while the number of landowners is small and diminishing. Very little of it comes into the market, and that is sold "at fancy prices" to rich men who can afford a country-seat. The working classes have become more and more wretched and dependent; all sense of any relationship, other than that formed by the payment and receipt of wages, is now lost by both the landowner and the people on his estate. "In fact, there is no longer a true rural population remaining, for the ends, political, social and economical, that such a population ought to fulfil. The landed yeomanry, insignificant in number, and a nullity in political power, are steadily disappearing altogether. The tenant farmers have lost the security of tenure, the political independence, the prospect of one day farming their own lands, which they formerly enjoyed. And lastly, the inferior peasantry not only have lost ground in the literal sense, and have rarely any other connection with the ground than a pauper's claim, but have sunk deplorably in other economical respects below their condition in former centuries. Thus a soil eminently adapted by natural gifts to sustain a numerous and flourishing population of every grade, has almost the thinnest and absolutely the most joyless peasantry in the civilized world." . . . "Once, from the meanest peasant to the greatest noble, all had land, and he who had least might hope for more; now there is being taken away from him who has little, even that which he has—his cottage, nay, his separate room. Once there was an ascending movement from the lowest grade to the highest; now there is a descending movement in every grade below the highest."

See Cliffe Leslie's *Land Systems of Ireland, England and the Continent.*

§ 84. Attempts are made to explain this state of affairs by ascribing it to the operation of causes that were equally and even more vigorously in action when the tendency was to the division and distribution of the land. Thus some ascribe it vaguely to the perpetuation of the feudal system and its land tenure in England. We have seen how the customary tenures of that system operated most powerfully to the advancement of the people at the expense of their lords. We have also seen how those forms of tenure, with their half-defined and therefore objectionable rights, were finally expunged from English law at the Restoration. And in fact the best landlords in England are those that retain under the new forms something of the old spirit that made feudalism endurable,—to wit, the sense of a personal relationship between higher and lower, and the sense of a duty to the land. Their tenants have security without leases, for they know that no unfair advantage will be taken of them. As they sometimes express it, their confidence in the family is as good as a lease.

Others ascribe the mischiefs of the system to the right of primogeniture, by which the whole estate passes to the eldest son, to the exclusion of his brothers and sisters. This no doubt is a mischievous rule, but it is one that tends to keep large estates undivided rather than to lead to the absorption of the small ones. No doubt it has the latter effect in an indirect way, by leaving large sums in the hands of the landowners to buy up these latter. But this right is not an invention of this century or of the last; it was in full operation long before the decline of the English yeomanry began.

Others urge the want of a proper system for the registration and transfer of land titles. This also is a grave mischief, but it is one of much longer standing than the mischief for which it is to account. It has not kept the rich from buying up the estates of poorer men.

§ 85. The true cause, as Coleridge pointed out, is the importation of purely commercial maxims into the rural economy of England. The trading spirit attained in England the ascendancy it has ever since possessed, about the time when the separation of the mass of the English people from the soil fairly began, viz.: the middle of last century. English political economy from Adam Smith down, with some notable exceptions, has been the exponent and the justification of that spirit. It has shaped public opinion, controlled the tenor of legislation, and controlled the direction of the industry of all classes. It has stripped the landlord of all notions of stewardship for the nation and duty owed to the land and the people who till it. It has led men to regard the production and cheapening of commodities as the one great end of all activity. It has sacrificed men and their personal interests to things.

Now in trade the law of parsimony is the supreme law. For trade aims at getting as large and as quick returns as possible, with the least possible expense in managing and collecting these. Trade can make no distinction between persons and things; it is (in a low sense) no respecter of persons. It sets aside the dearest friend or the worthiest object of pity, and takes the offer of the man who bids highest and offers the best security. Other things being equal, it prefers the largest purchaser to any other, and even abates the price in his favor; for the ultimate object being to get wealth enough to be rid of the trouble of getting it, the offer that involves least trouble is the best.

Apply these maxims to the management of an estate, and the problem becomes one of getting the largest returns with the least outlay in wages and food. All question of the well-being of the small farmer and the laborer is lost sight of. The holding of the former was taken in with other lands to make large farms, that the landlord might have fewer tenants to deal with and less trouble about his rents. The latter were systematically and designedly brought into a position of dependence, because they were thus the more easily managed. Their cottages and gardens, for instance, were let to the tenant-farmer with the understanding that he would see to repairs, and then the cottages were re-let by him without the gardens, that their sole dependence might be their wages. The wages-roll was cut down to the utmost, because the less labor the less expense; the majority of those who had lived by the land were driven to the cities, and only a fraction of the people of England now live by agriculture.

See Coleridge's Works; VI, 215–25 (Amer. Edition).

Did the English economists raise their voices in protest, when the highest interests of the nation were thus imperilled? They said: "We have nothing to do with those moral and political questions; we have no advice to offer. Only be it known to you that additional labor employed in manufactures is *more*, when employed in agriculture is *less* efficient in proportion." They left men to draw the inference that it was a national advantage when labor was withdrawn from work where it could not be effectively concentrated, and transferred to the cities and factories where it could. Furthermore they furnished them with the factory system for application to tillage,—the capitalist furnishing the means, and the actual worker on the land being reduced to the rank of a day-laborer. They applied to farming "the machinery doctrine of most produce from least labor," which is "the doctrine of starvation to the laborer, and dispossession to the small proprietor, and instead of belonging to the advance of knowledge is a retrogression" (Wren Hoskyns, M. P.).

"Political writers and speakers of this school have long enjoyed the double satisfaction of beholding in themselves the masters of a difficult study, and of pleasing 'the powers that be' by lending the sanction of 'science' to all established institutions and customs, unless, indeed, the customs of the poor. Instead of a science *of* wealth, they give us a science *for* wealth." (Cliffe Leslie.)

§ 86. The system may be a failure socially and politically; but the chief question for us here is—Is it an economic success or a failure? A study of its general features and a comparison with what we find in other countries leaves no doubt that, in spite of brilliant successes in many matters of detail, English rural economy is, on the whole, a failure, when regarded from an economic point of view.

(a) It has failed by displaying a lack of aggressive power. It has gathered up into large farms the areas previously cleared and brought under cultivation by the small farmers of the past;

it has in some degree improved upon their methods. But it has not evinced any ability to cope with and bring under tillage the vast area of English soil that still lies in a state of nature. A committee of the House of Lords of the session of 1873, after a searching investigation, reported that "the improvement of land, in its effect upon the price of food and upon the dwellings of the poor, is a matter of public interest; but that as an investment it is not sufficiently lucrative to offer much attraction to capital, and that therefore even slight difficulties have a powerful influence in arresting it." As we have seen, seven and a half millions of acres in England alone still yield no food for man or beast,—contribute simply nothing to the support of the nation. The only proposal made to attack these masses of unsubdued nature is, so far as we know, a proposal to divide them up into small farms. In some cases, especially in the Highlands of Scotland, the peasantry have been encouraged to enclose and fertilize small patches of waste ground that nobody else would touch. At the expiration of their nine years' leases they are commonly ejected, and their little *holms* or farms are taken into the larger farms. "I could name many," says a Scotch land-agent, "who use this crofting for their waste lands, and then turn out crowds of them and throw their land into large farms."

(b) It has failed to develop the natural powers of the soil. Were even the area that is now under tillage to be cultivated as experience, both in England and elsewhere, shows to be perfectly feasible, the country would be under no necessity of depending upon foreign harvests for her supply of food. English soil has been made to yield 57 to 60 bushels of wheat to the acre without exhaustion. The average yield is much less than half so much. It is so, because only the merest fraction of that soil has been treated as the scientific knowledge of our days suggests, and because the amount of capital laid out upon the land under the system of large farms is about half as great as would be expended by small farmers of thrift and intelligence.

(c) But the fundamental mistake and failure has been in the treatment of the human material of her agriculture. She has failed to bring into exercise one of the most powerful and efficient motives to thrift and industry that exists in the human breast, viz: the attachment of the small holder to the spot of earth that is his own, his home. That passion for the possession of land, which is elsewhere a source of public security and social permanence, she has made a source of public instability. By all the tenor of her legislation and the drift of her public opinion, she has helped in the work of sundering the workman from the soil, and of either driving him away from it to the city or retaining him in the pitiable position of a day-laborer at the lowest rate of wages consistent with bare life and shelter. She has taken no pains to diffuse the intelligence and scientific knowledge that would fit the rural classes to till the land as the needs of the country and the time demand. She has left them at the mercy of the squires and the farmers, growing every day more brutal and hopeless. "They are unable," says Canon Girdlestone, "to lay by anything. They are long-lived, but even in their prime are feeble; and at the age of fifty often crippled with rheumatism, the result of poor living, sour cider, a damp climate, hard work and anxiety combined. There remains nothing for them then but the parish-pay and the workhouse."

**87.** In Ireland the English conquest, begun in 1169, found the people still in the tribal state. The land generally was owned by the tribe, and the chief's rights extended little farther than to temporary maintenance during his constant peregrinations. The conquerors displaced the chiefs by Norman barons, who held the land under conditions similar to those which prevailed in England at that time. Not until the completion of the conquest, in the reign of Elizabeth, was there any disposition to disturb the common people. In that and the succeeding reign great areas of Irish soil were "planted" with English and Scotch settlers after the extrusion of the previous tenants, and the jurisdiction of the English common law was extended to the island, setting aside all the native customs of tenure and inheritance. The plantation of Ulster, chiefly by Scottish settlers, was the largest of these operations until the era of the Commonwealth. Cromwell, after the conquest of Ireland in 1652, formed a plan to drive the native population into Connaught and settle the three other provinces from the sister-island. This barbarous policy was carried out as far as was possible, and the people—rich and poor—stripped of their lands. At the Restoration a very imperfect restitution was effected, and the attempt to make the restitution complete under the reign of James II. was defeated by the renewed conquest of the island under William III. The destruction of Irish manufactures by hostile legislation in this reign produced a state of wretchedness worse than any caused by mere conquest and confiscation. It forced the people to secure land on any terms. They became tenants-at-will at rack-rents, with the certainty that the improvement of their lands would lead to a rise in their rents. For six generations past the labor of Irish tenants in reclaiming lands, erecting houses and fences, and adding to the value of their holdings has been confiscated by their landlords, who hardly ever lay out any money upon such improvements. There are exceptions, but this is the very general rule. As a consequence, the Irish people have had no motive to improvement. They became disheartened and wasteful farmers. As the English demand for meat and butter seemed to furnish a better return to the landlord, great bodies of the people have been at various times evicted from their holdings to make room for grazing-farms. If they could not manage to make their way to America, these tenants had to settle on any bare mountain-side or barren peat-bog, where they find shelter and obtain for a good price the privilege of growing, on land quite unsuited for the purpose, enough potatoes to keep them alive. The worst of these evicting landlords were those who obtained their lands on the sales ordered by the Encumbered Estates Court (1849–1859).

The inducement originally held out to Scotch and English settlers was the offer of "tenant-right"—*i. e.*, compensation for unexhausted improvements, and free sale of the good-will. This bargain was very generally broken by the landlords. Scotch settlers of Ulster found that they could not depend upon these promises, and to save themselves from ruin they emigrated in great numbers to America (1720–1770).

The recent land acts of 1870 and 1881 have for their purpose to terminate this confiscation of improvements and of tenant-right. They allow the land-courts to fix what would be a fair rent for the land, independently of the improvements the tenant has made. They punish with a heavy fine the eviction of tenants who are paying a fair rent, and they allow the tenant to dispose of his tenant-right when he decides to throw up his farm. The landlord himself can buy this at a valuation if he so wishes.

<small>See Prendergast's *Cromwellian Settlement of Ireland;* Sir Gavan Duffy's *Young Ireland;* Mr. Sullivan's *New Ireland;* and Mrs. Margaret T. Sullivan's *The Case of Ireland* (Philadelphia, 1881).</small>

In the Scottish lowlands the history of land tenure has run much the same course as in England. In the Highlands the tribal tenure lasted until 1748, the lands being the property of the whole clan, and the chieftains being chosen by the people and liable to be deposed if unpopular. In that year the British Parliament abolished the hereditary jurisdictions of the chiefs, and authorized the crown to give to each of them a baronial title to the lands of their clan, if they would surrender their chieftainship. Under this law the whole of the Highlands have been confiscated from the people and converted into private estates. The clansmen, from landowners, have become tenants, holding at the proprietor's pleasure. Great multitudes of them have been evicted to make room for deer forests and sheep pastures; others have seen their little holdings absorbed into large farms held by capitalist farmers. The towns, the sea-coast, and America have received the people of the Highlands, which now could not furnish one-tenth of the great military contingent which was raised eighty years ago for the war with France. The most cruel evictions were those of Sutherlandshire, in the second decade of the century. The whole interior of this great shire was depopulated, sixteen thousand tenants being driven to a barren sea-shore or to America. The heather was fired in early spring to destroy the pasture and force the immediate sale of their cattle. Their homes were burnt above the people's heads to effect their expulsion. Delicate women died of the shock, old people lost their reason; but not a hand was lifted in resistance or revenge. When removed to the seashore they were required, after hard and unaccustomed labor in fishing, to aid in the erection of new homes under the direction of the agent. For farming they had nothing except a few patches of soil on the ledges of the rocks.

See Mr. John Murdoch's "Letters on the Sutherland Evictions," in the *Mark Lane Express*. The history of those evictions has been misrepresented very elaborately in various works of reference, and in Mrs. H. B. Stowe's *Sunny Memories of Foreign Lands*, although their character was exposed very fully by the report of the Parliamentary Commission on the Scottish Poor Laws. One of the actual victims, a Highlander in Canada, prepared a reply to Mrs. Stowe's chapter on the subject, which he called *Gloomy Memories of the Sutherland Clearances*, but his sudden death just after his book was printed prevented its getting into circulation, and it is now exceedingly scarce.

In very few instances have the tenants of the large farms prospered in their new holdings. Many of them have thrown up their farms and left the country, and the landlords would be glad to relet to small farmers, but, having allowed the farm-buildings of the ejected tenants to fall into decay, they cannot secure such tenants without making large outlays in repairs.

§ 88. Passing from England to the Continent, we find the rival nations growing in the sort of strength that was once but is no longer the boast of England, the yeomanry. In France small proprietorship was the rule even before the Revolution. The old records abound in accounts of their purchases. It was their wretchedness under the excessive burdens of the Old Regime, when they paid nearly all the taxes, that led Arthur Young to prefer large farming; yet he admits that the peasants of many parts of France were prosperous, industrious and thrifty. They had risen to that state out of the deepest degradation. In the middle ages they could not stand against the English yeoman, because they were little better than slaves. The free play of economic laws steadily bettered their condition, and vested in them more and more of the soil. The Revolution abolished all customary tenures, but it threw the royal demesnes and the estates of the nobility upon the market, and abolished the right of primogeniture, besides releasing the peasantry from the burden of excessive taxation. The number of large estates rapidly declined; that of the actual landowners has immensely increased. The soil of France is now owned by more than four millions of her people. M. de Lavergne, often quoted by English economists as approving of the English system, says: "All the world accepts petty proprietorship not only as a necessity, but as a benefit. It is recognised as favorable to agricultural productiveness and to public security." To it France owes her vast wealth and her wonderful financial elasticity, exhibited in her management of the immense debt incurred by the last war. In many respects French agriculture has much to learn from that of England; but if the history of each for the last two hundred years be taken for comparison, the result will be a judgment greatly in favor of the former.

§ 89. Belgium is the strongest case in favor of small farms and intensive culture. The farmer in the Flemish provinces lays out twice as much on an acre as is done in England. Farms are continually divided, and with every division their yield of produce has increased. Vast quantities of horned cattle and of green crops are raised; wheat, indeed, is imported, but paid for by exports of meat and vegetables. East Flanders has and feeds 1800 people to every square mile of her barren soil. The small owner generally saves half his income, and is continually on the outlook for more land. The farms are mostly between five and seven acres in extent. Most of the land, indeed, is farmed at rack-rents on nine years' leases, with "customary" compensation for unexhausted improvements; but a large proportion is steadily passing into the hands of small holders, who, as in France, outbid all other competitors. So strong is the hunger for land that it is bought up with full knowledge that it will not give as high rate of interest upon capital as is offered by the money-market. The people are poor through the lack of all large industries and the market they give for labor and for food, and the consequent tax of the cost of transportation upon most of what they need besides food. But their poverty is disappearing; want and destitution are becoming more rare; agricultural methods are rapidly improving; the country is tilled like a garden, yielding several heavy crops every year, and presenting the most beautiful and civilized appearance of any in the world.

§ 90. In Prussia the mediæval system held its ground down to the beginning of the present century. The government "saw with terror, in 1808, how insecure was a state which had so great a claim on the bodies, and none at all on the hearts of its people" (Gustav Freytag). Some opposed change. The *bauer* was stupid, lazy and thriftless, it was said; nothing could be made of him. A government commission met at Memel in 1807 to draft a land-law that should effect the transition from the mediæval to the modern agriculture. They found themselves divided into two parties: on the one side the great statesman Stein, the great historian Niebuhr and his friend Stägemann; on the other a group of now-forgotten *doctrinaires*, who had studied English political economy under Kraus at Koenigsberg. The latter wished for a policy that would secure the maximum of production from the soil, independently of the welfare of the producers. "They held it indifferent whether the present feebler proprietors remained or not, if their place was supplied by wealthier ones, and thus the greatest possible amount of profit secured." They preferred, indeed, that the change should take that shape, following the English commercial maxim: "most produce by least labor." "Why," they asked, "waste the productive force of four proprietors and sixteen horses to do that which one proprietor and six horses can do better?" The other party "considered the promotion of the welfare of the actually-existing occupants of the soil as the true problem of the statesman;" else they "saw the likelihood of obtaining a class of proprietors who would have no moral interest in the welfare of the country, and they felt the importance of a numerous class of small landholders." Happily their counsels prevailed; the transition was effected by impartial legislation, and not on English principles nor by English methods. The peasant secured the complete control of his own labor, and rose from a state of villeinage to the freedom of a landowner; in return he ceded to his former master a portion of the land he had held, retaining the rest in fee simple. All restrictions on the sale of land were removed, and provision was made for cutting off entails. This measure was enlarged and extended to all parts of the kingdom in 1811. It aimed at the highest end of national economy, the welfare of the people; it secured the lower also—the maximum of production from the soil.

Since its adoption, the yeoman class has grown in numbers, wealth and independence. In Westphalia especially, land constantly passes into their hands by purchase. Its price has risen rapidly; it rose seventy-five per cent. between 1829 and 1843. The bulk of it is now in the hands of the actual tillers of the soil; the agricultural methods are very greatly improved, and the *bauer* is now proverbial for thrift and industry.

§ **91.** Switzerland takes rank next to Belgium in the perfection of its intensive culture, and the density of its population. Every foothold of ground is occupied; if the clefts of the rocks contain no soil, it is carried thither.

Norway with its rocky surface, and Denmark with its alternations of peat and gravel, would be—like Flemish Belgium—inaccessible to any sort of agriculture that did not bring into play the entire devotion and earnestness of their people. In both the greatest difficulties have been overcome and the largest outlays of labor rewarded.

Russia, in the emancipation of her serfs (1861), had to solve the problem that was before Prussia half a century earlier. The large proprietors and the students of English political and rural economy wished to see the land vested in the nobility, and the bulk of the peasantry reduced to the level of day-laborers. But the aristocratic party had lost its prestige through its failure to carry the Crimean war to a successful issue. The government secured to the serfs the right to purchase at a moderate rate enough arable and pasture land for the needs of each village, and undertook to collect the payment in small annual instalments and pay it over to the landowners. That the economic results of the measure are as yet anything but satisfactory must be admitted. This is due (1) to the virus of slavery still poisoning the minds of the people and leading them to regard work as a curse and a disgrace; (2) to the system of taxation, by which the public burdens are thrown chiefly upon the peasantry; and (3) to the fact that the system of communistic land tenure is still kept up in Russia, and in such a way as to deprive the peasant of many of the most powerful impulses to industry, improvement and thrift.

In Italy, the plains of the north are under petty culture, and the excellence of the agriculture is proverbial. In Tuscany the lands are farmed in larger portions on the *metayer* system, the landlord and tenant dividing the crop equally. To pass from Lombardy to Tuscany, is to go from better to worse; but to cross the Tiber to what was the Papal States and Naples, is to come into a country of large farms, in which beggary and bad tillage deface the earth. The yield is much smaller, and the rural methods are those of the days of Hildebrand, if not of Cato the Censor.

§ 92. Another chief point in the economy of land is to secure and preserve an equilibrium of the three great elements of the industrial state—the agricultural, the commercial and the manufacturing. To cherish and foster agriculture alone is not to cherish it at all. The farmer's work, unless misdirected and wasteful, produces more than furnishes food for himself and his household. Were it otherwise the whole population would have to be employed in agriculture, as was the case in the earliest period of the art. The existence of such a surplus sets free a part of the population to engage in work of producing other things that society counts among the necessities and comforts of life. When this class, and the number of persons needed for the exchange of the products of both classes, are large enough to consume the ordinary surplus product of the farming class, the three classes stand in equilibrium; the farmer is assured of a market for his crop, and of a fair exchange of other objects of desire for what he can spare. But if these two classes are not large enough to consume his surplus, the equilibrium does not exist, and the farmer must suffer accordingly. His labor goes for nought; his crop rots in the fields, or if gathered and taken to market, brings a trifling price because farmers are underbidding each other for the small sales that are possible. In our Mississippi valley, for instance, the equilibrium of the two classes has not yet been attained. "The burning of corn for fuel in the West, of which we hear dismal stories once in seven years, is an indication that too many people there are engaged in farming and too few in manufacturing" (*The Nation*, New York, 1869).

In the absence of a sufficient home market, the foreign demand for breadstuffs and other farm produce is the only dependence of the farmer. For reasons hereafter given, the exchange of raw produce for manufactured goods between distant points can never be a remunerative one for the producer of the former. Were the rural economy of every nation wisely managed, no such exchange could take place; save in years of extraordinary scarcity the transportation of large quantities of breadstuffs and the like across the seas would not be thought of. The foreign market can therefore last no longer than the bad management of a few densely peopled countries lasts; with every advance in agricultural methods and rural economy it must threaten to disappear.

And even while it lasts it is the most uncertain of all markets. The farmer who depends on it takes the risk of two harvests instead of one. If the foreign country have a bad harvest, and so need much grain, while his own country's harvest is not too good, he may get as fair a profit as the nature of the case permits; in any other combination of circumstances he will not. Still more complicated are his chances when other nations nearer the foreign market are competitors to supply its needs. In that case his success depends upon their comparative failure also. Worse still, the price he can get for what he sells at home is fixed and regulated by that of what he sends abroad; if a large surplus, raised for the foreign market, be left on his hands, prices will rule low in the home market also, because he and his fellow-farmers will be underselling each other in competing to supply its demand.

§ 93 The farmer who depends upon a distant market can never carry on his farming by the best methods. He cannot raise that variety of crops by which the pressure of tillage upon the resources of the soil is lightened; for such crops cannot be transported to a distance. He must grow the great staples that meet the foreign demand, year after year, to the exhaustion of the most important elements of his land. He cannot make such returns to the soil as will keep up its fertility; the refuse of the factory and the town are not to be had. The highly nitrogenized forms of animal manure he can procure in trifling quantities only, as his own cattle and those of his brother farmers are the only beasts of the sort in his neighborhood, and are far fewer in number than if he had a town close at hand making large demands for meat and dairy produce. He can only farm thriftlessly and wastefully; in our Eastern sense of the word his place is not a farm, but a wheat factory or a corn factory. The farmer who lives near his market is continually improving an instrument of great power and value; he who lives at a distance from his market is continually injuring it and breaking it. The one is adding every year to the wealth of the soil beneath his feet; the other is exporting that wealth to a distance, without the opportunity of making any return to the soil he is robbing of its fertility.

<small>The census of 1870 exhibits the undue preponderance of agriculture in the states we have referred to. In six Western States fifty-four per cent. of those who report any occupation were engaged in farming, while of the whole population of the United States so reported only forty-seven per cent. are farmers. In nine Southern States, from North Carolina to Texas, the proportion is as high as seventy-five per cent.

The six Western States have nineteen per cent. of the national population; but they raise forty per cent. of the whole corn crop, and forty-two per cent. of the wheat crop, while of all other crops they raise less than their share. Their industry lacks variety, being chiefly agriculture; their agriculture lacks variety, being chiefly the growth of cereals. In 1872, when the English demand for American breadstuffs was much above</small>

the average, Illinois produced enough to feed all her own population, and to supply the whole English demand, at that rate, for ten years. See a very able article on "The Farmers' Difficulty," by Edward Stanwood, in *Old and New* for September 1872.

§ 94. The theories of the national economy of land which pass current with the English economists seem to be suggested by their practice. Like the theory of population discussed in the last chapter, they seem designed to excuse the anomalies and miseries of English society, by throwing the blame on the natural laws which govern and condition the growth of society.

Indeed, the chief of the English theories about land grew directly out of the Malthusian theory of population. In the last statement of that theory, that Mr. Malthus made (1826) he concedes to his numerous opponents that so long as good land was to be had, "the rate at which food could be made to increase would far exceed what was necessary to keep pace with the most rapid increase of the population" possible. This shows that the whole question turns upon the relation of man to the soil.

The "theory of population" is therefore the parent of the "theory of rent" announced by David Ricardo in 1815, and designed to explain the way in which the growth of society makes the few rich and the many poor, by inuring chiefly to the benefit of a class of monopolists called landlords. In his view, rent arises from the insufficiency of good land to supply the entire people. The first settlers of a country take possession of the best lands; the second set of cultivators are obliged to take those that are worse, or pay nearly if not quite the difference in rent. When the second grade of land has been settled up, the next set must take up a third grade, or pay nearly if not quite the difference in yearly value for a share of the first or second. Thus as the growth of numbers requires the tillage of an ever larger area of the soil, each higher grade of land pays an increasing rent. With every advance in population men are driven to poorer and more wretched soils, and the monopolists of the higher grade of lands are able to live in idleness and plenty upon their continually increasing share of the growths of the soil. The only limit to the process will be reached when the only land that is unoccupied is too poor to repay cultivation. The rent that can be secured for any given piece of ground will be nearly if not quite the difference between its annual yield and that of the poorest lands under cultivation.

§ 95. To show what Mr. Ricardo asserts to be the *tendency* at work as a country grows in density of population, let us suppose the case of an island divided into a number of areas equal in extent but of various degrees of fertility, and each large enough to employ a hundred laborers. The best land in the series can produce (let us say) 900 bushels of wheat, giving nine bushels to each laborer if there be an equal division. The next best will produce (let us say) one-tenth less or 810 bushels, giving 1710 (or 900 plus 810) bushels to be divided between two hundred workmen; and so on. If the population double every twenty-five years, as Mr. Malthus says it may, the following table shows what the growth of population and of sustenance will be in two centuries :—

| Years. | Persons. | Bushels. | Share. |
|---|---|---|---|
| 1 | 100 | 900 | 9. |
| 26 | 200 | 1,710 | 8.151 |
| 51 | 400 | 3,150 | 7.875 |
| 76 | 800 | 5,670 | 7.0875 |
| 101 | 1,600 | 9,990 | 6.243 |
| 126 | 3,200 | 17,190 | 5.37 |
| 151 | 6,400 | 31,710 | 4.92 |
| 176 | 12,800 | 48,990 | 3.8 |
| 201 | 25,600 | 72,030 | 2.8 |

But on the theory of unequal division propounded by Mr. Ricardo, the owners of the lands last occupied would not get 2.8 but only 1.8 bushels each, and the amount which falls to them is just or almost the share that falls to the tenants of any of higher grade. The difference between that share and the actual annual yield is absorbed in rent. If the entire seven grades of superior land is leased to tenants, its owners absorb nearly if not quite 25,950 bushels as their royalty on the use of the land, leaving 46,080 bushels to the actual workmen. The denser the population, therefore, the greater the misery of the people, and every growth in their numbers increases their own poverty and adds to the wealth of these monopolists.

§ 96. This doctrine found even more acceptance with the English school, and elicited far less criticism and opposition, than that of Mr. Malthus on population. It was a more direct and explicit apology for the anomalous state of things in England; it explained how a nation might grow in wealth while a very large share of its people sank ever deeper in poverty and misery. It was a still more explicit and satisfactory verdict of "Nobody to blame,"—a still clearer excuse for the absence of effort to amend things. Mr. J. S. Mill goes so far as to pronounce this law of rent and of the increasing sterility of the land brought under cultivation, to be the very corner-stone of the science. "After a certain not very advanced stage in the progress of agriculture . . . in any given state of agricultural skill and knowledge . . . every increase of produce is obtained by more than a proportional increase in the application of labor to the land. This general law of agricultural industry is the most important proposition in Political Economy. Were the law different, nearly all the phenomena of the production and distribution of wealth would be other than they are." An American writer of the same school says: "It is natural—and if natural, proper—though we may not see the reason—that poverty and want, and disease and misery, should be the next-door neighbors of wealth and unbounded prosperity."

§ 97. On Mr. Ricardo's theory that land derives its value from the natural properties of the soil, and not from the labor expended on it, and that landlords are a class of monopolists who have possessed themselves of it, and thus managed to make the growth of society inure chiefly to their own benefit, the right of ownership in land is one that rests on no sufficient foundation, and one that many of the interests of society call upon the state to set aside and destroy. Mr. Ricardo himself was no friend of these "monopolists," and his school are as little so. Especially in late years they have been given to using phrases that strongly resemble the utterances of those communists, who would have the right to landed property, if not to all property, repudiated by society. They have held up the land-tenure of their country as the source of nearly all its social evils; they have insisted that the nature of landed property is such that it is both the right and the duty of the state to interfere with it in ways that would be public robbery if applied to other sorts of property; they have declared that the ownership of land—in contrast to the ownership of other things—is a public trust, a stewardship of which the nation may exact an account. The offspring of these teachings is the Irish Land Law of 1870, by which the landowner is forbidden to rent his land for the price that it will bring in the open market. All contracts are to be on terms that an Irish judge shall decide to be reasonable, and when the lease expires the tenant cannot be ejected unless paid for his good-will and improvements.

§ 98. Do the *facts* of history bear out this theory? If they do we shall find (1) that in any given area the amount of the produce of the land obtained in earlier times is greater in proportion to the number of laborers; (2) that of two countries, or two districts in the same country, if other things be equal, the one that is poorest in people is the one in which the average degree of personal wealth and comfort is the highest; (3) that the share that falls to the landlord increases, and that which falls to the laborer diminishes, as more land is brought under cultivation.

Not one of these results is sustained by observation. The facts alleged in the previous chapter in regard to the condition of savage nations, and of civilized peoples in the earlier stage, show us that the thinly-settled countries are those in which continual poverty prevails, and frequent famines occur. In the first and the second points, therefore, the theory diverges widely from the facts.

On the third point—the increasing *share* of the landlord, as distinguished from an increasing *amount*—the theory is equally at fault. With the growth of society in numbers, in intelligence, in the efficiency of its workers, the landlord obtains a continually increasing amount, but a continually decreasing share. His third falls to a fourth of the produce, but the fourth is more than the third was; the fourth becomes a fifth, but the actual amount is still increased. Adam Smith pointed this out as *the* difference between the times when feudal bondage existed in Europe and the whole crop fell to the landlord, and his own day when the landlord took a third or a fourth part of the produce, but got three or four times as much as the whole had once amounted to.

Mr. Malthus showed from official returns that in *England* the landlord in his day took but a fifth of the crop in rent, and yet got a larger quantity than in previous ages when his share had been one-fourth, one-third, or even two-fifths. We have it on equally high authority that between 1790 and 1833 the amount got by the landlord had doubled, while the improved condition of the laborer showed that the increase had not been at his expense. Mr. Senior says that the improvements in England between 1776 and 1836 had "more than doubled the wages of labor and nearly trebled the value of land."

<blockquote>These results are not open to question; they have been reached by competent statists, all of them of the school of Ricardo.</blockquote>

The official figures in regard to France show that of the gross produce of the culture of the soil, 35, 37, 43, 60 and 60 per cent., had been paid as the cost of cultivation at the dates 1700, 1760, 1788, 1813 and 1840, and that the yearly sum that fell to each family engaged in agriculture at each date was 135, 126, 161, 400 and 500 francs respectively. Comparing these figures with the price of bread at each date, we find that the people of France had not much over half enough to eat under Louis XIV.; about two-thirds of enough under Louis XV.; three-fourths under Louis XVI., and more than enough under the Empire. The minister D'Argenson in 1753, a year of no special scarcity, says: "Men die around us like flies and are reduced to eat grass." The Duke of Orleans brought a loaf of fern bread to the Royal Council, and placing it before the King, his brother, said: "Sire, see what your subjects live upon!" The returns to labor in France are by no means what they ought to be even now. France is more fertile than England, yet two-thirds of the French people are engaged in producing food for the nation, against one-third of the English; and with all, the latter are better fed and more prosperous generally. Furthermore, one-sixth of the soil of France is covered with forests; one-twenty-fourth of England. If Mr. Ricardo be right, this should mean that the pressure of population has not yet brought the French nation to the cultivation of the poorer soils, and that the acreage under tillage yields a larger average of bushels than in England. But notoriously the reverse of this is true. And if we compare department with department, it is found that the most populous parts of France are also those in which the yield per acre and the consumption of food per head are both greater, and the quality of the food better, than in the others.

§ 99. The study of the early history of land-tenures, begun since Mr. Ricardo's time, it is now admitted by English scholars, discredits his assumption that all the facts known to us can be traced back to the competition for the use of the soil. Such competition is quite modern in its origin. In former times land was not held by individuals, but by associated groups, bound together by kinship and by immemorial custom. The whole group held the soil in common as an inalienable possession, and assigned parts of it to single families for their use. While custom defined the rights of these families and prevented all intrusion upon them, custom also debarred the family from disposing of those rights. Where some chief or lord of the manor possessed a claim upon the services of the rest of its inhabitants, the kind and amount of this also were fixed by custom; and where a violent change of lordship overthrew existing customs, others of equal rigidity quickly grew up in their stead, and were quietly assumed to have held from time immemorial. No market for land, and consequently no competition for its possession existed among the actual cultivators. Only the extinction of these tenures in common, and the enclosure of the lands, created individual ownership in the modern sense, and with it competitive rents. Down to quite recent times the rent of land even in England was fixed by custom, not by competition, and much of it is still so held. But English economists, following Adam Smith and Ricardo, have always assumed that competitive are the only true rents, just as English lawyers have assumed that all customary rights are usurpations on the rights of the lord of the manor. Both opinions had their excuse in the almost if not quite universal ignorance of the historical fact; both have done great mischief to the common people, by fostering the notion that the traditional customary rights of the people to the land could be set aside without injustice.

"These tenures afford confirmation of the doubts suggested in Sir Henry Maine's *Village Communities* respecting the historical truth of the economic theory of the origin of rent. Early land-rents were not competitive rents; they were not at all in conformity with Mr. Ricardo's doctrine; they bore, for the most part, no relation to the fertility of the soil, or its vicinity to market, if there was any market at all. . . . Each manor was, as it were, a separate territory, inhabited by a distinct community. There was no competition for the tenure of farms from without; and within the manor the sole regulators of rent were the arbitrary will of the lord, and custom. The rent of the villein was at first, in theory at least, an arbitrary rent; in its next stage it was a customary rent, in labor or produce; in a third stage it became commuted into a money-rent, based on a valuation of the customary service or payments in kind. In the book before us [Blount's *Tenures of Land*] we have many examples of the customary rent in labor and in kind, and of the commuted money-rent; but there is not a single example of a competitive rent. Competitive rents only began with enclosures and the disruption of the old manorial community; and customary rents survive to this day in many a manor, in defiance of economic theory" (*The Athenæum*, 1874).

The only early instance of a rent not fixed by custom is that provided for in one of the old Irish laws, in which a member of one group, becoming an outcast, becomes the tenant of another. Of such a tenant as large a rent as could be exacted, might be justly demanded; but of a member of the sept itself only a fair (i. e., a customary) rent could be exacted.

§ 100. Mr. Ricardo is wrong in his very first premise. "The

elements of value to" the first settlers of a new country " are not the resources that are capable of development through industry and enterprise, but those which offer the readiest supply of the necessaries of life" (J. H. Burton). They do not begin with the best soil, and afterwards proceed to that which is worse, however natural and reasonable it may seem to assume that they do so. The best soil is usually not known to them as such; even if it were, it is nearly always inaccessible to them. Through its very wealth, it is not unusually covered with timber, whose clearance is impossible to them. More commonly it is marshy, and requires what would be to them a vast expenditure of labor to drain it. It lies in the lower parts of the country, to which the aqueous circulation has been for ages carrying down the richest elements of the soil. It is infested with malarias, bred of vegetable decay. It is utterly devoid of those natural facilities for defence, which in most situations are imperiously necessary to the settler.

The progress of civilization in all ages, therefore, has been from the thin and poor soils high up the rivers to the richer soils that lie nearer their mouths. The retrogression of civilization has been the abandonment of the richer soils and the retreat up the hillsides to those that are lighter and less fertile.

> The next chapter gives the historical proofs of these facts, and of the true law of settlement.

The great means that has enabled men to pass from the poorer soils to the richer is the power of coöperation that increases with the growth of numbers, unless some artificial obstacle has been interposed to prevent it. The sudden decline of numbers, or the diminution of the power of association, has had the effect of driving men back from the land that richly repays the labor expended upon it, to the soil that furnishes natural drainage, that can be ploughed with a crooked sapling and harrowed with a thorny bush. The labor expended upon such soil is slightly repaid; the crop reaped is therefore dear; but necessity has no choice.

## CHAPTER SIXTH.

**The National Economy of Land** (*continued*): **How the Earth was Occupied.**

§ 101. The historical refutation of Mr. Ricardo's theory, which is presented by the history of the settlement of the various countries of the earth, was first given to the world by Mr. H. C. Carey in his book *The Past, the Present and the Future* (1848). It is worthy of study, not only as a refutation of a dismal theory of the destiny of mankind, but for the light it casts upon the economic side of the world's history, and indirectly upon other sides also. It might be easily and fairly elaborated into an economical history of the earth, for that history is nothing but the story of man's victory over nature's resistance and the progressive mastery of her manifold utilities.

§ 102. The theory that we are discussing was devised to explain the condition of Great Britain, but no English antiquarian would have given such an account of the settlement of the country. When the Romans invaded England, it was at most about half as populous as at the date of the Norman conquest. "The woods must have been larger, the fens had not been partially reclaimed and made accessible by causeways; some of the tribes were unacquainted with tillage; the beech tree, which doubled our food for swine, had not been introduced; half the roots, vegetables and fruits, which now supplement our corn-crops, had not passed the Channel, and the great roads were not yet made on which the plenty of a fortunate district could be transported to parts where the crops had failed. The stunted British cattle, whose remains we constantly disinter, are proof that even if tillage was known, a large portion of the population lived upon milk. The best peopled parts of England were probably those which were most open and easy to cultivate; the home counties, Norfolk and Suffolk, and the south-western counties." A "mighty sum of toil has transformed the country throughout England. The fens and forests are a mere memory and a name; foreign trees grow in our hedge-rows; it is difficult to find a point within half a mile of which a road does not run; the climate has been modified as woods have been felled and marshes drained; our rivers are smaller than in the old days. Thanks to these labors, and to those marvellous changes in agricultural science, which may bear comparison with any triumphs of mechanics, England, left to her own resources, can now support four times the population that the country contained under Edward III., eight times our number at the period of the Norman conquest, and perhaps sixteen men for one whom Cæsar found in the island."

<blockquote>
In this and the following paragraphs quotations not otherwise credited, and much besides, are from Mr. C. H. Pearson's *Historical Maps of England, with Explanatory Essays* (2d edition, London, 1870). Mr. Pearson tries to account for many of the facts by military and political reasons, having no knowledge of the true law of the occupation of the land.
</blockquote>

§ 103. The Celtic tribes whom the Romans found in the island do not seem to have been either numerous or powerful, as the invading army that added the island to the Roman Empire numbered but 30,000 men. The home of the several tribes is in every case but one uncertain, but they seem to have been confined to the hills of the north and to the hill system of the south and west coasts, which opposes its cliffs to the currents from the Atlantic, and is divided from the rest of the island by the old Roman military road from London through Chester, which the Saxons called Watling Street.

The monumental remains of the ante-Roman epoch indicate this. "The earliest grave mounds are mostly found in the mountainous districts of the land,—among the hills and fastnesses; the later [Roman and Saxon] overspreading hill, valley and plain alike. Thus in Cornwall, in Yorkshire, in Derbyshire and in Dorsetshire, in Wiltshire and many other districts, the earliest interments are or have been abundant; while the later ones, besides being mixed up with them in the districts named, are spread over every other county. In the counties just named Celtic remains more abound than those of any other period. In Dorsetshire, for instance, 'that county,' as the venerable Stukeley declares, 'for sight of barrows not to be equalled in the whole world,' the early mounds abound on the downs and the lofty Ridgeway, an immense range of hills of some forty miles in extent,—while those of a later period lie in other parts of the county. In Yorkshire again they abound chiefly in the wolds; and in Cornwall on the highlands. The same again of Derbyshire, where they lie for the most part scattered over the wild mountainous region of the Peak,—a district occupying nearly one-half of the county, and containing within its limits many towns, villages and other places of extreme interest. In this it resembles Dorsetshire, for in the district occupied by the Ridgeway and the downs are very many highly interesting and important places. It is true that here and there in Derbyshire, as in other counties, an early grave mound exists in the southern or lowland portion of the county. . . . There are districts where there is scarcely a hill even in that land [of hills] where a barrow does not exist or is not known to have existed."

See *Grave Mounds and their Contents*, by Llellwyn Jewett. London, 1870.

§ 104. West of Watling Street lay (1) the ancient kingdom of *Cornwall*, which must have been densely peopled, as we learn from the Roman lists of towns, the traces of ancient agriculture and the abundance of ancient remains. Here is the seat of the events now clothed in poetry in the Arthur-Sagas. The land is now mostly abandoned by the farmer to the fisherman and the miner. (2) Wales, whose mountains were fought for as a prize by the two great branches of the Celtic race. (3) The Welsh kingdom of Strathclyde, which includes the Galwegian district of Scotland and the lake district of England. When the Roman occupation ceased, we find the Celts confined to this district and the south coast. Their literature " shows no acquaintance with the country east—let us say—of the second degree of longitude, beyond what a half-educated yeoman now might have of America. . . . Except perhaps in one case there is no authentic tradition of war with the Saxons or Angles in that region, or of British sovereignty there. The single exception is that of Kent." And yet the race is remarkably tenacious of traditions. It carried the Cornish Arthur-Sagas into Brittany; the Irish Fingal-Sagas into Scotland. It knew little or nothing of the east, of the rich lands containing nearly all the wheat-fields of England, while the west is devoted to grazing. What tribes were found there by the Romans were few and scattered. It was therefore open to Roman colonization, and a mixed multitude of Roman citizens and continental peoples was transplanted thither. Seventy thousand Roman citizens are said to have been killed in the massacres by which Boadicea began her revolt. This was the region that fell so easily into the hands of the German tribes, and after a few struggles became the site of Saxon kingdoms. As the Saxons pressed westward they encountered a fiercer resistance, and repaid it by enslaving the conquered people. At Domesday the percentage of slaves in the north and east was but $3\frac{1}{2}$ per cent.; in the five south-western counties 16 to 17 per cent.; and the intermediate degrees of serfage hold the same proportion. The west was the land desired by Saxon as well as Celt; its ranges of hills, that rise to mountains as they approach the sea, were the subject of protracted conflict, and it was the kingdom of Wessex that rose to such eminence that its king became Bretwalda or sovereign of England. "All the energy and enterprise of the Saxon name flowed naturally towards the west, and from the district of the West Saxons, at first only embracing Hampshire and a part of Wiltshire, went out all the conquering expeditions that wrested not only the south-west and the valley of the Severn, but the more southern of the Midland counties from the Britons."

§ 105. The early isolation of the Saxon kingdoms as of the Celtic tribes was largely due to the great lines of forest that ran across the country, and to the fens that covered much of its surface. To the former (as greatly increasing the annual rainfall) the existence of the latter was largely due. "The clouds which at present pass over our heads and break in another country or over the sea, were arrested by the simplest natural agencies; and the water that now flows down in a thousand drains to the river, was preserved in marshes and lakes, which in turn sent back what they had received in dank exhalations." The deflections of the Roman roads show that these were among their chief difficulties of engineering, while they show readiness to run over a hill instead of round it. In Saxon times these obstacles isolated closely related tribes, and forced them to advance from east to west, and to occupy the poorer soils on the high moorlands and the mountain-sides, where traces of the most ancient occupants are visible. We find the Saxon Saint Cuthbert praised because in his missionary tours "he was wont chiefly to go through those places and to preach in those hamlets which were high up on rugged mountains, frightful to others to visit, and whose people by their poverty and ignorance hindered the approach of teachers. He went out from the monastery often a whole week, sometimes two or three, and often also for a whole month would not return home, but abode in the wild places" and gave them lessons in husbandry and in finding and saving water (Hughes's *Alfred the Great*, pp. 28-9).

§ 106. Throughout early English history the lands beyond the Humber are slightly or not at all connected with the southern shires. Of the midland shires, now the most fertile grain-lands in the island, we hear next to nothing. "The map of Saxon-England is singularly bare for that midland district, and the few names that mark it are mostly of towns which Edward the Elder founded as a military frontier. Few, indeed, are the charters that record gifts of land in its rich pastures; scanty and late the names of monastic foundations that sprang up in it." "A great district popularly called the desert stretched from Durham through the West Riding [of Yorkshire] to the Peak [in Derbyshire;] and to a period as late as the twelfth century, contained no town of importance... The site of Durham was occupied by a thick wood in the twelfth century. Down to a much later time, a lamp used to be hung from the old steeple of All Saints, York, to guide travellers across the forest of Galtres. The Domesday Survey tells us that in Derbyshire five ' hundreds' out of six were heavily wooded; and that in Lancashire a quarter of a million of acres was covered with a network of dense woods." With the Normans begins a new era for these midland shires. "Generally the north of England, Kent and Gloucestershire, were the parts most thickly peopled under the Romans, while under the Saxons Wessex and the eastern counties were on the whole the best governed and developed. . . From Derby, with its one borough, to Wiltshire, with at least eight and perhaps sixteen, or Suffolk with six, is a great ascent. But it points to different conditions of country." "With the Norman dynasty came new conditions of national life. Wiltshire and Somersetshire declined in relative importance. . . Under King John Lincolnshire alone contributed a fourth of the exports between Newcastle and the Land's End. The midland districts of England were now neither desolate nor martial." Yet we still find districts now fertile named in mediæval history as morasses which threatened the destruction of armies; and the rich grain-fields of South Lancashire were in the reign of Elizabeth a quagmire that daunted the antiquary Camden. Oliver Cromwell was one of a "company of adventurers" who undertook to drain the fen of Huntingdon and Cambridge shires by diking the channel of the Ouse.

Northumberland during the Roman period was densely settled; Roman remains are numerous; Roman cities were frequent and of great size on its "naturally sterile" soil. It afterwards sank into comparative unimportance. The eastern lowlands of Scotland were at first an outlying part of this kingdom; the castle of Edinburgh is built on the site of a Northumbrian fortress designed to defend the northern frontier.

§ 107. The earliest history of the kingdom of Scotland goes back to the occupation of the Western Highlands by Scotch tribes from the north of Ireland and their subjugation of the

Picts. But the prehistoric remains, such as the subterranean dwellings and villages on the upper reaches of the river Don in the slopes of the Highlands, go still farther back. "The country is crowded with hill-forts, small and great; they may be counted by hundreds. They consist of mounds of earth or stones, or both, running round the crests of hills." Every spur of the Cheviots is crowned with remnants of old fastnesses whose builders are unknown to us.

As to the Irish occupation of the Highlands it has well been said that " one acquainted with the agricultural resources of the north of Ireland at the present day, might question the inducement of a people to leave that region for the sake of settling in Western Scotland. But it is observable of the Celts as of other indolent races, that the elements of value to them are not the resources capable of development through industry and enterprise, but those which offer the readiest supply of some of the necessaries of life. . . The geological character of the country would supply them with a limited quantity of alluvial soil for immediate cultivation. It was found on the deltas of the mountain streams, on the narrow straths around their margin, and occasionally in hollows containing alluvial deposits, which might have been the beds of ancient lakes. These patches of fruitful ground the first immigrants would find ready for use. Modern agriculture has indeed been able to add very little to their area, and has wisely determined that sheep-farming is the proper use of those tracts of mountains among which the alluvial patches are thinly scattered. It is a curious coincidence worth remembering, that those very lands in Northern Ireland which the ancestors of the Scots Highlanders abandoned, were in later times sought and occupied by Scots Lowlanders as a promising field of industrial enterprise."

See Burton's *History of Scotland*, Chapter V. (Edinburgh, 1873).

As in English history, we find a Celtic kingdom (Strathclyde) occupying the western hills and Cumberland, while the more fertile Lothians lie open to the invader and yield to the Teutons with hardly a struggle. But even in the Lothians the richer soils—as along the Tweed—are of more recent occupation and were forests and swamps two centuries ago.

§ 108. The comparatively bare and now insignificant islands that lie around the coast were once prizes. The Romans seized the Orkneys and perhaps established a garrison there, and the remains of cyclopean works attest a still earlier occupation of the Islands. In the Ossianic traditions they formed a powerful kingdom. In the middle ages they were pledged to the King of Norway as security for a sum of money that would now more than purchase their fee simple. To the west lie the far more barren Hebrides, which, with the Isle of Man, Dublin and the south-east of Ireland, once formed a powerful Danish kingdom. These islands, once " rich and powerful," we find afterwards " sinking into poverty," while the others have merely " preserved a respected position in the British Empire, as maintaining a valuable and industrious population."

The Duke of Argyle, President of the Cobden Club, in his book about Iona tells us the story of the settlement of that island and the adjacent highlands. " At a time," he says, "when artificial drainage was unknown, and in a rainy climate, the flats and hollows, which are now generally the most valuable portions of the land, were occupied by swamps and moss. On the steep slopes alone, which offered natural drainage, was it possible to raise cereal crops. And this is one source of the error which strangers so often make in writing on the Highlands. They see the marks of the plough high up upon the mountains, where the land is now very wisely abandoned to the pasturage of sheep or cattle; and seeing this, they conclude that tillage has decreased, and they wail over the diminished industry of man. But when those high banks and braes were cultivated, the richer levels below were the haunts of the otter and the fishing-places of the heron. Those ancient ploughmarks are the sure indications of a rude and ignorant husbandry.

" In the eastern slopes of Iona, Columba and his companions

found one tract of land which was as admirably fitted for the growth of corn, as the remainder of it was suited to the support of flocks and herds. On the north-eastern side of the island, between the rocky pasturage and the shore, there is a long natural declivity of arable soil, steep enough to be naturally dry, and protected by the hill from the western blast.

"And so here Columba's tent was pitched and his Bible opened, and his banner raised for the conversion of the heathen."

§ 109. Ireland (as that best of judges Arthur Young says), taken acre for acre, is more fertile than England. Yet in her earlier history, when the whole population consisted of a few hundred thousands gathered into clans, its "pressure upon land and food" caused frequent famines, and led to large emigrations into what we regard as the poorest parts of the sister island. Such was the exodus of Scots that established the Celtic kingdom of Dalaradia, and laid the foundation of Scottish nationality. Such also was the invasion and occupation of North Wales by the Gadhelic or Irish kingdom of Gwyned, just about the time of the Saxon incursions on the east.

The Scotch and English colonies in the north had a long struggle with the natural obstacles to settlement, among which want of drainage and consequently malaria and agues were the chief. Within the memory of people now living, large districts have been brought under culture, and the yield of the land immensely increased wherever the density of population was such as to make it both possible and profitable. The malarious type of disease—including that offspring of the union of hunger and malaria, typhus fever—have comparatively disappeared.

§ 110. In America, the Pilgrim Fathers and the Puritan colonists fixed their homes on the barren shores of Massachusetts Bay; and even when they penetrated the country to found new commonwealths, they chose high and dry spots like Newport and New Haven. The richest soils under cultivation in New England were reclaimed within fifty years. Other lands, quite as rich, if not richer, lie untilled, while old mountain settlements in Berkshire county and other districts are being emptied of their inhabitants and ancient farmhouses left untenanted. But much of the long-occupied lands have grown in fertility, as agricultural methods and appliances have been improved. "Our soil," says Emerson, "is capable of as great and increased productiveness as that which England has attained. Concord is now one of the oldest towns in the country,—far on now [1858] in its third century. The selectmen have once in five years perambulated its bounds, and yet in this year a very large quantity of land has been discovered and added to the agricultural land, and without a murmur of complaint from any neighbor. By drainage we have gone to the subsoil, and we have a Concord under Concord, a Middlesex under Middlesex, and a basement-story of Massachusetts more valuable than the superstructure. Tiles are political economists. They are so many young Americans announcing a better era and a day of fat things."

> Mr. Emerson sees the bearing of all this, for he adds: "There has been a nightmare brought up in England, under the indigestion of the late suppers of overgrown landlords and loomlords, that men bred too fast for the powers of the soil,—that men multiplied in a geometrical ratio, whilst corn only in an arithmetical. The theory is that the best land is taken up first. This is not so, as Henry Carey of Philadelphia has shown, for the poorest land is the first cultivated, and the last lands are the best lands. It needs science to cultivate the best lands in the best manner. Every day a new plant, a new food is found. Thus political economy is not mean, but liberal, and on the pattern of the sun and sky; it is coincident with love and hope. It is true that population increases in the ratio of morality, and the crops will increase in like ratio."

§ 111. In *New York* the first lines of settlement ran along the dry and sandy hills from Manhattan Island and the Highlands to the Mohawk valley. The settlements on the edge of that beautiful and fertile region are much older than those within it. Rich and fertile districts like Geneva have not a history of more than seventy years, while the more remote and less fertile lands along the Pennsylvania line were settled very early, their elevation and their consequent exemption from malaria being an especial recommendation. The New York farmer of our days finds that "knocking the bottom out of a swamp" is one of the most profitable things he can put his hand to, and his less-knowing neighbors stare at the crops that follow.

*New Jersey* was preferred by the first Quaker settlers to the west bank of the Delaware, because of the abundance of her light, sandy soils, which were the more easily got at. Hundreds of their clearings, which have long been abandoned, may be found in these districts. The Swedes across the river followed suit. They built Christina, Lewistown, and other towns of *Delaware* that have become decayed and insignificant places.

§ 112. Penn had the same preference for high land. His first choice for the site of Philadelphia was twelve miles farther north. The early maps of the province show us miles of small farms running from the city along the tops of the ridges, while the richer and lower lands on each side are marked as uncleared and uncultivated. Hence the origin of the Ridge Road. A large part of the banks of our rivers above the city, are still unsafe as building-sites, while below us lie undrained swamps that will yet be the farm-gardens of our city. Much of the best land in the interior of the state is still unoccupied, especially in the valley of the Susquehanna, while comparatively barren places on the slopes of the Alleghenies and its related ranges were settled at a very early date. The old roads of the state go twisting about as if in search of hills to clamber along—even in the limestone valleys, where there is no malaria—while the new ones run along the streams and through the valleys.

The vast immigration from the north of Ireland that went on during last century found homes in the Alleghenies and their spurs, which they entered through Pennsylvania and North Carolina, and then spread over the whole Apalachian system from what are now the Oil Regions to Huntsville in Northern Alabama. Their choice was not prompted by want of better lands,—for such lay unreclaimed on both sides of the mountains;—nor by indolence (as Mr. Burton charges upon the Irish settlers of the Scotch Highlands), for no race is more industrious;—nor by any special safety of their position, as they had to bear for half a century the brunt of our Indian wars. They took the lands that lay most open to them, as did their brethren, who passed by Maine to settle the Granite State.

§ 113. The same course of settlement may be traced in every Western state. Everywhere the rich valley-lands are avoided as the seat of malaria. In Wisconsin the first settlement was made in the patch of highlands called the Blue Mound, and the lines of settlement ran out along the sandy hills as in the east. The richest and the most fertile spots on the prairies were in earlier times the sloughs or "wet prairies"—the terror of travellers, but now under combined and patient exertion "fair as the garden of the Lord." One such in Southern Illinois, occupied by Paisley weavers turned American farmers, recalls the most carefully tilled bits of the British Islands. This whole district, commonly known as Egypt, and spreading from the Mississippi far east of the Wabash, is perhaps the richest in the whole North. Yet the Southern planters on their way to occupy Missouri, passed it by in disdain, and left it to "poor whites" of the South, who occupy such dry and sandy ridges as they find accessible, where the rudest agriculture suffices to supply their very primitive wants. The rich creek bottoms are inaccessible to its rude and scanty population, who have hardly any notion of their value and no capital sufficient to master them. A man, whose lands if rightly tilled would feed a New England town, will live in a log-hut of two rooms, with a loom and spinning-wheel on the "stoop," and ride to a Hard Shell church, with a saddle of raw hide and stirrups of straw. Every family has its package of quinine, and "the Egyptian shakes" are a proverb.

If we ascend the various branches of the Mississippi, we find tillage approaching the river if the population is dense, receding from the river to the barer lands that furnish natural drainage if it be sparse.

Descending the river we reach the vast levees that protect the richest plantations of the continent and testify to the growth of man's power to command the services of nature with the increase of numbers. East of this southern valley lie the South Atlantic States. In North Carolina the richest lands are still undrained, while labor is expended upon others that yield from three to five bushels of wheat to the acre. The Cotton States contain millions of acres still inaccessible to agriculture through lack of population, because a large outlay of intelligently directed labor would be required to occupy them.

In *Texas* the first Spanish colony at Bexar and the first American colony at Austin, high up on the Colorado, were both settled by men, who passed by millions of acres of better land as inaccessible, to reach an exceptional elevation.

§ **114.** Looking at the entire area of the earth's surface, we find (1) that no nation occupies a territory incapable of supporting its actual or even its probable population. Norway comes nearest to forming an exception, but the Scandinavian peninsula is manifestly designed for the home of one nationality. Sweden raises more cereals than her people eat, and a very considerable area of her arable lands is still covered with dense forests. England is clearly no exception; she is capable of producing on her soil four times as much food as her people use; but her agriculture lags far behind the general average of her skill in the invention of better methods and in the application of scientific principles.

(2) The pressure of population upon subsistence and upon the land exists in sparsely-settled regions, and there only. It is a providential agency to stir men to greater exertions and wiser methods, and these exertions are always abundantly rewarded.

(3) The richest areas of the earth's surface lie still unoccupied, and in many cases the richest districts, within national boundaries whose population is dense enough to take possession of them, are untilled and undrained.

(4) The area of culture may be indefinitely extended in both directions. It is now—we may say—the belt of land that lies between districts that are too poor and districts that are too rich to repay culture. The former as well as the latter may be mastered, as the sciences advance in their mastery of the secrets of nature; chalk downs and sandy deserts may be transformed into fair garden fields and orchards at the touch of man, as great

natural forces and resources are brought into his service. The wilderness and the solitary place shall be glad, and the desert shall rejoice and blossom as the rose.

(5) The value of the land of a country is chiefly—or in truth entirely—due to the labor that has been wisely expended upon it, and is proportional to that. The price of a Belgian farm, for instance, is twelve times as great as that of the same amount of waste land in the same country, and the latter brings even that nominal price only because (1) it furnishes a field for labor to produce utilities possible but as yet non-existent; (2) because the labor already expended on other adjacent pieces of land, and the growth of numbers and of the power of association, have made it possible to bring this one under tillage. Were the same piece of land to be transferred to the Andes, its market value would be *nil*.

In fine, if in any case a people, with the strength of numbers and the strength of skill, should come to such a state that great wealth should be found side by side with deep poverty and its accompaniments, misery and sordid vice, the cause of such a state of things is not to be sought in " the pressure of population upon land and food," but in bad national thrift. *Somebody is to blame!*

# CHAPTER SEVENTH.

## The National Economy of Labor.

**§ 115.** The industrial age, in which national economy has become a science, is also the democratic age, in which the governing class are no longer regarded as composing the state or possessing an exclusive right to direct its policy to the promotion of their own interests. It is no longer possible, therefore, to call a nation wealthy and prosperous because large masses of capital are in the hands of a few men, if the great body of the people are ill-fed, ill-housed and ill-clothed, or struggling on the brink of pauperism. The prosperity of "the most numerous class, that is, the poorest," is coming ever more to the front as the great problem of modern statesmanship.

In an *industrial* age this problem resolves itself into the question of the rewards of labor. Modern governments can no longer undertake to support great numbers of people in idleness on the produce of the industry of other classes, as was done in the Greek republics and the Roman Empire. Those others, with the advance of political equality, claim equal rights and care. The aim of national economy is therefore to secure "a fair day's wages for a fair day's work," to all who are willing and able to work.

In modern industry, the operations are so complex in method and so extensive in scale that unassisted labor would be unable to undertake them. Those who by their savings, or by the inheritance of other men's savings, have come into the possession of a large amount of the results of past labor, naturally and necessarily take the work of organizing industry and directing its forces. These men are capitalists, and their accumulations are called capital.

**§ 116.** Of the net product of the joint application of labor and capital, what proportion should fall to labor and what to capital? Is there a natural and necessary rate of distribution or does it vary arbitrarily according to the contract made?

The English economists generally accept the former alternative; they believe that there is a natural and necessary rate of wages; that no efforts of the workman can permanently raise wages above that rate, and no efforts of the capitalist can permanently depress them below it. For, say they, if wages be raised above the natural rate, the rate of increase in the population will be accelerated, and after a time the number of workmen will be so great that they will underbid each other for work, and the rate will be depressed again. If it be depressed below the natural rate by this or any other cause, then the rate of increase of the population will be diminished, and the labor market will be scantily supplied, so that wages must rise. Between the two extremes of this oscillation, there is a middle point of stability,—the natural rate of wages, that which will neither accelerate the growth of population till it surpasses the growth of capital, nor the reverse. This natural rate is the amount necessary to supply to the unmarried workman the real necessaries of life, and whatever other things his class regard as such.

The theory is commonly stated in another form, which also accepts a natural rate of wages, and one which is reached far more swiftly. All the money in a country that is available for the payment of labor is taken in the mass and called the wage fund. This fund is divided pretty equally among all the laborers in the country. The apparent inequalities in the distribution are not real; higher wages can always be traced to payment for undergoing danger or doing work that is disagreeable or discreditable, or work that involves special capacity or preparation. The amount of the fund to be divided depends upon the amount of capital in circulation. The rate of division depends upon the number of claimants. The workingmen have no power to increase the amount of the fund, but they can limit the number of those among whom it is divided, and on their doing so depends their welfare as a class.

This theory in both its shapes grows out of the supposed

"law of population," and must stand or fall with that. Like that, its motive is to show that the misery of the working classes is not to be attributed to any mismanagement on the part of the ruling class, but to the operation of natural and unavoidable laws. Its verdict is, "Nobody to blame," when the growth of a nation in wealth and numbers, and the distribution of wealth among those numbers, do not go on together.

The first form of the theory is fully refuted by the ascertained fact that the poorest classes are the most thriftless, and the least likely to take thought for the future. The second, by the proofs that workingmen actually have, by combination, raised the rate of wages, without any such increase of circulating capital, or the resulting "wage fund," as is here demanded as a preliminary to that increase.

<blockquote>The facts are abundantly given by Mr. W. T. Thornton (*On Labor*, 1870), and by Mr. Cliffe Leslie (*Systems of Land Tenure*, 1868).</blockquote>

§ 117. If the English theory as to the relations of labor and capital be true, then there is no hope for the essential improvement of the workingman's condition so long as the existing order of society holds its ground. What labor gains on one side it for ever loses on the other, and as often as it rolls the Sisyphean rock—the rate of wages—up the hill, it rolls down again to crush and destroy the workman. All the old pictures of foiled effort, with which the Greeks peopled their Hades, become but pictures of the efforts of the working classes to raise their condition above the wretched standard called "natural wages."

Those who are striving to rouse the working classes to overthrow the frame-work of modern society and its economic basis, the right of property, are not slow to discern this. Thus the leader of the German socialists, Lasalle, based his fierce denunciations of modern civilization and its proprietary rights upon the recognised doctrines of the English school, claiming to be "equipped with all the knowledge of the age" on this subject. His chief opponent, his successful rival in the love and allegiance of the working classes of Germany, is Schultze-Delitzsch, who has devoted his life to showing the working classes that they can improve their condition simply by removing unnatural obstacles to improvement, by availing themselves of the great drift of society towards an equality of condition, and without for an instant lifting their hands against the accumulations and the vested rights of the rich. In doing so, he ranged himself on the side of the German-American school of economists founded by List and represented by H. C. Carey, telling Herr Lasalle that if he had taken the pains to go over the whole field he would have found better teachers and better principles than those of Malthus and Ricardo.

"If any one object," he says, "that the economical principles of the writer are devoid of authority, it will suffice to answer that these principles have been established by the work of one of the most philosophic minds of our epoch, the celebrated American economist, Carey. That work is entitled *Principles of Social Science.* It was finished in 1860; some years later gave us a German translation of it (München, 1863-4, published by E. A. Fleischmann). We commend it to the public as one of the most eminent publications that have appeared in this branch of human knowledge.

"All that is false and damnable in the economic theories of the modern English school, especially those of Ricardo and Malthus,—theories which furnish the starting-point for the thesis defended by Lasalle,—there meets with a triumphant refutation; and it is truly astonishing that our opponent, 'armed with all the knowledge of the age,' had not even known of the aforementioned labors of the eminent man, who, during the last twenty years, has discovered a great number of truths that are now accepted as axioms in political economy."

John Stuart Mill, in his *Autobiography*, shows us that the gloomy outlook for the future of the majority of mankind, presented to his mind when he studied the world through the spectacles made for his eyes by Malthus and Ricardo, led him to at least approximate to the theory of the St. Simonian socialists. They proposed to abolish all rights of inheritance; to reconstruct the government out of the ablest men in each of the professions; to make the state everybody's heir, and to redistribute all property as fast as its present possessors died. In Mr. Mill's *Principles* (ii, xiii, § 2) he speaks of "the industrial system prevailing in this country and regarded by many writers as the *ne plus ultra* of civilization," as "irrevocably condemned," unless it prove itself competent to solve the population question by bringing sufficient motives to self-restraint to bear upon the classes "dependent on the wages of hired labor."

§ 118. The English theory that the power of competition

fixed all the status of industries, and that all things found their level, led to the inference—adduced above—that the wages of labor are essentially the same in all departments, and that any difference in payment could be traced to an implied payment for facing some danger, or something disagreeable or disgraceful in the work. Closer investigation shows us that *custom* is as large an element as competition in determining the rate of wages, although the latter is gaining upon the former steadily in modern society. The great change going on all around us is from customary status, that fixes the rate and price of all things by tradition, to one in which they are fixed by free contract. But the change is anything but complete in any department of life, and as to wages it is simply impossible to say why some classes of work are paid so high and others so low. To give a reason for the difference would be to trace to reason what had not its origin in reason; or if it ever had, it was in a past so distant that we cannot reconstruct it.

§ 119. Capitalists are, of course, more ready than workingmen to listen to the English arguments in favor of the necessity and naturalness of a low rate of wages. But the effort to keep the workingman down to such a rate ignores the very nature of the instrument that is to be used. It is to adopt as a maxim of economy the fundamental falsehood of slavery,—that a man may be treated as a thing. The law of parsimony is a wise one in dealing with the material, but not with the workman. Every needless pound of iron on the locomotive, every needless pound of coal in the fire-place, is so much waste of the moving force. Every unnecessary ton of iron on the girders of the bridge merely adds to the weight to be sustained, without proportionally increasing the strength that sustains it. So in regard to cost of material; what is needless is waste.

But when we come to apply the law of parsimony to the complex being called man, we discover by experience that there are very decided limits to its application. Here at least " there is that scattereth and yet increaseth, and there is that withholdeth more than is meet, and *it* tendeth to poverty." The lowest wages that you can get a man to live on, will not get the best work out of him. Put a whole people on such wages, and keep them there—if you can—for two or three generations, and you will have crushed the energy, the spirit, the heart out of that people, and made them a very inferior and unprofitable class of workmen. You will have taken away from the great mass of them the means of advancing in intelligence; their physical character will have deteriorated greatly; their social morality—their good-will, and public spirit, and ready helpfulness, and brotherly feeling—will have been pretty thoroughly eliminated. Factories will be full of the inflammable human stuff, to which demagogues furnish the spark. The stability of the social edifice, and consequently the security of property, will be endangered. Instead of cheerful, pains-taking, thrifty work, eye-service alone will be rendered, and profits will suffer from waste more than they would from high wages.

On the other hand, wages that put heart and hope into a man, that make him feel that his personal efforts and his best work are needed to keep them at present rates, that offer him the prospect of becoming his own master by frugality, that enable him to educate his children to fill a place like his own intelligently, or perhaps to rise to a higher place,—such wages are in the long run the best of investments. It cannot be said that capitalists any more than workmen, have always been alive to this substantial harmony of their interests. When the higher rate of wages has been adopted, it has too commonly been after a conflict between the two classes, through which much of its good effect upon the workmen has been destroyed.

§ 120. Men are morally responsible for the terms on which they purchase labor. When the workman makes his contract singly, the capitalist has a power to dictate its terms, which does not exist in ordinary transactions. In case of disagreement as to terms, it remains to be seen which of the two can hold out longest. Labor cannot: the laborer would starve. Capital can live on its accumulations. If I refuse to buy the baker's loaf, because I think it too dear, he loses but little in waiting till noon for another customer. I have therefore no means of dictating to him. But "labor is the most perishable of commodities." He who cannot sell his morning's labor before noon, can never sell it; it is gone. The producer of other commodities can at least stop producing, and lose only the interest on his capital, when the prices are unsatisfactory. But he who has labor to sell cannot stop producing, cannot cease to offer his single commodity for such price as he can get.

§ 121. The history of labor shows the wisdom of generous dealing with the laborer. In the earliest ages, he was generally a slave; but it was found that slave labor was dear at any price. Homer says:—

"The day
That makes a man a slave, takes half his worth away."

Pliny tells us *Coli rura ab ergastulis pessimum est, et quicquid agitur a desperantibus* (It is the worst possible tillage that is carried on by slaves, nor are they more fit for any other sort of work, because they are devoid of hope). A southern slaveholder told Frederick Law Olmstead: "In working niggers we must always calculate that they will not labor at all except to avoid punishment, and they will never do more than just enough to save themselves from being punished, and no amount of punishment will prevent their working carelessly and indifferently." Why should it? "Fear," says Bentham, "leads the laborer to hide his powers, rather than to show them; to remain below, rather than to surpass himself.... By displaying superior capacity, the slave would only raise the measure of his ordinary duties; by a work of supererogation he would only prepare punishment for himself. His ambition is the reverse of that of the freeman; he seeks to descend in the scale of industry, rather than to ascend." And just the same must be the effects of a system in which the workman's wages are fixed by his necessities and not by his work.

See Prof. Cairnes's *The Slave Power* (1862); Chapter II. "The Economic Basis of Slavery."

§ 122. The history of European serfdom in the middle ages tells the same story. The great mass of the population of Europe was in a state of villeinage, which varied in its forms, but was commonly little short of slavery. They were worth so little as workmen that it took all but a small percentage of the population to raise food for the whole, and vast numbers were employed in herding swine and cattle. In the worst cases, which were very numerous, the villein had no right to the produce of his labor; the landlord took the whole, and gave the serf what he pleased,—generally the refuse. Hence, as Gurth the swine-herd (in *Ivanhoe*) says, the cattle bore Saxon names (ox, pig, calf, sheep), while they lived and needed care, but Norman names (beef, pork, veal, mutton), when killed and turned to food.

Afterwards these villeins began in great numbers to buy their time, and then their freedom,—a fact which shows at once the greater worth of free labor. Those feudal masters were too poor to give anything for nothing; they sold their slaves to the slaves themselves, because the latter could afford to pay more than any other purchasers; and because the purchase-money earned in half freedom was the full price of the slave's work. What we see in our own century in Prussia went on in England: the emancipated serfs bought land of their lords, creating a new market for it. The Prussian masters complained of the Stein legislation (§ 90) as an invasion of vested rights, but that great statesman told them that a generous policy would benefit all parties. They now admit the fact; what their serfs gained they did not lose. Between 1829 and 1843 land rose 75 per cent. in Westphalia, while there has been an incalculable improvement in the condition of the peasantry—some of whom still remember the time when they were called *sclaven*.

§ 123. We begin to hear of free laborers in England in the fourteenth century, and from this time laws are passed on the one hand to protect them and increase their number, on the other to keep their wages down to a minimum rate. These laws tell us themselves that such short-sighted policy could not reach its end. "The price of labor continually rose; the price of food constantly fell" (Thorold Rogers). This must have been the consequence of a great increase in productive power of labor acting in harmony with capital. The logic of facts drove wages up, and every successive change was to the advantage of all classes. The workman rose in freedom, self-respect and efficiency.

Between the Restoration and the Revolution the week's wages of a farm hand was four shillings. In 1680 an M. P. complained that the English mechanic was demanding a shilling a day, though he would still work for less. In the century ending 1830, the wages of a carpenter at Greenwich Hospital rose from 2s. 6d. to 5s. 8d. a day. Bread, indeed, had risen equally, but all other necessaries had fallen. The weekly wages of a farm hand for various periods, if translated into wheat values at current rates, gives this result: 1680–1700, 54 pints; 1701–1726, 64 pints; 1727–51, 78 pints; 1752–64, 80 pints; 1770, 79 pints; 1780, 82 pints; 1824, 89 pints; 1832, 90 pints.

§ 124. In France this matter has been very carefully investigated, and it appears that the rural population of France had half as much food as they needed in the time of Louis XIV.; two-thirds under Louis XV.; three-fourths under Louis XVI.; while from the time of the Empire the laborer's budget begins to show a surplus instead of a deficit. D'Argenson writes in 1739: "At the moment when I write, in the month of February, in the midst of peace,—with appearances promising a harvest, if not abundant, at least passable,—men die around us like flies and are reduced by poverty to eat grass." A fern loaf was brought to the council table by the King's brother that his majesty might "see what his subjects lived upon." With the increase of wages, labor has risen to such efficiency that one fourth of the soil formerly devoted to grain is now set free for "industrial crops," and the food of a much larger population is raised upon the other three-fourths. At the same time a much larger proportion of the people is set free to engage in manufactures of all kinds.

§ 125. In the colony of New York in 1773, when cheap and fertile lands were plenty, and every mechanic could turn farmer if he pleased, day laborers were paid 45 cents a day; ship carpenters, three times as much; house carpenters, $1.10; journeymen tailors, 56 cents. Adam Smith, who gives us these data, says that the London rate was lower than this, but that of the other colonies was not. Has the rate diminished since the country became more densely settled? In 1850 our factories employed 731,137 men and 225,922 women, whose daily wages was respectively $.88 6-10 and $.49 2-10, for each person. In 1860 they employed 1,040,349 men and 270,900 women, at wages of $1.02 and $.59 respectively. In 1870 the number was 1,615,598 men and 323,770 women, and 114,628 young persons, a total of 2,053,996 workers, at an average of $1.18 *per diem;* a gain of 37 per cent. in ten years.

§ 126. What is true of different periods in the same country is equally true of different countries at the same date :—Ill paid labor is dearer as a rule than well paid. Two Englishmen will mow as much hay as six Russians, and although their wages are much higher, the hay costs the farmer only half as much. Arthur Young saw that the Essex laborer was cheaper at half a crown a day than the Tipperary laborer at 5 pence. This is still true of Irish labor outside Ulster and the Dublin Pale ; capitalists pay less for it and yet find it at least no cheaper. The *Edinburgh Review* denies that labor is cheaper on the Continent than in England in spite of the difference in wages, and Mr. J. S. Mill says " the cost of labor is frequently at its highest when wages are lowest." He says that labor is probably no dearer in the United States than in England. When the Revolution of 1848 banished the English navvies who were working on the French railroads, it was found that twice as many Frenchmen could not do the work. But when these had been put for a while on the beef diet of the English navvies, they came up to the English standard, and two could do almost as much as five had done.

§ 127. It is not only through the growth of the laborer in thrift and skill that his condition is bettered. All the accumulations of capital in other men's hands coöperate to make his work more efficient and to secure him a larger share of its rewards. All the work that has been done already adds to the value of the work that he is now doing. Hence, in the course of natural development, the power of labor over the accumulations of the results of past labor, grows with the growth of those accumulations. Past work never brings market price, because its very existence makes present work more effective than it was. "The share assigned to the laborer almost always bears a much larger proportion to his labor than his employer's share bears to the labor which his capital represents" (W. T. Thornton).

The price of a thing being fixed by the cost of its reproduction, every improvement in the methods of production lowers the price of what has been already produced. Suppose that any European kingdom or American state were brought into the market as a whole, it would sell for the sum needed to bring it up to its present state of improvement in the present condition of labor. Such a sum would represent a mere fraction of the labor that actually was required in its past history to do the same work. Thus the worth of the fee simple of the real estate of England (including roads and mines) is reckoned—or was a few years ago—at £2,000,000,000. This represents much less than the labor of five million men for ten years at present English rates; yet it would purchase the results of the labor of millions spread over the thousand years through which the English nation has lasted (§ 102), because it would now achieve as much as those millions did. Value is not determined, therefore, by the cost of production, but by the cost of reproduction, and with every improvement in method, and even with every accumulation of results, the latter falls below the former.

With the growth in the productive power of labor, an increased proportion of the increased product falls to the laborer. The improved instruments with which he works are themselves the products of more efficient labor; their value has fallen while his has risen. The capitalist cannot demand as much for the use of them as before; the workman's ability to become himself a capitalist has increased, and that ability is one of the points to be considered in their contract. The capitalist's share increases greatly in quantity, but is a less proportion of the whole amount. For with the diminution of nature's resistance, the whole dead stock employed in production declines in value while man's value rises, as he is by all these changes the master of larger utilities. The power of his labor to command the service of capital rises; that of capital to command his labor declines; the inequality of laborer and capitalist tends to disappear.

> The Italian economist Ferrara in the introduction to the twelfth volume of the *Biblioteca degl' Economisti* (Turin, 1852), says of this definition: "Carey [in 1837], and after him Bastiat [in 1850], have introduced a formula *a posteriori*, that I believe destined to be universally adopted; and it is greatly to be regretted that the latter should have limited himself to occasional indications of it, instead of giving to it the importance so justly given by the former. In estimating the equilibrium between cost to one's self and the utility to others, a thousand circumstances may intervene; and it is desirable to know if there be not among men a law, a principle of universal application. Supply and demand, rarity and abundance, etc., are all insufficient and liable to perpetual exceptions. Carey has remarked, and with great sagacity, that this law is the labor saved, the cost of reproduction—an idea that is, as I think, most felicitous. It appears to me that there cannot arise a case in which a man shall determine to make an exchange, in which this law will not be found to apply. I will not give a quantity of labor or pains, unless offered in exchange for a utility equivalent, and I will not regard it as an equivalent, unless I see that it will come to me at less cost than would be necessary for its reproduction. I regard this formula as most felicitous, because, while on the one hand, it retains the idea of cost, which is constantly referred to by the mind, on the other it avoids the absurdity to which we are led by the theory, which pretends to see everywhere a value equivalent to the cost of production; and finally it shows more perfectly the essential justice that governs all our exchanges."

§ 128. In regard to the quality and the rewards of labor, therefore, the same law of progress holds as in regard to food and land. As society advances in numbers and wealth, there is, unless bad economy prevent, a constant progress from worse to better. With the growth of wealth and of numbers, the power of combination increases, with great increase in the productiveness of labor and the power of accumulation.

What are the chief forms of bad economy that prevent the laborer from profiting fully by the growth of society?

(1) When the steps in the progress of improvement are very sudden and great, a considerable amount of suffering is often inflicted; but this is temporary and, to much greater extent than is commonly supposed, can be avoided. The introduction of labor-saving machinery is an instance of what we mean; a much more striking one was the transition during the last quarter of the eighteenth century from hand to steam power, and from the workshop to the factory system.

The old school-books used to tell us that "it takes ten men to make a pin." But since that day an inventive mechanic has put together a machine that only needs to be fed with wire, well oiled and supplied with steam-power, to turn out complete pins, sort them, and even thrust them into the papers in the right numbers and in straight rows. What is to become of the ten pin-makers? In any community in which industrial progress is constant, there will be openings for their work. Even Mr. Mill, who believes that such inventions have not "lightened the toil of any human being," admits that "they have enabled *a greater number* to live the same life of drudgery and imprisonment." Why is this the result? Because pins made by the new process are so much cheaper than before, that the demand for them is greatly enhanced, and when this demand has reached its natural height the whole number of persons employed in the manufacture (including miners, machine-makers, engineers, &c.) is greater than it was before. As the money then needed to buy pins for a family is much less than it was, there is something left to buy other things, and to pay the men who produce them.

Furthermore, machinery supersedes muscle but not brains, force but not intelligence. It drives men from low-priced, mechanical work, to employments that demand a higher capacity and command higher pay. Increasing the productiveness of labor, it increases also the workman's share of its results. And this share is not to be conceived as lying idle in the hands of those that earn it. It is again expended in employing other workmen by purchasing necessaries and comforts.

The change in methods of work (by its demand for adaptiveness), and the quality of the new kind of work, both demand a large measure of intelligence in the workman. The amount of suffering and privation involved in such a change, is exactly proportional to the ignorance and general backwardness of the working classes. For this society is directly responsible.

§ **129.** The transition from industry organized on a small scale to the larger industry of the factory system was begun in Lancashire in 1790 by Richard Arkwright, and has been one of the greatest of industrial revolutions. It grew naturally out of the invention of the steam-engine, and the application of a power that moves a hundred looms or spinning jennies as easily as a score. It has introduced the precision and effectiveness of military discipline into industry, divided labor more thoroughly, assigned to every workman his position, and reduced the loss of time and of material to a minimum. It thus rendered the labor of the workman far more productive than when he wrought in isolation, flinging the shuttle and tramping down the treadles by the force of his own muscles. It consequently increased the wages of his industry, while it diminished the value of all manufactured goods. The transition to the industry of the factory did not begin in the United States till the second decade of the present century, but since that date the wages of workmen have been doubled, and that of workwomen trebled, while the purchasing power of both has advanced at a still swifter rate.

It may be questioned, however, whether the change was not more sweeping than it need have been if the working classes had been fully alive to their own interests,—and therefore more injurious, temporarily, to their interests. Large intelligence and large capital went together in effecting the change. It was assumed on all hands that the steam-engine can only be employed with economy as the motive power of a large establishment, which experience shows to be untrue. Small employers shared in the prejudice of their workmen and the uneducated generally against the new invention. Instead of accommodating themselves to the logic of facts, they resisted the change, and were swept into the large factories by the force of circumstances, before they knew. The restoration of petty industry in a new form, with all the advantages of discipline, intelligence and machinery, is one of the most desirable of changes in the future.

§ 130. (2) A French workman has well said that "when two workmen run after one master, wages fall; they rise when two masters run after one workman." Had he said "two sorts of masters," it would have been even truer. "There is rarely competition for labor *within* a trade in a particular place, unless there be competition for it from *without*" (Leslie). The more openings there are for the laborer to invest his capital (which is his labor), and for the capitalist to invest his (which is the accumulation of past labor), the better each will be remunerated. Hence the connection between varied industry and fair wages, as well as fair profits. In any country (or even district) in which that is wanting, labor will be but poorly paid, and especially so, if agriculture is the only pursuit open to the great body of the people. Furthermore, that form of industry, as a rule, furnishes employments that are suited only to able-bodied men, and consequently, if there be not a fair admixture of manufactures, those who are not equal to hard, out-door work, are left dependent upon those who are. With the rise of a varied industry, the number of workers rises to a maximum, that of idlers sinks to a minimum. A field sown with various sorts of grass seed yields a larger crop than if one kind only be used, because each finds special nourishment in some single element of the soil; and so is it with the employment of all the elements of industrial power.

In later English history, the manufactures have become concentrated in London and in the midland and northern shires. Between 1770 and 1850, wages rose 66 per cent. in the twelve northern shires and 100 per cent. in Lancashire and the West Riding of Yorkshire: in eighteen southern agricultural shires, only 14 per cent., although food and cottage-hire were far dearer. In the former two sorts of masters run after one workman; in the latter the growth of population has no outlet save in farming; local capital, of which labor is the most *perishable* form, has no other investment, and two workmen run after one master. In Ireland the principle is seen still more clearly. The south is now not over populated, but under populated; whole districts are desolate and idle; yet nowhere are wages above eight shillings a week, though food is nearly as dear as in England, to which everything is now carried. In the north, the eastern three counties have a very different rate of wages. "In that vast system of manufactures, which now stretches over several counties, it is around towns in which population has doubled in half a generation, that agricultural wages are highest" (Leslie). The north, from the first days of the Ulster plantation, has had two sorts of employers running after every workman.

§ 131. (3) Laws made in the interest of the upper classes very greatly interfere with the well-being of the working classes, especially the farm-hands. Till very recently the right of the workingmen peaceably to combine to secure higher wages was denied and its exercise punished on both sides of the Atlantic although no law forbade the employers to combine in depressing wages. Till very recently the treasurer of a Trade's Union in England might rob it with impunity; the law would not punish him. The Unions were outlawed, though their members since 1824 were not.

Laws not made for any such purpose have often been perverted in their application to the great injury of the working classes. Thus under the old English poor law, the farmers in many districts by combined action beat down their workmen's wages to such a point, that the latter were forced to "come upon the parish," by asking relief as out-door paupers. The guardians were required by the law to find them work, which they did by supplementing their wages up to the point required for their subsistence. Thus able-bodied men, who fairly earned a living, were degraded to the rank of paupers in order that the whole community might be forced to contribute to the farmer's profits.

"He was virtually able to put his hand into the pockets of the neighboring rate-payers to make up the deficiency to those whom he employed" (Fawcett). The consequences were most disastrous; the spirit of the people was broken, and pauperism increased so vastly that it absorbed in some parishes more than half the rent of the land. In some cases the land was actually offered to the paupers to till for themselves and refused; they preferred to live on alms. Could there be a worse economy of the wealth-producing forces of a nation than the destruction of the thrift, the self-respect and the hopefulness of the common people?

§ 132. The method of prison discipline commonly adopted in this country tends to do injustice to the working classes. In order to make the prison self-supporting, the labor of the prisoners is hired out to a contractor, or some industry is practised by the prisoners, and its products sold for the benefit of the State. In either case the tendency of the system is to force down the wages of the free workman. The State cannot bring its bondsmen into the labor-market either directly or indirectly in such a way as to secure the full market price of their work. No man will hire convict-labor except on terms specially favorable to himself. No State can dispose of the articles made by convict-labor except at lower rates than are usual for such goods. There is no objection to making convicts work; on the contrary, every one recognizes the usefulness of work as a moral discipline. But the work should be in the production of articles needed for the prison's use. In this way the prison should be directly self-supporting by supplying all its own wants of food, clothing, furniture and the like.

§ 133. (4) The disproportionate outlay of the workingman's savings upon objects of luxury, instead of a wise saving, is justly alleged as a cause of misery to the class. Thus the expenditure upon spirituous liquors is a heavier tax upon the earnings of the laborer than all others put together. But the remedy and therefore the responsibility of this state of things is partly with society at large. It is in the improvement of the homes of the poor, and in furnishing them with mental resources and proper places of resort. So long as the gin-shop and the bar-room are to the modern workman what the church was to the peasant of the Middle Ages, viz.: the only clean, warm and well-lighted room that he is welcome to visit in his hours of leisure,—so long will he go to them. "The main exciting cause of drunkenness is, I believe, bad air and bad lodging" (Chas. Kingsley). Alcohol is sought as the only accessible relief from the physical prostration and mental depression that bad habits of living produce. Drunkenness was once universal in the highest classes of society; "drunk as a lord" was an English proverb. It has decreased, no doubt with the growth of habits of personal cleanliness, and with a larger intelligence as to the conditions on which good health may be enjoyed.

> In some parts of Swoden they have effected a thorough reform of the tavern, without attempting to abolish it. The right to sell liquor in a district is put up at auction by the government, and bought in by an association of the friends of temperance. They open the number of houses that the law prescribes and at the legal hours only. They sell other drinks and food as well as pure liquors, and allow of no solicitation to purchase the latter. No person who has had "enough" can get any more. The association furnish pleasant rooms to which the workingman can invite his family, and provide books and periodicals. The proceeds, after paying all expenses, go to local charities.

The diffusion of education will both directly and indirectly work to the same end. When this has multiplied the number and elevated the character of his enjoyments, the workman will no longer seek happiness in sordid physical gratifications. Perhaps he will then come to learn—as no class has yet learned—the vast importance of the way in which a people disposes of the small surplus left it, after the necessaries of life have been provided. Everything that impoverishes mind and heart tends to increase the outlay upon articles of false luxury which are rather hurtful than helpful.

§ 134. (5) Grave injuries have been inflicted on the laboring classes by the conflict between labor and capital. In the absence of any knowledge of the essential harmony of their interests, or at best from the notion that the interests of the workmen were consulted by keeping down wages to the natural level, English employers, with the approval and support of English economists, have striven to get their work done at a minimum rate of wages. The workmen, finding individual resistance useless, organized for combined effort, and fixed rates of wages for their respective trades. Their right to associate and to refuse to work for less than this seems plain enough, but the governing classes denied the right, and treated these Unions as unlawful conspiracies. Being thus put out of the pale of the law, the Unions unhappily, but not unnaturally, fell into lawless methods of securing their ends. They had the right to use all persuasive methods to induce those who did not belong to the Union and comply with its rules, to become members, and failing in that to refuse to work in the same shop with them. But they went beyond all lawful limits to force outsiders into membership, and to force them from work during "strikes," as they called the temporary suspension of work intended to force masters to raise wages. "Rats," as these outsiders were called, had their tools destroyed, their persons assaulted, their houses attacked, sometimes by explosive substances; and in a number of cases their lives were taken.

It is a question whether the Trades' Unions have accomplished the ends of their organization. The figures presented by Mr. Thornton in his work on *Labor* seem to show conclusively that they have; that the hours of labor have been reduced, and that rates of wages that would never have been attained without combined action, have been thus secured, and that the end of the process is not reached. This indeed is contrary to the teachings of English economists that there is a limited wage fund subject to the demands of labor, and that the average share of each workman can only be increased by reducing the number of claimants or increasing the fund. "Workmen are solemnly adjured, in the name of political economy, not to try to get their wages raised, because success in the attempt must be followed by a fall of profits, and bring wages down again. They are entreated not to better themselves, because any temporary bettering must be followed by a reaction that will leave them as ill off as before." "To go on reasserting that unionism *does* not raise wages, and that to all appearances permanently, would now-a-days be running too completely counter to every-day experience. To assert that it *cannot* raise them, is the utmost extent to which any but the hardiest theorists still venture to go" (Thornton). True it is that strikes have frequently, perhaps in a majority of cases, ended with a victory for the masters; but the very rise in rate thus successfully refused has been almost always conceded afterwards to prevent a renewal of the strike; and the gain thus made, when the aggregate of increase is computed, has been such as to cast into the shade all the sacrifices and losses incurred during the strike.

§ 135. Trades' Unions' strikes need not succeed if the masters would unite as closely and coöperate as heartily as the men. As a rule the employers are taken in detail. The strike for an advance is made in a few establishments, and those that it throws out of work are supported by the members of the Union at work elsewhere. Succeeding in these establishments, they then make the same demands in other quarters, and with the same result.

Strikes have utterly failed in a few cases, where the masters throughout a whole trade have at once discharged all members of the Union, thus retaliating by what is called a "lock-out." But as a rule the employers of labor have not the means of effecting close association, that their workmen possess. Business makes them rivals; they are often blindly exulting in the embarrassment of a brother capitalist, when they might well read in it a prophecy of what is coming on themselves. Nor have they any of the vigorous class feeling and opinion, which enables the workingmen to compel unwilling associates to fall into line.

§ 136. These Unions, originating in England about half a century ago (at first merely as Benefit Societies, which most of them still are), have spread into France and Germany, and the United States. They were brought across the ocean by English and Welsh operatives, attracted to our shores by the superior advantages possessed by our working classes. They are still an exotic on our soil; their strikes are generally in the hands of persons of foreign birth; they have never attained the completeness of organization and the effective management that characterize those of England. This is due to the fact that there is really no such need of them in a country where every man can leave the workshop and become a farmer if he will; where the supply of skilled workmen generally falls far below the demand; where the utmost freedom of association co-exists with the habit of spontaneous action; where wages are steadily and materially advancing; where public sentiment gives no support to the doctrine that low wages are best; and where social and political prestige is rather on the side of numbers, than on that of wealth and the capitalists. They have unquestionably checked the growth of some of our industries by limiting too much the number of persons who may be admitted as apprentices, a rule that does far more mischief in a rapidly expanding country than in one that is nearer the limit of its industrial capacities. But after all, it must be borne in mind that united action is in many cases the best and most effective means for labor to secure fair terms in dealing with capital; and that there is in the Trades Union itself, apart from the outrages sometimes perpetrated in its name, nothing to call for reprobation.

§ 137. Labor and capital in conflict are in an unnatural state; harmony is their true relation. For reasons already given, capital finds its account in the cheerful service of labor, not in its discontent. To labor, capital is a benefactor in the highest sense; were the whole class of capitalists with all their accumulations to be annihilated, labor would be reduced to indigence and a struggle for existence more severe than can easily be conceived. The capitalist is the captain of industry, who takes the unorganized mob of men, drills it into a disciplined army, supplies them with weapons, ammunition and a commissariat, and leads them to industrial conquests. He is able to do so because he has accumulated instead of merely consuming; his right to his million rests on exactly the same ground as the workman's right to his week's earnings.

By what method to restore a lasting harmony between the two, is a great question of the day. The first and simplest method is by *arbitration*. Where it is possible to obtain referees, in whose impartiality and intelligence both parties have confidence, and where both are ready to submit their case, disputes are easily settled and harmony restored. The ordinary courts of justice are not available for the purpose, because they cannot adjudicate the terms of contracts not yet made, and because the judges have no special acquaintance with the matters at issue. The establishment of tribunals of arbitration chosen from both masters and men, with the sanction of government, has been successfully tried in England, and these have put an end to several recent strikes and lock-outs. Something like these, though more official in their character, were the *Conseils de Prudhommes* of mediæval France, which were revived by Napoleon I. in 1806; but the latter are rather government courts of selected experts to decide legal issues.

§ **138.** A second solution is offered by the system of *coöperation*, whose advocates would abolish the conflict between capitalist and laborer, by uniting the two functions in the same persons. They would have workingmen unite their savings to establish a workshop of their own, to be managed by foremen of their own selection under rules adopted by the whole body.

Instances of this industrial method are to be found very early in our own country. The Greek merchant marine is based on the same principle, and it has secured, through the zeal and energy of its sailors, nearly the monopoly of the carrying trade in the Mediterranean. But the first proclamation of the method as a means to revolutionize industry and commerce was made by the socialist Robert Owen. His design was to set up coöperative stores rather than workshops; to abolish the profits of middlemen rather than to get rid of the wages system. About 1824–30 many societies were formed on this basis to make "every man his own shopkeeper." The most successful was the

"Rochdale Equitable Pioneers," organized in 1844. The political troubles of 1848-50 called attention to this method and to successful applications of it to industry in France. The Christian socialist party (F. D. Maurice, Chas. Kingsley, Thos. Hughes, J. M. Ludlow, &c.) urged its general adoption as a remedy for the deadly competition of the wages system. Every man was to be his own employer as well as his own shopkeeper. In spite of many failures, coöperation has an honorable record of successes to show in France, England, Germany, Spain and the United States.

If considered as intended to supersede the wages system entirely, coöperation is open to serious theoretical and practical objections. In the light of the true law of social progress (§ 30), it will be seen to be a decline in industrial organization, when duties and functions that have been distributed among several persons are united in the same person. It would be a loss on all sides, were the captain of industry to cease to exist, and were his functions to be vested in the whole body of workmen. The singleness of purpose, the clearness of outlook, and the energy that large industrial operations demand, could never be brought into play by an association of workmen, or by delegates chosen from their ranks and subject to their control. As a rule, the possession of capital is itself the gauge of business capacity, and of the power to organize and administer an establishment. To exclude those who possess these from their present position, would be to deprive industry of its natural and trusted leaders. Now if coöperation were to become universal they would become mere money-lenders, or else their capital would be entirely withdrawn from the sphere of production,—a loss of the results of past labor that would be eminently deporable.

In practice it has been found difficult to secure the right sort of men to take the place at the head of coöperative establishments. Men of the necessary qualifications are generally able to command their own price elsewhere, and are too well satisfied with their positions to give them up to begin a mere experiment here

And if they did, the estimate put upon their services by their new associates is commonly much below their deserts, so that they would soon be glad to go back to their old places. In the absence of first-class men, it is commonly not the second class that are chosen, but rather men of an inferior grade but more showy qualities.

§ **139.** Less open to objection as a solution of the question is the plan of *industrial partnerships*. In this, the proprietor of an establishment agrees to pay his workmen the current rate of wages, and also to distribute among them at the end of the year all or part of the net profit above a certain percentage, say 15 or 20 per cent. This method identifies the interests of labor and capital without confounding their functions. The men are stimulated to do their utmost,—to avoid all waste as tending to diminish profits, and all careless work as injuring their market, —and to keep each other up to the mark by the force of public opinion.

This plan also is no novelty in our own country. Thus in Albert Gallatin's Glass Factory (established in 1794 at New Geneva, Pa., being the first west of the Alleghenies), every workman had a direct interest in the profits, besides regular wages. The whale fishery and the China trade were managed on the same principle. It was first urged upon the attention of Europe by Charles Babbage in his *Economy of Manufactures* (1829). A Parisian house-painter, after making trial of the wages system in 1842, took his workmen into this limited sort of partnership, with moral and financial results that attracted very great attention, and led to its imitation by a considerable number of establishments in France and not a few in England. It has been found that the plan restores thorough good feeling between masters and men, where the worst irritation has existed for years; that it makes the workmen eager to adopt improved methods, which they would previously have resisted to the utmost; that it diminishes the amount of drunkenness and thriftlessness, and reduces to a minimum the number of holidays spent in dissipation; that it creates a vigorous public opinion against eye-service and waste, and leads men to pride themselves upon giving good work for their wages. In some cases the amount of profits reserved to themselves by the firm, was fixed at a higher percentage than they had ever earned; and yet at the end of the year they had a surplus to divide with their workmen.

The plan has been adopted in a good number of American establishments, but it may fairly be hoped that it will be extended to many more, as it seems to be the least objectionable and the most effective of all the new solutions of the labor question. Of course circumstances will demand manifold modifications of the principle. The number of laborers employed in proportion to the capital invested, must determine what is the proportion of the surplus that will fall to capital and labor respectively. In case the business has suffered losses, it might perhaps be both wise and just to recoup those losses out of the profits of following years. All these details are open to equitable adjustment at the start, or to arbitration as cases of disagreement arise; but the great thing is to get the workman to feel that he is working for himself and has something to hope for as the result of his skill and diligence.

§ 140. Another modification of the principle of coöperation is that introduced in Germany by Schultze-Delitzch. In that country industry is not so generally organized on the grand scale as is common in England, France and America; a great part of their workshops are very small establishments, often managed by a single family. If these were to have their materials at the lowest price they must buy them at wholesale to save commissions; to this end there were organized raw material associations, that they might combine their capital for such purchases. Then came the establishment of public bazaars by these or similar associations, for the sale of their wares. But it was found that these workmen had but little capital and no credit; they could offer no sufficient security to induce the banks to lend them even the small sums that they needed; for a workingman's capital is his health and strength, and his death or serious illness destroys it. But if the single workingman has no credit, a large body of them organized on the principle of mutual security would have credit enough ; if one or a few died or were ill the rest would be the bank's security. Associations were therefore formed to establish loan banks or people's banks, as they are variously called; and these banks make advances to their shareholders on such terms as put them on an equality with the rich.

> The movement began in 1850. In 1872, after twenty-two years of slow and steady growth, there were 442 associations for purchase of raw materials and sale of wares; 2220 banks to make advances to workmen. Of these banks, 807 reported 372,742 members; loans, 359,519,200 thalers; capital, 21,373,529 thalers; deposits and borrowed capital, 77,188,731 thalers. (A thaler is seventy-two and a half cents.) This group of banks is connected with a central bank, which negotiates loans for them in the money market.

§ 141. The question of the rate at which woman's labor should be paid, and of the employments that should be open to her, is one of the living issues of our time, and must not be passed over.

The rate at which she is paid is often alleged as an instance of the power of custom, and unjust custom besides. For doing exactly the same sort of work, it is said, and doing it quite as well, she receives far less pay than a man does. Custom, no doubt, has its influence here; the more rapid advance of woman's rate of pay seems to indicate as much. But there is reason as well as custom for the difference.

(1) Men are more steady workmen than women are. The latter, rightly or wrongly, all but a small minority, look forward to marriage and the care of a household as their true career. For this reason they do not concentrate their attention upon their calling with the same singleness of eye as men show. Nor have they, as a rule, the same power of continuous application, although they have far more natural quickness. The superintendent of the Elgin Watch Factory told me that the women employed there learnt far more during their first fortnight than men did; but there they stopped, while the men went on learning all their lives.

(2) Through the limitation of the number of employments open to women, they are driven to underbid each other for work. By "employments open to women" are meant those that their prejudices will allow them to enter, not merely those that are fit for their sex to undertake. The position of household servant, for instance, is one that very few American-born white women will now accept. Nor is it of any use to argue the question, or to hold up the example of a few ladies of high culture and slender purse; the position of direct control by an individual will, that is bound by no rules save such as it extemporizes from time to time, is become intolerable to them. They fly from it to the store, the factory, the school-room, and finding all these insufficient, they will sew for slop-shops and die of slow starvation rather than go to the kitchen. German and Irish women, and Chinese men, are the only material to be had to fill these vacancies, to the varied discomfort of the mistresses of the households.

The plan of coöperative housekeeping in cities and towns offers a solution of the difficulty. By this, cooking would be conducted in a large central establishment, under the management of superior *chefs*, and the purchases made by experienced caterers under the direction of a committee of housekeepers. This change would be in the same line as that which removed the work of spinning and weaving from the list of household duties; it would cheapen living to both rich and poor, by enabling wholesale purchases; it would give an opportunity for the application of scientific principles to the art of cooking; and it would furnish congenial and well-paid work to a large percentage of the women now out of employment. Nor would it be impossible to apply the same coöperative principle to other parts of household work, and relieve the mistress of the family from the necessity of depending on the services of a class, who —with some exceptions—are certainly not improved and humanized by their position.

## CHAPTER EIGHTH.

### THE SCIENCE AND ECONOMY OF MONEY.

**§ 142.** The progress of society from slavery and poverty and isolation to freedom, wealth and association, involves not only a progressive differentiation of its members and of their functions, but also a constantly increasing interchange of services between these. The more developed the society, the greater the interdependence of its members, and the more numerous and rapid these exchanges. With the solitary backwoodsman they have no existence, and he must overcome nature's resistance and master her utilities unaided. But when the country begins to be settled, these exchanges begin; if a town spring up, they become more numerous and rapid; if the town grow into a city, the system of mutual service becomes complete.

These exchanges are at first effected by barter, or the direct exchange of commodity for commodity. But a little experience shows this process to be both awkward and wasteful. The artisan might waste more time than he spent to produce his commodity, in searching for a customer whose wants and possessions were the exact complement of his own. Where a single article that varied in the value of its parts, such as the carcass of a cow, had to be divided among a great number of customers, the adjustment of values was nearly impossible. This led to the setting apart some one commodity which should be the representative of all estimable values, and should be the instrument of these exchanges and therefore of human association for mutual help. Cattle (*pecus*), being the first form of personal property (*peculium* or *chattels*), was first used as money (*pecunia*). Afterwards silver, and probably somewhat later gold came into use. The scarcity of these precious metals, and their eminent fitness for making ornaments, had, doubtless, brought them into general demand and caused them to be held at a very high price. The transition to their use as money was gradual and natural. It is impossible to trace the early history of their adoption. The oldest historical records tell us that they were already in use, though not yet coined, in the patriarchal age,—that is, at a time when the family was still the largest social unit among peoples that afterwards played a part in ancient history. The first coins were in the form of animals, as indicating that they were substitutes for cattle. Afterwards they were coined in small, flat masses of equal weight and a recognised degree of purity, with an image and superscription, which now give these pieces a great historical interest.

Money is therefore *the instrument of exchange and of association*. It is more usually defined as "the instrument of exchange and the standard of value." In a popular, not a scientific sense, it serves as an instrument for the comparison of values. But as value is the measure of nature's power over man, and as money, like every other commodity, falls in value with the growth of that power, it is more scientific to regard labor as the standard of value, that being the means by which nature's resistance is overcome. It is true that in setting aside any commodity for use as money regard is had to its comparative fixity of value. This is the consideration which determined the selection first of cattle, and then of the precious metals. But neither these commodities nor any other possess that fixity which entitles them to rank as scientific standards alongside the standards of weight and measure.

This usual definition errs also by defect. Money is *the instrument of association* as well as of exchange. The absence of it tends to isolate men, to prevent the formation of industrial relations among them, and to keep labor down to an unproductive level. Its abundance enables the organization and drill of the industrial forces, and the direction of their energies to the best purpose.

*Association* is the largest fact in economic experience. It is the exchange of services not only within the range of contract, but among millions who never see each other. The payment of two cents for a morning newspaper brings its purchaser into association, to that extent, not only with the people actually engaged in its editing, composition and press-work, but with paper-makers, ink-makers, miners, lumberers, telegraph-agents and so forth.

§ 143. The adoption of any form of money as the instrument of association and exchange was a clear advance upon barter. In barter every commodity discharges two functions at the same time; it is both goods and money. In the new method of exchange the two functions are separated; money and goods become separate things. Nor is a vast amount of material thereby withdrawn from other uses: a very small amount of money suffices to effect a very large number of exchanges, and no country needs anything like as much money as it has property; it might as well have wagons and railroad carriages enough to convey all its movables at once. Very much of its property never changes hands, except by inheritance; a still larger amount not once in a long series of years. At most a very small amount changes hands in the course of a single day, and there is no use for as much money as will represent this amount. The same sum (be it coin, or notes, or credit represented by a check) may be used repeatedly in the same day, and thus discharge many times its own amount of indebtedness. The most perfect money is that which changes hands with greatest rapidity; the more rapid its circulation the greater its usefulness. "The proportion borne by money to commerce decreases in advancing societies" (Carey), and by consequence its rate of interest, or the price paid for the use of money, falls with every advance in its usefulness. Brutus got fifty per cent. a year; Rothschild will lend at four.

The precious metals have many qualities that fit them for use as coined money. They are not liable to rust; they are easily alloyed with baser metals and as easily separated; they receive a stamped impression easily and retain it firmly; they are not easily worn or abraded; they are readily distinguished from other metals. Their defects are their weight, their intrinsic value as commodities, and hence the real loss of value by such abrasions as they suffer. So long as we use as money what possesses a very considerable value for other purposes, and is liable to be diverted to other uses, we cannot be said to have attained the complete separation of the function of money from that of commodities.

That these metals should be used at all as money is a matter of convention or general agreement merely. But that convention once established, their value in circulation, like all other values, is not conventional, but is determined by the cost of reproduction. If, however, the general agreement to use them as money were to cease, and they were to be demonetized, the excessive supply for other uses would cause their purchasing power to decline very greatly. Their intrinsic utility would, indeed, be more generally made use of, since they would be far more generally employed in the arts than at present, and in this respect there would be a net gain to mankind in the change. Their use—especially that of gold—as ornaments would cease on this decline in price, and this would make them still cheaper. However well fitted their color and brilliancy to attract the eye and please the fancy of childish savages, the refined taste of civilized man would cast them aside as barbarous. They still hold their place in the toilet because they are "condensed wealth, the trophies of industrial warfare," analogous to the savage's string of scalps. Very few of the articles made of them have any artistic merit.

§ **144.** They are difficult of reproduction, and therefore valuable, because they are scanty in supply and hard of access in their natural deposits. Gold especially is found in very small quantities, and to dig for it is—considering the number of persons employed in it—the most unprofitable of human employments. It has the fascination of a lottery, in which a few succeed, but thousands fail. The Mexicans have a saying that he who mines for copper will grow rich; he who digs for silver may or may not; he who seeks gold never will. Were it otherwise, success would defeat itself, through the decline in the value of its products.

These metals are, therefore, a very expensive instrument for effecting exchanges. They require a vast outlay of capital, labor and intelligence, that might otherwise be expended in producing what would directly meet and satisfy the primal needs of humanity. "It is a heavy price, and each ounce of gold represents so much labor withdrawn from agriculture and other industrial pursuits, which minister directly to the comforts and necessities of mankind."

See R. H. Patterson's *Economy of Capital* (1864).

These two metals do not circulate equally in all parts of the world, nor is their purchasing power the same everywhere. Since 1771 gold alone is "legal tender" for large payments in England; *i. e.*, is such an offer of payment as the creditor must accept or forfeit his claim to interest.

At the beginning of our own government both gold and silver were made legal tender, but owing to circumstances silver was the metal chiefly employed. In 1834 the standard of our coinage was changed from 1 : 15 to 1 : 16, thus favoring the use of gold. Silver-using countries of Europe sent us gold in exchange for our silver, thus effecting a profit to themselves at a loss to us. In 1873 a law was passed, without much consideration, demonetizing silver; but in 1878 this law was repealed. Silver was again made legal tender, and its coinage in limited quantities for government account was ordered. The law of 1873 was prompted by the change which had taken place in Europe. In 1871, Germany, taking advantage of the large accumulation of gold in her treasury through the payment of the French war-indemnity, determined to substitute that metal for the silver of which her coinage had been made chiefly. A few of the lesser states followed this example of demonetizing silver, and the states of the Latin Union which still retain it in use have been forced to suspend its coinage. Germany was moved to take this step partly by the example of England, and partly by exaggerated reports of the productivity of our Nevada mines. She has sustained serious losses in consequence of it, since she has not been able to dispose of the silver which she called in, except at a much lower price; and the knowledge that she holds large amounts for a rise in the market has tended to keep the market depressed. Besides the discredit thus brought upon silver by laws for its demonetization, its price has been affected through a serious interruption of its outflow from the silver-producing to the silver-using nations. Formerly the East India trade carried to the East a large amount of surplus silver every year. But since India became heavily indebted to England through loans raised in England to pay for railroads and other public works in India, the East Indian government has to meet the interest on these bonds in London by large sales of exchange on Calcutta. As a consequence the export of silver to pay balances of trade due to India has been stopped, and this surplus accumulates in Europe to the disadvantage of the holders of this metal.

It is generally recognized that this process of discrediting silver by demonetization must come to an end, and several international conferences have been held to secure its general restoration to the coinage of the world. But thus far there has been no result from these, as the nations which employ gold exclusively show no disposition to retrace their steps, and the others will not resume the coinage of silver until they do so.

It is argued by the opponents of the restoration of silver that the supply of that metal has been excessive and irregular for years past, and that there is no reason to expect anything but a continuance of this. The figures, however, show that the annual product of gold and silver taken together is much more constant and regular than is the product of either of them. It is also said that silver having fallen below its former value, remonetization would only result in flooding the world with a debased coinage. But the fall of silver is due, not so much to any increase in the product, as to the cessation of the demand for it in the mints of the world. A general agreement on the part of Europe and America to restore the free coinage at the old ratio would retrieve and maintain its price.

On the other hand, the continued demonetization of silver must cause such a diminution of the supply of coin as cannot but result in the most serious disturbances to domestic and international commerce. The mischief already done by demonetization cannot terminate until other countries have been forced to abandon silver. They cannot afford to go on using a metal which their neighbors have discredited, and which they refuse to take in payment of balances of trade. Their business, in so far as coin is necessary to it, will have to be transacted by means of the very inadequate gold coinage they possess or can procure. In Europe this will be felt much more quickly and severely than in America, for the present conditions of international trade and those we fairly may expect for the future, tend to transfer to America a large part of the gold supply of Europe.

In the East gold has never been a circulating medium; China will not accept it in payment for her teas and silks; in India gold mohurs are coined, but have never been legal tender. During the panic of 1866, Calcutta merchants offered 20,000*l.* in gold at the banks, but could not obtain even bank notes in exchange. To demonetize silver in the West would be to interpose a serious obstacle to commerce with the East. This commerce is of importance, as covering many articles to be found only in the East.

> Cowries, a species of shell, are used in the native kingdoms of Central Africa and some parts of India. Part of the land revenue of Orissa is paid in them, at the rate of 6000 or 7000 to the rupee. Similar were the wampum belts of our Indians. Carthage had a coinage of metal enclosed in stamped leather; Sparta had an intentionally cumbrous one of iron. Russia during the present century tried to get coins of platinum into circulation, but they were bought up and withdrawn because of the too great variation in the commercial value of platinum. Copper and bronze have been commonly used for coins of small value, but latterly an alloy of nickel and copper has been adopted by several of the most enlightened nations as the best material for small coins.

§ 145. The "precious metals" are often spoken of as "the standard of value," which is true only in a restricted sense. A standard must remain the same, however other things change; and this is certainly not true of gold and silver. Their purchasing power has been continually varying, generally declining, as the natural deposits of their ores have been laid bare, and the resistance of nature to those who searched for them has diminished. Vast quantities of them were furnished to Europe by Spanish America from the conquest of Mexico and Peru, till the revolt of those colonies in 1810. During the thirty years that followed, the supply was largely interrupted, and the supply of money in other forms was hindered by restrictive legislation. It was a time of great popular distress, and of embarrassment to the money markets of the world. Commerce and manufactures were growing, but the instrument of exchange was nearly a fixed quantity. In 1840 Russia began to work the Ural mines: the gold discoveries in California (1848) and in Australia (1854) came next. Since then the annual increase of coined money has been nearly quadrupled, and a vast extension of commerce and manufactures has followed throughout the world.

While both the periods of increase have seen a decline in the purchasing power of gold and silver, in neither of them has it fallen in anything like the ratio of increase. Humboldt estimates that in the eighteenth century there were thirty times as much coin in circulation as in the fifteenth; yet money had, on the very highest estimate, only twelve times as much purchasing power at the era of the Reformation as at present. When the new flow of gold into Europe began, economists of the English school (Chevalier, Cobden, etc.), predicted a rapid fall in its value; others of the same school (Cairnes, Jevons, etc.), claim that this has been the case to some extent, say ten or fifteen per cent. But even this much is not universally admitted. "We have seen," says R. H. Patterson, "three hundred million pounds added to the general currency within fifteen years, with so little effect that it is still doubted by many authorities whether there has been any depreciation at all." A small depreciation seems, however, to have taken place.

§ **146.** On the principles generally accepted by the English school, and first enunciated by David Hume in 1752, the rate of decrease in value should have been exactly proportional to the increase in amount. He says that "the only influence which a greater abundance of coin has in the kingdom" is "by heightening the price of commodities and obliging every one to pay a greater number of these little yellow or white pieces for everything he purchases." He admits indeed a *temporary* effect of quite another kind: "In every kingdom into which money begins to flow in greater abundance than formerly, everything takes a new face; labor and industry gain life; the merchant becomes more enterprising, the manufacturer more diligent and skilful, and even the farmer follows his plough with greater alacrity and attention."

Mr. J. S. Mill applies the well-worn formula of demand and supply to the subject in this way: "The demand for money consists of all the goods offered for sale.... The money and the goods are seeking each other for the purpose of being exchanged." Again: "If the whole money in circulation was doubled, prices would be doubled; if it was only increased one-fourth, prices would rise one-fourth." Mr. Mill does not appear to be aware of the fact that all but a small percentage of purchases are paid for by offset (checks, bills of exchange, etc.), without the use of coin.

§ **147.** The element of truth in this mechanical theory is separated from the falsehood in Mr. Patterson's statement: "An addition to the currency of a country is not necessarily a benefit. ... If the currency be doubled, *while the productions of that country and the demand for money remain as they were*, the double amount will do no more than the lesser one,—only all prices, wages, rents, etc., will be doubled in amount. The prices which a farmer or manufacturer gets for his goods will be increased; but so also in similar proportion will be the amount of his outlay in rent and taxes. It is like adding to both sides of an equation. It would be a sheer waste of money. ... A case like this, however, never occurs in the actual world." And why? Because in the actual world money is always drifting to the nations whose industry and enterprise give it the highest utility,—to the nations whose increased productiveness and increased demand for money furnish a sphere of usefulness to the increase,—to the nations whose worth, honor and intelligence make them the safest depositaries of the world's loose cash, and thus the centres of credit. England has raised her coin circulation to 150,000,000*l.*, but her annual savings are between a hundred and a hundred and thirty millions. The vast quantities of the precious metals that flowed into Europe after the discovery of America, may well, in the absence of new enterprises and industries to employ it, have had a different effect, and produced "a dearness of all things without a dearth of anything." Europe—especially Spain—was industrially inert, incapable of safely absorbing so large a quantity of the precious metals, incapable of receiving the industrial impulse they would most naturally have imparted. The lack of stimulating influence on a stagnant and stationary society is seen in India and China, which absorb every year $50,000,000 in silver, only to hoard it away.

§ 148. The influx of money into a progressive country is one of the most powerful promoters and increasers of production. To money (as to labor) "time is money;" whoever possesses it must seek an investment for it, or lose the profits; when it is plenty, all sorts of productive work are stimulated; labor is the master of capital, and industrial enterprise gains a more than proportionally larger return for its outlay, with every increase of the outlay. Labor becomes more productive as the instrument of association is more universally accessible. Its price rises while that of commodities falls.

The drain of money away from a country does not make it—as some have said—"a good place to buy in but a bad place to sell in,"—just the reverse. It makes it a bad place in which to buy anything but special products of its soil or climate, because although labor is cheap, the commodities produced by labor are dear through its inefficiency. It makes it, therefore, a good place for the sale of the merchandise of countries more happily situated. "To him that hath shall be given." Money tends to where money is; start a shilling in circulation in Thibet or Central Africa, and the chances are that it will turn up in London. It will do so, because the presence of great accumulations of capital in England, have made English labor productive to a degree that outweighs all other considerations.

§ 149. For the same reason, the money market in poor countries always tends towards stringency. However great may have been the recent supply, it is speedily drawn off into a thousand side channels, and the main stream is diminished. The effect of this is far more than proportional to the amount involved, for this market is extremely sensitive. On the first intimation of a scarcity, the rate rises, and they who must have money to pay the current expenses of large establishments, or to meet their outstanding obligations, are at the mercy of the lender. The captains of industry, and, through them, their laborers, are no longer the masters but the servants of capital.

§ 150. A second form of money, and one that is in many respects superior to coin, is paper-money. It is open to none of the objections that we have presented to the use of gold and silver. It wears out sooner, indeed, but can be replaced at a trifling cost; its production withdraws no large portion of the race from productive industry; its use abstracts from the arts no substance of intrinsic value; it circulates more rapidly than gold because it represents great values by a smaller bulk, and is easier of transfer. And when, as can be accomplished by wise legislation, the public have security that the note is really issued by the firm that it professes to come from, and that that firm is able to meet all just demands upon it, the last objection to its use is removed. If barter may be compared to the rude mode of transportation on human backs, and coin to transportation in carriages drawn by horses, paper-money is the steam-carriage, whose use calls for larger precautions against danger, but whose superior utility far outweighs that consideration.

The earliest form of paper-money was the bill of exchange. From a letter of Cicero to his brother Atticus, directing him to obtain a sum of money at Athens, we learn that this or something equivalent to it existed in antiquity. It was reinvented in the Middle Ages, not by the Jews, but by the Caursins, a class of money-changers employed by the Papal See in the collection and transmission of its revenue from all parts of Europe to Rome or Avignon. The Hanse towns adopted it, and it passed into currency as one of the ordinary methods of commerce between distant traders.

By this plan a debtor in Hamburg, who wishes to pay his London creditor, goes "on 'change" and buys of a discount house a draft on London for the amount. This draft has previously been drawn by some Hamburg merchant upon his London debtor, and sold by him to the discount house for a trifle less than the market rate of exchange. This exchange is "in favor of Hamburg" when drafts on London are plenty and sell for a small percentage less than the "face value." It is "against Hamburg" when the reverse is the case; and unless the course of exchange changes, some specie will in that case have to be exported from Hamburg to London to restore the balance. The amount of the discount or the premium on bills of exchange can never be greater than the cost of transmitting specie, including interest and insurance. By this method, it will be seen, the debts of London merchants to Hamburg merchants are paid by set-off against the debts of Hamburg merchants to London merchants, and the amount of money exchanged between the two cities is reduced to a minimum.

§ 151. The advantages of this plan are so great that the advantage of something like it for the transaction of business within each city was readily seen, and banks of deposit and issue were established as early as the fifteenth century. The first Italian banks, however, were mere associations of the public creditors in each city for the joint care of their interests, and when they became banks in the modern sense, they did not begin the issue of paper-money, but dealt only in money of account, which is yet to be described. The same is true of the banks of Amsterdam, Hamburg, and Stockholm. By 1673 we find the Bank of Genoa issuing bills of pretty large amount, which passed into circulation for wholesale transactions. About the same time the English goldsmiths began the practice of issuing bills which circulated in the same way, and when in 1694 the

Bank of England, and in 1695 the Bank of Scotland, were established, the issue of these bank-notes to those who borrowed money was a feature of each institution. These were at first "time-notes" bearing a low rate of interest, and consequently certain to be presented for redemption. Growing a little bolder, the Bank of England issued demand notes that bore no interest, and these passed rapidly into circulation, imparting a vigorous impulse to all sorts of business. As the country really needed these, it was almost impossible that any large quantity of them could be presented for redemption at once, except in cases of extraordinary panic. Of course the bank was enabled to extend its discounts far beyond the amount of coin at its command. For the bank did not—no bank could—keep on hand specie enough to redeem its entire circulation. It was sufficient if it kept as much as experience showed would meet the largest ordinary demand for it.

Such was the genesis of the modern bank-note, which has been one of the most powerful agents to promote and fertilize industry. To establish a bank of issue in a community where none has existed before, is to coin the mutual credit and confidence of the people into available money. It is to bring men into closer and more helpful association, by furnishing a new supply of the instrument of association and of the exchange of services. It is to put the means of industrial activity into the hands of those captains of industry who will open avenues of useful employment to the idle and the dependent. It is to recall from distant banks, and to draw out of old stockings and cash-boxes, the accumulated savings of the community, and make them doubly efficient in the promotion of local interests. By adding to the rapidity of societary circulation it adds new profits to every bargain, and gives a new efficiency to every blow on the anvil, a new value to the crops in every field.

Sir Walter Scott says of the Scotch system of banks of issue "The facilities which it has afforded to the industrious and enterprising agriculturist or manufacturer, as well as to the trustees of the public in executing national works, have converted Scotland from a poor, miserable and barren country into one where, if nature has done less, art and industry have done more than in perhaps any country in Europe, England not excepted. Through the means of credit which this system afforded, roads have been made, bridges built, and canals dug, opening up to reciprocal communication the most sequestered districts of the country; manufactures have been established, unequalled in extent or success,—wastes have been converted into productive farms,—the productions of the earth for human use have been multiplied twenty fold, while the wealth of the rich and the comforts of the poor have been extended in the same proportion. And all this in a country where the rigor of the climate and the sterility of the soil seemed united to set improvement at defiance. Let those who remember Scotland forty years since bear witness if I speak truth or falsehood."

See "Malachi Malagrowther's" *Letters on the Proposed Change in the Currency* (Edinburgh, 1826).

§ 152. The community, in using the notes of the bank as money, pass a vote of confidence in the general solvency. They are authorizing the directors to monetize a small portion of the capital of the neighborhood, that the utility of the rest and the facility of its transfer may be increased. They are passing, at the same time, a vote of confidence in the honesty and prudence of those directors.

"What security have we that the confidence thus extended will not be abused?" Two: (1) government inspection should be continually exercised over every such institution, and should extend to all the details of its management. Of course this implies no publication of the bank's affairs, save when the results are such as to justify its dissolution.

(2) Under restrictions imposed by general laws, any number of citizens should be as much at liberty to establish a bank as to open a store to sell dry-goods. The profits of legitimate banking are always large enough to attract thither capital sufficient to supply safely all the demand for paper-money and discounts. It

is only when the business is made a monopoly, and confined to a small number of firms, that their limited capital is unequal to the demand for money made upon them by the community. The best guarantee for safety is freedom.

The supposed danger that over-issues are practicable, and that they may not only bring the holder of bank-notes into a position of risk, but also derange the whole market for money, and with it all other markets, is in the main a mere bugbear. Banks do not break down because their note circulation is too large, but because the other departments of their business are so badly managed that their notes, be they few or many, have no guarantee behind them. A bank can ordinarily put into circulation no more notes than the community needs. The avenues of return are always more open to the public than those of issue to the directors. But one class of English economists have said "over-issue" so often that they are ready to stake their reputation as financiers upon this theory, which is sustained by no facts, and is disputed by the ablest men (Tooke, Ashburton, Fullarton, etc.) of their own school. "It was a pair of spectacles which the Bullion Committee [of 1811] left as a legacy to the subsequent generation, and which became the medium through which all our monetary difficulties were viewed. The increase of the bank's issues to the extent of a million or two above the ordinary amount, was held capable of producing the most momentous consequences. It 'depressed the currency,' and was the parent of our recurrent monetary crises. The upholders of this theory, it is true, never demonstrated by a reference to prices that the currency was depressed. They took that for granted, and a good deal more besides" (R. H. Patterson).

§ 153. The third and the most perfect form of money is *money of account*. It possesses in a still higher degree all the advantages that make paper-money better than coin. It passes in circulation most rapidly; it performs the vastest amount of service in proportion to its amount; its use involves no loss by wear; its production is so nearly costless that its cost hardly enters into men's thoughts. As much as paper-money is less material than coin, by so much is money of account less material than paper-money. As we have compared coined money in its efficiency and utility to a carriage drawn by horses, and paper-money to the car moved by steam-power, so might we conceive of money of account as a vehicle of transportation through the air, moving with electric swiftness, and impelled by some of those subtler physical forces whose mastery is yet to be achieved. It is the money of civilization; its use involves a degree of intelligent insight into the true nature of wealth and of exchanges, and a strong confidence in the general honesty and trustworthiness of mankind, that are impossible to the savage or the half-civilized man.

Money of account originated in the commercial cities of Italy, and its use was thence transferred to the great emporiums of Northern Europe—Amsterdam, Hamburg and Stockholm. The republics of Venice and of Genoa authorized their creditors to establish banks on the basis of the certificates of the city's debt. The Bank of Venice dates from 1171, when a forced loan was raised to fit out a fleet; that the burden might be felt as little as possible, the persons assessed were formed into a company for protection of their common concern and the receipt of interest; at the same time the debt was made easily transferable by order on the company, and thus its use for the discharge of obligations grew up naturally. At first it was a forced loan under special guarantees; then a desirable investment; then a means of payment. The first character of the deposits so entirely disappeared that government ceased to pay interest on the capital. Then to secure a uniform currency, it decreed that all wholesale transactions should be paid in the form of a transfer of bank stock, unless otherwise stipulated; so that whoever had a box full of coins, gathered from the four quarters of the earth through the manifold channels of Venetian trade, took them to the bank to get credit upon its books according to their weight and fineness. The standard by which their value was estimated was called "money of account," to distinguish it from the various moneys that were translated into it. The government treated these masses of coin as payment for the privilege of a credit on the bank's book, and all idea of their repayment was lost sight of. Yet for four hundred years, or until the conquest of the city by Napoleon I., this money of account circulated freely, and was at a premium (or *agio*) in coin; trade proceeded with a rapidity previously unknown; no Venetian ever raised his voice in complaint of an institution which was the pride of the city and the envy of Europe. When the French destroyed it, they found no funds to reward them.

The Bank of Genoa originated in the same way, but differed in some details of management, such as the issue of bank-notes. The Bank of Stockholm owed its origin to the fact that copper was the only coin in circulation in Sweden, and it was therefore necessary to translate this into a more convenient form of money. Hamburg and Amsterdam, the Genoa and Venice of the North in the sixteenth century, were equally embarrassed by the various weights and standards of the coin that flowed into their cities, and established banks of deposit and transfer to translate these into " money of account;" here also wholesale transactions were required to be settled in the shape of transfer of bank credits. As neither were based on government debts, and neither loaned money, the expenses were defrayed by a slight charge to the customers of the bank. Both cities reaped immense advantages from the system, in the rapidity and ease with which money of account passed from one person to another in effecting exchanges. The Bank of Amsterdam failed in 1790, as it was found that the funds on which its credit rested had been in part abstracted by the Dutch government. That of Hamburg still exists.

§ 154. A bank in the modern sense is more than any of these institutions was. It is a *discount* house, a firm for the *issue* of paper-money, a place for *deposit* of money, a *clearing-house*, and a branch of a larger clearing-house. It is the union of all the earlier features of such institutions, with the addition of others that grew out of the peculiar methods of modern business.

First, its *discount* business.  A bank is an institution that deals in credits by buying up debts,—that may be said to turn debts into credits for a consideration called discount. Except in the retail trade, the larger part of modern business is transacted by means of "mercantile paper."  The buyer does not transfer the amount due to the seller in coin or bank-notes.  He gives him a bill for the amount payable in (say) sixty or ninety days. The seller cannot afford to do without the money for so long a time.  He wants to "turn over his capital" as fast as possible; he would rather give up a percentage of his profits and get the money at once.  He takes it to bank to be discounted, after making himself responsible for its payment by endorsing it. If the directors are satisfied with the name of the endorser or of the drawer, or of both, they let him have the money, *minus* the interest for the time specified.  When the time is up the drawer of the bill must pay it, or if he fail its endorser must.

Second, its *issue* business.  A whole or a part of the money advanced to the bank's customer may be needed in such shape as will circulate among all classes.  If he be a contractor or a manufacturer he is dealing with people who keep no bank account.  He must, therefore, have money which they can use, and this the bank gives him, either in its own notes, or in those of some other bank.  In this way the banks put into circulation a much larger sum in notes than their whole paid-up capital would suffice to redeem, and this with perfect safety to themselves and great benefit to the community.

Third, its business as a *clearing-house*, which is the most important of its functions.  In most cases a customer of the bank who has had a note discounted would find it very inconvenient to be paid in any form of money; he prefers a credit to that amount on the books of the bank.  That is, the bank advances him a sum of money, and he at once "deposits" it with the bank, and uses the credit thus obtained to pay his debts by check, i. e., by the transfer of a portion of this credit to the account of his creditors.  A small percentage of checks are drawn in money by their holders, but in most cases they are paid simply by a transfer of credits. In this case the "deposits" on the bank's books become virtually part of the currency, and constitute a vast fund of "money of account" for the discharge of indebtedness. These deposits far exceed in amount all other forms of money in circulation, and move with greater rapidity and exhibit vaster utility in effecting exchanges. The deposit fund continually tends, indeed, to diminish in volume through the discounted notes maturing and being paid, as well as through the payment of depositors' checks; and it is only kept up through fresh deposits of cash or fresh discounts. When the demand for these discounts is not great, or the directors are hopeful and confident, the rate of discount falls. When the contrary is the case, it rises and the best security is required.

> This is particularly noticeable in countries where there is no legal limit to the rate of interest, such as England. In the United States a bank usually charges uniformly the rate fixed by law.

Fourth, to make the system more efficient and to give this money of account yet wider currency, each bank in our great cities is a branch of a larger clearing-house. When all the business of a city was done at a single bank, the transfer of its credits sufficed for all wholesale transactions. When several took the place of one, very large sums of money passed between them, as a check would not transfer credit unless both parties kept accounts at the same bank. But now each bank makes its statement in the clearing-house, of its claims against every other, and on balancing the account of each, the net indebtedness to (or from) it is ascertained, and paid from (or to) the clearing-house. These balances are the merest fraction of the gross amounts, and the system brings every bank, to a certain extent, under the supervision of the rest.

> This method of settlement was adopted by the dealers in the old French fairs, and enabled the merchants to transact a great deal of business with the exchange of very little money.
>
> The Scotch banks first adopted it for the mutual supervision and control of their circulation. They met once a fortnight in Edinburgh to exchange notes, and paid the net balances in coin.

§ 155. Note here that we must distinguish between the true character of money of account and the way in which it is mostly created in modern times. The method of buying and selling "on time" with which it is now associated is open to many objections; but if that method were utterly abolished, if the discount system were to cease, and all purchases were to be paid in cash, such a currency as this would be as necessary as ever for the transaction of business. The credit-fund would then have to be created entirely, as it now is in part, by the actual deposit of money in some institution like the Bank of Hamburg. Its volume would then be no longer liable to contraction or expansion with the hopefulness or distrust of bank directors. Were a money of account based not on deposits of cash, but on deposits of securities to a fixed amount, as in Venice, it would retain its power of circulation, with no reduction of its volume, in the worst seasons of panic, and would be continually available for the transaction of legitimate business. The possession of such a "money of account" was the secret of the mercantile stability of Venice and Genoa, Hamburg and Amsterdam; as the complication of our "money of account" with the discount system is a chief cause of our commercial fluctuations.

§ 156. No market is so sensitive as the money market. A very slight reduction in the supply raises the price out of all proportion, and leads to a rigid scrutiny of all securities offered as the ground of a loan. The banks at such a period are sensitive to the approaching stringency; they refuse discounts that they would else have granted; they refuse new paper, and put an artificial dam across the great stream of credit-payments, to the ruin of those who must go on and who must have money. In the fright that follows, as in all frights, men lose their wits; the business community is demoralized. Credit, faith in anybody, in anything but visible and tangible money, disappears. There is a general falling back upon the more primitive and material methods of payment. The great credit-fund of money of account loses its currency, or hold upon public confidence, because created by discounts and bound up with the uncertain fortunes of the discounting banks. Then begins a "run upon the deposits." Those deposits were in great part created by credits granted, and were never intended to be paid in money of any sort. The banks should have the option of paying them in legal tender, or in certificates of deposit, good at the clearing-house; but they have none. They are demanded in visible and current money. In spite of the reduction of discounts, their amount is still too great to be thus disposed of, and a suspension of the banks necessarily follows, upon which the panic reaches its height. All exchange of services, except the most necessary, ceases at once; the community relapses into the barbarism of mutual distrust. The history of banking, since the establishment of the discount system, shows us the necessity of such a reform as will sunder that system from banking proper, and secure the permanent currency and the free creation (under proper safeguards) of money of account.

No bank existed in England till 1694. During Commonwealth times the London goldsmiths, whose fire-proof and thief-proof vaults rendered them the natural custodians of large sums of money, began to exercise some of the functions of modern banking. They granted loans at high rates of interest, and issued these in demand-notes. A little experience showed them how much specie they must keep on hand to meet the possible demand for it on any one day. They paid depositors six per cent. interest for it. This continued till after the Revolution.

§ 157. It occurred to William Paterson, member of the Scotch Parliament from Dumfries, that government could raise money for the war against France without paying the high rate of interest exacted by the goldsmiths. He saw that a far larger sum than they could command would be obtained, if the government could give confidence to the multitudes who were hoarding small sums, and make it worth their while to lend them. He proposed a Bank of England, after the model of those of Italy and Holland,—i. e., for the issue of circulating paper-money, secured by the deposit of what we call government securities. After much opposition, the plan was adopted with some modifications, and the Bank of England began its career January 1st 1694 by lending its whole paid-up capital of £1,200,000 to the government at 8 per cent. interest. At first its notes were gladly taken in exchange for the light and defective silver currency of that day; but when the new coinage that was carried through under Sir Isaac Newton came upon the market, the notes declined in favor, although they bore interest and were much needed for the business of the country. In 1696 their redemption in specie was suspended. The Tory party, mostly country gentlemen, attempted to establish a land-bank as a rival. It also was to loan money to the government and to discount bills only on the credit of real estate. The plan failed utterly and caused great loss to the nation.

The Bank of England grew slowly into favor, and lost its bitterest enemies as the old race of usurers died out and none filled their places. It gradually perfected its methods; it established the system of book credits, with payments by check. It substituted demand-notes bearing no interest for time-notes that bore interest; these new notes passed quickly into the circulation, and were rarely returned for redemption. It issued smaller and therefore more useful notes, the first being never less than £20. It secured in 1706 a virtual monopoly, not more than six persons being allowed to unite their capital to establish any other bank in England. (This lasted 120 years, and was then confined to London and towns within 65 miles of it.) On the other hand it upheld the public credit, and greatly simplified questions of finance, by furnishing a channel through which the people could easily come to the support of the government in time of need, and could always obtain either a profitable investment for capital or a loan of money on easy terms. The rate of discount *down to* 1844 varied between 4 and 5 per cent., save a rise to 5½ and 6 in the last half of 1839. Other banking houses grew up in London and throughout the country, but all subordinate to the great national concern in London.

§ 158. As a state bank it shared in the vicissitudes of the government. It had to stand a run on its specie in 1745, when the Pretender was on his way to London, but the city merchants stopped this by publicly pledging themselves to stand by the bank. In 1772 and 1783 panics were caused by "over-trading" in foreign goods; in the latter the bank for the first time adopted the policy of cutting down its discounts, till the drain of specie from the country should cease,—an effectual but rather "heroic" remedy, as every reduction of the circulation intensifies the panic.

In 1793 and 1797 panics recurred; that of 1793 caused partly by over-trading, partly by the political disturbances of the time; that of 1797 entirely by the latter. In both cases the bank made bad worse, by refusing discounts and thus allowing wealthy and solvent firms to go down unaided. Happily the government restored confidence by an issue of exchequer notes. In 1810 the revolt of the Spanish-American colonies led to immense over-trading and a consequent panic. Cargoes of skates had been sent to cities where ice and snow were never seen, and others had received Epsom salts enough to physic their entire population once a week for fifty years. The bank having suspended specie payments since 1797, came to the aid of solvent firms with large amounts of notes, and the government ordered an issue of £6,000,000 besides.

§ 159. In 1815 the bank began to get ready for a resumption of specie payments by cutting down discounts and reducing circulation. It thus reduced the currency by £12,000,000, a mere trifle as compared with the money value of the nation's property; but the whole circulation for a time stopped and an artificial panic was produced. In 1821 it resumed specie payments, after a suspension of twenty-four years, thus altering at once and greatly the terms of all contracts made in the interval and not yet executed. All who had land, labor or produce to sell, or contracts to fill, were placed at great disadvantage. Creditors— i. e., the wealthy, capital-holding class—gained greatly, except where their debtors were absolutely ruined. Mills stopped, land fell in price, labor was thrown idle, and in peace men suffered more than the calamities of war.

In 1825, 1837 and 1839 panics similar to that of 1793 occurred—i. e., they were caused by over-trading and intensified by the selfish policy of the bank. In 1840 a parliamentary commission began to investigate the reasons of these crises, and in 1844 Sir Robert Peel's famous "Bank Act" was passed, with a view to prevent their recurrence. Rejecting the opinion of Adam Smith—that if bank-notes be issued only on the discount of merchantable bills of undoubted character, and founded on a real transaction, they cannot be excessive,—English financiers had adopted the theory of over-issues as explaining the whole matter. That theory grew very naturally out of their mechanical theory of the effect of an increased supply of money (§ 146).

§ 160. The Act of 1844 was directed to the regulation of the English currency through the Bank of England, to prevent a fancied "depreciation." It severed the banking department proper from the department of issues, and transferred to the latter £14,000,000 in government obligations as security for bank-notes of that amount. It required that, if the note circulation exceeded that sum, the bank should have gold in its vaults equal to the excess. At the same time it provided that the bank-note circulation of the country banks should be limited and diminished, never increased. In other words, it made the amount of paper-money in circulation in England dependent upon the amount of bullion in the vaults of the banks.

The measure betrayed a total want of apprehension of the true nature of the discount and deposit system. It did not put the vast currency created by the bank's advances and those of its rivals, under any specific limitations. It allowed the bankers to create currency *ad libitum* on the pages of their ledgers, provided they did not print it on bits of silk paper that passed from hand to hand. In ordinary business times it could therefore put no restraint upon the real circulation of the country. Rather it set before the bank the strongest inducement to multiply that currency and stimulate speculation when money was easy, that it might "make hay while the sun shone" and get its superfluous issues into circulation. Heretofore the rate of discount had ranged between 4 and 5; from this date the extremes are 2 and 10. The office of a regulator is to moderate extremes; but the bank has really intensified and exaggerated them. And when we speak of the Bank of England, it must be remembered that it controls all the lesser banks. By its immense size, its vast prestige, its special privileges, it is able to fix the rate to be paid for money throughout the kingdom.

But in other than ordinary times, when this great credit-fund loses its currency, when the business community is demoralized by panic, and the demand for other and more tangible forms of money recurs, the act becomes at once powerful for mischief. In such a case the actual supply of notes and specie is manifestly unequal to the vast demand made upon it by the business of a great nation; and not only the Bank of England, but all the banks of the country are hand-tied so far as regards any help they can give. Their notes may be as good as gold. Since 1823 they have always been so. But they can issue none until the government step in and put an end to the panic by suspending the act which was meant to prevent panics.

>All these objections were very ably presented before the act was passed, by Lord Ashburton (head of the house of Baring Bros.), T. Tooke, (author of the *History of Prices*), John Fullarton (*On the Regulation of the Currency*), Charles Scott (a Montreal banker), and others; but to no purpose. The "sound views on currency" represented by Peel, Lord Overstone (Mr. Jones Lloyd), Torrens, McCulloch, &c., carried the day.

Worse still, the act conduces to purely artificial panics. The causes that lead to the diminution of bullion in the bank vaults are various, and most, or indeed all of them, are without any significance as to the general soundness of the English money market. If a large amount of foreign stocks or government bonds have been subscribed for, gold must go out to pay for them. If schemes of improvement in India are on foot, English gold must buy on the Continent the silver that is to pay the Hindoo workmen. If any country has sold as much as usual to England, but has bought less than usual, specie must be exported to pay the balance, since bills of exchange are not to be had. If a failure of the English grain crop necessitates a larger import than usual of Russian or American wheat, Mark Lane must pay for it partly in gold, unless the exports to Russia or America be unusually great. Any one of these causes or a concurrence of several will diminish the bullion in bank. Were there no Act of 1844, and were the directors wise by past experience, the decrease would not matter. It might be treated as a petty backset, that the course of trade would speedily compensate for.

But as it is, the bank raises the rate and diminishes the amount of discounts as the bullion diminishes, in order to keep the circulation down to the level of the bullion, instead of taking any steps directly to replace the loss. It does not go to the Continent to buy or borrow bullion; it throws the whole pressure of the distress upon the business men of the nation. Holders of stocks of domestic and even of foreign goods, who are in want of money, must throw them on the market at any sacrifice, and sell them at a bargain to some rich capitalist at home or on the Continent who is on the outlook for such chances. English stocks and foreign stocks held in England are sometimes sacrificed to an extent that exceeds the maximum of bullion in the bank vaults. In this way a purely artificial drain of specie homeward is produced, and the bank is satisfied. In the meantime great establishments have broken down under the pressure, a few because they ought to break, others in spite of their complete solvency. In many cases, after the affairs of such houses have been wound up by the costly processes of an English bankruptcy,—which absorbs 45 per cent. of the estate,—every creditor has been paid in full, and a handsome fortune left to the partners.

§ 161. Three years after Peel's Bank Act was passed came the crisis of 1847, occasioned partly by the drain of gold to buy food abroad because of the failure of the potato crop, partly by the great railway speculations of that period. The Bank Act failed in its purpose, as even its author confessed; the government suspended its operations to allow the bank to come to the assistance of business men. The same took place in the great crises of 1857 and 1866, and in a less degree in 1874. In 1857 mercantile extravagance was not rife in England; business was quiet and moderate as compared with 1852, when the bank stimulated speculation to the utmost by lowering the rate to two per cent. But Peel's Act necessitates a crisis in England whenever any of England's customers are in trouble. The American crisis caused a drain of specie from Europe to the United States, and all England was put "under the bank's screw" to turn the tide of gold back to England; prices were forced down twenty-five per cent., and large amounts of the products of industry passed out of the hands of their rightful owners into those of capitalists who could take advantage of their necessities. Every crisis takes from the poorer and more active to give to the richer and idler classes, and adds to the inequality of wealth that is so ominous a sign for the future of England. It destroys also a part of the moral capital of the nation,—the confidence and hopefulness of its captains of industry.

England possesses, therefore, a highly artificial banking system, one which is nominally armed with great powers to protect the industrial interests of the nation, but certain, if rigidly adhered to, to use them to oppress and injure those interests.

§ 162. In Scotland, on the other hand, we find an eminently natural banking system, created not *for* the people, but *by* them, acting down to 1845 with the most perfect freedom in the extension of its operations, the increase of its credits and the amount of its circulation. And the safety has been exactly proportional to the freedom. Scottish bank-notes have been at par; the people will take guineas instead, if they must, but they pass them off as soon as possible as a pretentious, unthrifty, eminently un-Scottish kind of money, much inferior to a native bank-note issued in any corner of Scotland.

The business men of Edinburgh, having heard that their countryman (Paterson) was planning a bank for the English, and that he had been successful in obtaining a hearing, asked an Englishman named Holland to devise a Bank of Scotland. He did so, and put his proposals before them. They knew nothing of banking, but were willing to learn. They abounded in objections, but saw the point of his answers. And so, in 1695, the new institution was launched, under a charter granted by the Scottish Parliament, being the first private joint-stock bank that the world had ever seen. It had a monopoly for twenty-one years; its profits were very large, and the benefits that it conferred on an impoverished country were immense. Other companies came into existence, and the jealousies were extreme; every bank was eager to break the rest, or at least injure their credit. In 1752 better counsels prevailed. Legislation was had to put an end to some abuses, including the practice of refusing payment of notes till six months after demand, and the issue of very small currency. The banks associated closely in a sort of national clearing-house, for mutual protection and mutual surveillance. The bi-weekly exchange of claims in Edinburgh was adopted, serving as a powerful check upon unsafe business. Nowhere in the world has an extensive banking system been carried on with so little loss to the public, and no country has derived so much benefit from banking.

The distinguishing feature of the Scottish banks is their system of *cash credits*. Whoever can get two satisfactory bailsmen to endorse his bond, can open an account for its amount in the bank. He is charged four per cent. on the amount that he actually draws, and is allowed two per cent. on sums deposited when the bank is in his debt; that is, after every day's transactions his account is balanced and he is paid interest at the lower rate or pays it at the higher rate,—according as he is the bank's creditor or its debtor—till the next transaction alters the balance. But the payments are mostly in notes, and not by check; paper money, therefore, plays a large part in Scotch banking, as notes constitute almost the entire currency of the kingdom. They are not aristocratic notes like those of England, of £5 and upward, but very largely £1 notes for the use of the people. It is to exchange these notes and pay their balances in coin that the banks meet twice a week, and thus they are enabled to form an estimate of the extent and safety of the business of each. In

1826 the English ministry proposed, "for the sake of uniformity," to abolish this useful and popular currency; but the proposal was received with such an outburst of opposition from all classes and parties (Sir Walter Scott took a very prominent part), that it was abandoned. In 1845 all further increase in the amount of this paper-money was forbidden—i. e., it was enacted that, however great Scotland's need for more money in the course of her growth, she should have no more. She has now actually less, as the failure of a Glasgow bank has caused the lapse of several hundred thousand pounds. In times of panic these cautious Scotchmen exercise the higher caution of mutual help. In the run on the Union Bank of Edinburgh in 1857, there was in Bank street a double flow of gold—frightened depositors carrying away their money to other banks, and bank clerks carrying it back again. The results fully justify this confidence; for over a century the public have lost nothing by the banks and the banks have lost nothing by the public. Stockholders have lost in a very few instances through dishonest or silly management.

§ 163. The first Bank of France was established in 1716, when the country was bankrupt, business suspended, and the misery of the people at its height. In two years it had revived trade of every kind and restored the public credit. Unfortunately its projector and manager, a Scotchman named John Law, held the theory that a country could not have too much money, and that it could safely have and usefully employ as much as the entire value of its property. Sustained in his schemes by the Regent, he extended the circulation to four thousand millions of dollars, bought up the royal revenues, the colonies and the entire foreign trade of France, and went into immense speculations in trade. To keep up the value of his notes, false dividends were declared, and specie was forbidden to pass as money except in small amounts. Of course the attempt utterly failed, and the bubble burst, leaving France in a worse plight than before.

In 1776 another bank was started, but not under that name, as France was afraid of banks. This one shared in the great struggle carried on by Turgot and Necker, to redeem the public credit—and in the failure of the struggle. It came to an end with the Revolution, and was succeeded by a joint-stock bank, established by the Parisian bankers.

The present Bank of France was founded by Napoleon in 1800; it was given a complete monopoly of banking—a state of things that has been again restored through the provincial banks being united to it. Throughout its history it has been characterized by public spirit and a generous policy. Thus it did its utmost to carry French commerce through the exciting times of 1848 without reducing its discounts; and when the government authorized it to suspend specie payments, it really never did so. It has repeatedly raised bullion by loan or purchase to meet a drain, instead of making the business community meet the emergency for it. Since 1857 it has adopted the principle of raising the rate of discount in stormy times, but apparently it does not materially decrease the amount. For this reason all sorts of disasters are predicted for it by English authorities on finance. France suffers less from commercial crises than England or America, because less engaged in foreign trade or indeed in wholesale operations of any sort. Her currency is mainly specie, and the extent of the credit system in proportion to her population and wealth is very small.

§ 164. In France, Belgium, Germany and Russia, the problem of establishing banks on the credit of real estate has been successfully solved, and these banks are now very widely established to grant discounts to landowners and thus promote agricultural improvement. The great difficulty and expense of proving land-titles, and of legally recovering money loaned on land, seemed to condemn this class to pay high rates of interest. In Scotland, however, there is a very simple system of land-registry, and recovery of debts is a cheap and easy process. The Scotch banks, by their cash credits secured by bond, have solved the problem for their agricultural customers. The landowners of Silesia, finding themselves utterly impoverished by the wars of Frederick the Great, adopted a scheme proposed to them by a Berlin merchant, named Büring. They unitedly pledged the whole land of the province to the government, which raised money on its own credit as if for a public loan, and lent it to the association at the rate it paid for it. This loan is put on the market in the form of land-stock, guaranteed by the government and transferable at pleasure. Besides this public association, private ones have been formed in great numbers, and have done much to improve the agriculture of the Continent. These private land-credit banks take mortgages bearing a fixed rate of interest upon landed property, paying for those mortgages not in money, but in their own obligations bearing a lower rate of interest, which obligations the mortgagor sells, mainly to small local capitalists.

§ 165. Although proposals were very early made for the establishment of joint-stock banks of issue in the American colonies (especially in Boston and in Philadelphia), land banking was the first that was adopted. The colonial governments' land offices made loans in paper-money "on bond and mortgage" at low rates of interest, thus furnishing a circulation for local trade and helping the settler to reclaim his land. The depreciation of public credit by the vast issues of paper-money during the Revolutionary War put an end to the practice. But these colonial issues did not stand at par; they ranked differently in different colonies, and so gave rise to that curious complication by which a pound meant one thing on the right bank of the Delaware, another on the left, but a pound sterling in neither case.

§ 166. Robert Morris, a merchant of Philadelphia, was much struck with the need of a public bank to facilitate the business of the colony, and was about to ask a charter for one when the Revolution put a stop to his plans. Being the Superintendent of Finances during the closing years of the war, he had great difficulty in raising loans, and proposed to the Continental Congress his plan for a bank. It was formally approved, a charter secured from the State legislature, and the Bank of North America went into operation January 1782. The national

For some account of a system by which the advantages of the credit system have been extended even to the working classes, see § 140.

government took a quarter of a million in stock, and borrowed $400,000 from the bank. It did much to restore public credit and stimulate industry; it gradually became independent of government, while still rendering needed aid. In 1785 its charter was withdrawn by the state legislature by the votes of the country members, who wished to see the state's credit restored and the land offices reopened,—and who thought the bank was in the way. It continued operations without a charter, and was re-chartered in 1787, the farmers having found out their mistake.

Banks were soon after established in Boston, New York and Baltimore.

§ **167.** The old Bank of the United States was chartered by the U. S. Congress in 1791, on the recommendation of Alexander Hamilton, whose report on the subject is a masterly state paper. When the charter had expired in 1811, the party of strict construction—i. e., those who believed in giving the general government as little power as possible—were in possession of power and refused to renew the charter. The local banks chartered by the states alone remained, with capital by no means equal to the demands upon them. Great expansions were followed by sudden contractions of the currency, the banks always "protecting themselves" at the expense of their customers by sudden retrenchment of circulation, rather than sacrifice any part of the large amount of government stocks that they held. Well might Matthew Carey protest, "that abstracted from all attention to the interests of the community, it is supereminently absurd, impolitic, and injurious, as it regards the interests merely of the banks, to press citizens into the vortex of bankruptcy;" and "that those sudden vibrations of bank accommodation whereby money is rendered superabundant at one time and immoderately scarce at another, are favorable to speculation and the wealthy alone,—and are pernicious to morals, industry, trade and commerce,—that they tend to enrich the wealthy and impoverish those who stand in the middle and lower walks of life,—in a word, to make the rich richer and the poor poorer."

*Letters to the Directors of the Banks of Philadelphia* (1816).

§ 168. The second U. S. Bank was chartered in 1816, a charter granted two years previously having been defeated by the veto of President Madison. Its earlier years covered a period of great financial prostration (1816–24); its later period was one of great inflation and general speculation (1833–6); the nine years between were marked by a sober and steady growth in all the elements of national prosperity. The history of the bank and its national influence has been the subject of bitter and protracted controversy. We incline to the view that it rendered the nation great services in helping it out of the time of distress, and was in no wise responsible for the inflation and reckless trading that culminated in the crisis of 1837–8. It furnished a national currency that passed current in every part of the Union, at a time when the complexity of a score of different banking systems, and the existence of numbers of fraudulent banks, prevented the notes of any other bank from possessing more than a local circulation. It raised the public credit by accepting public bonds as subscriptions for bank stock. It evinced the solidity of its monetary basis by sustaining for years the attacks of a powerful political faction, headed by President Jackson. When at last it failed to obtain a renewal of its charter, and thus ceased to be a national and became a state bank, it was at the same time greatly weakened both in actual resources and in public confidence by the withdrawal of the government deposits. It engaged in speculations, and the failure of these, joined to the hostility of the then dominant political party, involved its ruin, but it cannot be held to have verified the prophecies of its enemies.

§ 169. From 1836 till the opening years of the recent Civil War, we had no National Banking system. Every state legislated according to its light, and hardly one of these state laws evinces any intimate knowledge of the workings of the credit system. Some had the wisdom to leave their people free to engage in banking to any extent they pleased, under general restrictions for the defence of the public who held bank-notes,—as in Scotland. Others by artificial restrictions kept capital out of banking, and thus prevented the business community from getting the amount of accommodation they needed. Thus Rhode Island, under a free system, had seventy-one banks, or one for every 2000 of its population, with an aggregate capital of nearly $15,000,000, and investments and loans of $19,500,000. Pennsylvania in 1850, under a restrictive system, had but fifty-three banks, or one to every 40,000 of its people, with a capital of $20,500,000, and loans and investments of over $50,000,000. Rhode Island had $100 a head invested in banking; Pennsylvania $8. The legislators who established this state of things, and conferred the monopoly of banking on a few favored establishments, thought they had provided for all risks by limiting the number of bank-notes, and requiring the banks to keep a fair proportion of specie on hand for their redemption. They did not see that they had left it in the power of the directors to create another species of currency without any limit except ordinary prudence, and yielding large returns for the loan of the bank's credit. If they saw a huge mass of "deposits" set over against a somewhat larger mass of "loans and investments" in the published reports, they probably counted it a sign of the high confidence that the bank enjoyed; they never thought of those deposits as a far more volatile and explosive form of currency, not issued in engraved notes, but created by a few strokes of the pen on the credit side of a bank-account. By limiting the capital invested, they had only furnished the chance and increased the temptation to excessive discounts, such as the actual figures show. Nay, they rather forced the banks to go beyond the bounds of prudence by subjecting them to an intense pressure on the part of the business community, which would otherwise have been distributed over a large number of establishments with a great aggregate capital. For the profits of safe banking are always large enough to attract thither as much capital as the business community needs, when the right to establish a bank is restricted only by such general laws as are necessary to protect the public.

§ 170. The banks of our three great seaports rendered very

effective service to the government during the opening years of the war, filling the empty treasury by a large loan of specie, and upholding the national credit.

The National Banking system which has grown out of Secretary Chase's financial operations, and now includes all the banks of issue in the country, recalls many of the features of early banking. Like the Italian banks, and the Bank of England in its first stage, the notes are secured by the deposit of government securities, but with the additional guarantee that the national credit is fully pledged for their redemption. The banks have a double source of profit; they receive the interest on the government bonds, and have besides the profits of their discounts. They are of course subjected to the closest examination as to the state and management of their affairs. Those who remember the state of the currency before the war, or have ever looked into an old *Counterfeit Detector*, will be forced to confess that this national currency has great advantages.

The valid objections to the system are two: (1) The laws to establish and regulate it are based upon a very imperfect notion of the credit system, and of the nature and extent of the credit employed by the bank in business. Like the old state laws, they take great pains to "hedge in the cuckoo" by limiting the issues of notes. They do not provide for the grouping of the banks in local clearing-houses for mutual supervision. They do nothing to keep the banks from "protecting themselves" in stringent times at the cost of the business community at large.

(2) The distribution of these banks was an artificial one, and was becoming more and more so with every year. In the original assignment the amount of their aggregate issues was fixed at a given amount and distributed among the states according to population. Several of the poorer states were unable to make use at once of all the amount thus assigned to them, and after a given date it was distributed among the older and richer states. Connecticut, Rhode Island and Massachusetts, for instance, got very much more than their share, the Western States very much less. With every year these poorer states were

growing in wealth and in the need for money, at a rate that surpassed the progress of the older states. With every year the preponderance of numbers and wealth shifted farther westward. But the new states were tied to just the amount of circulation that they could put upon the market at that date; and this, although they needed far more bank-notes in proportion to the extent of their business than the older states did, as with them the credit system is far less perfectly organized. Hence their outcry for more money, and their opposition to the measures taken to reduce the amount of national currency in circulation, unless it were replaced by some other form of paper-money. So far as this defect can be obviated without changing the basis of our banking system, it has been, by recent legislation.

(3) In spite of their bearing the name "national," our banks are confined to very limited localities in the transaction of business. A vast amount of money is paid in transactions between distant parts of the nation by the cumbrous and expensive method of drawing and negotiating bills of exchange. The sales of the Western crops and the purchase of Eastern goods in exchange are actually carried on as if they were transactions between the merchants of two different nations, and sometimes at an expense of several per cent. premium or discount to business men. While our present system offers the advantage that the national currency passes freely through the whole nation, and keeps the rate of discount down, its incompleteness leaves great openings for illegitimate business in drawing speculative bills of exchange based on no real transaction, but negotiated by collusion between distant banks or firms.

A national clearing-house established by government, with branches in every important city, and an understanding with all the national banks, would cheapen, simplify and add security to all our domestic trade. As local clearing-houses enable the banks to keep watch upon one another, so would this system bring the collective banks of each locality under the supervision of the banks of other places. The amount of money needed for the whole business of the nation would be greatly reduced. The balance due to (or from) any city from (or to) all the rest, could be ascertained at a central office and then paid from (or to) that office. There might also be lodged in this national clearing-house, as in the Bank of England, "the power to meet panics by temporary expansion," which "must be a power capable of being used promptly and with decision" (*The Nation*). Of course this institution would be debarred from all trading in money or commodities, and would be allowed to charge a small *per centum* or rather *per mille* to pay expenses.

(4) The laws which regulate these banks unhappily tend to accelerate rather than to retard the centralizing tendencies of the national money-market,—the tendency to gather the great mass of the nation's capital into one great monetary centre. Money flows naturally to the places where it is most abundant, just as water tends to run down hill; but as it is often the chief problem in hydraulics to overcome that natural law, so also is it a chief problem of national economy to bring the power of capital to bear upon the less developed and less wealthy districts of the country.

## CHAPTER NINTH.

### NATIONAL ECONOMY OF FINANCE AND TAXATION.

§ 171. The differentiation of function that accompanies the progress of society renders necessary the existence of a body of paid officials to carry on the government (including police and military forces), and numerous other expenditures. In the earliest time the head of the family—the chief of the tribe—the lord of the manor—bore rule within limited areas without receiving fee or salary. He was the lawgiver, the law-ward (lord), the executor of the law, by reason of his position as chief proprietor or as head of the kindred. But in the growth of nationalities a great step was effected when the king's judges rode circuit through the whole realm, with cognisance of all or nearly all causes, and when the king's shire-reeve (sheriff) took the place of the feudal and hereditary count at the head of the county. It was felt that there was a great gain in the increased responsibility and in the fairness of professional judges, though the new system was far more expensive. The remnants of the old system that exist to this day in England in the unpaid justices of the peace, chosen from the gentry and clergy, is felt by the common people to be a great burden. It gives the power and the interpretation of the laws into the hands of men who are swayed by the prejudices of a class. "Justices' justice" is a proverbially poor sort, and one of the chief demands of the working classes in the agricultural shires is: " Give us stipendiary magistrates!" So in Ireland, the "assistant barristers"— professional judges supreme on the local bench, though bearing a very modest name—are found to be the mainstay of the poorer classes in all matters of the interpretation of the law.

§ 172. As in the enactment, interpretation and administration of the laws, so in the enforcement of civil order and the national defence,—every class of transactions is a source of expense. The soldier and the policeman discharge duties that were once incumbent upon every male citizen; they set the citizen free to employ himself as he will, and he must pay for the release. And if the state interprets its vocation as extending to the sanitary and intellectual welfare of the people, the expense involved becomes still greater. It must take measures itself, or require municipalities to take measures, to keep its cities in such a state of cleanliness as shall bring up the average health of the people to a high standard. It must establish public schools and colleges, and training schools for teachers, that the rising generation may not grow up in ignorance. It must set up post-offices, to promote easy intercourse between the different parts of the nation. If it regard religious knowledge as essential to good citizenship, it may endow a clergy devoted to diffusing it. In these and a thousand other ways it comes to pass that a civilized nation is obliged to pay for the advantages of a free government, and the state must assess upon itself in some form taxes to secure a sufficient national revenue. Through fees, fines, costs of suits, &c., it can throw a part of the burden upon those who are most immediately concerned, but a large part of it must be discharged by the community as such.

§ 173. The problem of so imposing taxes that they may be as little burdensome as possible is one that has perplexed statesmen in all ages. Some of the methods taken to raise money for current expenses without taxation are sufficiently curious. Down to quite recent times *lotteries* have been thus made use of on both sides of the Atlantic,—the people greedily buying a "ticket," each acting in the hope that one of the great prizes will fall to him. This plan is now justly discredited as lowering the tone of social morality by giving a legal sanction to gambling, and fostering thriftless and reckless habits.

*Monopolies* have been another device of state-craft. The notion that the state possessed exclusive control of certain trades, and of various branches of commerce, was general in the middle ages. Even where no fee was exacted, it was usual to require a charter from the king for every trade-guild, and this was afterward made a source of revenue to the government. James I of England made himself especially odious to the mercantile classes by granting monopolies of trade in great numbers to his court favorites, and to those who would pay roundly for them. This system was in some cases not without its merits as a promoter of enterprise, apart from its relation to national revenue. In some cases great undertakings would not have been begun without the grant of a temporary monopoly like that given to the East India company, and to the companies that effected the first English settlements in America. Monopolies of the tobacco trade exist in France; of salt in British India. The licenses given in England to auctioneers, pawnbrokers, pedlars, and to those who sell tea and tobacco, and the licenses required in most countries to sell spirituous liquors, are something of the same nature.

The income from the royal demesnes was in early times a chief source of revenue. But these have been so largely reduced by alienation, and are so small in proportion to the revenue now required, that they play little or no part in national finance. The sale of public lands once brought a very considerable revenue to the United States, but through the preëmption and homestead laws this source of revenue is now almost closed.

§ 174. Taxation, direct or indirect, is now the chief source of revenue. The former is levied either (1) upon the people according to numbers, or (2) on their property, real and personal, according to its value, or (3) on articles of luxury in use and possession, or (4) on the annual income of the people. The latter is levied on articles produced, usually those that are not of prime necessity, or on imported goods, usually such as are luxuries, or can be made at home.

The comparative merits of direct and indirect taxation have been much disputed. Both forms exist in this country, the former being that chiefly employed by the state and municipal governments, while since the repeal of the income tax the revenues of the United States are mostly derived from indirect taxes.

§ 175. Indirect taxes are so called because they are not paid into the treasury by the person who really bears the burden. The payer adds the amount of the tax to the price of the commodity taxed, and thus the taxation is concealed under the increased price of some article of luxury or convenience. The distribution of such taxation by the payer among his customers is not so easy a matter as is supposed. English economists, applying their formula, "all things find their level," have treated this distribution as a thing of course. But experience shows that the incidence of taxation is not determined by laws as rigid as those of hydraulics. A tax is often paid directly and finally by the person on whom the law imposes it, and makes no change in prices. Were it otherwise direct taxation would be impossible, and the rich man, when assessed upon land, luxuries or income, would pass the burden on to his dependent neighbors.

It is claimed as a merit of indirect taxation that vast sums may be thus raised without exciting dissatisfaction, or even attracting attention; that duties which bring the government forty or fifty millions cost each consumer but a few cents a week, and are paid in almost daily instalments. As Theodore Parker—arguing against this method—puts it: "The people must pay and not know it; must be deceived a little, or they would not pay after this fashion." The expediency of the method is all the more questionable in view of this fact. In a free country, where public opinion is the force that directs and controls national policy, it is eminently desirable that the people should feel that they are taxed, and that every appropriation of the legislature comes out of their pockets. "A free people ought to know what they pay for their freedom, and pay it joyfully; and they should as truly scorn to be cheated into the support of their government as into the support of their children. In the next place, a large revenue is no blessing. . . . A revenue rigorously proportioned to the wants of a people is as much as can safely be trusted to men in power" (Dr. Channing).

Another objection is that nearly all indirect taxes are burdensome checks upon societary circulation and the interchange of services,—not the less really such because their action is not so easily perceived. The amount of water in the channels of business may be lowered but a few inches, but that few inches turns shallow places into shoals, and impedes the whole current. The poor especially suffer under this system; these little assessments come upon them pretty much in proportion to their numbers, not at all in proportion to their means. It is said that they can exempt themselves by ceasing to use the commodities taxed, none of which are articles of prime necessity. So they would, perhaps, if they realized how much they were paying in the course of the year, but the "few cents a week" is taken so quietly that it is not felt to be the burden that it really is.

It may safely be laid down that indirect taxes should be assessed only on those articles whose consumption it is desirable to discourage, and if it be possible with a view to discourage them, rather than to revenue. For this reason all internal revenue duties,—except on spirits, tobacco and the like,—all taxes upon the capital or dividends of corporations who have not received a monopoly of their business, should, unless urgently required for revenue, be wiped from the Statute Book.

Stamp duties are sometimes indirect and sometimes direct. The stamps put upon mercantile paper, receipts, and the like, come under the former head, and are objectionable. They resemble the *alcavala*, or tax upon every transfer of property that did so much to blight the industry of Spain. Taxes imposed in the same way upon inheritances and wills are not so objectionable, being direct taxes, but they are assessed upon property that is likewise subject to income or property taxes. They are not imposed in this country, although there are taxes upon "collateral inheritances" in some states; but the stamp taxes on beer-kegs and on cigar-boxes are instances of direct taxation by means of stamps.

§ 176. Experience shows that as a rule, lighter taxes of the indirect sort yield a larger amount of revenue than those that are heavier. In political arithmetic two and two do not always make four. Thus Sir Robert Peel and Mr. Gladstone achieved their great reputation as financiers partly through their raising a larger revenue through well-adjusted but lighter taxes. Similar to this was the immense increase in the post-office revenue through the lowering the rates of postage to two cents for half-ounce letters, and the use of postal cards. In each case the lowering of the price caused a great increase in the consumption which more than balanced the loss of revenue on each single amount. This fact of itself shows how much this method of taxation interferes with the business of a country and checks the exchange of services.

In other cases the imposition of a very high excise or importation duty leads to smuggling or illicit manufacture. The duty covers the risk of discovery and punishment, and those who have been engaged in the manufacture or the importation excuse themselves for defrauding the revenue by the plea that the government is oppressing their business and waging war upon it. In general the tone of social morality is not so high as to prevent this plea from having some weight in the public opinion of the country, and the detection and punishment of the offender become difficult and expensive. Thus, under the regime of high excise duties imposed 1864–7, whiskey sold in open market for a less price per gallon than the amount of the tax per gallon upon its manufacture. In this way the business passed for a time into the hands of illicit distillers, and all others were obliged to stop.

§ 177. Direct taxation is paid by the person who really and finally bears the burden. In most cases it is to a certain extent indirect also. Thus a heavy tax on real estate will raise rents, and a heavy tax on incomes will affect salaries. But neither the house-owner nor those who receive salaries are able to add to their receipts in anything like the same measure.

Of the three forms of direct taxation—capitation tax, property tax and income tax,—the first is the most objectionable, if employed to raise a large part of the revenue. A small capitation tax upon every citizen is not an unfair way of reminding the voter that the government is carried on at the expense of the people. But a heavy tax of this sort—much resorted to in earlier times—has all the disadvantages of indirect taxation except its popularity.

Property taxes are assessed either upon all forms of property, real and personal, in proportion to its value, or upon articles of luxury included among personal property; or upon real estate alone. The first is the method practised in the state of New York; the last is that in use in Pennsylvania, and is now generally thought the wiser one. So much of personal property is now held in the form of bonds, mortgages, &c., that can be sent out of the state as the day for making returns comes round, that the evasion of a law taxing this sort of property is very easy. But real estate cannot be hidden, and a tax upon it reaches all classes, though not equally. It raises house-rent, &c. As assessments upon real estate must be made by public officers, the collection of the tax is expensive and it is liable to great abuses through favoritism.

§ 178. The most modern and theoretically the fairest form of taxation is the income tax. It seems to make every one contribute to the wants of the state in proportion to the revenue which he enjoys under its protection; while, "by falling equally on all, it occasions no change in the distribution of capital or in the material direction of industry, and has no influence on prices" (McCulloch). No other is so cheaply assessed and collected; no other brings home to the people so forcibly the fact that it is their interest to insist on a wise economy of the national revenue.

The first English income tax was imposed by Pitt 1798–1802, and renewed 1803–1815. In the middle ages the feudal tenure upon military service saved large expenses for the national defence, and most of the domestic affairs of the kingdom were administered by local authorities. The income of the royal demesnes was supplemented by customary feudal fines and payments, and by a capitation or poll tax. At the outbreak of the Civil war the first excise taxes were imposed, but with the pledge that they would be abolished at the return of peace. The first Parliament after the Restoration was controlled by the landed interest; it abolished all duties on the land, whether of service or payment, and confirmed to the landowner all rights without duties  The feudal system came to an end at once. From this time excises and customs were multiplied by parliaments made up of landlords. At the Revolution the Whigs came to power, and the country gentlemen found themselves in a minority, but still strong enough to prevent the imposition of any but the most trifling taxes on land. The rate of these taxes was afterwards through their influence made permanent and the principal commutable at the pleasure of the landowner, and Mr. Pitt was defeated in his attempts again to make the land contribute its fair share. His income tax was a compromise that assessed the landlord's permanent revenue and the trader's precarious profits equally. At present the whole land-tax of England is about one-fiftieth of the revenue, while landed property constitutes a very large part of the whole wealth of the nation.

By 1840 the indirect system had attained the perfection humorously described by Sidney Smith: "Taxes upon every article which enters into the mouth, or covers the back, or is placed under the foot,—taxes upon everything which is pleasant to see, hear, feel, smell or taste,—taxes upon warmth, light and locomotion,—taxes on everything on the earth and the waters under the earth,—taxes on everything that comes from abroad or is grown at home,—taxes on the raw material,—taxes on every fresh value that is added to it by the industry of man,—taxes on the sauce that pampers the rich man's appetite, and the drug that restores him to health,—on the ermine which decorates the judge, and the rope which hangs the criminal,—on the poor man's salt and the rich man's spice,—on the brass nails of the coffin, and the ribands of the bride,—at bed or board, couchant and levant, we must pay. The schoolboy whips his taxed top,—the beardless youth manages his taxed horse with a taxed bridle, on a taxed road; and the dying Englishman, pouring his medicine which has paid 7 per cent. into a spoon that has paid 15 per cent., flings himself back upon his chintz bed which has paid 22 per cent., and expires in the arms of an apothecary who has paid a license of a hundred pounds for the privilege of putting him to death. His whole property is then immediately taxed from two to ten per cent. Besides the probate, large fees are demanded for burying him in the chancel; his virtues are handed down to posterity on taxed marble; and he is then gathered to his fathers to be taxed no more."

§ **179.** Sir Robert Peel imposed the new income tax in 1842, in a time of general distress, after a series of great deficits in the annual budget. It brought in so much revenue that he and his successors in the treasury were able to relieve the mass of the people from the burden of some indirect taxes and to lower others. This last step, it was found, still farther increased the revenue, and these reductions became a settled policy in British Finance. But the whole British system, the income tax excepted, must still be classed among the measures of bad policy by which the inequalities of condition are preserved and fostered. Seven-eighths of the revenue is still raised by indirect taxation, and the proposal to raise it all by the same means was made by Mr. Gladstone at the general election of 1874, but shared in his general defeat. The revenue is raised by duties upon a few articles in general use, such as sugar, tea, coffee, spirits and wine; while articles of expensive luxury, laces, satins and velvets, have been exempted. Cobden, Bright and some others advocate the removal of most, if not all, the existing duties and excises, and ask that the workingman's breakfast table be free from all taxation.

§ **180.** The objections to the income tax, however, are very strong. (1) That it is *inquisitorial*. It demands of the citizen a statement of his affairs for each current year, and this he must make to commissioners who are his neighbors, and perhaps his rivals in trade. This objection is hardly a sufficient one in case the tax returns are not published. If they are, there can be no doubt that it is a hardship for a tradesman to be obliged to inform the public that he has had rather a bad year of it, and has hardly been able to make both ends meet. In many cases it is well known that persons reported and paid taxes upon a much larger income than they actually received, purchasing thus a reputation for wealth and prosperity.

(2) Reports are more commonly dishonest in the other direction. To escape taxation, incomes are returned as much less than the fact. This has been frequently the case in England, where no publication of returns is made. Income from land and houses is indeed very easily ascertained, but that from trade and professions must be taken on the faith of the citizen. Certain London shopkeepers, whose stores were removed to make way for a city railroad, made claim for compensation on the basis of annual profits, aggregating five times as much as they had put on their tax-papers, and a jury cut down the estimate only to three times as much.

(3) The equal assessment upon all sorts of income is claimed to be unfair. The lump value of two incomes of $5000—one permanent as derived from real estate, and the other precarious as depending upon the profits of a trade—is very different; but the law taxes both equally. This may be obviated by careful legislation.

The great problem to devise an income-tax law that shall enforce honest returns without resorting to wholesale publicity, and shall duly discriminate between different forms of income, has not yet been solved. Till such a law is obtained, the least objectionable form of taxation must be that assessed on personal and real estate. To make direct taxation on personal estate effective, it should be levied on stocks through the company in which they are held, and deducted by the company from the amount of the dividends. To assess it on dividends merely would be a mistake. Many companies are so situated that they do not care to declare dividends, though they earn them. They go on year after year turning their net profits into principal invested, and the proprietors live on income from other sources.

No income tax will probably be again imposed in the United States for many years. But if the industry of the country should ever reach such a height of development as to enable her to furnish herself with the most of what she now imports from Europe, the revenue from customs will then be inadequate to the needs of the government. New revenue from some other source will take its place. If an income tax should be again adopted, one of the most important questions in regard to it will be whether all incomes, whatever their amount, should pay the same percentage. The law that Pitt devised, and all others in England down to 1861, made a discrimination between large and small incomes, and taxed the former more heavily. Since that year all incomes not exempted have been taxed equally, and the United States law was severely censured by some British writers for exacting a "progressive rate" of 5, $7\frac{1}{2}$ and 10 per cent. for different incomes. Now taxation should be proportioned either to income or to ability to bear it. If the former, then the English law is unjust in exempting incomes below £100; if the latter, the American law and the earlier English laws were not unjust in making a discrimination among taxed incomes. It would be unjust to make the discrimination excessive, and tax all incomes above a certain sum—50, 75 or 100 per cent.—as some wild theorists in France proposed. But the want of some discrimination must be reckoned among those defects of English legislation that have tended to perpetuate and increase the vast discrepancies in English wealth.

The practical objections to this form of taxation make a tax on land far less objectionable, especially in a country whose resources are imperfectly developed and its wealth unevenly distributed.

§ 181. Among the important points in the economy of taxation are (1) cheap collection; (2) popular certainty as to amount and time. Both these and every other wise principle were set at nought by the system of farming the revenue adopted under the Roman empire and in France before the Revolution, and still perpetuated in some Mohammedan countries. The taxes were sold at public auction to a class of persons who remunerated themselves by wringing the utmost farthing out of the poor.

The popular hatred and detestation of the publican class, disclosed to us in the Gospels, related to this custom, and was well deserved and universal throughout the empire. Jewish tradition records but one honest publican.

The second principle is also violated by unforeseen changes in the revenue system of a country that employs indirect taxation. Business men lose very much by every new piece of tinkering expended upon the tariff. They must, therefore, on the principle of insuring themselves, put a larger profit upon all commodities, so that the lack of a wise and steadfast national policy inflicts a tax upon the people that brings no return to the treasury.

§ 182. Ordinarily the taxation of a year should at least pay the national expenditure of the year. A nation that does not "make both ends meet" in times of peace and of no extraordinary calamity, cannot be regarded as wisely governed. But times that call for a vast extraordinary outlay of national wealth are incident to the history of every nation. In periods of great wars, for instance, the government must raise sums of money which far exceed those that it ordinarily raises by taxation, and national debts are incurred, to be gradually paid off on the return of peace. These debts are of no modern invention, but the fashion of paying them came in about the close of the seventeenth century. The power of one generation of a nation thus to bind not only itself but subsequent generations is now an accepted principle.

Are war debts really necessary? Perhaps not; any prosperous and free people that unanimously undertake a just war, and are not already encumbered by previous debts, could, by vigorous exertion, pay their way as they go. Prussia avoids war-debts; the wars of Frederick the Great left the country greatly depressed and exhausted, but without a dollar of indebtedness. The Hohenzollerns, it has been said, brought good business abilities with them from Nuremberg. England's great war with the first French Empire left the country the burden of £600,000,000 of debt. Had she begun the war with a clear financial record, and assessed every year the same amount of the total taxation raised during its continuance, she would have come out of it with a surplus in the treasury. Could the taxation have been raised one-third higher than it actually was during our recent civil war, and kept at that from first to last for five years, the country would have come out of the struggle with no indebtedness. This is the policy that all great writers on finance,—Hume, Adam Smith, Ricardo, McCulloch, &c.,—recommend. For political reasons, good or bad, it is never adopted. It is feared that a great increase of the immediate public burdens will strengthen the peace-party and weaken the government. It is thought that the people are not at first aware of the magnitude of the sacrifices required of them, and heavy taxes are not imposed till the war is coming near a close. For these and the like reasons the nation comes into the money market as a borrower. Thus, it is thought, the burden will be so distributed as to be imperceptible and lightly borne. But all such attempts at distribution add to its real weight and to the injury it inflicts.

§ 183. Governments generally borrow at a great disadvantage when great capitalists control the money market. The public credit is at the lowest point in war times, and no patriotism holds men back from taking advantage of this. In former times this was remedied in a vigorous way; Colbert cut down the capital of the public debt to the amount actually furnished by each lender, and treated the surplus as an illegal because usurious exaction. By this partial repudiation he brought up the public credit at once and was able to borrow at very reasonable rates. The British ministry in the reign of Queen Anne replaced all the old loans by others that paid interest at market instead of war rates; giving the lenders the choice between that and redemption. During the war that England waged with Napoleon her capitalists were on the outlook to prevent any renewal of that proceeding. The government was forced or induced to *fund* the debt as fast as it was contracted. That is, money was raised by selling perpetual annuities, redeemable at par, for such price as they would bring in the market. These annuities, considered as the interest upon the nominal principal, were at very low rates, but the principal itself was not paid in full to the government. The buyer offered to take the loan at thirty, forty or fifty per cent. discount, according to the state of the money market. Thus of the 600 millions sterling added to the national debt, only 484 millions was actually paid to the government. The perpetual annuities amounted to 3 per cent. interest upon the nominal, and 5½ per cent. upon the actual loans. With every rise in the national credit, the nominal value has become more nearly the actual one, so that even by purchases in open market the nation could now redeem its debt only at the par value, i. e., by paying a sum to its creditors that it never received from them. As capital is worth much more than 3 per cent., taking year with year, it is thought by many a saving not to pay the debt. Others oppose payment on the ground that its wide distribution imparts a certain stability to the whole political edifice by identifying the interests of the people with those of the government. Cobden, Bright and the Manchester school generally oppose its payment on the ground that it holds England back from engaging in new wars, by putting her under bonds to keep the peace. The population of England is twice as great, and her wealth four times as great, as when the debt was contracted two generations ago, yet its amount has been but slightly diminished. Few people seem to expect that it ever will be paid, and one Tory organ, denouncing Gladstone for his policy of harassing interests, expressed the fear that he would be for attacking the national debt next. Two measures, however, look toward its redemption. There is a Sinking Fund managed by commissioners, which uses such money as is placed at its disposal to buy up " consols," and hold them at interest, expending that interest in fresh purchases. Another measure of Mr. Gladstone's has been to sell terminable annuities chargeable to the budget, and buy up with the proceeds the perpetual annuities formerly granted. But at the present rate of redemption four centuries must elapse before the whole would be discharged.

§ 184. The United States have always acted on the policy of speedy redemption. The debt of the Revolution and that of the second war with England were discharged by 1835, less than sixty years after the former began. At the rate of redemption pursued since the close of the civil war, the nation would be out of debt by 1890, and much sooner if the national revenue be not reduced and the large sums that are now expended in paying interest are applied to paying the principal.

§ 185. The existing debt of the United States was not funded as fast as contracted; high rates of interest were offered rather than large discounts on the principal. Secretary Chase, whatever his mistakes, strove to keep the debt under national control, and even borrowed for periods that were far too short, so that some of his earlier loans fell due during the war. Afterwards three forms of bonds were adopted,—7-30s, 8-40s and 5-20s, the two latter being payable at option at any time between eight and forty years, &c., after issue. Yet, as in England, the real rate of interest upon the debt is much higher than the nominal one,—in some cases nearly eleven per cent. instead of six. The government had made large issues of paper money, which after a time depreciated in value very greatly, fluctuating with the course of our military history, as the public confidence in its redemption rose or fell. But vast quantities of this money were subscribed for United States bonds and accepted at par; so that the nation received on an average about fifty-seven cents in gold on the dollar for its obligations, on which it pays full interest and is bound in all honesty to pay the full principal.

This is the calculation of Prof. Bowen of Harvard College.

§ 186. So long as the government continued to borrow money and to accept this paper-money at par in subscriptions for loans, it was not strictly an inconvertible currency, and the country had to some extent the control of its volume. When the government ceased to borrow, it lost this redeeming feature, and became a currency of the most objectionable type. The question was then raised whether it should be allowed to continue thus, or steps be taken to bring it to par with gold. Here two parties were developed. One proposed to accumulate gold in the treasury, and fix a day for resumption. The other proposed to make these notes convertible into bonds bearing interest at 3.65 per cent. or some similar rate, and reconvertible into treasury notes at any time at the holder's option. The former plan prevailed, and was carried into effect January 1, 1879.

The steady appreciation of our paper-money under the steps preliminary to resumption caused great suffering to the debtor classes of the country. Farmers, for instance, who had borrowed money on mortgage when the dollar was worth sixty cents in gold, found themselves obliged to repay these mortgages in dollars worth one hundred cents. They very naturally resisted the policy which made this necessary, not only as regards their own debts, but also those of the government. Hence the rise of the Greenback Party, with its theory that money is the creation of a governmental *fiat*, its demand that the debt be paid in paper-money, and its proposal to substitute treasury notes for national bank notes. The party reached its maximum strength during the years of business distress which began in 1873, and declined with the actual resumption of specie payments and the revival of our industries. There is a possibility that its proposal to replace bank by treasury notes may come to the front again when the repayment of the outstanding bonds has gone so far as to deprive the banks of the basis on which their paper-money rests.' (See § 170.) Instead of devising some other basis of issue equally or sufficiently secure, it will be proposed to issue an equal amount of treasury notes. As a note is a debt bearing no interest, owed by the issuer to the holder, there would seem to be some fairness in asking that the privilege of such issues should be confined to the government. But any advantage which would be derived from making such issues a government monopoly would be more than counterbalanced by the loss to the country through the destruction of its local centres of issue, and the substitution of the Treasury at

Washington and its branches in the great cities as the only places of issue. Our monetary system tends too much to centralization already. This plan would increase that tendency tenfold. It would destroy many of the country banks, which depend on the privilege of issue for their profits, and in this way would deprive us of the most important agencies for the facilitation of association and the fertilization of industry.

§ 187. During the war the government found it necessary to establish a system of internal revenue taxation, by which a great number of articles were made to contribute to its support. When the necessity for such a revenue ceased, these taxes were removed, with the exception of duties on whiskey, tobacco, playing-cards, matches, patent medicines and bank-checks, and a tax on the capital and deposits of banks. The removal of all these except the two first is now accepted generally as advisable. But there is good reason for objecting to these two being made exceptions. Of course the appetite for whiskey and that for tobacco are as legitimate objects of taxation, with a view to discouragement, as anything can be. But these taxes fall upon the States with no fair reference to their ability to bear the burden they impose. In particular, the Southern States pay under the whiskey and tobacco taxes large sums into the national treasury which would be better expended on the education of their people and the payment of their debts. These taxes should be removed, not to give the country "free whiskey" or "free tobacco," but to enable the States to relieve their necessities from this very source of revenue.

§ 188. The United States government is one of a series of governments—national, State, and county or township or municipal—whose aggregate costliness is greater than that of any other system in the world. All our officials are paid, and we have more of them in proportion to the population than has any other country. Under the peculiar provisions of the national Constitution, the general government discharges fewer functions than in any other country, except perhaps Germany. It leaves to the States the local police and the most part of the management of civil and criminal justice, but it retains to itself several of the easiest and most popular sources of revenue, and compels the States to raise their revenue by direct taxation mainly. It alone can impose duties on imports. It alone can levy internal revenue taxes in such a way as not to discourage the production of any article in any particular locality. Ordinarily, the revenue of the general government must be much in excess of its legitimate expenses. This leads to very gross abuses in congressional legislation, by which large sums of this surplus are appropriated for public works which have no real claim upon the national treasury. It would be much better to arrange for its distribution among the States in proportion to population, as was done with the surplus of 1835. Such a distribution could be accompanied by conditions as to its expenditure in the education of the illiterate and the extinction of local and State debts. It would bind the States more closely to the national Union, while relieving their people of burdens which at present press with severity upon many of them.

## CHAPTER TENTH.

### THE SCIENCE AND ECONOMY OF COMMERCE.

§ 189. COMMERCE is the interchange of services or productions between persons of different industrial functions, effected either directly or through the intervention of third parties. The motive to such an interchange is found in the fact that the labor which each expends upon the production of the article which he gives is less than that which he would have to expend to reproduce the article which he receives. Thus each receives, therefore, what is of greater value to him, than what he gives.

§ 190. Commerce is therefore the outgrowth of the division of labor, and has kept pace with that in its growth. In the first stage, commerce existed only between persons of the same family or tribe, and involved no formal exchange of commodities. The savage husband undertook the dangerous duties of hunting, fishing and war; the wife the laborious work of the household and their petty agriculture. Both shared in the products. Afterwards members of the same tribe rendered each other certain customary services, such as mutual help in the pasturage of the cattle and the tillage of the *fields* of the *mark* (§ 80). Then through the rise of a difference of employments or possessions between the tribes, a piece of neutral ground became the meeting-place of a group of these tribes for mutual exchanges, in which exchange cattle were used, less as money than as a standard to estimate comparative values. Then arose a class of traders, whose business it was to facilitate exchanges by ascertaining the reciprocal wants of different persons, and to negotiate for terms advantageous to each. Either from the first or in course of time, these traders became possessed of capital enough to purchase what was offered for sale, which they then again offered to those who needed it, on terms advantageous to themselves.

The rise of this class was clearly an advance in social development. A function hitherto discharged by persons, who might be better employed, was transferred to more competent men. The trader knew the demand and supply of every article more thoroughly and readily than its producers or its consumers: to obtain that knowledge was his special work. Instead of spending much of their time in searching for a customer, producers found it to their advantage to employ his knowledge and skill, and to devote the time thus saved to larger production. While he added nothing directly to the amount or the utility of the products of industry, he helped to increase the amount of production indirectly by economizing the time of the producers.

One of the most important of these traders is the banker or dealer in money, whose function has already been discussed. All that is said in Chapter VIII. is, in some sense, a subordinate part of this chapter.

§ 191. Still the trader, the middleman or go-between of these exchanges, is but a means or instrument, whose end is commerce. And as in the case of other instruments, how to dispense as much as possible with his services is one of the problems of economic organization. His power over the producer and the consumer, which is measured by the proportion that his profits bear to the value of the article exchanged, declines steadily with the advance of society in intelligence and the power of association. In the early time he took a very large share, because the producer and consumer being at a distance from each other, knew little of each other, and because the risks and the expenses of his business were great. Afterwards his profits declined, mainly because with the growth of population and the advance of mutual knowledge, the chances of producer and consumer dispensing with his services and dealing directly with each other, increased. But even now his profit is a tax upon both, which should be reduced to a minimum. For he adds nothing to the real wealth of society. He neither directs and manages a vital change in the form of matter as does the farmer, nor a chemical and mechanical change in form as does the manufacturer. He merely transfers things from the place of their production to the place of demand: The products of other men's labor pass unchanged through his hands,—with their value increased by the cost of transportation and the amount of his profits.

> When Charles Fourier was young, he was on a visit to Paris, and priced at a street stall some apples of a sort that grew abundantly in his native province. He was amazed to find that they sold for many times the sum that they would bring at home, having passed through the hands of a host of middlemen on their way from the owner of the orchard to the eater of the fruit. The impression received at that instant never left him; it gave the first impulse to his thinking out his socialistic scheme for the reconstruction of society, in which, among other sweeping changes, the whole class of traders and their profits are to be abolished.

§ 192. It is evident that the amount of this tax upon industry is greatest when the consumer and producer are at the greatest distance from each other, and are consequently most dependent upon the trader. Where the producer has the market close at hand he is under no necessity of sacrificing any large part of his profits. Sooner than do so, he will be his own trader, and deal directly with his customers.

Commerce between persons in neighborhood is also a commerce of swift returns. The capital employed circulates much more rapidly, and accomplishes a much larger amount of service in proportion to its amount. Instead of considerable amounts of it being thrown out of possible use, because in transit between distant points, the whole is directly and immediately available; as soon as the manufactured goods have left the factory, they are ready for purchasers. As soon as the flour has left the mill, it is available for human food. The waste of time involved in more distant commerce is totally avoided or reduced to a minimum.

§ 193. Commerce between persons in neighborhood leaves little opening for those traders' speculations by which artificial scarcity is produced. Commerce between distant points involves the passage of large quantities of goods through single ports of entry and exit, on their way from the field of their production to that of their consumption. As they change hands at this point from one trader to another, their price to their final purchaser is mainly fixed. If a number of traders foresee a slight scarcity of supply, it is not unusual for them to club resources, buy up all that they can lay their hands on, and hold it for an advance. Unless some unforeseen circumstance defeat their plans, they are thus enabled to put into their pocket large sums, which represent simply no service rendered to society,—no benefit to either producer or consumer. Thus in the grain-trade, which centres so largely in Chicago, traders have repeatedly brought about a scarcity of this sort, and raised the price of flour to the Eastern and European consumer. Were the wheat-crop of the whole country, like that of Pennsylvania, consumed in the vicinity of the farms, "such corners in wheat," as they are called, would be impossible. Very different is the desert of those, who, foreseeing an enormous scarcity, buy up the present supply and hold it over till the scarcity occurs, or buy up in one district to sell in another. They diminish the present consumption and enforce economy of resources; they spread the dearness over a larger space and time, and thus prevent scarcity from becoming real famine by making the supply go as far as possible. Whatever the motive, a real service is rendered in this case.

This production of artificial scarcity is not an exceptional or difficult thing when the producer and consumer are at a distance from each other. When California was quite a young state, and depended almost entirely upon the Atlantic States and Europe for all supplies, the prices of all importations were kept enormously high by forestalling the San Francisco market. "It is a frequent occurrence that a few wealthy men combine together to buy up all of a certain kind of merchandise and then control the price." In Australia (§ 274), especially during the time when the country was dependent upon England for nearly all sorts of goods, the same system was "carried on in the most systematic manner" and has not ceased yet.

See *Restrictions on Trade, from a Colonial Point of View*, by David Syme (republished from the *Fortnightly Review*), Boston, 1872.

§ **194.** These facts are only extreme instances of the power of the trader to dictate his own terms, when the producer has to send his wares to a distant market. These conspiracies are but the extreme form of the general understanding that grows up between the body of capitalists, when the chief supply of an article is concentrated within a limited area and in a small number of hands. Such an understanding, easily reached in such circumstances, will, unless checked by some other competition, enhance the price of goods quietly and by degrees that escape notice, but are none the less burdens upon the producers and the consumers. The traders can "fix their own prices" in such cases.

The same power of the trader over the prices that rule in a distant market is sometimes displayed in producing an artificial but temporary cheapness, to be followed by such a rise of prices as will recoup him for the loss. Where the consumers of an article make an effort to dispense with his services and those of its distant producer, by developing resources for its supply that are nearer at hand, he not seldom finds it worth while to offer large quantities at less than cost price. He shares this sacrifice with the producer of what he sells, and both have the intention to hold fast the market, and retrieve their present losses by larger future gains. The effect is to force the new producer of the same article to cease operations, " unless he have a very strong back indeed," and can afford to go as far in making sacrifices as his longer-established rivals. As this is very rarely the case in the first stages of an enterprise, there is no choice but to cease producing, and the market is left dependent upon the trader and his partner, the distant producer, although every facility existed for producing the article more cheaply and abundantly at home.

See §§ 252 and 284. Coleridge says: (VI. 511) "It has already been shown, in evidence which is before all the world, that some of our manufacturers have acted upon the accursed principle of deliberately injuring foreign manufacturers if they can, even to the ultimate disgrace of the country and loss to themselves."

§ 195. Even as regards domestic commerce, there is large space for reform in the diminution of the number and the profits of the middlemen, who stand between producer and consumer. "Any one who inquires," says Mr. Mill, "into the amount that reaches the hands of those who made the things he buys will often be astonished at its smallness." This bears especially hard on the working classes; it deprives them as producers of the benefit of market rates for their workmanship. It taxes them more heavily as consumers than it does the rich who can afford to buy at wholesale. He needs most to economize, yet he pays the highest prices, a fact that does much to counteract the natural tendency towards an equality of condition; as Solomon said, "The destruction of the poor is their poverty." The earlier English economists regarded free competition as a sufficient corrective of this; if profits were excessive, more capital would flow into the trade, and the competition for custom would bring prices down. But while this has had its effects, it is by no means sufficient, especially in small communities; trades tend to become informal associations to keep prices up to a customary standard of profits, which in England averages about fifty per cent. of the wholesale price.

Coöperative stores are a means of obviating this difficulty, from which great things are expected, and perhaps justly. In these the consumers associate to establish a retail store by their joint contributions, and employ competent persons or some central agency to purchase the goods in large quantities and at the lowest wholesale price, as well as of the best quality. These are retailed for cash at a margin of profit that more than covers the cost of the operations, and the net profits are distributed at the end of the year in proportion either to purchases made or to stock held. Some of these stores sell only to their stockholders; others sell to accepted customers, and give these a small share in the joint profits proportional to their purchases; others sell to the public at large, and distribute the profits among stockholders only. In the third method (and in the second, in a less degree) the coöperative basis of their operations is given up; the establishment becomes merely a joint stock company to deal in a certain class of goods, and the ordinary dealers' motive to overcharge or adulterate goods comes into play. These stores originated with the Owenist party in England about 1830; they exist in great numbers in that country, in France and in Germany, where Schultze-Delitzsch has greatly promoted their establishment. Some look to them for a complete revolution of the retail trade and the abolition of the retail trader. But the destruction of any function in the organization of society would be a retrograde step. The chief service that these stores can render is in restraining the trader from adulteration, and in forcing down prices to a just rate; in substituting cash payments for book-credits, and perhaps in finally leading him to take his customers into partnership by dividing among them a share of his annual profits.

§ 196. Another questionable feature of modern commerce is its transaction of business on credit, or "on time," as it is called. The buyer of a quantity of goods does not pay for them in ready money of any kind, but gives his note payable in thirty, sixty or ninety days, which the seller can only convert into available money by having it discounted at the bank. If the buyer does not pay the note at the date specified, the seller has to pay it himself, and put the amount into his list of bad debts, unless the law gives him redress by a levy on the property of the buyer.

(As we have already said, this method of creating the credit-fund of money of account on the books of the bank might be abolished without abolishing the credit-fund itself, and the separation of the two—of our money of account from our discount system—is one of the problems that greatly concern the future of modern business.)

Now, of course, the seller cannot afford to put the goods at as low a figure as if he were paid in cash. He even in some cases designates different prices according to the length of the credit; in other cases, each house or each trade sells on time for a fixed number of days. And the difference is not merely the amount that he will lose by the discount of the note. He has to insure himself against bad debts by an increase of his profits on all transactions. He must charge more to good customers in order to insure himself against bad ones. This has a tendency to force up all prices, and to increase the value of the goods in their passage from producer to consumer without adding to their utility.

A transition to buying and selling for cash would greatly simplify business. It would separate transactions that ought to be treated distinctly and each on its own merits. It would rid good houses of the burden of this mutual insurance system, through which they suffer for the instability of others. It would separate the business of borrowing money at the bank from the business of buying and selling, and make "every tub stand on its own bottom." It would send every man to bank to borrow money on his own security, or that of his neighbors who know something of his affairs, instead of enabling him to borrow there on the credit of those from whom he buys.

§ 197. Whether and how far the change would be effectual in restraining the spirit of reckless adventure and speculation, without impeding legitimate enterprise, is a more difficult question. It would at least bring distinctly into view the question of the sufficiency of every person to whom an advance is made, without complicating it with the desire to make a sale to him. And this question would come before experts, whose business it would be to make themselves acquainted with the facts, instead of business men who have hands and heads full of other matters. As a rule it would come before a man's own neighbors and acquaintances, the directors of some local bank, instead of being settled in a city where the statements of a "Commercial Directory" or some similar institution, are the only data for proceeding. If joint guarantee were required it would have to be furnished as in Scotland by two or more responsible neighbors, who would need to know something of his standing before they risked what would be a large loss to them, while it might be in comparison a small loss to the wholesale firm in the city.

A great change for the better in this regard has been effected since the war. Six months' credit has been generally shortened to thirty or sixty days. The possession of a trustworthy medium of exchange, of bank-notes that circulate throughout the whole country, and that with a new rapidity, has done much good in this respect. The loss of a multitude of bad debts, and the consequent decline of confidence in distant customers, have done more. But there is still great need of improvement and perhaps of the abolition of sales on time. For instance, one of our largest dry goods houses made a thorough overhauling of its list of debtors during the panic of 1873, and found that it knew simply nothing of its prospect of ever getting any money from nearly a third of them.

§ **198.** When we know the function of the trader, and the part he has played in industrial history, we are better able to decide between the comparative benefits of home and foreign commerce. The question is not of merely theoretical interest; upon the answer generally accepted as correct must depend the public policy of each nation, for the revenue system of every country has its effect to encourage or discourage one or both.

Adam Smith and Jean Baptiste Say, the founders of the modern school of economists in England and France, pronounce in favor of domestic commerce as the more profitable of the two. Smith says that if a given amount of capital be employed in purchasing and interchanging goods within the same country, that country will reap twice as much advantage from the activity of that capital, as if it had been employed in purchasing and interchanging an equal value of goods with another country. For in the one case encouragement is given to only one native industry; in the other to two. Nay more,—the operations of domestic commerce being far swifter than those of foreign trade, the advantage to the country is proportionally great. In his day it was possible to effect twelve such exchanges at home for one abroad, making capital employed in the former twenty-four times as useful to the country as if it were engaged in foreign trade. (With modern facilities for transport, this ratio would of course be very much decreased.) In his view the amount of employment that a country can furnish to her people, depends upon the amount of capital in circulation; so that a pound employed in the purchase of British carpets for sale in the home market might furnish twenty-four times as much work to English workmen as a pound employed in trading with Portugal for wines. A trade, therefore, by which the merchant grows rich may be one from which his country derives no corresponding advantage. In asserting so much, Adam Smith certainly yielded the fundamental principle of his whole system, which was that if society will simply remove all restrictions from individual enterprise, and allow every one to do with his own what he will —what he finds pays him best—society will reap the largest possible benefit.

§ 199. The English school of course enter protest against this concession, and try to refute the reasoning on which it is based. Ricardo and McCulloch give substantially the same answer. They assume in their answer that goods must be paid for in goods; that if England and Scotland give up a certain commerce with each other, because the one can better supply itself from one foreign country, and the other from another, those countries will begin to purchase the products of English and Scottish labor to the same amounts, and nobody will be thrown out of employment in either country by the cessation of the domestic exchange. Now this assumption, which they do not put in so many words, but leave to be implied, is not to be conceded without evidence. Rather there is much evidence to the contrary. England and China have a large mutual foreign commerce, but, in spite of the Christian forcing the pagan to allow the importation of opium, millions upon millions of English silver are absorbed every year by the Chinese, in payment for teas and silks, which are *not* paid for in English goods. So also India absorbs yearly millions of silver coin in payment for her native goods, all that she takes from England being insufficient to pay for what England buys of her. The trade between our own country and Europe is after the same fashion. England and the Continent do not "call it square" at the end of every year, balancing our raw cotton and breadstuffs against dry goods and hardware. We pay over millions upon millions of gold and silver to balance our accounts. Europe takes no more of what we have to sell than she must; she sells us all she can. For us, therefore, these attempted refutations of Smith have no force, and unless some better be given, we must concede his position that American capital, if spent in encouraging the production of some of those articles that we pay Europe gold and silver for, would confer greater benefits on the country than if spent in importing them. The second part of his argument—that from the comparative rapidity of the two forms of commerce—Ricardo and McCulloch do not touch.

§ 200. "But after all, even when the balance is paid in gold and silver, still the fact is that the exchange is of commodities for commodities. For in that case gold and silver are themselves given in exchange as commodities, not as money. And it is in this new capacity alone that they are productive; in all other cases they merely facilitate interchanges of parts of the national wealth; but when exported as commodities, they procure in return other commodities that add to the aggregate of that wealth." So J. B. Say argues.

Under this reasoning lies the notion of the passivity of money,—that it plays no part in production, but only in exchange; that any increase of the amount of it in circulation, only increases in that proportion the money price of other commodities; that any decrease in that amount only diminishes the price. This notion runs counter to the observed facts in the history of money, as recorded by Humboldt and Arthur Young, for the last four centuries, and by Thomas Tooke (*History of Prices*), for the present century. A tendency to decline in the purchasing power of money with the increase of its amount, is indeed a very natural supposition; no doubt, in an unprogressive society, such would be and has been the effect, as has been shown by the vast decline in the purchasing power of silver in India, since the English began to trade with her people. But a progressive society is one that resists such natural tendencies; an influx of the instrument of association into such a country, tends to stimulate all sorts of productive industry. It finds—except in periods of financial depression—a host of persons waiting for this very instrument, to begin new lines of production, and it sets many new wheels moving. "Hence new uses will be found for it when it is abundant, new avenues of commerce will be opened, new branches of industry will be essayed, until increased production finds employment for the increase of money. If money has increased, industry and trade are increased; and thus the tendency to depreciation is met and strongly counteracted."

See Stephen Colwell's *Ways and Means of Payment* (Phila. 1859), p. 556.

§ 201. The drain of the precious metals from a country, though its effects are alleviated by the creation of the credit fund for domestic payments, is therefore decidedly injurious to its general interests. "It is not exactly true to say, as has too often been said over and over again, since Turgot first said it, that money is a commodity like any other. That proposition is untrue, except as it regards the metal of which money is made; but in so far as it is the means of exchange, it has peculiarities of its own, which clearly distinguish it from other commodities. If iron and cotton are scarce, those who need them suffer by the scarcity, but it has no effect upon the prices of other materials. If, on the other hand, money is scarce, the price of everything else is affected. Every one must make exchanges, must buy and sell; if, therefore, there is a tendency to a deficiency or a scarcity of the means of exchange, every one is straitened, and all transactions become difficult. Just as when the water falls in its rivers, traffic is interrupted because the vessels are aground; so, when money is diminished or disappears from the channels of circulation, articles pass from one owner to another with great difficulty. We have got to the point of dispensing, in the commercial transactions of advanced countries, with a great quantity of money by replacing it by credit in all its forms; but, given the quantity of money that is still necessary, its rarity produces an embarrassment, and sometimes even a general crisis."

See *Le Marche Monétaire et ses Crises depuis Cinquante Ans;* by Emile de Laveleye (1865).

The possession of a large quantity of money is, within limits that no progressive country has reached, a great advantage. It enables any country to organize its industry upon such a scale, and to carry its division of labor to such perfection, as will bring down the price of all the products of industry, while affording a large return to both the capitalist and the laborer. It therefore makes such a country a cheap place to buy in, mainly because of that accumulation of money, which was to make everything dear. And if any country have got the lead in this respect, an unrestricted trade with those that are not so well off for money will not correct but only increase the inequality. It will continually drain the precious metals out of those countries to increase its own store, because it will steadily keep the balance of trade in its own favor. It will sell others what it pleases, and buy of them what it must. If there are exceptions to this rule, they are to be found in those unprogressive countries, in which the wants of the people are so few that it is impossible, after selling them everything that they will buy, to balance the purchases of raw materials from them. Such countries are India and China.

This truth is the germ of the theories of the Mercantile school; it is a doctrine " combated by the great majority of economists," who travesty the principles of that school as if men like Colbert, Locke and Steuart held that one could eat or wear money. But these same economists, proclaiming the passivity or barrenness of money, save when given in exchange for foreign goods, would have us believe that those countries which receive it in that exchange are so grandly generous, or so blind to their own interests, as to give commodities of the highest utility for one that has no utility, or that only possesses it when it can again be sent abroad.

**202.** The theory of foreign exchanges now maintained by the English school, and first enunciated by Torrens (1808) and Ricardo (1817), is given in a very forcible form by Mr. J. S. Mill. It bases the advantage of the foreign trade exclusively upon the comparative productiveness of labor, or of different kinds of labor, in different countries. Each country exchanges with others goods that cost it less labor than those that it receives would have cost it if produced at home. Each saves labor by the bargain, and therefore each derives benefit from the exchange, even though it might have produced the same articles at home for less labor than they cost the other. For even if it be as easy to make iron in Pennsylvania as in England, yet if it pay better to raise wheat for exportation because England's need of wheat compels her to give more iron for our wheat than the labor spent in raising wheat would have produced, we are gainers by the exchange. Each country, therefore, should manage its economy not on the lines indicated by its natural resources, but on those that are indicated by the exchangeable value of its products in the markets of the world. Every nation, therefore, Mill says, instead of adopting a national policy that looks to the development of any species of industry, should allow things to take their natural course, being assured that to do the things that are easiest, and to buy in the cheapest market and sell in the dearest, are the most remunerative ways of procedure.

§ 203. We have already given some reasons why commerce between distant points is an undesirable thing, as open to the exercise of tyrannizing power by traders and their combinations. The next chapter will be chiefly devoted to showing that while individuals may find it to their account to buy in the cheapest market and sell in the dearest of those that already exist, communities will frequently find it more to their account to create new markets by cherishing a varied industry at home. At this point, therefore, we shall only remark :

(1) That exchanges are not, as this theory assumes, effected on the basis of labor expended, but of money price, which is quite another matter. We might be able to produce iron at a far less expenditure of labor in Pennsylvania than in England, and yet not be able to sell it so cheap in the world's markets as England does. Some of the manufactures of iron, such as cutlery, axes and saws, are actually so produced through the possession of better machinery, but they have not yet driven

English wares of the same sort out of the market. A recent report to the British government asserts the same of many forms of American dry goods, yet they do not sell in Europe. "What makes the difference in money cost?" Many things,—the extent and the method of taxation, the cost of capital, the rate of wages, the difference in the purchasing power of money, and the like.

Now, in view of domestic commerce, these elements of difference have no existence. It makes no difference to a country what is paid for an article of home production, provided there is no waste of labor in producing it, and provided there is a fair exchange of labor for labor. If tailor and hatter make an exchange of goods, whether they call the price a thousand dollars or one, is of no importance if only the values exchanged are equal. The standard of money payment, be it high or low, is the same for both.

§ 204. (2) The theory assumes that the chief end of national as of individual economy is to save labor, whereas the great problem is how to employ it productively. If buying in the cheapest market reduce the amount of employment, it will be for the nation that does it the dearest of all buying. A farmer who spends his idle hours in making a sled might have got one at the factory for the price of wheat that cost him less labor; but he may have been wiser in making than in buying, because those idle hours would otherwise have been wasted. The nation that spends its surplus labor,—and every nation has a surplus of it,—in working up its raw material into goods is gaining by the business, even though it may employ that labor less effectively than another that has more experience and capital. The people of Denmark spend their long and bleak winters in spinning and weaving home-made goods that England would furnish them cheaper than they make them. The nation says, with one consent, through its national government, "we will not buy of you what we can make ourselves, for if we did our time would be lost." England herself is an illustration of what we mean. "If every man and woman and child returned as a worker in the census had full employment, at full wages, for forty-eight weeks out of the fifty-two, England would be a perfect Paradise for workingmen. We should be in the Millenuium! Far other is the real state of affairs. Taking all the facts into account, I come to the conclusion that for loss of work from every cause, and for the non-effectives up to sixty-five years of age, who are included in the census, we ought to deduct fully twenty per cent. from the nominal full-time wages" of the lower classes as a whole.

See R. Dudley Baxter's *National Income of the United Kingdom.* (London 1868.)

The problem thus presented is not an insoluble one for any country. It is the problem of the due balance of the three great elements of the industrial state. England has missed its solution chiefly through the rending the people away from the land, the establishment of a system of agriculture which lacks aggressiveness and full productive power, and her consequent dependence upon foreign harvests. Millions of the English people who should be living by the land and owning it, sit prisoners in English workhouses, or crowd the lanes and back streets of her manufacturing towns. Our danger is in the other direction— an undue development of agriculture and foreign trade to the neglect of varied industry.

§ 205. (3) In adopting, therefore, a purely passive policy, we should not be accepting the natural order of things, but accommodating ourselves to a thoroughly artificial order. The false position in which England finds herself compels her to wage war upon the industries of other countries; for us to sit idle and passive while she does so by means of the vast masses of capital concentrated in the hands of a few capitalists, would be as weak as to sit idle and passive while her fleet bombarded Boston or New York. The English ideal—forced upon them by their position—is that their country should be "the workshop of the world" and all other countries her dependencies. She is, in their view, "like a vast city to which the less peopled parts of the civilized world are an agricultural country, which is glad to send its overplus of provisions [of raw materials] in exchange for the luxuries and conveniences of a manufacturing region" (Thorold Rogers). "England's position is not that of a great landed proprietor, with an assured revenue, and only subject to occasional loss of crops or hostile depredations. It is that of a great merchant, who by immense skill and capital has gained the front rank and developed an enormous commerce, but has to support an ever-increasing host of dependants. He has to encounter the risks of trade and to face jealous rivals. . . . England is more favorably situated than any country, except the United States, for manufactures and commerce. . . . The future rise of the United States into a great manufacturing and naval power, appears the most probable and certain cause which will place a limit to our national increased prosperity" (Dudley Baxter). The United States and British colonies "are young and rising countries; industries, as yet nascent, are thoroughly suited to the natural capacity of the region and of the people, the latter being of the same stock as the mother country, whose manufactures they prohibit or discourage. There is no reason, apparently, except priority in the market, why the industry of the old country should not be transplanted to the new" (Thorold Rogers).

In other words, England having by a bad national economy destroyed the equilibrium of agriculture and manufactures at home, and thereby made herself dependent upon other peoples for the supply of food and a market for her wares, must now do her best to prevent these new countries from attaining that equilibrium. If they attain it, that will " place a limit to her increase and prosperity," and unless emigration surpass everything that the world has seen, will produce first wide-spread misery and then domestic chaos. She must, therefore, use all her powers of capital and persuasion to keep off the evil day. Although she professes to believe, and persuades herself that she believes, in the solidarity of interests, and exhorts men

> From growing commerce loose the latest chain,
> . . . Till each man finds his own in all men's good,
> And all men work in noble brotherhood ;

yet she cannot but see in this national growth of the industry of these new peoples an injury to her own well-being. All English arguments and exhortations to passivity, however sincere, lie, therefore, under a just suspicion, as special pleadings. *Facile homines credunt, id quod volunt.*

§ 206. (4) The commerce proposed by this theory is the exchange of the raw materials of some countries for the manufactured productions of others. It is therefore an unfair exchange, [1] one side pays for the transportation of bulky and costly articles over great distances; the other pays for the transfer of goods of the same value but condensed in form. The burden of transportation, the chief tax upon production, falls therefore heavily upon the producer of raw material, lightly upon the manufacturer who exchanges with him. But as long as comparative cheapness is the one test by which an industry must stand or fall, the producer has no redress. He cannot say that he will sell to the nearer consumer and save the cost of transportation. His farming or planting may be a ruinous exhaustion of the land that does little or nothing to fill his purse, but there is nothing else for him, so long as the foreigner can undersell home-made goods, prevent the establishment of factories, and close those that have been established.

[2] The exchange is unfair through the unequal distribution of risks. The producer of raw materials depends upon a thousand contingencies for his success, of which other producers know nothing. A bad crop or harvest may leave planter or farmer with nothing to sell; a good one may overstock the market and pull wheat and cotton so low that the cost of transportation absorbs nearly the whole price. But the manufacturer can foresee demand and adjust the supply to it, running his mill over-time at one period, under-time at another. The English distribution of functions thus assigns all the certainties to one nation, all the risks to another.

§ 207. This contingency is the chief element in fixing the price of raw materials. Their supply vibrates between distant extremes of scarcity and plenty. Their producer finds a great loss in either. The manufacturer, through his larger power of adjustment to demand, can ordinarily avoid these ruinous extremes. The country that exports raw material is continually losing the fair returns of its labor through these variations, while it takes in pay goods at a price that is permanent and profitable to the manufacturer. Such a country is consequently a large exporter of the precious metals to pay for its importations.

[3] It was an old and a true jest of the manufacturing countries at the expense of those who supplied them with raw material and took manufactures in exchange, that these latter "sold the hide for sixpence and bought back the tail for a shilling." Take the case of a planter, who raises both cotton and breadstuffs for exportation, as the best illustration of the position of the whole country. His cotton is worth from ten to twenty per cent. more at the Manchester mill than when it left his plantation; so much has been absorbed by the cost of transportation, and of the whole bulk some ten per cent. is thrown out by the spinner as waste. His corn is worth four times as much in Manchester, being far bulkier in proportion to its value, and he has no means to raise its price above one-fourth of what it ordinarily sells for in England, as it then comes into competition with the harvests of England and the world. But it goes to feed Manchester workpeople, and is therefore part of the raw material of the cotton goods that come back to clothe his family and his work-people. He buys it back in buying those goods, paying a dollar for what brought him twenty-five cents, and another dollar for what brought him eighty. And then, besides, he must pay the cost of bringing it back from Manchester to his plantation. He had better have employed people to spin and weave his cotton and consume his corn at home, even though their money cost were much greater than that of Manchester goods. For as he is both a producer and a consumer, his interest is in the comparative price of the two classes of goods, not only in the cheapness of that which he buys. And if—as must be the case—a factory near at hand gives him, and the people dependent on him, a

larger share of manufactured goods, it matters very little whether the money-price that he pays is great or small.

[4] If there were no other reason for the policy that seeks to reduce foreign commerce to a minimum, a sufficient one would be found in its effect upon the human material it employs. Bentham thought the worst possible use that could be made of a man was to hang him; a worse still is to make a common sailor of him. The life and the manly character of the sailor has been so adorned in song and prose, and the real excellences of individuals of the profession have been made so prominent, that we forget what the mass of this class of men are, and what representatives of our civilization and Christianity we send out to all lands in the tenants of the forecastle. How could they be otherwise, unless gifted with superhuman powers of resistance to temptation, since they are ordinarily shut out from all the humanizing and elevating influences of human society and its natural relationships?

And then, be it remembered, their work, while the most difficult, dangerous and severe of human employments, is also the most unproductive, the most useless. John Fitch's application of steam-power to navigation has rendered no greater service to mankind than this, of reducing the number of those who are required to conduct the interchanges of commodities between nations.

§ 208. Domestic commerce, or the interchange of services and commodities between persons of the same nation, is one of the bonds that Providence employs to bring every people into closer and firmer unity. It grows out of that differentiation of function that characterizes organisms of a higher order of life. It weaves across the country a web of intercommunication, binding part to part in the bonds of mutual service and helpfulness. The national unity rests on deeper foundations (§ 23–25), but this is one of the natural expressions of that unity, which reacts upon and strengthens the unity itself. It tends to produce that individuality of type in the part, which again produces the strong coherence of the whole body politic. In every progressive nation this domestic commerce is continually gaining in its amount and in proportion upon commerce with other peoples. Its people are continually more and more employed in serving and helping each other—less and less in serving foreigners.

A nation that is declining in industrial coherence and independence grows faster in foreign than domestic commerce. Its people lose their diversity of pursuits, and conform more and more to a single type of character as of occupation, to the loss of true individuality. Their lines of transit run across the country in one direction,—to the seashore; they are the warp without the woof of the web. That people are sinking to a lower grade of social organization; the parts grow in likeness to each other, and their numbers, however great, are but the numerical repetition of a single specimen.

The amount of a nation's foreign commerce is therefore the worst possible test of its general prosperity. A disproportion of this to domestic commerce shows that the nation is not self-contained and self-sufficient, but dependent upon other nations either for the supply of its necessities or a market for its labor. Yet the increased returns of exports and imports are often gravely offered in evidence of the beneficent effects of a certain course of national policy. A fair test is to be found in the average consumption of articles of prime necessity per head of the population, which continually tells quite another story.

§ 209. Every nation contains within its own providential boundaries the means of making itself independent of all others as regards the supply of articles of prime necessity. There is, therefore, no need of employing a large number of its people and a large amount of its capital in transporting those articles across the ocean. They are always of a bulky nature, and therefore manifestly unsuited for long transport.

Legitimate and natural commerce moves rather along the meridians than along the parallels of latitude. It is the interchange of the products of one climate with those of another. Its mission is to " mix the seasons and the golden hours" (Tennyson), not to "carry coals to Newcastle" by bringing to each people the things that it could abundantly produce at home. From such natural commerce to "loose her latest chain" is the clear duty of every nation.

Or, if we take commerce in the largest sense, as meaning the whole intercourse of nation with nation, it will include the interchange of ideas, the naturalization of better political and industrial methods. And with this intellectual interchange there would naturally be associated a commerce in those articles whose artistic excellence and elaboration of workmanship cause them to present in a concentrated shape the very flower of the producing nation's intellectual life and spirit.

## CHAPTER ELEVENTH.

### The Science and Economy of Manufactures — The Theory.

**§ 210.** The progress of the industrial state, as of every other organized society, and indeed of organic life as a whole, is in the transition from the simple to the complex, from the state in which the parts resemble each other and the whole organism, to that in which the difference between the parts, and between the whole and the parts, is as great as possible. "As we see in existing barbarous tribes, society in its first and lowest forms is a homogeneous aggregation of individuals, having like powers and like functions; the only marked difference of function being that which accompanies the difference of sex. Every man is warrior, hunter, fisherman, toolmaker, builder; every woman performs the same drudgeries; every family is self-sufficing, and save for purposes of aggression and defence, might as well live apart from the rest" (Herbert Spencer).

With the advance of society, this uniformity disappears. From being "Jack of all trades and master of none," each member of the community confines his attention to a single pursuit, and does that one thing better and more effectively. Methods of work improve; a smaller number of workers and a less amount of labor is required to raise food for the whole community. The rest are gradually set free for other employments, some to tan skins into leather and make shoes; others to turn wool into cloth and make clothes; others to dig up iron and smelt it for tools, agricultural implements and articles of household use; others to mould clay into pottery or bricks, or quarry stone for houses; others to cut down trees and fashion them into furniture and other wood-work. Each of these trades, as the numbers of society and the consequent demand for their productions increase, is capable of continued subdivision of labor. The tanner ceases to make shoes, the carpenter to cut down timber the weaver to spin his yarn or to fashion his cloth into garments. And at every subdivision of function, the efficiency of the workman and the skill demanded of him are increased. Arkwright, the Lancashire barber, may or may not have invented the spinning-jenny, but he stamped his name on the history of industry when he devised the first factory, and taught the North of England weavers and capitalists to substitute coöperation as regular as clock-work for desultory and wasteful work.

§ 211. Every change of this sort is a real gain to society at large and to each member of it. The members of the nation who had before no need or less need of each other, become more helpful and useful to each other. The farmer finds, with the artisan within reach, a ready market for his produce. He can buy with its price plenty of clothing, utensils and furniture,— plenty of the things that add to life's comfort and take away its sordidness. He can purchase improved implements that make his work easier and more fruitful. He is more closely associated with his fellow-citizens than before; every wise purchase or sale that he makes is an interchange of services, by which both parties are benefited. There is a real and growing harmony of interests between all classes; the advance of either in wealth enables the others to find a better market for what they would sell; and as wealth leads to the expenditure of larger capital and thus to more productive work, the prosperity of each enables the other to buy of it to better advantage.

§ 212. The growth of the power of association is, at the same time, growth in individual freedom. The more closely men are thus united, the more free each one is to give full play to the bent of his own character. He is not forced to make his living by an employment for which he may have no taste, and in which he can therefore never use his natural gifts to the best advantage. He can consult his liking. And men's employments and daily industries react powerfully upon general character; variety of work produces and cherishes individuality. The parts of the body politic grow in diversity from each other and from the whole body; the societary type rises with that growth. The unity of the parts in the whole becomes all the stronger for the difference. The body is "fitly joined together by that which every part supplieth," when no part can say to another: "I have no need of thee."

All history illustrates this growth in social unity, through growth in individuality. Spain proscribed individuality and freedom; her only philosophers were, like St. Theresa and Ignatius Loyola, those who taught the absorption and annihilation of the man in the corporation; the consequence has been a growing lack of vital cohesion and unity in a monarchy that once aspired to universal empire. Germany was riven into fragments by feudalism, but her individualistic philosophy, whose first word is " I am I," has gone hand in hand with her industrial progress, in binding her into a compact and vigorous empire.

See Prof. F. D. Maurice's *Lectures on Social Morality.*

§ 213. This industrial growth is the natural course of all progressive societies. They grow more diversified in their work, if the constitution and course of their nature be not interfered with. Were there no possibility of interference, the whole process might be left to nature, except so far as legislation is needed to restrain those who are unwilling to give justice to the rest.

Interferences, however, do arise; some from within, some from without. Unjust laws, artificial panics, badly imposed or excessive taxes, unwise economy of labor, restrictions on home trade, the currency of doubtful money and false theories, the absence of general education and intelligence, and many other things already adverted to, prevent the industrial community from going forward as it might. To remove all such restrictions must be among the first duties of the statesman as an economist.

§ 214. But interferences come from without also. Sometimes these grow out of wars and conquests, as when the Philistines would not allow the Israelites to carry on the trade of the smith, lest they "should make them swords or spears," and he who needed a smith's help had to go down to Philistia. At others they grow out of the state of dependence in which one country stands to another. Colonies have been continually cramped and held back, that they might contribute to the profits of industry in the mother country, rather than develop a native industry of their own. In 1827 Mr. Huskisson of the British ministry told our Minister " that it was the intention of the British government to consider the intercourse of the British colonies as being exclusively under its control, and any relaxation from the colonial system as an indulgence, to be granted on such terms as might suit the policy of Great Britain at the time it was granted."

§ 215. But without the employment of either military force or political domination, it is possible and not unusual for one country to keep another in a state of industrial dependence and check its growth. Were all countries equal at the start and sure to remain so, this could not happen. If they had all the same command of capital, had they all equal skill and intelligence, were they all subject to the same taxation, then any aggression could be but temporary and would be punished by equal loss in some other direction. But this is by no means the actual state even of the nations called civilized. No two of them have reached the same point in industrial development, some are far ahead, because of an earlier use of natural advantages; others lag far behind, though they are striving with all energy to come up.

Suppose, now, that two nations that differ thus should establish full and free commercial intercourse between each other, what will be the necessary effect? At first sight it might seem that the rich nation would be conferring benefits upon the poorer one, which the other could but feebly return; that the difference between them would be gradually and steadily diminished through the poorer nation coming forward in industrial development, and taking an ever higher place, and that more rapidly than before.

But experience shows that just the reverse of this is the case. The rich nation becomes, for a time at least, richer by the exchange; the poor nation permanently poorer. The former, through its command of cheap capital, and, by consequence, its greater division and efficiency of labor, can continually undersell the latter in whatever it chooses to export to it, for it can send it manufactured goods at prices with which the manufacturers of the other cannot compete. The process of accumulating capital in the poorer country is decisively checked; its people are reduced from what variety of industry and mutual exchange of services they had possessed, to a uniformity of employment in which no man needs or helps his neighbor. Their power of association is destroyed; money, the instrument of association, is drained out of the country. Nothing is left them but the production of such raw materials as the richer nation chooses to buy, and how unprofitable a commerce of that sort is, we have already seen (§ 206). The country steadily declines in all the elements of productive power, even in the character of the single home industry that is left it (§ 92). "From him that hath not" is "taken away that which he seemeth to have."

§ 216. Here a sweeping objection meets us. A number of theorists tell us that "even if this be the result of unrestricted trade between two such countries, the weaker has no lawful power to put a stop to it. The sphere and duties of government do not extend to the direction and regulation of industry. It might as well undertake to tell its people what they are to believe, as to tell them what they must make, and where they must buy. The right to exchange one's property wherever one pleases, is a part of the right of property itself. It is robbery of the individual citizen, therefore, to say that he shall so manage his buying and selling as to foster a native rather than a foreign industry." "I assume," says Prof. Thorold Rogers, "that there are such rights as are called natural, and that these are the inalienable conditions under which individuals take part in social life. No one questions the natural right of free exchange."

This notion rests on the old exploded fiction that men passed out of a state of nature into the social state by a social contract, in which so much of their natural rights as were necessary to the being of society were given up, and all others were retained. But, as already stated (§ 23), natural rights of individuals have no existence in any real sense except in society itself, and wherever the *well*-being of society demands it, they must give way. It rests with the recognised authorities of the nation, those through whom the national will expresses itself, to say how far this is necessary, and when that decision is made, no one has a right to complain of spoliation. Else it would be the moral right of every citizen to refuse to pay school-tax, or a tax for any other purpose that the bare existence of the state did not involve.

This theory would introduce the most utter slavery, the despotism of the individual will, under the plea of liberty. It would give to every individual in the state the *liberum veto*, by which Poland was ruined. It would leave no choice with any nation but to follow a policy of inaction that would expose its people to the utmost suffering, and ultimately lead to the destruction of the bonds of society. And even if there were not one dissenting voice within the nation itself, still the unanimity could take no effect for lack of a proper organ for its expression. The uncertain agency of voluntary leagues and associations would be the only means,—a means altogether insufficient,—to carry out their purpose. When the sense of national necessity was clear and strong, the people would abide by such voluntary decisions, but in more ordinary moods they would begin to say: "What matter will it make if I buy this of one man, and not from another? It is but a drop in the bucket after all." Now the very function of the government is to express and embody the higher and purer will of the people, and not their lower, self-indulgent moods. The great and true ruler is the one who can distinguish between the two, and direct his policy accordingly.

The fragment of truth which gives this error all the validity that it has, is that the government, as a rule, is concerned with the industrial (as with the intellectual) life of its people *indirectly;* with some other provinces directly. It is, as the preamble of the U. S. Constitution very well expresses it, to "*provide* for the common defence" but to "*promote* the general welfare." Theorists who run to the other extreme would have government take as much charge of the one sphere as the other. They would substitute national workshops, for those of individual employers. They would put the rights of property under great restraints or abolish it utterly. But as the government is not the power that propels the ship of state, but the helmsman (*gubernator*) that steers it, this extreme is as false as the other, while it grew out of the other by a necessary reaction. Well did Edmund Burke say that to draw the line between what the state should do as such, and what it should leave to the activity of individuals, is one of the nicest questions in legislation. These sweeping and wholesale solutions of it, just because of their simplicity and directness, are under suspicion as false.

Another form that the objection takes is this : " The state should exact a tax from no man unless it be made payable into its own treasury and used for its own ends. But the difference between the price of the home-made article and that at which the foreigner would have provided it is such a tax; therefore it is unfair." In other words the state has no right to *promote* but only to *provide for* things and actions needful to the nation's life.

§ 217. In the state, therefore, inheres the right to promote the industrial development of the people, as necessary to their "general welfare." And the right is no less than a duty. If it be the first duty of the nation to provide for its own existence, there is involved in that the duty to promote the largest and fullest existence possible, the free development of all sides of the national life. If the state exist that justice may be done, that justice is not to be conceived merely in the jural sense ; as the popular phrase extends its application, the people must be allowed " to do themselves justice," and all obstacles to that end must be removed. If the state exist that freedom may be attained and realized for its people, then it must make such provision that its people shall possess real industrial freedom,— the freedom of neighborhood commerce and mutual service with each other. It puts restraint upon the international trade, that the far more important domestic trade may exist and be free.

15

"But are not its citizens at all times free to trade wherever they please, without its interference? If they think it best to buy of the home producer they can do so."

They are not free, if no one can undertake to produce what they need at home, for want of assurance and security. In such a case the right and natural thing is for the people to say, through their organ, the government, "Go ahead; build your factory; put in your machinery; we will buy of you." In so saying they are acting out their own freedom of choice to the fullest degree. They are saying, "We choose to have a free choice between the home and the foreign maker, and so we pledge ourselves that the former shall have a chance to establish himself." All freedom is won by sacrifice; the wise and far-sighted people is the one that will make the sacrifice—that will suffer the pains of a bloody revolution, as more endurable than the long, wasting misery that centuries of tyranny inflict. Such a principle will not be left out of sight when such a people enters the work-shop and the factory.

A writer in the *Fortnightly Review* (London) says: "An observant journalist has remarked that it is a singular fact that in Austria 'those who have vigorously struck down every ecclesiastical and political monopoly throughout the empire are the most vehement advocates of a restrictive commercial policy, while on the other hand those who are in favor of free trade are the most ardent supporters of ecclesiastical privilege.' Austria is not singular in this respect. In France the advocates of free speech and a free press are restrictionists; while imperialists, as a rule, are free traders. In the United States the abolitionists or Republicans are avowed restrictionists, while the Democrats are decidedly in favor of free trade. Precisely the same phenomenon may be observed in the British colonies. In Canada, Australia and New Zealand the party of progress has always been identified with a restrictive commercial policy, while the Conservatives are the most uncompromising of free traders. Indeed, it may be said that one-half the entire English-speaking race are, in one shape or another, in favor of a restrictionist policy, and of this half the great majority are advanced liberals. It is the national creed in the United States, Canada, and the leading Australian and New Zealand colonies. . . Strange as it may appear, it is nevertheless true that it is just because the party of progress in the colonies are opposed to monopoly in every shape that they are the advocates of restriction in regard to commerce. Instead of that policy savoring of monopoly, they maintain that it has exactly the opposite tendency; and their chief object in imposing import duties is to put down monopolies, by extending the sphere of competition."

§ 218. No violent transition from the sphere of the state's direct duties is needed to carry it into this of its indirect influence. Indeed, it cannot discharge the former without exercising the latter. It must make large purchases or manufacture in its own workshops large supplies for the army, navy and other executive branches (§§ 297, 302). In either case the choice between home and foreign industry is forced upon it. If it raise large sums by indirect taxation, it must select the method of imposing these,—whether by excises upon home productions or duties upon those of other countries.

Its provision for its own safety in case of war involves the cherishing of such industries as furnish the great necessaries of national use, and indeed requires their creation. "In time of peace be prepared for war" is a commonplace of statecraft. Now in war the government is of necessity a large purchaser of many sorts of manufactured goods. Foreign commerce is interrupted, either entirely or so much so as to render the importation of these goods—which are contraband of war—difficult and hazardous, and on a large scale impossible. The home manufacturers that might have supplied them cannot spring up in a night. The narrowness of vision, the lack of foresight, which prevented their being called earlier into existence, has its reward in national perplexity, often in actual defeat.

"How then is it," says Dr. Horace Bushnell, "that free trade science is going peremptorily to settle all the great questions of public economy? For if we set ourselves down to it as the test of economy, and say it is final, we are by and by obliged to ask: Is there nothing to be done or thought of in the world that is out of 'economy,' and rightly spurns it? May not the worst 'economy' sometimes be the best? To be fostering modes of production when the trade-balance shows a disadvantage wears a bad look certainly as respects the matter of economy. But how many and vast supplies are wanted that must not be left to the uncertainties of trade,—where to higgle over expense would be even a contemptible weakness? This is true in particular of all the supplies that are needed for the equipment of the state of war. Without these no people is a proper nation, or at least by any possibility a strong one. These, therefore, we must not only have, but must have the way of making at any cost."

See *Scribner's Magazine* for July 1871, article on "Free Trade and Protection."

**219.** It is sometimes urged as an argument in favor of unrestricted trade, that "the mutual dependence of the nations thus produced is eminently promotive of the cause of international peace. It will put the nations under bonds to keep the peace, by placing each of them in such a relation to the rest that a war with any other will inflict ruinous losses upon its industries, and therefore it will create within each a sentiment in favor of peace, and a class whose interests are bound up with its preservation."

An unhappy comment upon this rose-colored theory is found in the fact that the majority of modern wars have been undertaken, not for national honor or pride, but for the sake of trade, —"the fair, white-winged peace-maker." The communities most at war with the rest of the world have generally been those in which the spirit of trade predominated—Tyre, Carthage, Venice, England, &c. A great English military historian and general, Sir W. Napier, lays it down as a rule that the traders have begun the wars and the soldiers have ended them (See §§ 257, 278, note).

Furthermore, this argument assumes that war in and of itself, is the chief thing to be avoided in international affairs. It leaves out of sight the truth that a just and righteous war may be the clear vocation of a nation, and the preparation for it the very highest duty. If unrestricted trade unfits a people for the infliction of just punishment upon unrighteous nationalities, it unfits it for one of the very highest ends for which nations exist; —unfits it for rendering to other nations the very highest service possible,—the defending them against the unjust invasion of their rights, or the chastising them into a better state of mind. Such cases, do, undoubtedly, exist; but they are exceptional, and not happy exceptions either. Europe has no more pitiable spectacle than the sight of a nation foremost in wealth, culture and capacity for just and impartial indignation, yet bound hand and foot by trade motives, forswearing its better instincts, deserting its natural allies, and held back from exerting its just influence upon the world's politics.

Furthermore, the effect of such unrestricted commerce is to place the weaker and less developed of the two countries at the mercy of the other. The dependence is never fully mutual and equal, and in the nature of things cannot be. The one is fully provided with all the munitions and appliances of war; the other has all these to seek. Hence the rule of international law now coming into recognition, that neutral nations are bound to strict (not merely to impartial) neutrality, as the weaker of the two nations at war will derive more benefit than the other from the power of making unreserved purchases on neutral soil. This fact of the unprepared state of the more backward country cannot be hid from the other; in case of a disagreement, it furnishes a strong motive to overbearing insolence and aggression. It has been repeatedly alleged as a motive for rushing into hostilities, never for holding back.

§ 220. A comparative study of the financial methods of different nations discloses circumstances that render discrimination in favor of the home manufacturer the only fair mode of proceeding. One country makes efforts to be rid of the burden of debt, and to that end imposes a heavy direct or indirect taxation upon its people; another funds its debts in perpetual annuities, and has no intention of paying more than the interest. One country has adopted a very efficient but expensive system of government by paid and responsible officials; another possesses and employs a large class of men of wealth and leisure, upon whom the work of legislation and the local administration of justice can be devolved. One country has a very high ideal of the duties and responsibilities of government, and considers the health and intelligence of the people its charge, and taxes all property-owners accordingly; another leaves these matters to the care and interest of individuals. One country expects in all its people a certain degree of civilization implying a corresponding expenditure for fitting habitations, clothing, food, education, &c., and thence an adequate scale of wages to support this expenditure; another country is satisfied to see large masses of its population but slightly raised above the brutes, and toiling for a pittance. One country extends over a vast and sparsely-settled territory, and this fact adds to all the national expenses; the other has a small territory with a compact population. One country, through force of circumstances, has been compelled to ask very great sacrifices of its people for the national safety and defence; the other has long dwelt at peace. Any one or more of these circumstances make it just and fair to compensate for the weight of home burdens by duties high enough to give the home manufacturer a fair chance. Nothing could be more unequal than equality of duties in such cases.

These things are not superficial matters that may be adapted to the economic teachings of every new set of economists. The national methods of finance are the expression of the nation's life; their peculiarities are the expression of that in the nation's life which gives it individuality and historic distinctness. They need continual and steady reform, that they may be kept up to the national standard of right, and the national average of intelligence. But reform is not revolution; it is evolution rather. In these things there is for every nation a "constitution and course of nature," whose laws must be learned and followed in wise change and in wise resistance to needless change.

For these considerations the cosmopolitical school have no place; they think their consideration in connection with the question of wealth and economy an impertinence. They write as if there were no nations, or as if they were merely local and conventional arrangements for police purposes. With Cobden, they would gladly see all boundary lines wiped from the map; and like him, they regard nations as necessary evils. Their arguments are never based on the necessities of national life, and the means to attain the largest and fullest degree of that life; but on "the maximum of production throughout the world." They know of no interest save pocket-interest, whereas, as Mr. Mill well says, a man's interest is whatever he takes an interest in. And every good citizen will take an interest in the industrial development and independence of his own country. We might, as Dr. Bushnell does, concede the force of all their economic arguments, and then reject their conclusions on higher grounds.

*So much for arguments drawn from political theories and the replies to them. From these we pass to the purely economic arguments in favor of restrictions upon foreign trade, and first to those that would justify the imposition of those restrictions permanently, if need were. But first of all as to the methods of restriction.*

§ 221. The state, then, possessing the right to discriminate between home and foreign industry, and being prompted to do so by reasons of public policy as well as by a desire to promote the welfare of its citizens, has to make a choice of the best means to that end. It might directly encourage the worker at home by a system of bounties and subsidies; but this plan is now generally rejected as too artificial, and as open to great abuses. Or it may prohibit the importation of foreign wares, or discourage their importation by duties that will raise their price high enough to enable the native manufacturer to compete with them in the home market. Prohibitions are now properly regarded as unwise; discriminating duties are adopted as preferable by nearly all civilized nations.

Another question of method is the choice between specific and *ad valorem* duties. The former exact so much for each pound, yard's length or square foot of all goods of a given kind, with no reference to their comparative fineness or value. The latter taxes each class of goods a certain percentage on their sworn value. The specific form of duty is preferable, (1) because its proper amount is most easily and surely ascertained. It enables government to dispense largely or altogether with "Custom-house oaths;" renders false invoices as good as useless. (2) Because it gives the largest protection to the manufacture of those cheaper and bulkier articles which are of prime necessity to the nation. It thus furnishes a primary school of industrial education, in which the working classes and their captains of industry learn to make cheap things before they attempt those that require finer elaboration. (3) It diminishes smuggling. To bring in goods without paying duty requires a degree of concealment that is impossible in the case of the coarser wares; while the smallness of the duty upon the others, in comparison with their cost, makes it not worth while to run the risk of detection. (4) It does not, as *ad valorem* duties do, intensify the fluctuations in the price of an imported article, by admitting it at a low duty when it is cheap, and imposing a higher duty when it is dear. Especially in times of crisis and distress, when an industry is ready to perish, it does not, as *ad valorem* duties do, invite foreign rivals to complete the ruin, by allowing their goods to enter almost duty free; but by its unvarying defence against such assaults revives the fainting industry.

§ 222. Protective duties yield for a considerable period a large revenue to the state, but that is not the object of their imposition. Duties for revenue, i. e., too low to be protective, in spite of their appearance of moderation, are highly unjust. They inflict all the hardships of indirect and unequal taxation, without even the purpose of benefiting the consumer. Duties for protection, while they bring large revenue, have another purpose, and, as we shall see, benefit the consumer to a far greater extent than they tax him, while their amount is equally available for public uses. Their object is their own abolition, for they aim at such a development of the national industry as shall render impossible the importation of the dutiable articles. To impose revenue duties is to accept indirect taxation as a permanent method of finance; to impose protective duties is not.

§ 223. It would, of course, be absurd for a young or a poor

country to begin at once the production of everything that her people need. The limited amount of her capital and of her labor would not allow of this. Those coarser articles whose cost of transportation is great, and which a specific system of duties will do most to exclude, should be the first object; afterward those that are finer.

But even classes of goods that are under very heavy duties will continue to be imported for a good while. It will ordinarily take the lifetime of two generations to acclimatize thoroughly a new manufacture, and to bring the native production up to the native demand. It is from such imported goods as these that the customs' revenue is derived; and they will sell at a higher rate than before the duty was imposed. The very object of the duty was to raise the price of the foreign article; if it failed to do so, it would offer no protection. But it is a great mistake to suppose that such articles will sell for their old price *plus* the duty. A part of the burden will fall on the foreign producer and the importer. The amount of it that they will have to pay will generally be proportional to the amount of home production. When such duties are first imposed and the amount of native competition is very slight, nearly if not quite the whole of the duty is paid by the consumer; but the amount thus paid diminishes steadily as home production increases, and when the latter is nearly up to the home demand nearly if not quite all the duty will be paid by the importer and the foreign manufacturer. Hence the outcry raised by these two classes against protective duties; it is not from love of the consumer, nor yet from jealousy of the profits made by the native manufacturer, but from an unpleasant consciousness that through his efforts the amount of revenue that they are furnishing to the government is steadily increasing in proportion to their whole business, and to the reduction of their profits.

Here are two bits of information and confirmation from British trade circulars. A Sheffield steel firm says: "We have a very large steel trade in America, amounting to a large proportion of our whole business, and in that market there is, from various causes, much competition; and these two causes, large trade and competition combined, have induced me to be satisfied with a smaller average of profit there than we have realized on the average in our other markets." A London iron firm explains to its producing customers: "With the present out-turn, a material reduction of the American duty, or something equally significant, is necessary to advance the price of iron above £7 a ton." The very threat of a protective duty, i. e., the threat to foster native production and competition, has often had the effect to lower the price of the foreign article.

There are some very evident inferences from this fact. (1) The amount of a duty is not always nor often the same as the amount of the protection it offers. If the duty be seventy-five per cent., and the foreign manufacturer pay fifty per cent. of it,— i. e., if he sell his goods only twenty-five per cent. higher than before it was imposed, then the protection afforded is twenty-five per cent. and no more. Allowance, therefore, must be made for this fact in imposing protective duties. A duty is protective in intention when its object is to promote home production; it is protective in effect, whether it be low or high, when it does raise the price of the foreign article sufficiently to give the native producer a chance in the home market. It must therefore be so high that the foreign producer and his agents cannot pay it, and still have a sufficient profit on sales.

(2) Nothing, therefore, can be more misleading than some of the wooden calculations made by the opponents of protective duties. They reckon up the entire consumption of the home made article, and calculating—in the case supposed—that it sold for seventy-five per cent. more than the foreign article would have cost had there been no duty, they assume that the vast sum thus reached went into the pockets of native manufacturers, and was "taken out of the pockets of the consumer."

> For another false assumption in such calculations—the assumption that the home producer does or can charge up to the amount of the protection he receives—see § 241. Henry Clay used to tell a story of a Free Trade orator haranguing from the stump a crowd of Kentuckians. "Do you know, sir," said he to an attentive hearer, "that that coat on your back cost you a half a dollar a yard more than it need, because of this accursed tariff?" "Wal, stranger," was the reply, drawled out slowly, "I reckon it must be so since you say it. But this coat cost me by the yard just three bits" (three-eighths of a dollar).

(3) The notion that unrestricted commerce gives each nation

simply all the possible advantage that it can reap from the more advanced industries of others, and that nothing but a fair profit can be added to the cost of production and transportation, is utterly untenable. Were this the case, the entire duty would fall on the consumer from first to last. But in fact, the money received into the treasury is very largely drawn from the trader's excessive profits, and not from the consumer in any sense.

*The benefits reaped by a nation from a restrictive policy may be considered under four heads.*

§ 224. Firstly, it is a wise economy of the *labor* of the people. Now the national economy of labor consists, not in getting on with as little as possible of it, but in finding remunerative employment for as much of it as possible. If labor be the source of wealth,—and this is one of the few points on which all are agreed—then that country must advance to wealth which has work for all who are willing and able to do it. To find work for all is one of the greatest problems that a nation has to solve; none has yet attained to a complete solution of it; but none is so far from its solution as the country in which agriculture is the only employment open to the great mass of the people. For farming, as a rule, furnishes employment only to robust men and in the open air; all others—women, the young, the sickly—are left in idleness and dependence upon the farming class.

In districts of our own country, especially in the South, where agriculture is the only industry, a considerable portion of the people live on the verge of starvation for want of work. Maine was a by-word for poverty sixty years ago, when her people were either farmers or lumberers. Since she began to use her immense water-power, she has left many other states behind her, and has now work for all her people. Australia is a young country, with plenty of land, large natural resources, and no excess of population, and but a small percentage that are incapable of hard work. Yet she has been greatly perplexed to find employment for that percentage, especially for the young. A highly-respectable farmer from Ulster, who went thither about 1840, could get nothing for his boys to do, and actually made sailors of them to save them from idleness and worse. For this, among many good reasons, most of the Australian colonies foster home industries by restrictions on foreign trade.

The greater the variety of the industry the more the demand for labor and the better the laborer is paid; for instead of two workmen competing for every job, we shall have two masters, two sorts of masters running after every workman. "There is rarely competition for labor on the part of employers *within* a trade, in a particular place, unless there be competition for it from without. And in the absence of competition from without, what competition there is on the part of employers within a trade often tends to lower wages" (Cliffe Leslie). Thus in the northern and eastern shires of England, and the three north-eastern counties of Ireland, work is far better paid than in the other parts of those kingdoms, because in those agriculture and manufactures are competing for labor, while elsewhere there is little or nothing else than agriculture. So also in the Walloon provinces of Belgium, as compared with the Flanders provinces. In the latter farming has been brought to perfection, but industries exist only on a petty scale, for want of coal and water-power, and there is a considerable amount of misery. In the Walloon provinces farming is backward in comparison, but great industries abound, wages are nearly twice as high, and pauperism exists to hardly any extent. The notion that labor will in such cases transfer itself from the worse to the better market, is not borne out by the facts. The wrench of separation from familiar surroundings is terrible to the uneducated workman, and not very agreeable to any one. If it be made at all, generally a more distant field offers a still better prospect, and the man emigrates. The transfer around the world is easier than from shire to shire. Besides, the laws of many countries discourage the latter transfer, and tend to reduce the laborer to the condition of a serf, *adscriptus glebæ*.

§ 225. We sometimes hear it said in reply: "Skilled artisans are as well off in England under Free Trade as in America under Protection. Their week's wages will buy them more broadcloth, Sevres china, fine cutlery, &c., than it would in America." They ought to be much better off; a country that possesses the vast capital that England has, and can carry the organization of labor to the perfection it has there reached, should pay her workmen at rates with which the rest of the world could not compete. We ought to see a growing scarcity of skilled labor in America, through the emigration of our artisans thither. But, in fact, we find our workshops and factories full of her workmen, and an immigration of them to America since the restrictive policy was adopted, such as there never was before.

But all this is beside the question. The question is not between free trade and protection, but between the varied industry which England acquired by long persistence in protection, and which she will retain under any system, and the want of it, from which we can only be saved by following England's example rather than her precepts.

§ 226. Furthermore, the creation of a diversified industry introduces such a change into farming itself as enables the farmer to employ a greater variety of labor. A home market takes the place of the distant one, and crops are grown which require more care and attention, but repay it with larger profits. Farming passes out of its wasteful *extensive* phase into the *intensive* stage, in which its operations are more productive and profitable. And this "mixed farming" which pays best all the world over, is as varied in the sorts of labor it employs as in the products of the labor. Women and children can now be employed, as physical strength and endurance are no longer the sole requisites.

§ 227. Labor is benefited by the restrictive policy in that the increase of its productiveness, and consequently of its remuneration, is thus made possible. We have already seen the natural progress of the workman from wasteful, thriftless, mechanical, ill-paid work, to that which brings the whole man into service, mind as well as muscle, and uses all his powers to the best advantage We have seen that while both capitalist and laborer are benefited by the transition, the laborer receives the larger share of the benefit, and the power of labor to command the services of capital (of the accumulations of past labor, that is) grows steadily with the growth of society. A country that remains chiefly agricultural calls only for the lower, and lower-priced, sorts of labor; that which diversifies its industry creates a demand for those sorts that rank higher in their demands upon human capacity and in their rewards to industrial ability. It is therefore the interest of the laboring classes, even more than of their employers, to see to the naturalization of all the industries for which the country has any natural aptitude.

This argument has especial force as regards the people of the United States. The natural drift and bent of the American character towards the mechanic arts and the inventions that facilitate them, which a morning in the U. S. Patent Office would make clear to any one, would find little or no vent in the absence, or the undue subordination of the manufacturing industries. The strongest side of the national intellect and the brightest gifts of the people would be thrown into the shade.

A comparison of our manufacturing cities and districts with the city of New York and its working classes, discloses the fact that wealth is far more evenly distributed where industry is varied. In Philadelphia and Pittsburg, or Cincinnati, for instance, there are very few very rich men, and the process of accumulating large fortunes is a slow one. But more of the people own their own houses in Philadelphia than in any other city of the world. The working men of those cities, many of whom are foreigners, are generally well off and contented with their lot. They, too, have a stake in the stability and security of society, and taking the whole record, Philadelphia has had fewer strikes and lock-outs than almost any other city.

> Prof. Fawcett, indeed, has amused us by informing the English people that "the Manchester of America" has 119,000 paupers, or three times as many in proportion to her population as England has. The professor, unhappily for his country and his race, has lost his sight, and is therefore dependent upon those who read to him. By an inadvertence of some of these, the number of dollars expended in the relief of the poor of Philadelphia was transmuted into the number of poor who receive relief. Even

that sum is deceptive; as good salaries are paid to officials and the paupers are kept in such style that gout is a common disease at the almshouse. Philadelphia has something over three thousand in-door and about a thousand out-door paupers, nearly all unable to work.

As to being "the Manchester of America," Philadelphia may accept the compliment with qualification. She ranks above Manchester and next to London as a manufacturing city.

And these cities can claim no monopoly of prosperity. In Massachusetts, for instance, the number who receive relief from the state is reduced ten per cent. since 1855. *The Boston Traveller* says: "Fifteen years ago a visit to those districts in any of the cities of the Commonwealth that are occupied as homes by the working classes, revealed poverty and want in marked contrast with their present position. Then, the children, with bare feet and half covered with ragged garments, looked half-starved, as they really were. But to-day the visitor to the same district will find them comfortably clothed and shod, and having a cheerful look that gives the most unmistakable evidence that hunger is a stranger to them. The decrease in pauperism is therefore largely due to the better remuneration received by the working classes."

§ 228. Secondly, protection to industry is as much needed by the *farmer* as by the manufacturer. The farmer, and in general all the producers of the raw material of our industries and of food, need *direct* protection. The excessive grain-crop of the West, as we have seen, finds no outlet for more than a fraction of its amount in the European markets. What becomes of the bulk of it? It is mostly consumed by the people of the Eastern States, which might, but do not, produce enough food to feed themselves. Perhaps a great multitude of Western farmers could have found better work on the unoccupied land in the East; but as things are, they are secured the Eastern market for Western products by direct protection. If we had free trade with Canada, the farmers of that region, who pay little for labor and little for government, would be glad to sell their produce to New York and New England at prices with which the West could hardly compete. But a tariff on farm produce shuts them out, or keeps up prices so far that the Western producer has a chance.

So with other producers of raw materials. Our coal-mines have to compete along the seaboard with the mines of Nova Scotia; our salt-makers with the Liverpool exporters; our wool growers with those of Canada and Europe; our cotton planters once sought protection against the West Indies and may yet seek it again against those of Hindoostan; our sugar planters are and deserve to be protected. All these industries are carried on under a weight of national taxation that would make international free trade a bounty upon foreign importations. In every case the great body of protectionists and all their leading thinkers have urged generous consideration of the claims of this class of producers.

> A number of New England manufacturers have indeed taken another course. For the sake of getting the raw materials of their manufacture cheaply, they urge that we should admit free of duty whatever is " reproductively consumed," and impose duties on what is not. See *A Manual of the Currency*, by George A. Potter, New York, 1868.

§ 229. The benefits extended by national legislation to agriculture under the Nationalist policy does not stop at its protection. It is heavily subsidized by the nation. The Protectionists voted the Homestead Law, to enable the farmer to begin his occupation of new lands under the most favorable conditions. They also have always carried out the policy of subsidizing new roads and railroads, so as to give the farmer free access to his market. "A tariff *and* internal improvements" have always gone together in our political war-cries. The agricultural department of the government has been kept up for the benefit of the farmer, that a knowledge of the best methods of work might be disseminated, and new plants imported, acclimatized and scattered over the land. All these proceedings are capable of vindication only on the principle that it is wise and right for a nation to make sacrifices to promote industry; on free trade principles they are wrong.

§ 230. Just as the laborer's prosperity is measured by the relation of his wages to current prices, and not by the latter alone, so the farmer's is measured by the relation of the prices of raw and of manufactured goods—including food under the former,—and not by the prices of either one. Wherever the manufacturer is found at work, the prices of the two converge; wherever he is wanting, and the farmer stands alone, their prices diverge. On the Schuylkill, for instance, the price of a pound of rags and that of a pound of paper come very near to each other. Suppose there were no paper-mills elsewhere in the Union; then as one went west the prices of the two would diverge with every mile. At the foot of the Rocky Mountains rags would be as good as worthless, while paper would bring a far higher price than in the east. Just such is the relation of the price of raw materials of all sorts as compared with the price of manufactured goods of all sorts. The points where the lines of price almost converge are those at which the one is transformed into the other by manufacture. Free trade would, not completely, but in great measure, transfer those points to the other side of the ocean. Would the producer of food and of raw materials be benefited by the transfer? He would have to pay the heaviest tax upon industry, the cost of transportation in each direction. He would spend two bushels of corn in getting one to market, and then pay in equal measure for everything that he needed to bring back for his own use.

§ 231. Protection to industry gives the farmer an abundant and steady market for his breadstuffs, and creates a market for crops more remunerative than grain. The European market for our wheat and corn is furnished by England, and is the most unsteady that can be thought of. The amount that is needed depends, first of all, upon the character of the English harvest, which commonly furnishes from two-thirds to three-fourths of what is needed. Then Mark Lane turns to the wheat crops of the Baltic and the Ukraine (and the corn crop of Turkey) to supply the deficiency, as the English consumer prefers their round hard grain to the American. If they cannot get enough there, they send orders to the United States. The farmer ordinarily runs the risk of a bad harvest; our farmers take the risk of three. If two harvests abroad have been pretty bad, and that at home has been not too good, he will make money. Otherwise he may perhaps burn corn for fuel, as was frequently done in free trade times. One year England will purchase of us seven-twentieths of all the wheat that she needs; the very next year (1865) only one-twentieth. Her demand of us fell in 1872 to 8½ million bushels from 13½ millions in the previous year. The price varies, though not as much as the amount, and by no means depends upon the quantity taken, but upon how far that comes up to the supply. Thus in 1856 the quantity was nearly six times as great as in 1869, and the price was twice as high. Worse still, the price that England must pay for the petty quantity she takes, exercises a great influence upon that of the entire crop, destroying the stability of our home market.

§ 232. The policy which increases the number of those who are not engaged in farming, but must live on its products and pay for them, is that which secures to the farmer the best and steadiest remuneration. The average consumption of wheat in America is more than five bushels per head; on an average of years a native of the British islands consumes about a peck of wheat grown on our soil. It will, surely, be the wisest way to refuse to buy British goods, and thus draw her workmen across the ocean to manufacture the same articles here. It will pay better to feed them here than at home, and thus save the cost of transporting both their food and their manufactures, besides selling to each of them twenty times as much of the former. And besides, it will be wiser to attract a multitude of our own home population to manufactures, and thus create a steady home market for food. Free traders urge the farmer to secure the choice of two markets to make his purchases in, the home and the foreign. The American artisan has no such choice of two markets; he must buy his food at home. Even if he lives along the Canadian border he finds himself shut out from that market by protective duties on American produce.

§ 233. This fact, that the interest of the farmer and the manufacturer are identical, attracted the attention of Franklin.

He wrote home from London in 1771: "Every manufacturer encouraged in a country makes part of a market for provisions within ourselves, and saves so much money to the country, as must otherwise be exported to pay for the manufactures he supplies. Here in England it is well known and understood that wherever a manufacture is established which employs a number of hands, it raises the value of land in the neighboring country all around it. It seems, therefore, the interest of our farmers and owners of land to encourage our young manufactures in preference to foreign ones."

General Jackson, in a famous letter to Dr. Coleman, puts the case very forcibly: "The American farmer has neither a foreign nor a home market, except for cotton. Does not this clearly prove that there is too much labor employed in agriculture? and that the channels of labor should be multiplied. Common sense points out at once the remedy. Draw from agriculture the superabundant labor, and employ it in mechanism and manufactures, thereby creating a home market for your breadstuffs, and distributing labor to a most profitable account, and benefits to the country will result. Take from agriculture in the United States 600,000 men, women and children, and you at once give a home market for more breadstuffs than all England now furnishes."

§ 234. The creation of a varied industry enables the farmer to enrich himself without impoverishing the soil. It does so by bringing the farmer and the artisan into neighborhood, and giving the former facilities for making returns to the soil that he would not otherwise possess. It does so by creating a demand for less exhaustive crops than the great staples that are needed in the foreign market. It does so by promoting the cattle-farming that has turned large areas of Belgian peat and sand into the richest farms in the world. It does so by making it worth while to farm more carefully, through the certainty of a permanent local market, rather than to get out of the soil as fast as possible all the easily accessible elements, and then move on westward to take up new land. What has been the history of American agriculture thus far? It has mostly been the robbing the soil of its most valuable qualities to export its wealth across the ocean. "In my opinion it would be improper to estimate the total annual waste of the country at less than equal to the mineral constituents of fifteen hundred million bushels of corn. To suppose this can continue is simply ridiculous. As yet we have much virgin soil, and it will be long ere we reap the full fruits of our improvidence; but it is merely a question of time. With our earth-butchery and prodigality we are each year losing the intrinsic essence of our vitality" (Geo. E. Waring). In some parts of the country it is no longer a question of time. Districts like the region around Albany will now yield but a third the amount of wheat that the first settlers got from them. The New Englanders have been the most wasteful of our farmers. Wherever they have settled, as in western New York, the soil has been blighted under their feet. On the other hand, the grain farmers of eastern Pennsylvania, by their steady care to keep up the fertility of the soil, have made their lands more valuable with every year. Not that their methods are first-rate; any one who has seen a European farm knows how much they have to learn, especially on the utilization of manures. But by sowing clover, a plant whose roots thrust themselves down to the subsoil and take mineral sustenance from that, and by ploughing down the clover with lime, the land has been kept up to a fair degree of fertility. The possession of a home market, however, and the command of the refuse of our towns and factories, and the opportunity to keep large numbers of cattle and to alternate other crops with grain, have been the chief cause of their prosperity. The farmer who has his market at hand, unless he be unusually thriftless and wasteful, can go on year after year improving the instrument by which he makes his living; he who depends on a distant market has no choice, as he must go on, year after year, destroying it.

§ 235. Protection diminishes the risk of farming by giving variety to its products. The farmer who depends upon exportation puts all his eggs into one basket. Excessive rains or excessive droughts, insects and blights, wage war upon the few staple articles that he can find a market for. If he had the consumers at hand, he could sell them a great variety of crops; if one failed, the others would ordinarily—not always—escape. Green crops flourish under the rainfall that ruins wheat; the blight that spreads ruin among the grain is powerless over the hay. The soil that yields a poor and a risky return for one article is just the thing for another.

§ 236. Thirdly, the people of a nation reap a benefit from the restrictive policy, in that it applies the law of parsimony to the number of the *commercial* class, and to their profits.

A country is wealthy in proportion to the amount of its labor for which it can find productive employment, in directing either the organic or the formal changes of matter that fit it for man's use. But the trader and those whom he directly employs produce nothing; he only contributes to the productiveness of labor by saving the time that the producer might otherwise waste in seeking a purchaser. The more the service of the trader is needed, the less is the net benefit derived from him, because the greater in that case is the amount of the tax he imposes upon the article on its way from the producer to the consumer. This tax is ordinarily greatest when the distance between the producer and the consumer is greatest, and, as we have seen, is in that case not limited to the cost of transportation and a fair profit for his services. By practices and methods, of which artificial scarcities are but extreme instances, the price of the goods that he transmits is lowered or raised at pleasure, either to destroy competition in the market where he sells, or to reap the large profits that far more than repay him for that and other sacrifices. That these profits are ordinarily excessive in the absence of home competition is evident from the fact that he can afford to pay a considerable share of the protective duties designed to create home competition.

The restrictive policy brings the producer and the consumer into neighborhood, and thus diminishes their need of the trader, and weakens his power over them. The heavy tax of transportation is saved; men are set free from that most laborious and unproductive of occupations to engage in others which are productive, and which this very policy has called into existence. The buyers of an article are no longer dependent upon the trader as to the price they will pay; if it be exorbitant, they can go direct to the producer. The market can no longer be forestalled, because the great and necessary commodities are no longer concentrated in a few hands, but pass in much smaller parcels, and through much fewer hands, from those who produce them to those who need them.

§ 237. Not that this policy destroys international commerce; it only transforms it and makes it more equitable. From an exchange of raw materials for manufactured goods, it raises it to an exchange of manufactured goods on each side. Even if the value of international exchanges is not reduced—and protection often increases them—their bulk and the cost of their transportation are reduced, and that very decidedly. Men have, thereby, more power to command the use of ships, and less need to use them. It gives men at once more power over ships, and ships less power over men—which is the law of progress in regard to the *instruments* of wealth. It restores the equilibrium of foreign exchange, and puts an end to the export of specie from the poorer to the wealthier countries, retaining it where it is most needed by increasing its utility and purchasing power.

A country that continually develops native wealth and industry by a consistent Nationalist policy grows in power to purchase those articles that its own manufactures do not yet supply, or that can only be produced in another climate than its own. The country that has the most diversified industry is best able to patronize the finer industries of other countries. The servant girls of the Northern States before the war bought more English silks than did the slaveholding aristocracy of the South. Every country that carries on an unrestricted trade with another much richer than itself, purchases a less and less valuable class and amount of goods with every generation, till at last its demand counts for nothing in the markets of the other. In so far as a richer country persuades the poorer ones to follow this policy, she herself becomes less of a workshop and more of a mart; their raw products pass through her ports and factories with ever less of elaboration and an ever greater diminution in their amount. From carrying on commerce *with* the world she sinks to the position of a nation of shopkeepers and traders which carries on commerce for the world.

<blockquote>The relations of Ireland, Portugal and Turkey to England illustrate what we mean. See next chapter. England's very best customers are the Protectionist nations.</blockquote>

§ 238. The numbers and the prosperity of our own trading class that are engaged in foreign commerce show that the protective policy has not extinguished that occupation. They show likewise that the profits of manufacture under protection are not so great as to cause an excessive diversion of capital in that direction.

If we were to listen, indeed, to the complaints of some of this class, we should infer in them either a great want of common sense, or a sublime disregard of their own interests. They complain, without courting any comparison of their ledgers, that the profits of the manufacturing class are inordinately great,—that two or three hundred *per cent. per annum* are reached in this or that line of production. Then, why not leave importing and go to manufacturing? Oh, they are too moral! "Those who believe that a legal monopoly is a system of robbery protest against it on principle, and do not want to share its ill-got gains" (*Evening Post*). Or if this be incredible there is another reason. "The profits are so precarious that before the year is up we may lose everything by a reduction of the tariff" (*Ibidem*). There would be very little danger of a reduction were it not for the zealous warfare that these gentlemen wage upon the tariff. If our manufactures are an unsafe investment, it is they who make them so. In doing so they not only keep those profits up, if they are high, by checking the flow of capital in that direction, but make those (supposed) high profits right and reasonable, as covering not only a fair return for the invested capital but a fair insurance for the risk thus created.

§ 239. Fourthly, and especially, the restrictive policy fosters and encourages the growth of manufactures, and is often the only way to create a varied industry in a new or a poor country that does not possess it.

In imposing a protective duty upon the products of foreign manufacture, the aim is not dearness or scarcity, but the reverse. Prohibitory duties or the legal monopoly of a manufacture by a few persons might produce a scarcity; but protective duties operate in exactly the contrary direction.

If dearness—and we measure that by the labor-cost always— were to be the result, and even the permanent result of such a policy, it might yet be vindicated as a wise measure, for all the reasons we have already specified,—reasons that relate to the economy of labor, of agriculture, and of commerce.

But a rise in price can be but a temporary result of the protective duty, while only prohibitory duties can create scarcity. And even if we leave out of view those compensatory advantages that accrue to the community from the first, the temporary sacrifice involved in the temporary increase of price is a measure of wise policy quite in the line of the best statesmanship in other fields of national life.

The establishment of a post office, which in a country like the United States will not pay for itself for centuries to come, is a measure whose wisdom none disputes. It binds the people in one, promotes intelligence, helps the popular education, renders services that far outweigh its cost. Yet a consistent free trader must oppose the measure, as taxing the mass of the people for the benefit of the classes who use the post office; if he defended it, it would be on grounds of indirect benefit that would justify a like sacrifice in the protection of home industry.

Our public school and college system is another instance of this. Consistent free traders, like Herbert Spencer and Gerritt Smith, must oppose the measure. It is taxing all classes for the benefit of one class of "producers," the fathers and mothers;

it is the expenditure of public money for other ends than those of police at home and defence abroad. It can only be justified on the ground that it pays in the long run, and indirectly to all classes, as protection does. And protection itself, as Mr. Mill very forcibly puts it, is a method by which producers are "educated up to the level of those with whom the processes have become habitual."

Not only the education, but the rearing of children, which the Christian state imposes upon the parents by its laws to give perpetuity to the relationship of marriage, and to punish infanticide, is a business involving large sacrifices for an ultimate benefit. Were not the natural affections too strong for logic, we might have zealous advocates of free trade urging men to give up this wasteful business, and import full-grown men and women from Europe, where they are to be had so cheap.

In short, wherever we turn we find the farsightedness that makes the sacrifice, and the nearsightedness that refuses to make it, set over against one another, and the one approved as wisdom by the consent of mankind, which rejects the other as folly.

§ 240. Protection, adopted for these ends, has the sanction of nearly all the great free trade authorities. Adam Smith conceded that, "by means of such regulations, indeed, a manufacture may sometimes be acquired sooner than it could have been otherwise, and after a certain time may be made as cheap or cheaper than in the foreign country." His chief French disciples are Say, Blanqui, Rossi, and Chevalier. *Say* taught that "protection granted with a view to promote the profitable application of labor and capital might be productive of universal benefit. New modes of employment, though destined to result in great advantage when the workmen have been trained and the preliminary obstacles surmounted, were liable, without the aid of government, to cause heavy loss to the undertaker—a result carefully to be avoided." *Blanqui* writes that "experience has already taught us that a people ought never to deliver over to the chances of foreign trade the fate of its manufactures." *Rossi* declared that "in the conduct of a nation," as in that of a family, sacrifices needed to be made in the hope of thereby opening " new roads to affluence." *Chevalier* declares that " every nation owes to itself to seek the establishment of diversification in the pursuits of its people, as Germany and England have already done in regard to cottons and woollens, and as France herself has done in reference to so many and so widely different departments of industry;" that this " is not an abuse of power on the part of the government; on the contrary, it is the accomplishment of a positive duty which required it so to act at each epoch in the progress of a nation as to favor the taking possession of all the branches of industry whose acquisition is authorized by the nature of things. Governments are, in effect, the personification of nations, and it is required that they should exercise their influence in the direction indicated by the general interest, properly studied and fully appreciated." And in his opinion, " combination of varied effort is not only promotive of general prosperity, but is the one and only condition of national progress."

All these gentlemen belong to the free trade school, especially Chevalier. So does John Stuart Mill, who is of the opinion that " the superiority of one country over another in a branch of industry often arises only from it having begun it sooner. A country which has this skill and experience to acquire may in other respects be better adapted to the production than those earlier in the field; and, besides, it is a just remark that nothing has a greater tendency to produce improvement in any branch of production than its trial under a new set of conditions. But it cannot be expected that individuals should at their own risk, or rather to their certain loss, introduce a new manufacture and bear the burthen of carrying it on until the producers have been educated up to the level of those with whom the processes have become traditional. A protecting duty continued for a reasonable time will sometimes be the least inconvenient mode in which a country can tax itself for the support of such an experiment."

Mr. Geo. W. Smalley (of *The N. Y. Tribune*) asked Mr. Mill during his later years, " whether he still adhered to this statement?" " Certainly," was his answer; "I have never affirmed anything to the contrary. I do not presume to say that the United States may not find protection expedient in their present state of development. I do not even say that if I were an American I should not be a protectionist."

If there be any doubt as to the practical bearing of these concessions, especially the last, it is dispelled by Prof. Thorold Rogers : " Few statements made by any writer have, I am persuaded, been more extensively, though unintentionally, mischievous than this admission of Mr. Mill. The passage has been quoted over and over again in the United States, and in the British colonies, as a justification of the financial system which these communities have adopted. The circumstances in which they are situated exactly square with the hypothesis of Mr. Mill. The countries are young and rising,—industries, as yet nascent, are thoroughly suited to the natural capacity of the region and of the people; the latter being of the same stock with the mother country whose manufactures they prohibit and discourage. There is no reason, apparently, except that of priority in the market, why the industry of the old country should not be transplanted to the new. Hence, I repeat, Mr. Mill's concession is perpetually quoted, and is perpetually mischievous." Protectionists may now cease quoting Mr. Mill, and begin to quote Prof. Thorold Rogers.

§ 241. The object and the effect of protective duties, then, is to enable the home producer to furnish the manufactured goods more plentifully and cheaper than before the duty was imposed. " Though it were true," says Alexander Hamilton, " that the immediate and certain effect of regulations controlling the competition of foreign with domestic fabrics was an increase of price, it is universally true that the contrary is the ultimate effect of every successful manufacture. When a domestic manufacture has attained to perfection, and has engaged in the prosecution of it a competent number of persons, it invariably becomes cheaper. Being free from the heavy charges which attend the importation of foreign commodities, it can be afforded cheaper, and accordingly seldom or never fails to be afforded cheaper in process of time than was the foreign article for which it is the substitute. The internal competition which takes place soon does away everything like monopoly, and by degrees reduces the price of the article to the minimum of a reasonable profit on the capital employed."

So well ascertained and so necessary is this result as regards the profits of manufacture that Prof. Thorold Rogers alleges it as a reason against protection: "Unless the state were to go so far as to grant a monopoly of production to one or a few individuals whom it protects, it could not prevent the operation of that economic law which reduces profits, other things being equal, to an equality. Manufacturers crowd into the protected occupation, and the benefit intended to be secured by the policy of the government is distributed and annihilated by competition." Mr. Rogers does not seem to be aware that this is the very "benefit intended to be secured." But we have his word as to how that policy does and must work,—above all that it involves no monopoly.

"Competition being always free," says McCulloch, "among home producers, the exclusion of any particular species of foreign manufactured goods cannot elevate the profits of those who produce similar articles at home above the common level, and merely attracts as much additional capital to that particular business as may be required to furnish an adequate supply of goods."

> Neither of these two authors, it will be perceived, concedes that prices are brought down by protection to the foreign rate; but they both show that the foolish clamor as to the excessive profits of the protected manufacturer has nothing to go upon. Mr. D. A. Wells flatly contradicts his English teachers when he says: "It not unfrequently happens that the imposition of a tax in the form of a tariff on an imported article is made the occasion for very greatly and unnecessarily advancing the price of a corresponding domestic product."

§ 242. What are the reasons for this final reduction in price? It is because the obstacles to cheap production have been overcome, and the home producers are competing for the home market. These obstacles are manifold. (1) The lack of security deters the manufacturer from putting his capital into a large undertaking. He has to make great outlays, great sacrifices even, but he has no security that he will ever reap the fruits, unless the home market is secured to him. He fears the foreign competition more than that of his competitors at home, because the latter stand on an equality of power and capacity with him, while the former are able and ready to make large sacrifices simply to drive him out of the market and secure it to themselves. It is not a matter as to which we are left in any doubt that artificial fluctuations are produced for this purpose. "It has already been shown," says Coleridge in 1834, "in evidence which is before all the world, that some of our manufacturers have acted upon the accursed principle of deliberately injuring foreign manufacturers, if they can." "Experience," says Blanqui, one of the free trade economists of France, "has already taught us that a people ought never to deliver over to the chances of foreign trade the fate of its manufactures."

A report presented to the British Parliament in 1864 by a commission appointed to investigate the state of industry in the mining districts says:—

"The laboring classes generally in the manufacturing districts of this country, and especially in the iron and coal districts, are very little aware of the extent to which they are often indebted for being employed at all to the immense losses which their employers voluntarily incur in bad times in order to destroy foreign competition, and to gain and keep possession of foreign markets. Authentic instances are well known of employers having, in such times, carried on their works at a loss amounting in the aggregate to £300,000 or £400,000 in the course of three or four years.

"If the efforts of those who encourage the combinations to restrict the amount of labor and to produce strikes were to be successful for any length of time, the great accumulations of capital could no longer be made which enable a few of the most wealthy capitalists to overwhelm all oreign competition in times of great depression, and thus to clear the way for the whole trade to step in when prices revive, and to carry on a great business before foreign capital can again accumulate to such an extent as to be able to establish a competition in prices with any chance of success.

"The great capitals of this country are the great instruments of warfare against the competing capital of foreign countries, and are the most essential instruments now remaining by which our manufacturing supremacy can be maintained; the other elements—cheap labor, abundance of raw materials, means of communication, and skilled labor—being rapidly in process of being equalized."

So much for Tennyson's
> ". . . fair, white-winged peace-maker."

A greater poet had some excuse for making his Faust say :—
> "*Krieg, Handel und Piraterie*
> *Dreieinig sind sie, nicht zu trennen.*"

§ **243.** (2) The inexperience of the laboring class is not to be overcome in a day. Their lack of skill involves difficulties and losses; their industrial education, like all education, is an investment that pays only in the long run. The unprotected manufacturer is a captain of industry who must drill his men under fire, must expect to fight with them from the first day that he enlisted them. Foreign operatives, indeed, can be secured in some branches and for positions that require special skill. The non-commissioned officers of the industrial army may therefore be men of some experience, but the rank and file employed in a new industry are raw recruits. But when once the army has learnt its drill, work becomes as effective as anywhere else, and the labor-cost, and with it the labor-price of production, is as low as elsewhere, and lower at home, as the cost of transportation and the profits of a long string of middlemen are no longer added to the price while the article is on its way from the producer to the consumer.

And the captains of industry themselves need drill and experience as well as their workmen. The processes of a great manufacture are not to be learnt in a day, even if no changes in method are contemplated. But among the great advantages gained in the acclimatization of new industries, not the least is the gain in improved methods when an old industry is tried under a new set of conditions. Many of the most notable labor-saving inventions, beginning with Whitney's cotton-gin, owe their existence to the efforts of those who were engaged in prosecuting new and protected industries. Such has been the history of the sugar manufacture in Europe, which now actually pays duties that discriminate in favor of cane sugar from the West Indies, and yet partly supplies even the English demand The great advances made in the application of chemistry to manufactures, date from the efforts of Napoleon to make the Continent independent of England. Thirty years ago Dr. Wayland entered his protest against the duties that discriminated in favor of home-made cutlery, since "not a thousandth part of the cutlery used is made here." Since then, by the invention of new machines, England is actually surpassed in the production of all but the finest varieties.

*The Spectator* (London) declares that the new manufactures in Bengal will in a few years be strong enough to hold their own against English competition, but that at present, or so long as " coal is dear, *and the habit of manufacture upon the large scale not yet formed*," the removal of high duties would cause them first to languish and then to die out, as the native manufactures of India did half a century ago.

> An English *Trade Circular* of 1871 says: "Every Canadian season affords unmistakable evidence that some additional article in English hardware is being supplanted by the produce of the Northern States, and it is notorious how largely American wares are rivalling those of the mother country in other of our colonial possessions, as well as upon the Continent. The ascendancy of the Protectionist party in the States continues to operate most favorably for the manufacturing interest there, and it is no wonder that, under such benignant auspices, the enterprise in this direction is swelling to colossal proportions."

§ **244.** (3) The complete organization of industry, and the accumulation of the capital that make it possible, are not effected in a day. It is a commonplace of the economists that the products of industry are cheapened by extending the scale of production. Very often a manufacture already existing in the face of unrestricted foreign competition is carried on in a small, feeble and costly way for lack of assurance as to a large demand for it. But as soon as protection gives it that assurance the production is doubled, trebled, quadrupled,—and the price is pulled down to less than the previous selling rates instead of increasing by the amount of the duty imposed. Thus the selling price of American cottons fell after the tariff of 1842 imposed a heavy duty on English cottons, instead of rising. Something of the same sort in the hardware trade was evidenced by an

English circular of that year offering hardware at rates that after paying the new duties would still be a little lower than they had been before. The same was the case with the price of starch, and doubtless with many other articles, which at once began to be made in large quantities instead of small. Mr. Greeley illustrates this by the case of a newspaper; double its circulation, and the publisher can afford a better paper at a less price.

§ 245. Much is often made by the opponents of protection of a case in which the adjustment of duties is exceedingly difficult. It may be desirable to protect both the production of the raw material and of the finished product of an industry. This occurs more frequently elsewhere than in our own country, but the case of the woollen and iron industries brings this within the number of our tariff problems. Our present tariff on wools and woollens was adjusted on a basis agreed to by a joint convention of wool-growers and wool-manufacturers, but it is complained, by a small minority of the latter, that it forces them to pay an exorbitant price for certain grades of foreign wool which they must have to mix with native wool for the production of some classes of goods; and that the protection accorded them by duties on the goods is nullified by the duties on wool. The same complaint is made by some manufacturers who need a large supply of steel and iron, and who say that the steel that they can buy in the American market is inferior, or the iron too dear. These complaints may or may not have foundation in fact, but the true remedy seems to be the higher protection of the manufactured goods, rather than the proposed "removal of duties from articles reproductively consumed." The difficulty will disappear as the production of these raw materials of the manufacture is brought nearer perfection; and no one that believes in protection could consistently seek its solution in the removal of duties.

*In conclusion, a formal answer to a few of the more common objections may not be out of place.*

§ 246. (1) "Protection discriminates against the consumer, in favor of the producer." Who this consumer is, that is neither a producer as well, nor directly dependent upon the prosperity of other people who are producers, is hard to say. His name and the mysteriousness of his character would seem to indicate that he is the Devil. But most likely he is an innocent *ens logicum*, manufactured by the same process of abstraction by which the economists devised their economical man—"a covetous machine, inspired to action only by avarice and the desire of progress." That is, they cut away or stole away (abstracted) the better half of the real being, and persisted in treating the remaining human fragment (if we can call it human) as a living reality. "The consumer" always buys and never sells—has no soul and no patriotism—has no interest but the cheapness of commodities—belongs to none of the classes that make up the industrial state. His sole function in life is to devour the result of other men's labors, but he adds nothing himself to the sum of the utilities that make wealth. There may be a few exceptional persons in the nation that deserve to be called mere consumers—*fruges consumere nati*—but that the national policy is to be for ever directed in accordance with the interests of an insignificant and useless class, is a large assumption. And that their interest lies in the direction of dependence upon the farther producer, instead of the nearer, we have seen reason enough to doubt. "The consumer" must be as short-sighted as he is hard to find, if he thinks it does.

It is said that "the interest of the consumer is the interest of society, while that of the producer is the interest of a class." The interest of the mere consumer is in mere cheapness. His interest must be best secured in a condition of business and industry in which prices are the lowest and the producers are underbidding each other for customers. But that condition is found in what are called hard times. Either such times are a golden age, for whose coming we should pray, or the interest of the mere "consumer" and that of society are not identical.

§ 247. (2) "But it is every one's interest—his money interest, at least—to buy in the cheapest market, and sell in the dearest he has access to." Suppose that his buying in the cheapest market makes the difference of his having no dearest market to sell in, but only a cheapest market for that purpose also. Then manifestly his interest is found, if he have anything to sell, be it sweat of brow or of brain, be it wares or provisions, in the comparative rates of the two markets. Free trade simply forces him—forces all the producers in the country—to buy in the markets that now exist, be they good or bad, without giving them either right or power to create a new and a better market than any that exists.

The sole interest of a man is not in the spending the money he has now in his pocket, be it great or small. A larger interest for him is the getting more to replace it. And then the interest of those who have empty pockets, of the unemployed laborers of a country, runs still more strongly in the same direction. Terence could buy " as much for a shilling in Ireland as he can here for a dollar." Why then didn't he stay there? Because he " couldn't get the shilling," and he can compass the dollar.

It is not, then, anybody's interest to buy in the cheapest and sell in the dearest of existing markets, if by that operation he leaves himself, in the long run, without much or anything to buy with. Least of all is it the interest of a nation, which has the power to create for itself markets in which the relative cheapness and dearness is really in favor of all classes of buyers and sellers.

§ 248. (3) "Every country has its own natural advantages, from which Providence meant the rest to derive benefit. Each country should do the things that are easiest. Free trade proposes that they shall do so—Protection that they shall not. It is, therefore, a setting aside the course of nature; it is introducing an unnatural system of exclusion."

Every country has its own natural advantages, from which Providence evidently meant its own people to derive benefit. To that end Providence itself gives a certain measure of natural protection in the cost of transportation, &c. Were all the international relations of the people in a natural state, that natural protection would possibly be quite sufficient. But the purely artificial status of those relations, produced by an unnatural national economy of some of them, deprives others, the newer and weaker countries, of the opportunities of natural growth and development. It is the aim of protection merely to remove the obstacles to natural growth.

This natural growth is achieved in the equilibrium of the industries. If one wealthy nation has destroyed that at home, has impoverished her agriculture by driving out of that channel the mass of the population, and is thereby forced to find work for them in manufacturing goods for foreign countries, and food for them in the unequal exchange of those goods for wheat and corn, all her financial power is at once exerted in the direction of destroying or hindering the growth of the equilibrium of the industries elsewhere. That she may manufacture for the rest of the world, the rest of the world must confine itself to raising food and raw materials for her.

Is it "natural" that any nation should keep its farms on one continent and its workshops on another? Is it "natural" that cotton, on its way from the grower to the wearer, should go half-way round the globe and back again? Is it "natural" that a large part of the race should be employed in carrying bulky articles—raw materials and coarse goods—from some countries to others in the same climate and of the same general capacity? Is it "natural" that a country with millions of tons of iron on the surface of her soil, and square miles of good coal not far below it, and most of her labor running to waste for lack of employment, should send for railroad iron thousands upon thousands of miles? (See § 282.) Is it not a most unnatural and artificial system? Or is there no test of what is "natural" in this connection, except present cheapness in money price?

Protection is natural resistance to an unnatural state of things. If to the superficial eye it wear the appearance of artificiality, it shares in the reproach of many a just war, which, although defensive in reality, wore the appearance of being offensive.

**§ 249.** (4) "Protection can change the direction of capital, but does not add to its amount or efficiency. It can only divert it from more to less remunerative channels, without in the least adding to its power to employ and fertilize labor, or increase the national wealth."

This argument has been partly refuted in the exhibition of the effects of a varied industry upon labor. Its chief author, Adam Smith, gives us its refutation in another direction, when he calls attention to the greater rapidity of movement of a capital employed in a home manufacture than a foreign trade, a consideration that has great weight when a country of limited capital is under discussion. We have also seen that the capital that is wastefully and feebly employed in a native manufacture under free trade, becomes far more efficient when a protective duty gives it a larger market. Far less than double capital will do quadruple the work, when the demand is quadrupled.

But the chief answer is that capital grows steadily under a nationalist policy, and declines as steadily in its absence. For capital grows as the power of association is increased, and the social circulation is accelerated; declines with the decline of either. Men can save only when they have plenty of work, and that work is remunerative. A nation that leaves its labor largely unemployed is unable to make those accumulations of the results of past labor that we call capital. A nation that secures its people as much and as varied industry of a productive and remunerative kind as the case permits, is on the road to wealth. In the latter case the results of labor are more evenly distributed than in the former; they are represented by the houses owned by well-paid workmen; the accounts kept at the saving's banks; the possession of better furniture; the better education of the children. In the former the gains effected gather into the possession of a few men of great fortune; they make a greater display, but the mass of the population are in penury.

Even if this objection were true in the sense in which it is meant, the advantage of protection would be great. To direct a part of the capital out of the channels in which alone it would earn a return under free trade,—the channels of money-lending, land speculation, transportation and agriculture—would prove a great gain to all classes, by increasing the rapidity of commerce at home, by diversifying industry, and adding to the mutual helpfulness and interdependence of the people. For a new country, in the present state of the world's industry, the question is not between this manufacture and that; not between "manufactures suited to the character of the country, and therefore remunerative," and others that "must be carried on at a loss." It is substantially between agriculture associated only with a few of the rudest industries that supply its direct wants, and the equilibrium of the industries, in which manufactures hold their due place. Under all these smooth sayings lies this harsh alternative, which is carefully hid away from the popular sight by round words.

§ 250. (5) "Protection does not protect." This paradox bears two senses: 1. "Production does not increase prices, and, therefore, does not stimulate home production. Look," we are told, "at its effect on copper. A heavy duty was imposed, and the effect was that the article reached figures so low that several mines had to stop, and its price at home is more governed by the prices that it brings in the foreign market than ever before." This is quite true, and yet the aim of the protective duty was accomplished. The American producer was secured control of the home market; if he went into over-production he made a mistake from which no national policy or legislation could save him. That he began to export pig copper, and thus to make himself dependent upon the foreign market, is not the fault of the tariff. He merely repeated what has been pointed out as the great mistake made by the farming interest. Meantime, what becomes of the theory that protective duties add just their amount to the price at home?

2. It is also said to mean: "Protection makes production so expensive that the home manufacturer is shut out from competing in the foreign market. The amount of our exports declines, and the national wealth is diminished."

In 1860 the value of our export of manufactures was $42,100,000. In 1881 it was $77,300,000, or including all manufactured foods, $165,874,000. But even if it were much less than this proportion, we should have every reason to be satisfied. The chief problem for the country is to secure such an equilibrium of our industries as shall employ as many of our people as possible in serving each other, and thus diminish our dependence upon foreign products. The growth of domestic commerce under the protective policy far more than compensates for any loss it might have inflicted as regards commerce with foreign countries. And a manufacturing system which has the patronage of fifty millions of people can afford to dispense with a good deal of foreign custom.

It is quite true that America will obtain a very large share of the world's commerce in the not distant future. Her share in it now would have been much greater than it is if she had adopted the policy of subsidizing steamship lines, by which the English producer has been brought near to every foreign market, and has been enabled to send his goods abroad at less than the real cost of transportation. The quality of our exports of manufactures is what has made for them the foreign demand which does exist. We make more honest cottons, more ingenious and serviceable tools, and better adjusted machinery than our rivals. Had we followed the free-trade principle, which exalts mere cheapness above everything else, we should not have effected these gains.

But it must be borne in mind that the amount of its exports is no safe criterion of the general prosperity of a country. That notion originated in countries that have made themselves dependent upon the vicissitudes of foreign trade. If we export less because we have the power to consume more at home so much the better. This must certainly be true of the United States under the present tariff. The manufactures of the country have vastly increased, and if we send less of their products abroad, it must be because we have grown wealthier as a nation and individually—able to command the use of more commodities.

§ 251. (6) "Protection discriminates against the poorer and more thinly settled districts of the nation in favor of the older and the richer states." We have partly answered this in showing that it did not discriminate against the farmer.

The tariff is no more designed for the East than for the West. Even if it had only the effect of bringing the Western farmer's market to buy and sell from across the Atlantic to our own seaboard, the West would have saved that much—the tax of transportation across the sea, the uncertainty of foreign demand, &c. The only industry that the West could cultivate without the tariff is the raising large quantities of wheat, to be sold in London or Liverpool at $1.40 per bushel put down, after paying railroads, grain-dealers, shipowners, and the like.

But the official figures show that the West is benefiting by the tariff even more than the East. While the increase in the entire value of our manufactures between 1860 and 1870 was 128 per cent, in the seven principal Western States it was over 400 per cent., and the increase in all the Southern States also outran the national average, in spite of the vast destruction of property and the prolonged suspension of industry there during the war.

These facts are sufficient for our purpose here, but to the advocates of the Nationalist policy they are not satisfactory. The South and West might have done far better than this; would have done so were it not for the wide dissemination of the notion that the tariff is a law for the benefit of Eastern and Northern manufacturers. Even in regard to material interests imagination governs men greatly. The West and South are both awakening to this fact. Georgia is ambitious of becoming the centre of the cotton manufacture, and Chicago and Minneapolis are destined to become two of the greatest manufacturing centres of the world.

> My old classmate, the postmaster of Charlotte, N. C., tells me that he found the people of his neighborhood so completely possessed with this prejudice, that he could hardly induce them to begin manufacturing their own cotton instead of exporting it. By taking advantage of every occasion, public or private, he at last persuaded them to organize companies

to start spinning-mills and weaving-factories, so as to find a local investment for their little savings. The result has been that employment has been found for large numbers who would otherwise have remained idle; the water-power that was running to waste has been utilized; profits larger than those of the Northern manufacturer have been realized; the price of cottons in the neighborhood has been reduced, and the general well-being of society generally promoted.

**§ 252.** (7) " The doctrine of protection leads on logically to the platform of the Communists. It teaches the people that it is the business of the state to provide for the prosperity and employment of the people. The next step is to assert that the people have a right to employment, and that if the competition of individual capitalists fail to furnish them with that, the state must step in to establish national workshops for the benefit of those who are out of work. From this, to the monopoly of all industry, and consequently of all property by the state, is an easy descent."

<blockquote>
*The Nation* (April 9th, 1874) speaks of "European socialism, the seeds of which were naturally found in Continental centralization, and were brought to this country in the protective system."
</blockquote>

Protection cordially accepts the existing order of society, the present distribution of wealth and the lawful freedom of individual action, as right and proper. Its chief advocates (Thiers, &c.) have been zealous opponents of Communistic socialism, and the ablest defenders of the rights of property. While it asserts that the industrial growth and welfare of the people must be among the first cares of the statesman, it does not teach—what all experience refutes, that this can be attained through the direct action of the state as the employer and organizer of labor in general, while it with consistency accords the state a monopoly of a few departments, such as the post-office.

That the protectionist principle bears some resemblance to the false positions of the Communists, or can be made to do so in clever but hostile statements, we do not care to deny. It contains the truth of which communism is the counterfeit falsehood,—the truth that it is the duty of the state to " promote the general welfare." It thus furnishes the best refutation of communism, for error is never defeated and put to rest by bare contradictions, but by the statement of the truth that lies nearest to them, or even involved in them, and that gives them what vitality they have. If the assertion of that duty leads on to communism there is unhappily no escape for the American nation; the country stands already committed to it by the preamble to the United States Constitution. That that preamble pointed to a protectionist policy is clear from the expressions of popular feeling while the Constitution was under discussion, and from the legislation adopted by the first Congress under the new government.

Throughout the earlier chapters we have seen two great contrasted theories of the nature and effects of social progress under the existing constitution of society. The one declares that the world under the freedom of individual action is drifting steadily toward distress and misery; that whatever progress is achieved enures only to the benefit of the few, and rather detracts from than adds to the well-being of the many; that it is in the interests of the rich to keep the wages of the poor as low as possible so long as free competition is the law and rule of industry. Whoever holds with this teaching must vibrate between the theory of state passivity or free trade, and that of the renovation of society by the destruction of the existing rights of property and methods of distribution. He will incline to the former whenever he is least hopeful of the future of society, or least alive to its miseries. He will favor the other whenever he is awake to those miseries, but confident that they are not the necessary lot of mankind.

The other body of teaching declares that power and freedom go hand in hand in the world's progress; that except by artificial interference every gain for man in power over nature is a gain for all; that wealth naturally tends to an equable distribution among all classes; that the interest of the capitalist is to pay well those whom he employs so as to develop their power to the uttermost; that labor continually and naturally grows in power over all the accumulations of past labor that we call capital. If the latter teaching be likely to lead some of the *thoughtless* into communism or socialism, is it not far more likely that the former will lead thither those of the *thoughtful* who are not able to think their way out of these doctrines?

And we are not left to conjecture here. Mr. Mill is certainly, after Adam Smith, the most distinguished writer of the Free Trade School; in his *Autobiography* he discloses the fact that his hearty acceptance of the doctrines of Malthus, Ricardo and his own father, had led him to such gloomy conclusions as to the results of the existing organization of society and its distribution of property, that he had come to the conclusion that it would be a change for the better were some modification of socialism to be substituted so as to put a limit to the great and growing inequality of wealth and extension of poverty that he saw around him. He also tells us, what is the fact, that Bastiat adopted in part the views of the Nationalist school in order the better to fight the Communists who attack landed property. What Schultze-Delitzsch and his opponent Lassalle have to say on this question has already been told (§ 114).

## CHAPTER TWELFTH.

### The Science and Economy of Manufactures.—The Practice.

§ 253. The theory and the practice of national economy, as already remarked, (§ 6), do not always go hand in hand. The theory in some cases is much better than the practice; men see and approve the better course and follow the worse. In other cases it is worse than the practice, or lags behind it. In all the more necessary and practical affairs of life, men are not left dependent upon the possession of correct theories. They do instinctively the right thing, having no conscious reason, or only a bad one; and after their practice has been repeatedly subjected to the censures or the mockery of shallow theorists, it is at last vindicated by the riper judgment and clearer insight of wiser men.

It is, therefore, a mistake to suppose that the practice of national economy at a time when correct or current theories of the subject had not yet begun to be formed, is unworthy of our study. Men "builded wiser than they knew" in many things; the great and wholesome instincts that grew out of the national life into which they were born, and from which their own life derived half its value, led them aright where they had no theory; and only shallow *doctrinaires* would depreciate the results as having no right to exist, because not attained logically.

§ 254. The ancient writers on political philosophy confined their attention chiefly to the jural state. But the actual rulers had a clear notion of economic policy. Boeckh has shown (as against Heeren) that Athens took measures to protect home industry, to develop its various forms, and to make the state independent of its rivals for the necessaries of life. The low conceptions of political morality that prevailed, allowed of the use of means to this end which are not capable of vindication. If an ally of Athens had corn to sell, it must be brought to the port of

Athens (the Piræos), and a certain proportion must be sold for use in the city itself, and at a fixed price, before any could be disposed of at competition prices to the merchants of other cities. The effect of these measures was limited by the nature of the political constitution of Greece. In this as in other matters every city legislated for itself; nothing was done to benefit Greece as a whole, and to bring her different divisions into the close and friendly relations of mutual helpfulness. Even the structure of the country forbade this; it was easier and cheaper to feed Athens with corn from the Chersonesus than to carry food over the mountain passes from Bœotia. That the country never became an industrial whole, is connected with the fact that it was never a political unit. It fell into subjection through the weakness of its social constitution.

Rome also adopted a Protectionist or Nationalist policy in earlier times, when she was still a people among the peoples. Already she was a great industrial city, competing with Carthage for the commercial preëminence of the Mediterranean. When she became an empire, the enemy and the destroyer of nationalities, she of course abandoned that policy.

§ 255. In the middle ages industry was in the hands of chartered guilds, and was a matter of privilege and prescription. The states that awoke to the importance of the industrial life of the community all took measures to protect and cherish local industries. In Italy the great prosperity of Venice was largely owing to the care with which she protected all the interests of her merchant princes, and the rival cities of the mainland followed hard in her footsteps.

Charles V., of Spain and Germany, studied the maxims and methods of Venetian policy, and adopted them in Spain. But when the industries of his kingdom sprang into life, he loaded them down with oppressive and vexatious burdens, in order to raise money for his wars. The *alcavala* imposed a tax upon every transaction, the intercourse between the provinces was put under a heavy tariff of duties, and the right to collect these was farmed to individuals who were often foreigners. Every wise maxim was set at nought, and the country languished in ever-deepening poverty.

§ 256. In France, the leading statesmen had learnt the same lesson from the Italian cities, but to better purpose. Sully, indeed (anticipating the *Economistes* of the last century), wished to promote agriculture alone, and regarded manufactures as promoting luxury and waste. But France owes to the care and patronage of his wiser master, Henry IV., the transfer of the growth and manufacture of silk from Italy to her own soil.

Colbert, the greatest statesman of the reign of Louis XIV., was recommended to the confidence of that monarch by the Cardinal Mazarin as his last act. The King " might with truth and justice say that, in giving him Colbert, God had done much for the prosperity and glory of his reign. France might add that she owes to his wise counsels the wonderful development of her industry" (Thierry). His "spirit has apparently never ceased to influence the councils of his country" (Dr Travers Twiss, in 1847). He found the finances in a ruinous state, and that the industrial interests of the country had been sadly neglected during the period of confusion that had elapsed since the death of Henry IV. As Adam Smith says, he combined great integrity and great clearness of intellect, with the habits of a laborious man of business. His weakness was undoubtedly his too great faith in the virtues of legislative interference. He did not know when to stop. He found the frontiers of the provinces lined with custom-houses for the collection of unnatural duties upon domestic commerce, and these he wisely transferred to the frontiers of the nation. He developed the French marine by a system of bounties. He removed excessive burdens from the shoulders of the agricultural class, and then did them more than equal harm by prohibiting the export of wheat. In 1664 he had enacted his great tariff law, by which duties were taken off exports, and imposed upon manufactured goods imported from other countries. That the effect was "the prodigious development of France under the encouragement which it afforded them" (Blanqui) is admitted even by the Free Traders, who deplore the means he adopted. Those light and graceful fabrics, in whose production the skill and nice taste of this Celtic people find exercise, were naturalized in France by Colbert; without him, as Irish history shows, these national gifts might have lain idle. "France," says J. B. Say, "at present contains the most beautiful manufactures of silk and wool in the world, and is probably indebted for them to the wise encouragement of Colbert's administration." Some English writers urge, indeed, "that France showed signs of revived prosperity and augmented wealth under the administration of Colbert, was to be attributed to the re-establishment of order in the finances of the country, and the removal of various obstacles which impeded the operation of certain branches of industry" (Twiss). It is certain that France was a richer and more prosperous country than at any previous period, partly in spite of the meddlesome trifling of the regulations which Colbert imposed upon the industries he had called into existence. The man could put no restraint upon his wonderful gift for arranging details; he irritated the French merchants till they told him that what they chiefly asked of him was to "let them alone" (*Laissez faire*); and one of them declared that Colbert, after getting the coach out of the slough on one side, had tumbled it back again on the other.

France did not long reap the benefits that Colbert's system conferred. Louis XIV. had no sense of the importance of industry. He wrote to Charles II.: "If the English are satisfied to be the merchants of the world, and leave me to conquer it, the matter can easily be arranged. Of the commerce of the globe, three parts to England and one part to France." He, therefore, wasted the national wealth in unsuccessful wars, and generally bought peace by granting treaties which pledged him to remove duties from foreign manufactures. That of Nimeguen, in 1713, completed the work of destroying the protective system. Colbert died of a broken heart in 1683, amidst general distress; two years later a still more deadly blow was struck at French industry at home; the edict of Nantes (1598), by which the Huguenots received full toleration, was revoked (1685), and half a million of the most industrious and intelligent class of French manufacturers and tradesmen were driven into England, Holland and Germany. "They carried with them the skill and intelligence, and the secrets of trade that made France great, and many of the most important industries of England, especially, are traced back to those expatriated Frenchmen." "They are at this time improving the manufactures of your majesty's enemies," pleaded Colbert against the measures of intolerance undertaken even during his lifetime; he himself afforded them all the protection in his power. No greater service could be rendered to the Protestant cause outside France than was rendered by the intolerance of Louis XIV.; it laid the foundation of the industrial, and, consequently, of the political predominance of the Reformed nations, by supplying just the element that their manufacturing methods most lacked. The reign that opened with such bright promise in 1661, closes in 1715 with a universal depression of every material interest of France.

The history of the financial policy of France between this period and the accession of Turgot, in 1783, is a story of makeshift and extravagance, in which the Law episode is merely the most fantastic passage. Turgot was theoretically a free trader of the school of the *Economistes*; but he seems to have shrunk instinctively from any steps to realize these views, while he took the boldest measures to destroy monopolies and to release labor from traditional shackles of all sorts. His successors in 1786 negotiated a treaty with England, by which France was flooded with English goods, and in two years the manufacturing industries of France were almost annihilated. Distress became so universal that the government was forced to call the States-General, and the Revolution—whose first and loudest cry was "Give us bread!"—began.

§ 257. Napoleon restored the policy of Colbert. He united all Central Europe into one vast empire, with perfect freedom of trade between all its divisions, and in so far allowed the devel oped industry of one part to cramp the development of that of another, knowing that France chiefly profited by this. But he shut out from the Continent the manufactures of the power that had long kept all the rest in industrial subordination, and everywhere throughout Europe manufactures began to spring up again. He had as little liking for English doctrines as for English goods. In 1803 he forbade J. B. Say to publish in France the work in which he had systematized the views and theories of Adam Smith. He said: "If an empire were made of adamant, political economy would grind it to powder." But he had thoughts of his own on the subject. "Formerly there was only one kind of property, land; another has now arisen, industry." He would defend the one as well as the other from invasion by "the nation of shopkeepers."

England had control of the seas, and Europe drew her supply of sugar mainly from the British colonies. Prussian chemists had been making experiments on the extraction of sugar from the beet, under the patronage of Frederick the Great, who was like Napoleon a very decided protectionist. At the Prussian king's death, the experiments ceased for lack of means to carry them on. They were again resumed under Napoleon, and the French Institute appointed a commission to look into the matter. The first attempts were failures, and France went on for years paying fifty cents a pound for foreign sugar. In 1810, the matter was taken up again under imperial patronage; special schools of chemistry were founded, and a large area of land was devoted to the culture, and in 1812 nearly 5,000,000 pounds of beet sugar was in the market. The industry survived the Restoration, for the Bourbons did not bring back permanent free trade. "For thirty years nearly every law passed on customhouse matters has been intended either to establish or to consolidate the system of protection and prohibition" (J. B. Say, 1826). Beet sugar now holds its own against the foreign competitor, and pays a tax to the government. It occupies an ever-increasing area of Flemish, German, Swedish, Polish, Russian and French soil,—millions of acres of the last. Its production has invigorated other industries, especially agriculture; the refuse pulp furnishes an excellent food for vast numbers of cattle, and their manure, with the other refuse of the factories, has added greatly to the fertility of the soil. No district produces less wheat, for having begun beet culture; generally more. It furnishes winter work, and work for women and children, giving employment to a great number of persons, who would else be idle. The *Journal des Fabricants de Sucre* for January 4th 1866, says: "One of the most remarkable and interesting facts of the past year is the export of considerable quantities of sugar from France to England, a country that, not many years ago, tried to stifle the beet sugar industry in its cradle."

§ 258. Under all changes of government, France clung to the commercial policy of Colbert and Napoleon, down to our own times. That she advanced most rapidly in the development of every material interest, is as clearly proved by the official returns to the government as anything well can be. Between 1820 and 1857 the growth of wheat rose from 5.4 to 6.8 bushels per head of the people, so that she feeds all her people, and has food to spare, though her population is nearly three times as dense as that of Pennsylvania. Between 1836 and 1856 the value of her exports increased 131 per cent., though the population had not increased five per cent. The increase in the value of British exports for the same period was 120 per cent.; and the amount of these that were paid for in imports was fully one-half, while that of France was not more than a fifth.

In 1860 the superior person who had made himself Emperor of the French, and afterwards unmade himself, set aside all the traditions of French finance and negotiated a commercial treaty with England, providing for a reduction of import duties on both sides. The English free traders; Cobden, Gladstone, &c., who were engaged in the negotiation, set at nought the traditional maxims of the school. "We want trade," said Mr. Ricardo, "not treaties of commerce; for they are opposed to our principles." The great body of the French people, especially the opponents of Napoleonic personal government, opposed the treaty and its principles most strenuously; but English liberals elaborated it in secret conferences with the agents of the French empire, and rejoiced when the imperial will forced it upon "the most Protectionist of European lands," as one of Cobden's eulogists says. On the one hand England removed all duties on French manufactures and lowered the excise duties upon French wines and spirits; on the other hand French duties on English manufactures, if more than thirty per cent. *ad valorem*, were to be reduced to that amount at October 1st, 1861, and to twenty-five per cent. three years later. The effect was no doubt to increase very greatly the trade between the two countries; they bought of each other many things that they had been accustomed to make at home, and employed a larger number of people in carrying these articles back and forward, instead of setting them at productive work. Some industries in each country gained at the expense of corresponding interests in the other; they had been doing well, and they did better. Other industries in each were very greatly injured by the change, and numbers of people thrown out of employment. This gain was thought a sufficient off-set among the friends of the treaty. France employed a far larger number of her people in serving foreigners, and made them dependent upon the vicissitudes of the foreign market. Hitherto she had suffered little or nothing from commercial revulsions and panics; from this time they began to affect her money-market and her industries. She lost in the stability of employments, wages and profits. But she lost much less than if she had made the experiment thirty or fifty years earlier; the gains of her long era of consistent and persistent Protection, made her able to sustain the hazard of the new era. She had become a rich country, with abundance of cheap capital, industrial skill, popular intelligence and enterprise. She could afford some competition, and even the imperial charlatan did not design to try unrestricted competition. The duties preserved,—if we consider the stage of skill, industry and capital that France had reached—were really as fully protective as many that have been enacted in our own country with a view to protection. One of the emperor's organs, the *Journal des Débats*, boasted that he had outwitted the English statesmen, and that the thirty per cent. duties would be really protective.

> Our staunch friend, Count Agenor de Gasparin, in his *Un Grand Peuple qui se Relève*, asserts that the French Treaty is actually more prohibitory than the Morrill Tariff of 1861. Yet French manufacturers complained of its terms. Although the duty on iron was $12 a ton, it was said that the production of iron in France was impossible. In 1868 the Chamber of Arts of Roubaix, the leading centre of the wool-combing industry, and the neighboring city of Tourcoing, protested against the renewal of the treaty, and the workingmen petitioned to the same effect. The manufacturers of Lille and Amiens united in the protest, and the *Moniteur Industriel* complained that the treaty "has carried 20,000,000,000 francs to the debtor side of our national credit sheet."

Since the French people obtained the control of their own affairs by the overthrow of the Second Empire, they have revised their general tariff in a protectionist sense. For the treaty of commerce of 1860 they have refused, after negotiations prolonged over years, to substitute any other, unless it were one much less favorable to free intercourse with England. The duties on cottons and woolens were the matters of most difficulty.

§ 259. England owes her industrial greatness to the persistency with which she adhered to the Nationalist policy. Five centuries ago she was little more than an agricultural country. She produced an abundance of excellent wool, but her workshops were on the Continent, among the Flemings, whither English wool was carried to be converted into cloth. "The ribs of all people throughout the world are kept warm by the fleeces of English wool," (Matthew Paris). "Most articles of clothing, excepting such as were produced by ordinary domestic industry, were imported from Flanders, France and Germany. The names of the articles to this day indicate the places where they were manufactured. Thus there was the mechlin lace of Mechlin, the duffle of Duffel, the diaper of Ypres (d'Ypre), the cambric of Cambrai, the arras of Arras, the tulle of Tulle, the damask of Damascus, and the dimity of Damietta. Besides these we imported delf ware from Delph, venetian glass from Venice, cordovan leather from Cordova, and millinery from Milan" (Smiles).

The last term formerly included all sorts of fancy and ladies' wares. Edward III., "the greatest of the Plantagenets," a sovereign of the same class with Frederick and Napoleon, took the first step to bring the nation out of this industrial dependence. Some Flemish workmen had fled into England, and this seems to have suggested to him the idea of importing Flemish skill rather than its products, of bringing the farmer and artisan into neighborhood. An act of Parliament was passed in 1337, forbidding under heavy penalties the exportation of wool and the importation of woollen goods. This heroic remedy probably caused some embarrassment, for the English did not possess the skill to produce the equal of Flemish fabrics; but the Flemings were in worse straits. "Then might have been seen throughout Flanders weavers, fullers, and others living by the woollen manufacture, either begging or under stress of debt tilling the soil." A large number listened to the invitation held out by the English government, and finding themselves cut off from the English market so long as they remained at home, came over into England and brought their trade with them. Old manorial rolls and charters from this time on, contain great numbers of unmistakably Flemish names, especially those that relate to the Eastern shires. As to the exportation of wool, that became a monopoly of the king's exchequer, and added much to the revenue at a time when the kings were much in need of such supplies. England then declined to compete with and began to emulate Flanders; artisan and farmer were brought into proximity, and the price of manufactured goods approximated to that of the raw materials.

> The penalty for a first violation of this law was a fine; for a second, maiming; for a third, imprisonment; for a fourth, death. In 1746 the last was changed to seven years' transportation. In 1334 all were abolished.

From this time woollens were the great English staple. Other branches lay under comparative neglect. Even iron was imported from the Continent for the use of English blacksmiths, and its cost was an important item in the expense of a farm

(§ 77). The coming in of Protestant refugees from the Low Countries and France, which began about 1550, was so extensive that an investigation showed the presence of 40,000 that year in London alone. Queen Elizabeth planted a great number at the then decayed town of Sandwich, describing them as " men of knowledge in sundry handicrafts," such as " the making of says, baize and other cloth, which hath not been used to be made in this our realme of England." Both Norwich and Sandwich were recovered to prosperity by these foreigners. They introduced, besides the spinning and weaving of new fabrics, the art of dyeing, of which the Flemings had preserved the monopoly. " The native population gradually learned to practise the same branches of manufacture; new sources of employment were opened up to them; and in the course of a few years England, instead of depending upon foreigners for its supply of cloth, was not only able to produce sufficient for its own use, but to export the article in considerable quantities abroad " (Smiles). They brought over the manufacture of lace and cutlery. They also put an end to the importation of cabbages, onions, and other vegetables from Holland, by establishing kitchen gardens, first at Sandwich and then at London. In 1621 the 10,000 strangers in London were plying 121 different trades. The unwise intolerance of Continental governments led to these transfers of skill and experience, and pointed out the wisdom of the policy that brings the workshops of a nation home to its own soil, to the neighborhood of its farms. The industrial life of the English people took a great advance; from the uniformity of a single occupation, they rose to that varied industry, which is the mark of a civilized people.

§ 260. Under the Protectorate of Cromwell the foundation of England's merchant marine was laid by the Navigation Acts. The Dutch possessed a monopoly of the carrying trade, which was open to all. Even the produce of the British colonies was brought to England in Dutch bottoms. The new acts prohibited the importation of any but European goods in any but English ships, manned three-fourths by Englishmen. Upon European goods imported in foreign ships, they imposed discriminating duties. A cry went up at once that England was ruined; the goods that must be had from abroad were far more in amount than could be brought by the existing merchant marine, or any that could be procured for years to come. But Cromwell persisted, and by the end of his reign the Navigation Acts were so popular, that the first Parliament that met after the Restoration reënacted them in full at the very opening of its session. They took care, however, to exclude Scotland, which Cromwell had treated as part of England, from their scope. England was a self-sufficient and independent country, more necessary to other countries than other countries were to her. At the date of their repeal she had given up that position; it had become necessary almost to her existence that she should have free access to the markets of the world. The Dutch sought to maintain their supremacy on the seas by force, but the victories of Blake confirmed the legislation of Cromwell.

§ 261. Under the later Stuarts the policy of naturalizing every species of industry was carried out with more or less energy. In 1677 appeared "*England's Improvement by Sea and Land. To Outdo the Dutch without Fighting. To Pay Debts without Moneys. To set at Work all the Poor of England with the Growth of our own Land.* . . By Andrew Yarranton, Gent." The author had taken pains to see how foreign tradesmen turned out the goods that were in such demand; he would have his countrymen come up to them in all things. Let them import the skill of the German and the Dutchman, set up the linen trade and the iron manufacture at home, and improve their woollen staples by getting foreign machines and workmen. From this time the statute book abounds in acts to accomplish these ends, and unforeseen occurrences coöperated with them. The last great persecution of the French Protestants began, and the best skilled laborers of France were flying across her border to find a home among strangers. England, the old refuge of the persecuted, got her full share of them, at least 100,000 skilled artisans. The wares made in England were only plain articles for common use. "The chief manufactures among us at this day are only woollen cloths, woollen stuffs of various sorts, stockings, ribandings, and perhaps some few silk stuffs, and some other small things scarce worth the naming; and those already mentioned are so decayed and adulterated that they are almost out of esteem both at home and abroad" (Fortrey, 1693). "France had long been the leader of fashion, and all the world bought dress and articles of vertu at Paris. Colbert was accustomed to say that the fashions were worth more to France than the mines of Peru were to Spain. Only articles of French manufacture, with a French name, could find purchasers amongst people of fashion in London... So soon as the French artisans settled in London they proceeded to establish and carry on the manufactures which they had practised abroad; and a large portion of the stream of gold which before had flowed into France now flowed into England. They introduced all the manufactures connected with the fashions" (Smiles). The hat trade especially was transferred from France to England, so that the French nobility and even the Roman cardinals had their hats made by the Huguenots at Wandsworth. Every species of woollens, linens, and fine hardware, glass and paper, known to trade was produced on English soil; the silk manufacture, which previous attempts had failed to transfer to England, now took root, and England soon exported large quantities of silk fabrics. To cherish the industry, the duties on imported silks were trebled, and then their importation prohibited. Strange to say, all classes of Englishmen still seem to think there was some gain to the nation in this importation of French skill, and in buying goods at home rather than in sending over the seas for them. The historians of English industry point to this era as one of the turning-points in the development of England's industrial greatness, and justly pride themselves on the fact that it was the readiness with which the nation opened an asylum to the persecuted of all nations that led to the building up her manufactures and the improvement of their processes. On their own principles they should see no difference between making these things at home and buying them in France.

§ 262. In 1771 the iron trade was taken under the protection of the nation, heavy duties on its importation being imposed. About 1787 very great improvements in the method of its manufacture were effected, and from this time English iron was increasingly protected by successive tariffs, till in 1819 the duty was £6 10s. a ton, although for years previous to this English makers had undersold all others in every European market. In 1834 it was reduced to £1 a ton.

But woollens were still the great staple of English manufacture in the 17th and 18th centuries, and every care was taken to protect their makers from foreign competition. In 1678 Indian cotton goods were denounced in petitions to Parliament, as threatening the ruin of the woollen trade. Between 1700 and 1736 their importation *and use* were prohibited; then the law was relaxed to allow the manufacture of mixed woollen and cotton goods; in 1774 the manufacture of cotton goods was legalized, as a thing which "ought to be allowed under proper regulations," among which were provisions to make sure that all that was worn was of British manufacture. When England began this manufacture, India could supply her with cottons at a third the cost of home manufacture, and indeed their import was a chief business of the East India Company. But by strenuous protective measures, she developed the skill of her people, secured the invention of better machinery, made great accumulations of capital. The tariff of 1819 still prohibited the importation of cotton goods made east of the Cape of Good Hope, and imposed 50 to 67 per cent. *ad valorem* duties on those that were made in Europe. She can now carry the cotton of Hindostan and Georgia over land and sea, spin and weave it into stuffs, and then carry it back to undersell the American and the Indian manufacturer, who sees the staple growing under the windows of his factory. Having reached this point she throws off all protective duties and invites the world to imitate her magnanimity.

The manufacture of cottons (coatings), seems to have begun at Manchester about 1640, the material being imported from the Levant. The name occurs much earlier, but really designates woollen fabrics.

One measure of protection to English goods was the prohibition upon the export of machinery for spinning, weaving or printing any sort of fabric; persons who "enticed any artificer to go to foreign parts in order to practise or teach his trade" were liable to severe punishment. As late as 1842, the export of flax machinery was still forbidden.

§ 263. Since the time when the chief American colonies declared and secured their independence, that is within the space of a century, great changes in the industry of the world have taken place. It has been, in another sense than the old phrase meant, "a century of inventions." James Watt devised the condensing steam-engine; Hargreaves the spinning-jenny; Arkwright the spinning-frame and the factory system; Crompton the mule-jenny; Cartwright the power-loom; Whitney the cotton-gin; Fitch the steamship; Oliver Evans the high-pressure engine; Stephenson the locomotive; Morse the telegraph; Howe the sewing-machine. All these and a thousand less-noted inventions have added new arms and legs to capital and endowed the rich with the power to add to their wealth, to make steam and iron do the work of a vast multitude of human hands. No country has profited so vastly by these inventions as England; none has guarded with such jealousy the material interests upon which she now bases her claims to greatness among the nations. On her small area she has gathered machines that do the work of four hundred and fifty million people. Improved means of communication have put her at the door of every other people under heaven. Vast accumulations of capital and the command of money at a low rate of interest, have enabled her to watch the shifts and changes of the market, to destroy hostile competition by temporary sacrifices, and to undersell every foreign manufacturer at will. Yet not until almost our own days has she ever pretended to open her own markets to the competition of other nations, and in very great measure this pretence is only a pretence.

§ 264. We have seen that Napoleon closed the market of Europe against her wares, and shut her out from all parts of the Continent. Even Russia, by the Peace of Tilsit (1807) joined the Continental system. The declaration of war in 1803 by England, when the ink on the peace of Amiens (1802) was "hardly dry" (Talleyrand), was largely due to the commercial jealousy of England. "The emperor," Talleyrand wrote to Fox in 1806, "does not think that this or that article of the Treaty of Amiens has been the cause of the war; he is convinced that the true cause has been the refusal to make a treaty of commerce against the industrial and manufacturing interests of his subjects." But the overthrow of Napoleon, and the release of European nationalities from the imperial yoke, did not bring to England the permanent open market that she expected. France did not for an instant relax her protective system; the Bourbons watered what the Corsican had planted. Germany suffered for a time the misery of a sudden paralysis of her new-born industries, but the rise of the Zollverein put an end to this. Russia and the United States, after a period of Free Trade and industrial depression, both went back to Protection in 1824. Much the same was the course of events all over Europe.

The revolt of the Spanish-American colonies in 1810, and the consequent destruction of the Spanish monopoly of their trade, gave an opening for the export of large quantities of English goods, which was eagerly embraced. The thoughtfulness engendered by free competition was finely illustrated; cities received consignments of Epsom salts sufficient to physic every inhabitant once a day for two or three generations to come; to others, in which ice and snow had never been seen, whole cargoes of skates and pattens were sent. This reckless trading to the supposed Eldorados of the West, had its necessary results in a violent commercial panic.

§ 265. Up to 1832 England was governed by the upper classes, "the landed interest," who had influence enough to return the majority of her House of Commons. By the Reform Bill of that year, such a redistribution of seats was effected, as transferred the power to the middle classes, who were chiefly interested in manufactures. "Since 1832 we have had a systematic course of legislation, in which the wants and the wishes of the middle classes have been carefully attended to, and their interests habitually consulted. But we have seen no signs of the same solicitude with respect to the necessities and interests—certainly not less pressing nor less important—of the working classes."—(*London Morning Post*). This gradually gave a new direction to the industrial policy of the country, and led to changes in the legislation. The old restrictive duties upon foreign manufactures were removed or greatly reduced, in the hope that the example would have the effect of leading other peoples to throw open their markets to British goods. The protection given to British agriculture by the Corn Laws, was removed, in order to secure cheaper food for the English laborer, and keep "the natural and necessary rate of wages" at the lowest point, so that the loom-lords might be able to sustain competition in the price of their fabrics. From this era England has steadily and unceasingly preached the beauties and benefits of unrestricted trade, and professed her repentance for the worse than blunders of her former method, declaring that her own "experience has fully proved the injurious effect of the protective system and the advantage of low duties upon manufactures." (*Government Minute*, 1859). *Homines facile credunt id quod volunt* (Cæsar).

> "Mr. Pitt in 1787 found our customs-law a mass of intricacy and confusion. 'The mode in which he proposed to remedy this great abuse was by abolishing all the duties which now subsisted in this confused and complex manner, and to substitute in their stead one single duty on each article, amounting, as nearly as possible, to the aggregate of all the various subsidies already paid.' Also, 'in some few articles,' for example timber, he meant to introduce 'regulations of greater extent,' but such was the general scope of his arrangement. During the war and during the first years of peace, many augmentations of duty took place, some for purposes of revenue, but with the effect of enhancing the stringency of protection; some for protective purposes alone. The tariff underwent a general revision in 1819, . . . and again under the government of Lord Grey, a large number of minor duties were reduced in 1832 and 1833, but it was in the interval between these two periods that the most important relaxations of the prohibitory and protective system were introduced into the law, first by Mr. Wallace [1823], and afterwards and principally by Mr. Huskisson [1823–27]. Still it continued to contain some prohibitions and a very great number of prohibitory rates of duty; and no approximation to unity of principle was discernible in its structure as a whole. In 1842 it was attempted to make an approach to the following rules:

(1). The removal of prohibitions. (2). The reduction of duties on manufactured articles, and of protective duties generally, to an average of 20 per cent. *ad valorem.* (3). On partially manufactured articles to rates not exceeding 10 per cent. (4). On raw materials to rates not exceeding 5 per cent. The duties were then reduced on about 660 articles." (Gladstone.)

The tariffs of 1845–6 still further reduced duties, leaving those on silk at 15 per cent.; on made-up fabrics of other material, 10 per cent.; not made-up, free. The corn laws were finally repealed in 1849, and the discrimination in favor of colonial sugar abolished in 1851. The tariff of 1853 fixed 10 per cent. as the maximum on all manufactures except silk, and abolished various unproductive duties. It substituted specific for *ad valorem* rates. The French Treaty of 1860 abolished the duties on French manufactures. The chief changes since 1853 have been the removal or reduction of revenue duties on articles in general use,—tea, sugar, and the like. All these tariffs admit the *principle* of discrimination in favor of home industry.

**§ 266.** With the very partial exception of France (§ 258), no continental people has followed English example. "There is no doubt," says *The* (London) *Economist*, "that Free Trade is one of the most unpopular things in practice in the world." It has not enabled England to hold the position of industrial superiority that she once did. "We have now," says a Free Trade authority, "many rivals, where thirty or forty years ago we had none; we formerly supplied nations, which now partially or entirely manufacture for themselves; we formerly had the monopoly of many markets, where we are now met and undersold by young competitors. To several quarters we now send only that portion of their whole demand, which our rivals are at present unable to supply. A far larger proportion of our production now than formerly is exported to distant and unproducing countries, . . . to our own colonies and our remote possessions. More, relatively, is sent to Africa and America, and less to Europe. Countries which we formerly supplied with the finished article, now take from us only the half-finished article or the raw material. Austria meets us in Italy; Switzerland and Germany meet us in America; the United States meet us in Brazil and China. We formerly sent yarn to Russia; we now send cotton-wool; we sent plain and printed calicos to Germany, we now send mainly the yarn for making them. All these countries produce more cheaply than we do,—but as yet they are not producing *enough;* we therefore supplement them . . . Henceforth our manufacturing industry can increase only, not by underselling or successfully competing with our rivals, but by the demand of the world increasing faster than our rivals can supply. This is . . . preëminently the case with our chief manufacture, the cotton." .(*The North British Review,* 1852.) Be it noted that these rivals who now compete on equal terms with England in the markets foreign to both, are nations who first refused to compete with her in their own home markets. They developed under the shelter of protective tariffs the skill and the capital, which have enabled them to *emulate* her as a producing and an exporting nation.

§ **267.** Even in the English home market the competition of foreign manufacturers has been keen and effective. Many minor branches of trade, which cannot secure a voice in Parliament and some sort of indirect protection, have been nearly ruined. For instance, the cheap labor of Norway and Belgium and the access to abundance of timber, have enabled those countries to export doors and window-frames at prices with which English house-carpenters cannot compete, and great numbers of them have been obliged to emigrate. The larger industries have not escaped. The abolition of duties on French manufactures in 1860 simply destroyed the extensive manufactures of silk in Coventry and Macclesfield, and sent hosts of their workmen to the poor-house. The importation of French silks was quadrupled. English statesmen looked on, suppressing all national instincts for the sake of a theory, and exhorted the silk-weavers to improve their machines and processes, or else take to something else. Formerly Coventry and Macclesfield competed with Lyons for the American market. Now the competition is only between the French and the American silks. So in less degree of the iron trade, the paper trade, and even the cotton trade. Thirty Prussian locomotives are running on one English railway, and the massive girders of the new St. Thomas's Hospital, under the very windows of the Houses of Parliament, were forged, framed and fitted in Belgium, after a free and open competition in which a dozen English manufacturers joined. Englishmen ask why is this, and find the answer: The foreign workman outdoes the English in effectiveness, because he is better trained and educated, and the natural organization of labor has been carried almost to perfection. The Continental states do not leave everything to the scramble of free competition; they have no faith in the *Laissez faire* maxim. They make temporary sacrifices, such as the outlay on popular education, both directly to schools and teachers, and indirectly by protective tariffs, and reap benefits manifold.

See an article on "Continental Iron Works Supplying English Markets," copied into *Littell's Living Age* for May 23d, 1868, from *The London Review*. The writer tells this story:

"An English manufacturer met a friend the other day in London. 'What are you doing here?' he said. The other told him in confidence that he was waiting to know the result of a competition for a large quantity of work. 'I fully expect the order,' he said, 'for I have tendered at a price by which we shall lose, merely to keep the works open.' The other asked if he had any objection to exchange figures with him, as all the tenders were in, and he had himself tendered for a Belgian firm. The Englishman named his price. 'You may go home then!' said the other. 'I am fifteen shillings a ton below you, and it will pay our firm very well at that price.'"

In 1874, when the iron trade at home was especially depressed by the sudden cessation of the demand in many parts of the world, following the panic of 1873, the English government sent out a commission to inquire upon what terms and of what quality Belgian iron, especially ship-plates, and bars and sheets used in ship-building, could be imported for the Admiralty. They did so because they found that Belgian iron in general could be had at 10s. to 20s. a ton cheaper in London than English could; and because this particular class of iron was monopolized by a few firms, and cost £10 a ton more than it would in Belgium. On free trade principles, the government was perfectly right. "Buy where you can buy the cheapest," is the first maxim for governments and for peoples, laid down by their English exponents. But there is a difference between "your ox" and "my bull." The English correspondent of an American paper tells us how Englishmen took the news of this commission:—

"So far as I can ascertain little sympathy dwells in the English heart towards the commission. Pecuniary advantages when opposed to national advantages must ever be ousted. And I think, with many others, that the present is a question wherein the former would operate antago nistically towards the latter. If government specifications were distributed exclusively amongst our foreign competitors, they and their workmen would proportionately swell in opulence and manufacturing supremacy in the departments embraced, as ours descended. Further, it is regarded as most significant that a Tory government should have ventured even upon a preliminary investigation of the policy of going out of the country for government iron. We are now thirty years from 1844. What would have been thought of the prophet who should have committed himself to the prophecy that in 1874 Mr. Disraeli would seriously think of buying foreign iron for our own ships of war? To buy foreign bread for our own mouths was considered bad enough, but to buy abroad our very bulwarks would have been thought absolute treason."

§ 268. Will England persist? Possibly she will. Her middle classes, at least, retain their faith in the sacredness, the almost divinity of free competition, and their belief that the sphere and duties of government extend no farther than to keeping each man's hands off his neighbor's throat and pocket. With Mr. Gladstone, they pity the benighted protectionists abroad, as a zealous Christian pities the heathen. " I venture," he says in 1871, "that there is not the prevalence of enlightened views upon the subject that we desire in America; although it has a strong free trade party, yet the prevalence of these opinions is by no means assured. In our own colonies—I say it with deep regret—in our own colonies there are very strong and considerable tendencies towards the establishment of what we call the exploded system of protection. I also must say, and it is with much pain, that the course of affairs in France is very different from that which we wish it to be." They still exult in the consciousness that they, and they alone, have found the key to all industrial problems, and lament the invincible ignorance of political economy that prevails in the United States (*Spectator*, 1874) and other protectionist countries. As this class gives us pretty nearly all the English literature of our days, it is the common impression that there is no dissent from its teachings.

"It would seem as though we free traders had become nearly as bigoted in favor of free trade as our former opponents were in favor of protection. Just as they used to say, 'We are right: Why argue the question?' so now, in the face of the support of protection by all the greatest minds in America, all the first statesmen of the Australians, we tell the New England and the Australian politicians that 'We will not discuss protection with them, because there can be no two minds about it among men of intelligence and education. We will hear no defence of national lunacy,' we say. If, putting aside our prejudices, we consent to argue with an Australian or American protectionist, we find ourselves in difficulties. As far as we in our island are concerned it (*i. e.* free trade) is so manifestly to the pocket interest of almost all of us, and at the same time on account of the minuteness of our territory, that for Britain there can be no danger of a deliberate relapse into protection."—Dilke's *Greater Britain.*

§ 269. But the Reform Bill carried by Mr. Disraeli in 1868, by establishing household suffrage, has effected a second transfer of power in England, to wit: from the middle to the lower classes. The latter gave no hearty support to the great agitation for the abolition of the corn laws. Ebenezer Elliott, the poet of that struggle, wrote in 1849, "It is remarkable that free trade has been carried by the middle classes, not only without the assistance of the working classes, but in spite of their opposition." Senior expressed his fear that if the extension of representative government should increase the power of public opinion over the policy of nations, "commerce may not long be enabled to retain even that degree of freedom which she now enjoys." Chalmers says: "This is a subject on which the popular and philosophic minds are not at all in harmony," and expresses the same fear as Senior does, as to what would result from "the very admission into Parliament of so large an influence from the will of the humbler classes." Kingsley speaks of the artisans of the great cities as "sneering and growling at Mr. Cobden's harangue—'Cheap bread! curse him, he means cheap wages!'"

§ 270. What direction will this new political element, as it gradually makes itself felt in Parliament, give to legislation, especially as regards economical matters? English students of its tendencies say that (1) it will be intensely Nationalist. It will insist on the nation having a foreign policy of its own; it will fight when its blood is up, whether Manchester suffers or not. It will look at matters through English spectacles, not cosmopolitan ones, and trust more to national instincts and impulses than to fine-spun theories. A Parliament, then, that really represented this class would not sit with folded hands and see Macclesfields and Coventrys go to ruin, because somebody had made a book argument about free trade that was thought unanswerable. (2) The theory of government held by this class is very different from the *Laissez faire* notion of the class just above it. It has not been the vigorous, strong, prosperous part of society that chiefly wanted the state to get out of its way. Rather it has been in great need of a helping hand from the constituted authorities. The state (apart from the policeman, to whose functions the "let alone" school would reduce government) has mostly been the workingman's best friend and protector. He has no scruples and no grudges about giving it pretty large scope of action. If any one will make it pretty clear to him that the drift of legislation can help him to more work and better pay, he will look for that help. (3) Being themselves very directly a producing class, they are not so likely to see the axiomatic force of the free trade maxims: "Every man's interest as a consumer is the interest of society; every man's interest as a producer is the interest of a class. Let all legislation be for the good of the consumer, because his interest always represents the interests of society and the good of the whole nation."

The agitation against free trade which began in England among the working classes soon after the American Civil War has spread also to the farming class, under the stress of American competition. It is still confined to a minority, but the minority is growing; and this issue has sufficed to decide several elections of members to the Imperial Parliament. It does not want for representatives among the intellectual classes, and it is admitted that Mr. Cobden's work is now subjected to an amount and degree of criticism which would have been thought quite impossible at the time of his death. The main answer to the protectionists is that they can propose nothing which will furnish any practical solution of the difficulties they complain of. Mere protection will certainly do nothing for England, unless as accompanying measures to restore the English people to the use and enjoyment of the land of England (§ 86). Protection is useful only as it tends to a healthy equilibrium of the industries (§ 33). At the time of the Reformation two to one of the English people were engaged in agriculture. At present the proportion is less than one to three, a sixfold change in three hundred years. For this disaster the "Fair Traders" have no remedy. They propose a system of retaliation, which England cannot afford and her working people would not endure. The land question is everything, and there is needed, not a break-up of the great estates, but a return to small farms.

§ 271. The colonies who form part of the British empire are as slow to adopt the English theory as are industrial nations nearer home. Canada until 1879 imposed a tariff for revenue upon imported manufactures, which fostered a few of her weaker industries, and thus excited unfriendly comment in England. Her policy was sketched as follows by Mr. (now Sir Alexander) Galt, her Finance Minister, in a speech made in England in 1859: "The fiscal policy of Canada has invariably been governed by the amount of revenue required. It is no doubt true that a large and influential party exists who advocate a protective policy; but this policy has not been adopted by either the government or the legislature, although the necessity of increased taxation for the purposes of revenue has to a certain extent compelled action in partial unison with their views, and has caused more attention to be given to the proper adjustment of the duties, so as neither unduly to stimulate nor depress the few branches of manufacture which exist in Canada. . . . The government have no expectation that the moderate duties imposed by Canada can produce any considerable development of manufacturing industry; the utmost that is likely to arise is the establishment of works requiring comparatively unskilled labor, or of those competing with America for the production of goods which can be equally well made in Canada, and which a duty of twenty per cent. will no doubt stimulate." So willing was the Canada of that day to serve as an appendage to the industrial system of England.

Three years later (1862) Mr. Galt assured the Manchester Chamber of Commerce that Canada had no purpose to close its market on them. "The best evidence that could be offered against the charge of Protection was that the effect of the tariff had not been to produce manufactures. The manufactures of Canada were those that might be expected in a new country—nails, steam-engines, coarse woollens, and other articles necessary in a newly settled country. There was not at this moment a single cotton-mill in Canada, nor a silk manufactory. The imports of earthenware and glass, hardware and iron, had gone on increasing every year from 1859 till the present year."

Even this meekness was not enough; he was asked why Canada did not raise her revenue by direct taxation on land and income; these revenue duties had been thrown in their teeth in Europe. It had been said: "Can you expect us to throw off all duties on British goods, when your own colonies tax them fifteen per cent?" He retorted that such questions would come with better grace if England did not raise £28,000,000 a year by customs, and £17,000,000 by excise duties. Direct taxation might be best; but it was also a luxury that a poor and thinly-settled country could not indulge in.

Knowing that a mere passive policy was not sufficient to build up a new country, Canada pursued with zeal and energy the traditional policy of directly aiding immigration from the Old World, instead of attaining the same end indirectly by making the Dominion a place eminently well worth settling in. She used the money raised by taxation to pay the expense of these new-comers; if she had taxed foreign productions at a higher rate, they would have come without her help. But she was "all the time pouring water into a cask with a hole in it. Allowing for great exaggeration in the reported numbers of French-Canadian emigrants to the United States, we fear that for two emigrants whom, with much expense and with great labor, we bring over, we probably lose three. But little account is taken of the emigrants who are lost, because they are mainly withdrawn from manufactures, and agriculture is the government's sole care" (*Canadian Monthly*).

Canada had bought in the cheapest market and sold in the dearest that she could find, with no thought of creating better, nearer and steadier markets than any she could find ready-made. Her wise marketing did not prevent her from being a poor and backward country. She did the easiest thing, and made no sacrifices from the first; had lived from hand to mouth; was wise with her pennies and foolish with her pounds; saved at the spigot and wasted at the bung. And, therefore, the tide of population moved over her border into the United States—away from the land of low taxation and free choice of markets to the land of high taxes and home markets. She could not keep the Europeans who came into her ports with half a mind to stay. Her own people sold land and houses at a sacrifice, and sought a home in New York and New England.

" By describing one side of the frontier," says Lord Durham in a celebrated report, " and reversing the picture, the other would be described. On the American side all is activity and bustle. The forest has been widely cleared; every year numerous settlements are formed, and thousands of farms are created out of the waste; the country is intersected with common roads. . . . . On the British side of the line, with the exception of a few favored spots, where some approach to American prosperity is apparent, all seems waste and desolate. . . . . The ancient city of Montreal, which is naturally the capital of Canada, will not bear the least comparison, in any respect, with Buffalo, which is the creation of yesterday. But it is not in the difference between the large towns that we shall find the best evidence of our inferiority. That painful but most undeniable truth is most manifest in the country districts, through which the line of natural separation passes, for a distance of a thousand miles. There on the side of both the Canadas, and also of New Brunswick and Nova Scotia, a widely-scattered population, poor and apparently unenterprising, though hardy and industrious, separated from each other by tracts of intervening forests, without towns or markets, almost without roads, living in mean houses, drawing little more than a rude subsistence from ill-cultivated land, and seemingly incapable of improving their condition, present the most instructive contrast to their enterprising and thriving neighbors on the American side. . . . . Throughout the frontier, from Amherstburgh to the ocean, the market value of land is much greater on the American than on the British side. In not a few parts this difference amounts to a thousand per cent. . . . . I am positively assured that superior natural fertility belongs to the British side. In Upper Canada, the whole of the great peninsula between Lakes Erie and Huron, comprising nearly half the available land of the province, is generally considered the best grain country of the American continent."

In 1856–1866 we had a treaty of reciprocity with Canada. She admitted free a few of our coarser manufactures, on condition that we should throw open our markets to her agricultural products. When the arrangement was made it was not very unfair, but it became so after the adoption of the protective policy by America in 1861. When the time fixed for its expiry came, America refused to renew it, and has repeated that refusal as often as it has been asked.

A much broader proposal than that for reciprocity has been made on both sides of the border. Canada and America are parts of a great area which seems to be designated by nature for unrestricted intercourse. Each of the three groups of provinces of which the Dominion is composed has closer relations naturally with the adjacent American States than with the other provinces. The customs line which sunders the two countries is excessively costly to both. A customs-union, if effected on the basis of a common protective tariff, with distribution of receipts proportionally to population, would bring Canada into closer relations to the continent to which she belongs naturally, while it would enable both countries to confine their custom-house line to the seashore.

The possibility of such an arrangement has been increased by the adoption of a Canadian protective tariff in 1879. In that year the Tory party, then in opposition, took up this issue at the general election, and, to their own surprise and that of their enemies, secured a working majority in behalf of this national policy. Of course manufactures carried on within so small an area and for the benefit of so small a population as that of Canada cannot be expected to exhibit the rapid and vigorous growth which is seen in those of America. But already the new tariff has done much for the welfare of the Dominion in diversifying her industries, furnishing employment for her surplus labor, and bringing the farmer and the artisan into close and helpful relations.

See Isaac Buchanan, M. P., *On the Industrial Resources of America* (Montreal, 1864), a chaotic compilation edited by Henry J. Morgan. Mr. Buchanan is the leading Protectionist of the Dominion, and belongs to the school of Henry C. Carey. The most original and able writer of the party, known to us, is John Maclean (*Free Trade and Protection*, Montreal, 1868).

§ 272. The Australian colonies have been much more decided and independent than those of British America, a fact largely due to the enterprising, wide-awake character of the population, whom the gold discoveries took thither. They have made fair trial of free trade, which they now scout as "an antipodean doctrine," while protection is their national creed. It commands an ever-increasing majority in the colonial legislatures; it is the avowed principle of "all their first statesmen;" it is especially the doctrine upheld and acted upon by the liberal and progressive party, while the old sheep-farming aristocracy are at once the Conservative and the Free Trade party. The policy of cherishing a varied industry is drawing the colonies closer together, and has led to the first steps towards a Federative Union. All classes but one are full of enthusiasm for the industrial independence of Australia. "No BRITISH GOODS SOLD HERE" is the sign by which an Australian tradesman wooes popularity and custom. Dishonest dealers tear off the British labels from imported goods, and substitute one which marks them as COLONIAL MAKE. This people are straining every nerve to develop a varied industry and bring the farmer and the artisan into neighborhood; they have no idea of keeping up workshops at the antipodes. They "would rather import that which should produce the commodities than the commodities themselves." They want a free trade that will not mean the "monopoly for British manufactures," "and their chief object is to put down monopoly by extending the sphere of competition."

§ 273. "But you are taxing your consumers for the benefit of the producers. As well break all the windows in your houses in order to keep glaziers in work." No proof that a percentage of loss is incurred by protection deters them. "A digger at Ballarat told me that he knew that under a protective tariff he had to pay higher for his jacket and moleskin trousers, but that he preferred to do this, as by so doing he aided in building up in the colonies such trades as the making up of clothes, in which his brother and other men, physically too weak to be diggers, could gain an honest living. . . The Australian diggers and western farmers of America are setting a grand example to the world of self-sacrifice for a national object" (Dilke).

"Australia is but a young country yet, with plenty of available land for settlement; with exuberance of resources, mineral and agricultural; and hitherto not greatly overburdened with population; and that, too, of a class consisting probably of a smaller number of the physically incapable than any other country in the world. Yet for years past the great difficulty has been to find employment for the rising generation. The question of tariffs there has been eminently a social one" (Syme). It is a fact known to the present writer that immigration thither from the North of Ireland was deterred by the reports which came back that fathers of families in very comfortable circumstances had sent their sons to sea in despair of finding work for them. The Australians found that "their youth was growing up in a state of semi-barbarism, without education, without employment, and without hopes for the future," while their country was becoming "a huge sheep-walk."

§ 274. Those who are familiar with the facts of the commercial history of Australia are not so ready to admit that her people are making their own goods at a loss. (1) The Australians are much less at the mercy of speculators than when they depended entirely upon a distant market, and by consequence they are now in so far free from the vast fluctuation in prices produced by "forestalling the market" or "getting up corners." "There is scarcely a commodity imported into Australia but has at one time or another been manipulated in this fashion. The practice is carried on in the most systematic manner. There are individuals there who make it their special study to create an artificial scarcity. No sooner is there the slightest prospect of even the most temporary deficiency in the supply of any commodity, than some one immediately begins to buy up every parcel in the market and every shipment to arrive. Once in possession of the bulk of available stock, he is in a position to demand his own price from the consumers" (Syme).

Hittell's *Resources of California* (p. 333), gives an account of the same system as pursued on the Pacific coast.

(2) Australia, like other countries that did not manufacture, was not ordinarily furnished with goods at the lowest price that her British friends could sell them for, but whenever she tried to begin their manufacture she got them "at a sacrifice." She had tallow in abundance and all the materials to make soap and candles; her people repeatedly undertook to make them, and it was found that they could do so at prices much below the ordinary price of the imported articles. But no sooner was this known in England, than large shipments of soap and candles were thrown upon the market at prices with which the home manufacturer could not compete. One maker after another was crushed by the unequal competition, until the Victoria tariff of 1871 took this industry under protection.

Again, Australia produces maize, while England has to import it. Yet maizena, a well-known preparation from that grain, was imported from England and sold for a shilling a pound. A native firm began its manufacture and sold it at five pence, and afterwards at two pence per pound, but has had a hard fight with foreign competition, and would have been swamped but for the confidence in success that buoyed them up against losses.

Again, Victoria produces vast quantities of very superior wool, yet in 1870 the importation of woollens amounted to £817,087. A factory at Geelong earned a fair dividend and a high reputation by the manufacture of a class of tweeds, which wore well. A Yorkshire firm got a sample of the fabric and made a cheap and inferior imitation of it, with which the colony was soon flooded. The factory would have been closed had not the legislature imposed a protective duty upon all imported cloths, and the colony is now spinning and weaving its own wools at a rate that will soon make it independent of Yorkshire.

These are not the only cases. An old colonist declared at a public meeting in Sydney, that he "had seen a large number of industries perish in this country, not because they had not inherent strength, but because they had been strangled, as it were, by the competition of other countries. . . . Unless a man had a very strong back, he could not bear up against them till he could establish his industry."

See Sir Charles Dilke's *Greater Britain*, but especially "*Restrictions on Trade: From a Colonial Point of View*," by David Syme. Republished Boston, 1873.

§ **275.** Two of England's dependencies—Ireland and India—have had no discretion as to the direction of their economic policy,—no power to set up barriers against the beneficencies of free trade. Both of them have been, throughout the period of their relation to her, relatively inferior in capital and skill, and both have illustrated the result of free competition between nations so situated.

Ireland possesses many natural advantages, but labors under the absence of others. Acre for acre her soil is better than that of England, but her immense rainfall—in some places in the west it rains two hundred days in the year—renders grain-farming gambling. Since the failure of the potato crop, she has been chiefly dependent upon green crops and dairy farming, and she is unsurpassed in both. She has mines of gold, silver, and iron, but very few of coal; a great geological convulsion seems to have stripped her of her coal measures, paring the top from the island and leaving bare the vast limestone plain, intersected with peat bogs, which forms its centre. But English coal can be put down on her seaboard as cheaply as in the south of England; more cheaply than in France. Her vast area of fine pasture land and her peculiar climate, render the wool of her sheep exceptionally fine, and therefore for centuries back in great demand to mix with the coarse wools on the Continent. But her wool is not woven and spun at home; she exports it together with large quantities of food. Her Celtic people are of the same blood with the French across the Channel, and possess the same capacity for the development of fine taste, and the artistic feeling for form and color; but these lie undeveloped while they remain at home. The Irishman only flourishes after being transplanted from his native soil, although he feels for that soil the most passionate attachment. His qualities as a workman, which have been so abundantly useful in our country, lie dormant at home.

§ 276. The spirit in which the English government and people used to deal with Irish industry finds its most striking illustration in the suppression of the woollen manufacture at the close of the seventeenth century. The manufacture of woollens and linens began very early; under Henry VIII. the importation of Irish woollen thread was prohibited. Under Charles I. Wentworth used all his tyrannical energies to suppress the woollen manufacture, and promote that of linen. The overthrow of the King and his party left the Irish free to spin and weave what they would, and not till after the Revolution of 1688 did the complaints of the English manufacturers induce the government to restrict them from producing woollens for the supply of the home market. The English House of Lords (1698) took the initiative, and begged the King to take measures to confine the Irish to the linen trade, as the rapid growth of their woollen trade was drawing English spinners and weavers to Ireland. The House of Commons followed, and the King promised to do what was desired. The Irish Parliament was in no sense a body that represented the nation; they imposed a prohibitory duty on the export of Irish woollens, while the English Parliament prohibited their export save from six Irish to six English ports. Irish industry received a shock from which it never recovered, and even English industry felt the recoil. The wool-workers flocked over into England, and overstocked the labor market, or by competing for the trade, cut down the profits. Others took their skill and industry to the Continent, and contributed to the improvement of the foreign factories. A great part of the people were thrown out of employment, or thrown back upon farming, and the era of rack-rents began. "Upon the determination of all leases made before 1690," says Dean Swift, "a gentleman thinks he has but indifferently improved his estate if he has only doubled his rent roll. Farms are screwed up to a rack-rent—leases granted but for a term of years—tenants tied down to hard conditions, and discouraged from cultivating the land they occupy to the best advantage by the certainty they have of the rent being raised, on the expiration of their lease, proportionably to the improvements they shall make." The value of Ireland as a customer for English goods was very greatly diminished; where once they had bought large quantities of the better wares, they now took only the coarser, and in small amounts. Well might Swift, with savage wit, refuse to respond to the toast, "Ireland's Prosperity," on the ground that he "never drank to memories." "Ireland," he wrote in 1727, "is the only kingdom I ever heard or read of, either in ancient or modern story, which was denied the liberty of exporting their native commodities and manufactures wherever they pleased, except to countries at war with their own prince or state; yet this privilege, by the superiority of mere power, is denied us in the most momentous parts of commerce." With every generation her trade declined, except that in linen, conducted chiefly by the Scotch and English colonists in the three north-eastern counties. These are reams are so richly charged with natural salts that they will bleach without the addition of chemicals. Even this was envied; in 1785 Manchester sent up a petition with 117,000 signatures, asking the prohibition of Irish linens. The implied pledge made to foster the Irish linen trade was never kept; bounties were given to English and Scotch producers only. But the Irish maker held his own, and the annual value of Irish linen is now half that of the rental of the kingdom.

§ 277. This act was but the worst of many conceived in the same spirit. The export of cattle to England in 1663 was prohibited in order to protect the English breeder. The manufacture of glass was put down in the same way as that of woollens. "The easiness of the Irish labor market and the cheapness of provisions still giving us the advantage, even though we had to import our materials, we next made a dash at the silk business, but the silk manufacturer proved as pitiless as the woolstapler. The cotton manufacturer, the sugar refiner, the soap and candle maker (who especially dreaded the abundance of our kelp), and any other trade or interest that thought it worth its while to petition was received by Parliament with the same cordiality, until the most searching scrutiny failed to detect a single vent for the hated industry of Ireland to respire" (Lord Dufferin). The country was forbidden to trade with the East, with the Mediterranean, with the Colonies.

Not till the rising of the Irish Volunteers in 1778, and the consequent concession of the independence of the Irish Parliament in 1783, was the weaker island treated as possessed of any industrial rights that the stronger was bound to respect. From that period till the Union of 1801, Ireland had control of her own industrial policy, and one of the first uses that she made of it was to impose a duty upon the importation of certain English goods which it was felt could be made as well at home. Those eighteen years were a time of rapid industrial growth; Irish manufactures began to show themselves. "There is not a nation on the habitable globe," wrote Lord Clare in 1798, "which has advanced in cultivation and commerce, in agriculture and manufactures, with the same rapidity in the same period." But one of the provisions of the infamous compact which terminated the country's legislative independence, was the gradual removal of these duties. Those on cotton goods were to be removed between 1808 and 1821; those on woollens by the latter date; that on cotton yarn in 1810. As the process went on, the Irish factories closed with the same beautiful regularity. The protected silk, flannel, stocking, blanket and calico manufactures of Ireland are now extinct. By 1840 the woollen manufacturers of Dublin had fallen off from ninety-one to twelve; their workmen from nearly 5000 to about 600; woolcombing and carpet-weaving was almost gone. Six thousand weavers and combers in Cork were reduced to 478 by 1834.

Once again the people were thrown back upon the land; the merciless competition of British capital was as effective as the merciless legislation of the English Parliament; English Free Trade undersold Irish manufactures out of existence, and reduced the Irish people to the uniformity of a single employment. The only field of enterprise left was competition for the possession of a few acres, as the last refuge from starvation. " Some well-meant but vain attempts have been made from time to time to promote manufactures in the country, in the form of what is called an Irish manufacture movement, that is, an agitation to induce a general undertaking or resolution to use articles of Irish manufacture rather than English, without reference to their relative quality or cheapness" (J. N. Murphy). But in vain; because the people had no power to "give effect to their judgment respecting their own interests," all attempts at such concert being ineffectual, "unless it receives the sanction and validity of a law" (Mill). "It is well known that almost all the manufactured articles used in Ireland, save linen, are British or foreign products. There are British and French millinery and silks; British, French, Danish and Hungarian gloves; English soap, candles, ironmongery, hardware and glass; in fact, almost everything in use by rich and poor—all imported and paid for by Irish raw agricultural product"

(Murphy). England has 740 occupations relating to trade, commerce and manufacture; little Scotland 501; Ireland only 261.

§ **278.** "Some human agency must be accountable," says Lord Dufferin, "for the perennial desolation of a lovely and fertile island, watered by the fairest streams, caressed by a clement atmosphere, held in the embraces of a sea whose affluence fills the noblest harbors of the world, and inhabited by a race—valiant, generous, tender—gifted beyond measure with the power of physical endurance, and graced with the liveliest intelligence."

Many are the solutions! 1. "The Irish are an idle, thriftless race," says prejudice. Their record in the colonies and in America, as in England itself, disproves the slander. "We are apt to charge the Irish with laziness," says Swift, "because we seldom find them employed; but then we don't consider that they have nothing to do." "They are priest-ridden, ignorant Catholics," says bigotry. They bring their religion with them to new fields of labor, but it does not prevent their prospering. They are of the same creed as the industrious and prosperous Belgians; of the same race and creed as the French. "They are turbulent; the country is so disturbed by popular outrages, that capital shrinks from Ireland as a field of investment," say the lovers of peace and quiet. It is admitted that Ireland is disturbed because of the poverty and misery of the people. It is a miserable circle, if the effects of their misery are such as to prevent the application of the remedy. Is not the effect put for the cause here?

2. "The misery of Ireland arises from the excess of her population," say the old-fashioned economists. Between the Union and the Famine (§ 66) the rate of increase of population in Ireland was less than in England; since that date there has been a decrease of one-third through emigration, without any corresponding improvement in the condition of the people. Although England consumes over fifty million bushels of grain in the manufacture of liquor, she manages to feed, in ordinary years, two thirds of her population or fourteen and a half mil-

lion people—taking the census of 1868—on the produce of twenty-five and a half million acres of arable land. Belgium on six and a half million acres feeds nearly five million people. Ireland with fifteen and a half million acres of better land than either England or Belgium can show, is overpopulated with a people that number something over five and a half million souls! "But since the famine and emigration brought down the numbers, things are much better in Ireland. Mr. Disraeli, you know, says that the 'famine did more for Ireland than a long succession of statesmen had been able to do.'" The famine and emigration did reduce the population from something like eight millions to the present figures, a decline of 32 per cent. But the best judges pronounce that this reduction has effected no material improvement in the condition of the people, which is improving only where the farmer and the artisan are in neighborhood, and where the farmer sells his crop to his neighbors, *i. e.*, in the three or four north-eastern counties. Everywhere else, the Irishman at home is "selling the hide for sixpence and buying back the tail for a shilling." "The disproportion of the opportunities of employment to population," as Lord Dufferin expresses it, is the real state of the case; not the disproportion of natural resources and land to the population. But this explanation confesses judgment against those who have control of the industries of Ireland. For the rapid and enormous multiplication of any people, if it outrun the development of their industrial resources, is a proof and a consequence of the wretchedness and poverty that first made them reckless and hopeless. It is the well-to-do workman, the one who has a social standing and prospects, that considers his ways.

See § 68, *note*. The only evidence we can find for the assertion of a rapid increase in the population is the fact that the Registrar-General reported an enormous birth-rate in Ireland. But the official figures of the Irish census show that this must have been balanced by a still more enormous death-rate, as indeed is highly probable (§ 71). Yet Mr. Mill gives from Quetelet a table of annual increase which puts the Irish rate far higher than that of England, and indeed th- *als leaat* in Europe.

**§ 279.** 3. " The misery of Ireland arises out of the wretched system of land tenure," say the new-fashioned economists, Mr. Thornton and his disciples; " her people are reduced to tenants at will, they are rack-rented; they have no inducement to improve their land, because the better they make it, the higher the rents will go. They hide their savings from the landlords, and get two per cent. interest on them, instead of putting them into the land. They need security of tenure and compensation for unexhausted improvement. Till they get them, as Mr. Caird says, ' what the ground will yield from year to year, at the least cost of time, labor and money, is taken from it.' " The inference is that the Irish landlords, and the middlemen to whom they let their properties, and who again sublet it to the farmers, have been the vampires who have destroyed Irish prosperity, and driven her people beyond the seas. But where the same land tenure has coëxisted with manufactures the people have prospered; and where the two have not been associated, the landlord has often been broken in fortune as well as the tenant. The commissioners sent out to relieve the sufferers by the famine, found in the Connaught poor-houses men of estate and family, who had served as the High Sheriffs of their counties. One-third the landlords of Ireland were swept away in the common ruin. A very large portion of the land of Ireland has changed hands in late years; £25,000,000 worth in the ten years (1849–1859), during which the Encumbered Estates' Court sat in Dublin. Of the estates thus sold, the ownership was often only nominal; the landlord an unpaid pensioner on his own land. And it is a mistake to suppose that rack-rents are necessarily high, except in relation to the means of the tenant. " The rents of Ireland are comparatively low. This, I believe, is generally admitted, though there are flagrant exceptions; even a rent that is absolutely low, may be beyond the means of an indigent or unskilful tenant" (Lord Dufferin.) They are in fact much lower than farmers with the command of a home market easily pay in other countries; much higher than the Irish farmer can often afford.

After all, what is the charge brought against the Irish landlords and their middlemen? That they acted on the principles of English Political Economy, and sold their commodity in the dearest market they could find. "The moral responsibility of accepting a competition rent is pretty much the same as that of profiting by the market rate of wages. If the first is frequently exorbitant, the latter is as often inadequate, and inadequate wages are as fatal to efficiency as a rack-rent is to production; though each be the result of voluntary adjustment, it is the same abject misery and absence of an alternative which rule the rate of both. . . . The disproportion of the opportunities of employment to population has resulted in universal pressure and universal competition—competition in the labor market; . . . . competition in the land market only to be relieved by the application to more profitable occupations of so much of the productive energies of the nation as may be in excess of the requirements of a perfect agriculture. . . . . How powerfully the development of manufactures in the North of Ireland has contributed to the relief of the agricultural classes of Ulster, by giving the tenant farmer an opportunity of apprenticing some of his sons to business, . . . . and by enabling the cottier tenant to supplement his agricultural earnings with hand-loom weaving, and by a general alleviation of the pressure upon the land, I need not describe. . . . . Had Ireland only been allowed to develop the other innumerable resources at her command, as she has developed the single industry in which she was permitted to embark, the equilibrium between the land and the population dependent upon the land would never have been disturbed, nor would the relations between landlord and tenant have become a subject of anxiety" (Lord Dufferin). But the Irish land laws of 1870 and 1881 both seek to put a limit to the competition for land by legal restriction, rather than to put an end to it by removing its cause—by creating and cherishing a varied industry. They did so with eyes fully open to the source of this unhappy competition. In the debate on the former Bill in the Commons the line of argument adopted by the Government, according to *The Spectator*, was this : " Free contract implies free contractors ; however, partly from historical circumstances but *chiefly from the absence of alternative employments, the poorer tenants of Ireland are not free ;* at least half the adult population are compelled by the coërcion of hunger to. agree to any terms which will secure them the use of the soil. It is because they are not free that a penalty is affixed to capricious eviction,— that a court is to settle the terms on which leases must be granted, that even on the expiring of the lease, good-will is to revive like a plant out of the ground." On reading this, we are obliged to ask : Are there no resources at the command of statesmanship, by which these " alternative employments " could be called into existence, and the Irish problem solved without tampering with vested rights, and recalling into existence that " system of limited, imperfect and half-developed rights, natural only to a low civilization," which all Europe has taken such trouble to be rid of. There is a resource which has always been found fully equal to the occasion, but unfortunately it is called *Protection*. And from the most trusted leaders that the people of Catholic Ireland ever had, a demand for it has been distinctly made.

" What sort of legislation would follow the establishment of a separate Irish Parliament, if any legislation at all, might easily be anticipated, if it were not distinctly foreshadowed in a tentative declaration of some Catholic clergymen, drawn with great ability for its purpose, and assuredly not put forward without the private sanction of higher authority than it claims. It is enough to say it is declared that Political Economy will not do for Ireland, that the Irish manufacturer cannot compete with the English, and that the natural energies of the Irish people must be developed—that is to say, properly speaking, repressed—by Protection and prohibition"—(Cliffe Leslie (*Land Systems of Ireland, England and the Continent*, pp. 35–6.) Mr. Leslie recognises the fact that the absence of manufactures is a chief source of Irish poverty and retrogression. However, he believes that Ireland is not a manufacturing country, because her land tenure laws are so bad that the capitalist cannot secure sites for factories, and he seeks to substantiate this reasoning by adducing some half-dozen cases of hardship. The land tenure is the same in England as in Ireland ; the same in Ulster as in Connaught. It was the same in 1783–1801 as it is now, when no such difficulty as to the sites of factories was experienced.

Did not the Gladstone ministry and their majority in Parliament " declare that Political Economy would not do for Ireland," when they resolved to set aside freedom of contract between landlord and tenant? " If English landlords, millionaires and economists have an economical conviction, it is in favor of freedom of contract. Yet a house led by the greatest of living economists has abandoned it. . . . The Bill does interfere directly with their claim to do as they like with their own. . . . .

Mr. Lowe, when taunted with his old economical arguments, acknowledged that the Bill was not intended to increase wealth, which is the object of Political Economy, but to save society" (*Spectator*).

§ 280. (4) "Ireland is miserable, wretched, unprogressive for lack of capital to undertake the industries that would give her people sufficient employment," says the practical man. Solomon anticipated him when he wrote, "The destruction of the poor is their poverty;" but of what use is it to tell the Irish people that the reason why they are so ill off is because they were not in the past able to lay by for the present, and therefore will not now be able to do so for the future ? "We frequently hear Irish aspirations after English capital; and loud are the popular rejoicings when an Englishman settles in Ireland, with a few thousand pounds, to establish some branch of industry; and these rejoicings are not so much for the example he sets, as for the capital he brings with him. We find, too, the English press occasionally warning the people of Ireland not to frighten away by their turbulence English capital, which, if not so deterred, would be devoted to the development of Ireland, instead of being sent for employment to the antipodes,—a warning which implies that Ireland must look outside herself for the capital necessary to develop her resources. . . . Capital may be defined as past labor laid by to aid future. . . . The capital of Great Britain and other civilized nations has grown from weak and scanty beginnings. . . . The capital, or saved labor of any country, must in the aggregate come from the labor of that country. It cannot come from any other source. Another country will not supply it. Capital is not parted with unless in exchange for an equivalent. The more the labor of a country is productively employed, the larger will be the amount of its saved labor. The greater the activity of industry, the energy of production, the process of perpetual consumption and reproduction, the greater will be the capital created within the country" (J. N. Murphy). But even savings are not capital unless they are reproductively employed in the country itself; and the productive classes of Ireland save large sums of money, for whose investment there is absolutely no opening in Ireland. An average of £16,000,000 is deposited with the Irish banks at 1½ per cent. interest, and is invested in the London money market by the bankers. And the amount of these savings would be very much greater, were it not for the vast number of the unemployed and unproductive class who live off the national income. These are the two extremes of Irish society,—the landlords who draw incomes from Irish estates and spend them in Paris or Naples, instead of devoting themselves, as captains of industry, to the development and improvement of their estates; the great host of beggars, paupers and dependent persons, who find nothing to do, and live in idleness off the earnings of others, some of them inside, but most of them outside the workhouse.

> Even Lord Dufferin joins in this talk about Ireland's need of capital:— "Let capital overflow her soil, and though her superficial area remain the same, the stimulus to her powers of production would be equivalent to an accession of territory sufficient to support thousands in affluence, where at present hundreds find a difficulty in extracting a bare subsistence." Ireland has, and under any free trade regime would have, to compete with the industrial skill and the division of labor which has been the slow acquisition of centuries of English history. Irish labor is dear, as all unskilled labor is. As her people say, "their fingers are all thumbs" at manufacturing, and Lord Dufferin himself tells us that "even the traditions of commercial enterprise have perished through desuetude." The nascent industries of Ireland would be "strangled in their cradle," unless the new capitalists had—as the Australian expressed it—"a pretty strong back" to bear up against the sort of competition that Manchester and Bradford, Sheffield and Birmingham would bring to bear upon them.

§ 281. What will England do for Ireland? Almost anything except protect her industry or repeal the Union and concede the "Home Rule" that would enable her to protect herself. Everything, that is, but the one thing that will be of permanent use.

She will even interfere with the rights of property, and put the competition of the land market under restraint. But she will suffer no restraints upon the market for cottons, woollens, hardware, soap, candles and glass; *its* competitions are something unspeakably sacred, on which none may lay irreverent hands. And then, is not British prosperity bound up with the doctrine that men have the right to buy in the cheapest and sell in the dearest market, and do what they will with their own,—provided it is not land in Ireland? Only one English voice is raised in protest: "The destruction of Irish industry by the ancient English policy is not only a case for repentance, but for restitution, or at least compensation. Like other sinners, we are very willing to confess that we have done wrong; ready even to promise that we will do so no more. But a proposal that we should give any Irish industry, or even any English industry on Irish ground, a partial and temporary advantage, so as to place Ireland, as nearly as we can, in the same state as if she had always been fairly treated, as an integral part of the empire—a proposal to make up for past delinquencies and really restore industry to its natural channels—I say such a proposal, just and natural as it is, would at present be received in England with derision." . . . If this were done "England's gain in the result cannot be calculated. But she will be no loser even in the process. The wealth that native manufactures will at once pour into Ireland's lap will not be *abstracted* from the United Kingdom, but *created* in Ireland" (Judge Byles).

<small>See *Sophisms of Free Trade*; Chap. XVI.: "Free Trade for Ireland." Also Lord Dufferin's *Irish Emigration and the Tenure of Land in Ireland;* and Mr. J. N. Murphy's *Ireland—Industrial, Political and Social.*</small>

§ 282. India was a manufacturing country when English merchants first began to establish their factories or trading stations along the coast of the Bay of Bengal. Down to quite a recent period a great trade in the fine cotton goods of India— "so fine that you can hardly feel them with your hand"—was carried on. "On the coast of Coromandel and in the Province of Bengal, when at some distance from a high-road or principal town, it is difficult to find a village in which every man, woman and child is not employed in making a piece of cloth. At present much the greater part of whole provinces are employed in this single manufacture," whose process "includes no less than a description of the lives of half the inhabitants of Indostan" (Col. Orme, 1805). The manufacture was very ancient: "the weaver of Dacca on his clumsy loom produced in the days of the Roman empire that 'woven wind,' the transparent Indian muslin,—the human gossamer, of which a whole dress will pass through a finger ring. Any other nation than our own, I suppose, would have cherished the manufacture of a fabric, the most perfect probably in the whole world, and certainly the most ancient that can be specifically identified: had it fallen naturally into disuse, would have held a little state money well spent to preserve it. Not so we English. We have well-nigh annihilated the cotton manufacture of India. Dacca is in great measure desolate; the population, from 300,000 has fallen to 60 or 70,000; its most delicate muslins are almost things of the past. We imposed prohibitory duties on the import of Indian manufactures into this country. We imported our own at nominal duties into India. The slave-grown cotton of America, steam-woven into Manchester cheap-and-nasties, displaced on their native soil the far more durable but more costly products of the Indian loom. . . . "

See J. M. Ludlow's *British India, its Races and its History.* Two vols. Cambridge, 1858. Also, his *Thoughts on the Policy of the Crown toward India.* London, 1859; and Chapman's *Cotton and Commerce of India.*

England brought India juster and cheaper government, an era of peace, lighter taxes and improved methods of management. But under the Christian rule of Britain the industry of the country has been blighted, and "the manufactures of India were, it may be said, completely ruined by a general lowering of import duties [in 1813] on articles the produce or manufacture of Great Britain, without any reciprocal advantages being given to Indian produce or manufactures when brought home. Next, inasmuch as the sale of opium,—a government monopoly in Bengal and Behar—was greatly impeded by the competition of free-grown opium from the native states of Malwa, prohibitory duties were imposed at all the Presidencies on" the latter, " and the native princes of Malwa were actually induced to prohibit the cultivation of the poppy for British behoof,—being suitably bribed for thus ruining their own subjects" (Ludlow). By 1833 not a single piece of cloth was exported from India, and for the ruin inflicted on its artisans Lord William Bentinck, the Governor-General, could find " no parallel in the annals of commerce." English writers tell of " the enormous and undeniable falling off in the commercial activity of India; the decay of those flourishing marts with which the whole coast was once studded; . . . the contraction, and in great measure the ruin of trade; the neglect of public works; the depreciation of agricultural produce;" which last " is observed to be a marked feature of our rule. . . . The numerous local markets created by the existence of the native princes," and by the wide existence of a class that had other means of subsistence than farming, "and which, by serving as centres of money circulation, enhanced the value of produce on the spot, disappeared." " The trade of India is so trifling, as compared with its agriculture, that the trading classes, except the village bankers" or usurers, " form a very small item " (J. M. Ludlow). " A great part of the time of the laboring population in India is spent in idleness. I don't say this to blame them in the smallest degree. Without the means of exporting the crude and heavy agricultural produce, and with scanty means, whether of capital, science or skill, of elaborating it on the spot, they have really no inducement to exertion beyond what is necessary to gratify their present and very limited wishes" (Chapman).

In fine, there is nothing left in India save an impoverished agriculture and a lifeless trade. The Hindoo cotton-grower produces the raw material to clothe his countrymen; but it reaches them by way of Calcutta and Manchester; the skill of his wonderful manufactures is being lost. He pays for the strip of cloth that covers his own nakedness twenty times the amount of cotton that it contains. To carry his cotton crop even to the river on bullocks costs on an average five cents a pound, and employs vast numbers of the people and of cattle in laborious and unproductive work. He has lost the power of association with his fellows; no man needs or helps his neighbors; all need and help the foreigner only. "Half the human time and energy of India runs to mere waste," says Mr. Chapman; and elsewhere he says that of the cultivable surface of all India one-half is waste. In 1831 the cotton weavers and merchants of Bengal petitioned the English Parliament for reciprocal free trade. They found their "business nearly superseded by the introduction of the fabrics of Great Britain into Bengal, the importation of which augments every year, to the great prejudice of the native manufacturers." Knowing "the immense advantages which the British manufacturers derive from their skill in constructing and using machinery, which enables them to undersell the unscientific manufacturer of Bengal in his own country," they were "not sanguine in expecting to derive any great advantage in having their prayer granted;" but with the meekness of the Bengalee they ask it "as a manifestation of your lordships' good will."

> Dr. Bowring, a leading champion of free trade, said on the occasion of this petition:—"It is a melancholy story of misery so far as they are concerned, and as striking an evidence of the wonderful progress of manufacturing industry in this country. Some years ago the East India company annually received of the produce of the looms of India 6,000,000 to 8,000,000 pieces of cotton goods. The demand has now nearly ceased. In 1800 the United States took nearly 800,000 pieces; in 1830, not 4000. In 1800 1,000,000 pieces were shipped to Portugal; in 1830 only 20,000. The poor India weavers are now reduced to absolute starvation; numbers of them have died of hunger. And what was the sole cause? The presence of the cheaper English manufacture,—the production by the power-loom of the article which they had been used for ages to make by their unimproved and hand-directed shuttles. It was impossible that they should go on weaving what no one would wear or buy.' But at this very period the exportation of this better machinery, and even the inducing skilled artisans to emigrate, was forbidden under heavy penalties by English law. At the same time, as we shall see, every trade exercised in India, and every tool it employed, was heavily taxed."

Some feeble attempts to revive by mild protection the cotton manufactures of India have latterly been made. One member of the Manchester Chamber of Commerce, assailing the Canadian Tariff (see § 271), told Mr. Galt: "This part of the country has been very restive lately under the India duties of five per cent.," and another that "Exactly the same process is going on in Canada that led to the erection of cotton-mills in Bombay." The tariff in force at the era of the Rebellion taxed British cotton, silk and woollen goods, and metal goods, 5 per cent.; those of other countries twice as much; cotton yarn and twist from England 3½ per cent.; from other countries 10 per cent. This was changed in 1859 by abolishing the discrimination in favor of British goods, fixing the duty on thread and twist at five per cent., and putting a duty of 20 per cent. on haberdashery, hosiery, millinery, and some other classes. Mr. Jas. Wilson, the founder of the *Economist*, becoming Finance Minister of India in that year, changed all duties on manufactured goods—including yarns—to 10 per cent. But the pressure of direct taxation has again forced a resort to high duties, and the people, with the co-operation of English capital this time, are again taking to manufacturing. Manchester protests, but it can't be helped. *The Spectator*, edited by an Anglo-Indian, says that if the tariff be kept long enough these manufactures will survive its removal; but that as long as coal is dear, "and the habit of manufacturing on a large scale is not yet formed," they would first languish and then die out under free trade.

§ **283.** The revenue from duties on imports being destroyed, the necessity of raising money to pay the British troops and officials, and carry on the government, led to a most oppressive system of taxation and the creation of monopolies. Former Indian governments drew the revenue from a land tax, at first payable in kind, but after the Mohammedan conquest exacted—at least in part—in money. The English adopted the same method, but (1) they carried it out with a thoroughness impossible under any Oriental government,—with the hard rigidity of a Shylock. (2) They insisted on payment in money exclusively, forcing the tax-payer to find a market for his goods, and requiring the circulation of sums hitherto never employed in India, yet the value of Indian coin declined. Silver was nearly as valuable in India as gold in Europe; but the establishment of absolutely free intercourse and competition with a European nation brought its value down to the European standard. On the other hand, the people were thrown into the hands of the native usurers who had control of the great mass of the coin in circulation; these vampires form the only class that has prospered under English rule, and desires its continuance. (3) The destruction of Indian manufactures has brought down the price of raw produce and food by removing the workshops of India to the British islands. It is by the export and sale of these, in a country till recently almost destitute of roads and means of transportation, that the land-tax is raised. In many instances, from 60 to 70 per cent. of the crop was thus employed, and outside the Deccan the average was fifty per cent. (4) The land-tax levied by the native princes was expended in the neighborhood; if in money, it was spent on articles of native manufacture. By the policy of centralizing the government, the same fund was now expended mostly in distant parts of the country, and much of it in paying salaries in London, still more in the payment of high salaries to foreign officers " without root in the country, who either save money for the purpose of carrying it away, or spend it for the most part on articles of British growth and manufacture; they being moreover few in number and residing only in the chief towns " (Ludlow). "Formerly," the native would say, "the governments kept no faith with their land-holders and cultivators, exacting ten rupees where they had bargained for five whenever they found the crops good; but in spite of all this *zulm* (oppression) there were then more *burkut* (blessings) than now. The lands yielded more returns to the cultivator, and he could maintain his family better upon five acres than he can now upon ten" (Col. Sleeman: *Rambles in India*).

But this oppressive land-tax is not sufficient for the needs of the government, and *monopolies* have been created to supplement it. (1) When the English began the conquest of India, its people were noted for "their total abstinence from spirituous liquors and other intoxicating substances" (Warren Hastings). The government have set up distilleries, and supplied "arrack," a fierce alcoholic drink, to licensed venders. It used its facilities to establish new depots for the sale where none were known before. The price is low; the sale immense; the spread of drunkenness is going on over the whole land; and petitions for a prohibitory law come to England from the most public-spirited of the natives. (2) The Hindoo lives very largely on rice and fish, consequently needs a considerable amount of salt,—far more than those who live on wheat and flesh. Instead of a light tax imposed by previous rulers, the E. I. Company established a monopoly of the manufacture by which the price was raised to famine rates, and it needed three months' work of a ryot in the interior to provide salt for a small family, while fish were carried inland half-salted or unsalted, and used in a state of half-putrefaction. Fortunately the English salt-makers could not be excluded from the Indian market, and their importations forced down the price, while it diminished the demand for labor. "Imagine," says Mr. Ludlow, "the possibility of Cheshire salt, produced in a damp and comparatively cold climate like ours, under all the disadvantages of rent and royalty, rates and taxes, interest on capital and a high price of labor—after being carried, bulky as it is, to the other end of the world—being sold to one of the poorest populations of the world cheaper than that manufactured on their own coasts, where evaporation takes place with extraordinary rapidity; where labor is at two pence a day; by a government which pays neither rent nor royalty, rates nor taxes!" Yet even since this alleviation, salt sold (1855) for 14 times its cost at Madras, and £72 a ton wholesale in the interior; and the average consumption was one-third as much per head of the people as the company supplied to its Sepoys. And in many ways the monopoly checks industry, restricts the fisheries, and hinders the keeping of cattle. (3) The monopoly of opium of Bengal began in 1795, the object being to supply the article to the armed smugglers who introduce it into China in spite of the efforts of the government to exclude the pestiferous drug.

See *The Opium Trade, as carried on in India and China*, by Dr. Nathan Allen. Lowell 1850. 2d Edition, 1853. The attempts of the Chinese government to suppress the traffic was the chief if not the only cause of the "Opium War" between England and China in 1840-1. In a petition addressed to the English government by the merchants engaged in it, it is said, "That the trade in opium had been encouraged and promoted by the Indian government under the express sanction and authority, latterly of the British government and Parliament, and with the full knowledge also, as appears from the detailed evidence before the House of Commons on the renewal of the charter" of the E. I. Company in 1833, "that the trade was contraband and illegal." When it was proposed in Parliament to suppress the monopoly, and thus put an end to the contraband trade, a committee reported : " In the present state of the revenue of India it does not appear advisable to abandon so important a source of revenue, —a duty upon opium being a tax which falls principally upon the foreign consumer, and which appears upon the whole less liable to objection than any other that could be substituted." The Emperor refused to legalize what he could not put a stop to, declaring "nothing will induce me to derive a revenue from the vice and misery of my people."

But wherever opium is grown it is used; and the company's servants tell us that "One opium cultivator demoralizes a whole village; and that one-half the crimes in the opium districts,—murders, rapes, and affrays,—have their origin in opium-eating." The ryot was not allowed to profit much by the crop; before planting the poppies he must make an engagement to sell the juice at a specified price, and to the government alone; when they were ripening, his fields were examined, the amount of the yield estimated, and another engagement to furnish at least that quantity was made. If less was furnished, he was heavily fined for neglect; if the government advanced him money—as was commonly done—to buy seed and get the crop in, he paid twelve per cent. interest. Nor had he his choice as to whether he would plant the poppies; he was forced to give up a portion of his land to them. (4) Equally oppressive and exacting were the methods pursued in carrying on the monopoly of tobacco on the Malabar coast. But these are only a few out of a multitude of monopolies resorted to in order to avoid taxing the importation of British manufactures. The *moturpha*, one of the worst abominations of Moslem finance, was levied upon the exercise of every trade and occupation, sometimes in the form of a license, sometimes as a tax upon the tools employed, often at six times their cost. A tax was laid on every cocoanut tree; on the knife with which the tree was tapped for its saccharine juice; on the pot in which the juice was boiled. The fisherman paid a tax for the very stone on which he beat his clothes. A petition sent to England by the natives of Madras complains of the practice of annually " leasing out to individuals certain privileges, such as the right of measuring grain and other articles; the right to the sweepings of the goldsmiths' shops; the right of dyeing betelnut; of cutting wood in the jungle; of grazing cattle; of gathering fruit and wild honey; of catching wild-fowl; of cutting grass for thatch, and rushes for baskets; of gathering cow-dung, and innumerable other such rights of levying taxes on the poorest of the poor." In Malabar the company claimed all the wax made by the bees, leaving only the honey to the keepers; and actually destroyed several branches of industry by exacting a license for their exercise.

§ **284.** The progressive peoples are in every case those who have fostered and protected national industry by national legislation.

(1) *Belgium*, "that old cockpit of Europe," is inhabited by two peoples, "who speak different tongues, intermingle but little, are jealous of each other, and inhabit different halves of the kingdom. The one occupying the northern half of the kingdom," the Flanders provinces, where Flemish is spoken, " is now famous for its husbandry alone, though once as famous for its manufactures." Its linens, woollens, and other fabrics held the markets of the world until the seventeenth century, when the protective policy of England and France fully acclimatized these manufactures on their own soils. Its superior skill in linen weaving enabled it to retain a large measure of that industry, until the invention of spinning and weaving machines superseded the spinning-wheel and the hand-loom. Its deficiency of coal, and the prohibition upon the export of linen machinery from the British Islands, *kept up till* 1842, forbade competition with the power-loom, and the country was reduced to a number of small local industries." For till 1844 Belgium was a Free

Trade country. Under the imperial rule of Napoleon she shared in an unusual degree in the impulse that the continental system imparted to the manufacturers of the Continent. Her cottons and woollens were noted for their excellency, and commanded the French markets. But the cheaper price of the inferior goods with which England flooded the Continent on the return of peace inflicted great injury upon both manufactures, especially that of cottons. Being transferred from Spain to Holland by the Treaty of Vienna, Belgium had free access to the markets of the latter and its colonies. But the Revolution which gave her independence in 1830 closed both these against her. The new government, taking its cue from the English Whigs, who had given it moral support, announced the purpose that Belgium should be an agricultural country, contented with " the commerce of commission and transit " as a port of entry for English goods on their way to the Continent. The Liberal party upheld this course, but some of the clerical party, notably the Abbé Defoer, contended for protection to home industry. They pointed to the increasing prostration of manufactures; to the repeated failures of new enterprise through their exposure to unfair compction, English goods selling at one-fourth less than the London price, as long as any one attempted to make them in Belgium, and French agents acting for years together under general orders to undersell the native manufacturers. They showed that although coal and iron had been found in close proximity in the southern (Walloon, or French speaking) provinces, yet no general success had attended the attempts to develop this and the other vast resources of the country. Associations and companies had been formed; there had been a sort of mania for industrial associations, but they came to nothing. At last a government inquiry into the state of Belgian commerce and industry was ordered, and in 1842 it reported; in 1844 the first Belgian protective tariff was adopted, and Holland followed the example in 1845; in 1846 a commercial treaty on the basis of reciprocity was effected between the two countries, in order that this new tariff might in no way interfere with their old commercial relations. The results are known to all the world in the rapid and vast development of manufactures in the Walloon provinces, which now compete with the English in the British markets and those of the world. Even in the north "steam factories are now rising in Flanders—the excellence of its flax, and the industry and manipulative skill of its numerous rural population, may go far, as regards the manufacture of linen, to compensate for the total absence of iron and coal." Two Englishmen, selected by the iron masters to ascertain the reasons of this, made inquiries on the Continent, and report that, "with the advantage of possessing the best and most skilled workmen in the world, Belgium and France have been thrusting us out of foreign markets to an extent which the public will hardly credit, and of which the trade itself is hardly aware." . . . . For instance, in Spain, "England is thrust aside, defeated by Belgium and France. We cannot compete with their producers either in price or in continuousness and certainty of supply. Nor is this all. Even at home these industrious and pushing people are challenging our supremacy, and that not infrequently with success. In bar iron, in rails, in engines for agricultural purposes, and even in locomotives for railways, they have lately been obtaining orders in our own market."

It is easy to believe that this is rather an overstatement of the case, but it has truth enough to be unpleasant reading in Birmingham. Upon it they base a plea that English workmen should be contented with lower wages, in order that their employers may compete with the cheaper labor of the Continent. But the development of manufactures in Southern Belgium has caused a great advance in the rate of wages, and by furnishing the farmer with a near and steady market, has made him fully able to pay these. Protection has also naturalized in those provinces new species of tillage, such as the culture of beets for sugar, from which the bulk of the sugar now used in Belgium is derived. "The Walloon farm laborer earns two francs a day, and often more, while the Fleming earns but one." "The line of division between high and low wages closely corresponds with the line of division between the two races;" it is also like the same line in England, the line of division between the purely agricultural and the manufacturing districts. Liége lies on the line; three miles south of it farm wages are twice as high as they are three miles north of it. The northern provinces, in spite of the unequalled agriculture, which has turned Flanders into a garden, are afflicted with pauperism. When hand-loom weaving ceased it was at its height; in 1848 there were nearly 200,000 "indigents," one-fourth of whom were women who had lived by spinning. The blow fell heavily on the farming class also, as the small holders lost the employment by which they eked out a living, and lost the home market for their flax. But even Flanders is rallying under the shelter of the protection that might have saved her workmen from beggary in the process of adopting better methods of manufacture.

"If any one," says a Belgian Free Trader, "had left the country in 1835, after having visited our principal manufacturing centres, and were to come back to it now," in 1861, "he would be struck with the transformation that they have undergone, the advances they have achieved; he would find a numerous, intelligent and active population of working people, where, a quarter of a century ago, he would have seen nothing but country houses scattered at wide intervals over extensive plains. As a consequence, production, except of articles of food, has outrun the needs of the population, although it has increased in numbers and in wealth, and we are obliged to seek for foreign outlets."

> See J. F. Constant: *Du Régime Protecteur en Economie Politique*, Bruxelles, 1842. II. F. Matthysens: *La Hollande, l'Angleterre, et la Belgique;* Anvers 1850. De Laveleye; *L'Economie Rurale de Belgique* (largely reproduced in Cliffe Leslie's *Land Systems and Industrial Economy.*) Ejusdem: "The Land Systems of Belgium and Holland" in *Cobden Club Essays on Systems of Land Tenure;* London 1870. II. H. Creed and W. Williams, Jr.: *Handicraftsmen and Capitalists;* London.

§ 285. (2). Germany is now taking her place among the great industrial nations, through the removal of all restrictions upon internal commerce and the legislative fostering of home industry. The second king of Prussia, gruff old Frederick Wilhelm, and his son, the great Frederick, began the work of raising the land to the place to which its vast resources, its intellectual vigor and its past history entitle it. "Frederick," says his greatest biographer, "was the reverse of orthodox in 'Political Economy'; he had not faith in free trade, but the reverse; nor had ever heard of those ultimate evangels, unlimited competition, fair start and perfervid race by all the world (towards *Cheap-and-Nasty,*' as the likeliest winning-post for all the world), which have since been vouchsafed to us. Probably in the world there never was less of a free trader. . . . The desperate notion of giving up government altogether, as a relief from human blockheadism in your governors, and their want of even a wish to be just or wise, had not entered into the thoughts of Frederick. . . . Many of Frederick's restrictive notions, as that of watching with such anxiety that 'money' (gold or silver coin) be not carried out of the country, will be found mistakes, not in orthodox Dismal Science as now taught, but in the nature of things; and indeed the Dismal Science will generally excommunicate them in a lump, too heedless that fact has conspicuously vindicated the general sum-total of them, and declared it to be much truer than it seems to the Dismal Science. Dismal Science (if that were important to me) takes insufficient heed, and does not discriminate between times past and times present, times here and times there."

"In improving the industries and husbandries among his people, his success, though less noised of in foreign parts, was to the near observer still more remarkable. A perennial business with him this, which even in time of war he never neglected, and which springs out like a stemmed flood whenever peace leaves him free for it. His labors by all methods to awaken new branches of industry, to cherish and further the old, are incessant, manifold, unwearied, and will surprise the uninstructed reader who comes to study them. . . . Certain it is, King Frederick's success in National Husbandry was very great. The details of the very many new manufactures, new successful ever-spreading enterprises, fostered into existence by Frederick; his canal-makings, road-makings, bog-drainings, colonizings and unwearied endeavorings, will require a technical philosopher one day, and will well reward such study and trouble of recording in a human manner, but must lie massed up here in mere outline on the present occasion." Excepting some small mention of two Prussian chemists, that are busied, with aid and comfort from this protectionist king, in getting sugar out of beet-juice—Herr Margraff, 1747 till 1773, and after him a French Monsieur Achard, refugee for his religion. This latter finds a second partner in Napoleon, with notable results for France (§ 257).

See Carlyle's *Frederick the Great*, Book XVI., Chapter VIII. Also Book XXI., Chapter II., where the younger and greater Mirabeau's *Monarchie Prussienne* (Paris 1788), a free trade pamphlet in eight octavo volumes, is noticed with the summing up: "M. le Comte, would there have been in Prussia, for example, any trade at all, any nation at all, had it always been left 'free'? There would have been mere sand and quagmire, and a community of wolves and bisons, M. le Comte."

In Mr. Carlyle's earlier works he accepts the results of the Dismal Science—as he was the first to nickname Political Economy—as a "Divine Message," though "perhaps as small a message as ever there was such noise made about before," (*Latter Day Pamphlets*, 1850). He seems to have now got beyond that, converted by the evidence of facts.

§ 286. Frederick's unfriend, the Empress Maria Theresa, and her son and successor, Joseph II., labored much the same way for the promotion of industry in Austria. They all made the mistake of leaving domestic industry under manifold restrictions, which went far to balance the protection against foreign invasions. The practice of trade was confined to limited corporations; heavy excise duties and monopolies kept back home production; instead of one national Prussian tariff there were sixty-seven, for every boundary line that divided province from province was a line of customs' duties, shutting out the home manufacturer from his rightful market. Equally unwise, but quite in keeping with this, was the prohibition of the importation of certain manufactured goods, and of the export of raw materials. The numerous privileged classes were exempt from the action of these laws, and could bring in what they pleased. Smuggling was made a science, and supported by public opinion; of the great mass of officials required by the system, very few were above taking bribes. These mischiefs came to a head under Frederick's worthless successors, who intensified all the faults and neglected all the good points of his system. Adam Smith's doctrines were becoming popular in Germany; Kraus of Koenigsberg and others taught them from professional chairs. A new generation of officials grew up under this teaching, who detested their country's meddlesome and vexatious fiscal policy for its faults, without understanding its merits.

At last free trade became a recognised maxim of Prussian policy. The king proclaimed, during the struggle with Napoleon, that all prohibitions were cancelled, and all duties were reduced to 8½ per cent. in the provinces not in possession of the enemy, and when the " War of Liberation " broke out in 1813, the proclamation was renewed. In the meantime the Continental system had been extended to Germany; British and Colonial goods were excluded from her markets, while those of France came thither free of duty " by right of conquest," without any grant of reciprocity. " German industry made admirable progress during that time, not only in the different manufacturing branches, but in all branches of agriculture, though laboring under all the disadvantages of the wars and of French despotic measures. All kinds of produce were in demand, and bore high prices; and wages, rent, interest of capital, prices of land, of all sorts of property, were enhanced" (List). The lower Rhine, as having been longest under the French rule, made the greatest advance. Perhaps Saxony, hitherto a free trade country, and the great depot for the dispersion of British goods over Central Europe, came next in point of industrial progress. Germany enjoyed prosperity without example at the very time when her people were drinking the bitter cup of national humiliation. The victories that restored the independence of European nationalities brought disaster to their material interests; it threw open their markets to the competition of their insular ally, and set up all the old lines of demarcation that divided Germany into a few large states and a host of microscopic despotisms. Twenty-seven of these custom-house lines—one-third of the whole number—lay across the Rhine, and at each of them commerce was impeded with duties and delays. The German merchant had no field of activity outside his own little principality; Germany enjoyed protection in each of its members from all the rest, and at the same time virtual free trade with the foreigner. The cry of ruined merchants and unemployed workmen led Prussia to undertake an elaborate investigation of her own industrial needs. The ministry of Hardenberg and Van Bülow had proposed to keep up the present low tariff, but make it specific in the nature of the duties imposed, and to abolish all provincial restrictions on commerce. The matter was referred to the Council of State, who recommended the appointment of a special commission of inquiry, and the king selected one under the presidency of Wilhelm von Humboldt. After a prolonged investigation, in which all interests had a hearing, the commission decided in favor of a moderately protective system, with the removal of all prohibitions on exportation or importation, and of all local restrictions upon trade. There were only two dissenting voices—both disciples of Adam Smith—in the commission; only three in the Council of State; the results were embodied in the Prussian tariff of 1818.

> As if with a view of illustrating both sides of the case at once, Prussia in 1822 demanded reciprocity with England in the matter of the Navigation laws, and in 1824 Mr. Huskisson granted it. "The effect of reciprocity upon the Prussian mercantile navy," says an ardent free trader, "has been to diminish it most materially in amount, while British shipping gains an ever-increasing share in her carrying trade. This case is quite sufficient to show what would inevitably be the result of a fair and free competition between British shipping and the shipping of any other country (in this hemisphere at least), with which it comes in contact," (W. P. Adam: *The Policy of Retaliation*; London, 1852). The Prussian shipping fell off 44 per cent. in the number of vessels and 27 per cent. in their tonnage between 1806 and 1839, although the commerce of the country increased vastly. See Porter's *Progress of the English Nation*, p. 396.

§ 287. At the same time a movement in favor of protection to German industry and the removal of all custom-houses to the German frontier was going on in the centre and south of Germany. Friedrich List, then a professor in the University of Tuebingen, was put forward as its spokesman. It aimed at a national tariff system for all Germany, and in 1820 succeeded in securing a preliminary treaty at a conference of German ministers at Vienna, and then a special conference at Darmstadt. Then followed the establishment of three Zollvereins,—one for Northwestern and Central Germany, headed by Saxony, Brunswick and Hanover, with low revenue tariff; one for Southern Germany, including Bavaria, Wurtemberg, and some minor states; a third in the North, consisting of Prussia and the minor states in her immediate neighborhood (Hesse, Nassau, &c.), who adopted the tariff of 1818. At last, in 1833, the last two and those of the first that lay in Central Germany united on the basis of that tariff, including in this great *Zollverein* about twenty-six millions of the German people. Austria on the south, and Hanover, Brunswick, Oldenburg, Mecklenburg and the Free Cities on the north, alone stood out. Hanover, Brunswick and Oldenburg, under English influence, formed in 1828 a *Steuerverein* with a tariff of low duties for revenue; as they shut out the Zollverein from the North Sea, the latter attempted a union with them in 1841, but found that it could only be secured at the sacrifice of protection to native industry. In 1853 the annexation was secured, on condition that Hanover should receive seventy-five per cent. more than the share of the revenue to which her population would otherwise entitle her. From 1849 Austria strove to either break up the Zollverein or get admission to it with all her dependencies. Many of the minor states favored this latter proposal, and it seemed likely that Prussia, in resisting it, would bring on war. But in 1853 a reciprocity treaty between the two powers put an end to the struggle.

*Zollverein* means Customs' Union; *Steuerverein*, Imposts' Union. The latter was an imitation of the former, without its protective purpose.

In the Zollverein each state has an equal vote, although

Prussia had till 1852 more than half the population. Another sacrifice made by Prussia for the general interest was in the distribution of the customs' receipts on the basis of population; small states with a farming population, got far more than their true share; Prussia got half a million thalers a year less, and asked no more, although Frankfort-on-Main in joining the Zollverein in 1835 received a larger share than her population would justify. The duties are assessed on the basis of the tariff of 1818, subject to modification at the conference of representatives. These modifications are of a sort to show the Protectionist purpose of that tariff, and of the Zollverein itself. Thus in 1843–5, the duty on cotton goods fixed in 1818 at $12\frac{1}{2}$ per cent., was very decidedly increased to meet English competition; in 1844 the duties on iron were increased for the same reason. The duties on all importations are estimated to average 12 per cent., but as a great part of these are low duties on the raw materials of manufacture, the duties on manufactured goods must be sufficiently high. Dr. Bowring, who was sent out by the British Government to examine and report upon the Zollverein in 1841, clearly showed the Protective character of the tariff. Professor List estimated the duties on manufactured articles in common use at from 20 to 60 per cent. "The most popular object of this great social movement is, by a prudent and well constructed tariff of duties, to protect and encourage German manufactures, to exclude by duties the foreign producer from the German market [?], and to extend the exportation of the products of their own industry to foreign markets" (S. Laing). One of the best and most protective features of the system is its imposition of specific duties, changed in their amount according to a periodical observation of the market prices. No room was left for false invoices; none for the foreign exporter to throw foreign goods on the market at a merely nominal price, after paying merely nominal duties, so as to undersell the German maker at a small sacrifice. At the same time the duties fell more heavily upon the cheaper and more commonly used articles, whose production at home is of the first importance, and though requiring less of skill in the workingman, gradually educates him in the skill and taste necessary for the production of finer wares.

§ 288. The carefully prepared statistics of the business of the Zollverein, in home production and consumption as well as importation, give us the data for estimating the effects of the system. We find (1) That protection has vastly increased the power of the German people to command the services of other peoples. The importations have risen steadily in amount and quality, instead of decreasing. "If we look at its practical effects upon British industry, we are warranted in the conclusion that the wealthier and more industrious our neighbors become, the better customers they are in the world's markets, in supplying which British industry and capital are embarked" (Laing.") (2) The wages of labor have been very largely raised, for both farm hands and factory hands. Not only has more money been paid for a day's work, but so much more as enables the workingmen to command a much larger amount of material comfort. (3) The farmer has not lost what the manufacturer has gained, but has gained equally with him; the prices of raw materials and of manufactured goods have steadily approximated, as the market has been brought nearer the farm. (4.) The total consumption of articles of prime necessity has increased in a ratio that far exceeds the growth of the population. (5) The enormous difference between rich and poor has been diminished and the middle class of prosperous and intelligent people has gained greatly in number. (6) The development of home industry has not been effected at the expense of that unhappy victim of tariff legislation, "the consumer." Even the small class of consumers, who are not also—directly or indirectly—producers, find their profit in it. As Dr. Bowring shows, the home market is supplied with better and cheaper goods than England could furnish, and Prussia is now competing for the possession of even the English markets.

"The Zollverein, according to the census of 1867, comprises a territory of more than 90,000 geographical square miles, with a population computed at over thirty-eight millions. Since the realization of commercial freedom" between the parts of the empire, " German industry has increased in an unprecedented degree, and, to a certain extent, competes successfully with that of Great Britain. The character of the foreign commerce of Germany has entirely changed. Instead of exporting raw materials only, she sends out the products of her own manufacturing industry, creating a market abroad which keeps her actively employed at home. The German woollen manufacture has recovered the ground lost in the middle ages, and its fabrics at present form the chief part of the Zollverein exports. The manufacture of cotton and silk has made equal progress, although the materials have to be imported. The linen trade has not yet begun to compete with that of England, but in steel and iron goods, in glass, paper and silk manufactures, in pottery, stoneware and porcelain, in chemicals, in the refining of sugar and beer, Germany abundantly supplies her own wants, and yet reserves a surplus for foreign interchange" (Yeates's *Recent and Existing Commerce*—Free Trader). The linen trade, also, has become of importance, in later years.

(7) The German people, once dissevered by the frontiers of petty principalities, have been mightily drawn into national and political unity by the industrial policy that recognised the identity of the material interests of these severed parts. It was the Zollverein that made the ideal of German unity popular, though it did not originate it. It was the public sentiment thus created that enabled Prussia in 1866 and 1870 to put herself at the head of a united Germany, and reduce the petty sovereigns of the country to the rank of a landed aristocracy. It was, as Mr. Laing points out, the same growth of public sentiment in power and control over the government, that compelled Prussia to replace her autocratic institutions by a representative system, in which the popular will finds a free and regular expression. Since that time, Dr. Bowring tells us in 1840 "the sentiment of German unity has been brought out of the regions of hope and fancy into those of the positive and material interests." "Germany in the course of ten years," says List in 1841, " has advanced a century in prosperity and industry, in national self-respect and power." "The German people," says Mr. S. Laing in 1842, " are for the first time united in one great object of material interest; . . . and for the first time they have made the influence of public opinion an effective state power in their in-

ternal affairs. . . . The German commercial league is, in its result, the most important and interesting event of this half century." "Their exaggerated expectations are that Germany is to run the same career as England; to attain the same national wealth; to force or persuade Holland, Belgium, Hanover, Hamburg, Denmark, to become members of the league; to exclude all but their own goods and manufactures from the Continent; to become an acknowledged political power; to have a common flag, common revenues; to have fleets, armies, colonies, and to be a great naval power on the ocean." "According to every true German, the league is to be the grand restorer of nationality to Germany, of national character, of national mind, national greatness, national everything to a new, regenerated German nation. They are to spin and weave themselves into national spirit, patriotism, and united effort as a great people."

In 1864 Prussia, following the example of France, reduced her tariff from a protectionist to a revenue basis. The competition thus challenged proved most disastrous to many of the great industries which had been developed by the earlier protective policy of the Zollverein. In 1879, after making full proof of what free trade could do for Germany, the protective policy was restored again.

§ 289. (3) Russia became a European power in the time of Peter the Great. He and some of his successors—notably Catharine II.—labored to foster industry by their patronage, but as the people were too unskilful, it was largely by the importation of foreign artisans. The merchants being mostly Old Believers (or Raskolniks) did their utmost to keep foreign manufactures out of holy Russia, but large quantities were brought in, especially from the Leipsic fairs. The peace of Tilsit included Russia in the Continental System, until the war broke out again in 1812. At the return of peace and the restoration of ordinary relations with Western Europe, Russia had an extraordinary season of prosperity. The failure of the crops in the West made a great demand for her grain, and money flowed into the country. Under the influence of Storch, a Russian disciple of Adam Smith, the Emperor Alexander adopted the free trade policy. The ruin of a great part of the Russian manufactures speedily followed. "It is only the first shock of free competition," said the theorists; "wait a little and you will see the tide turn." But the tide did not turn; England shut out Russian corn to protect her own farmers, and the ruin grew worse. Count Nesselrode came to the conclusion that Russia must keep herself. In a ministerial circular of 1821, he says: "Russia sees herself compelled by circumstances to adopt an independent industrial system; the products of the empire find no access to foreign markets; domestic manufactures are either ruined or on the point of ruin; all the moneys of the empire flow abroad; and the most solid business houses are on the brink of failure." The tariffs of 1820 and 1822 put an end to this period of dependence, when, as Mr. Cobden told his countrymen, a cessation of English exports would have the effect "to doom a portion of her" Russia's "people to absolute nakedness." Since that date every year has seen great industrial advances. "In no country in Europe has the march of civilization and progress in modern times been more rapid, decided and systematic;" all this "having been effected by the energy and wisdom of a few master minds." "The manufacturing industry is not yet fifty years old. It required nursing under a system of protection, but is now so far developed as to admit a great deal of competition" (Barry's Russia in 1870).

The cotton manufacture doubled in a few years after the tariff; its products are now worth $125,000,000. At first it imported four-fifths of the thread used; but since England removed her prohibition on the export of spinning-machinery, the proportion has changed, and only one-sixteenth of the yarn used is imported. The amount is seven times what it was in 1822, and employs 175,000 people. Native cottons have driven the imported out of the great Russian fairs, and the export is much greater than the import. They are "capital in quality and neat in design; far prettier and neater, I think, than our own" (Barry). Since 1830 the silk manufacture has been protected, and two-thirds of the silks used are now made at home, and compete in excellence with any foreign goods, while, like all home-made Russian fabrics, they are much better adapted to the popular taste. . . There are also 800 woollen factories, employing 110,000 workmen and making goods of the value of $50,000,000 annually. The absence of large capital, the lack of popular education, the low grade of intelligence, the large use—as in Germany—of fabrics spun and woven in the households, all tend to keep back Russian manufactures; the Russian workman does as he is bid, or as he sees others do, but cannot be left with any range of responsibility. But the people are making large advances, especially since the emancipation of the serfs, and in the absence of other teachers, the discipline and the work of the factory is of itself sharpening their faculties and quickening their perceptive powers. The somewhat lower tariff of 1869 imposes duties of at least thirty-five per cent. on foreign manufactures. "Everything is now done to stimulate trade; every inducement held out to encourage manufactures; factories are springing up fitted with native-made machinery. Branches of industry are started, which before were thought to be impossible for Russian ingenuity to master, and trade flourishes as it never flourished before. Ever since the Crimean war the amount of interchange of commodities has been increasing" (Barry).

§ 290. Sweden began to develop her manufactures by protection in the time of the great Gustavus Adolphus. During the later Middle Ages the country was kept in a state of poverty through the oppressions of the Hanseatic League and the backwardness of its people. Even after its emancipation from the Danish rule it formed no higher ambition than to export raw materials in exchange for the small quantity of manufactured goods this commerce could afford her people. Gustavus formed and executed the purpose to make his kingdom a manufacturing country. His protective policy has been maintained from that day to this, with great results to the kingdom. The first and only departure from it was in 1845. Sweden was almost the only country that responded to the proposal—reciprocity as to navigation laws—made by England. English authority describes her present tariff on goods as "having the unfortunate distinction of disputing with Spain the debatable honor of being the highest in the world, the Russian only excepted." Till 1824 the prohibition policy was followed, under "a more liberal but thoroughly protective (*tres-protecteur*) system," her manufactures were more than trebled in thirty years, and her agriculture so much improved that she now has large quantities of grain for export, instead of depending, as was once the case, upon the granaries of Finland.

*La Suède et son Commerce,* par le Baron Knut Bonde; Paris, 1852.

(5) *Denmark* is and was a protectionist country. "She stands alone in her corner of the world, exchanging her loaf of bread, which she can spare, for articles she cannot provide for herself, but still providing for herself everything she can by her own industry. . . . This home industry of hers is protected by heavy import duties on all foreign articles which could compete with her own manufactures; and these are avowedly imposed, not for revenue, while a lower duty would be more productive, but for protection. . . . The object is simply to secure a living to that portion of the population which is not engaged in husbandry, and which, without protective duties on all that interferes with their branches of industry, would become a burden on the rest of the community."

See S. Laing's *Denmark and the Duchies;* London, 1852.

§ 291. (6) *Spain* was one of the first to adopt the prohibitory system, and that by which revenue was raised by duties on the commerce between the different provinces of the kingdom; she was also one of the last to give these up. The system was often as ruinous to home industry as it was meddlesome; thus in 1720 she adopted a tariff which was ingeniously mischievous. "Its provisions discriminated against the export of Spanish goods to the colonies, and in favor of foreign manufactures and of contraband trade. The industry of the nation, arrested first of all by the competition of Italy and the Low Countries, afterwards by that of England and France, ceased its development. It remained backward it was paralyzed, while the other countries by means of Cadiz carried on the commerce of its colonial possessions, and drew from them the raw materials and the precious metals which they produced. The tariff of 1778 which imposed heavy duties upon goods produced abroad came too late; the mischief was accomplished, and the industry of Spain was all but annihilated" (J. F. Constant). It had no time to rally before the Napoleonic wars completed her misery. She has suffered more this century than any other country from internal discord and civil war. The country is rich in the elements of material wealth, but poor in population, being next to Scandinavia and Russia in the sparseness of population. The first really national and simply protective tariff was adopted in 1845; it abolished all provincial tariffs and most of the prohibitions, and reduced the duties on a good many articles without in the least giving up the principle of protection. That Spain has advanced rapidly in industrial development during the thirty years that have elapsed is universally conceded. "Progress," wrote M Block in 1850, " is so rapid that the figures of to-day are left behind to-morrow. On every side we see factories and workshops rising, established either by Spaniards or by foreigners. These latter crowd into this country of great expectations, where so much land still awaits active and intelligent occupants, who bring hither their talents and their capital."

    See *L'Espagne en 1850, Tableau de ses Progres les plus recents;* par Maurice Block. Paris, 1851.

The new tariff of 1869 reduced the duties on a great number of articles without giving up, either in fact or in intention, the principle of protection; after its adoption the revenue, which had fallen off since 1864, considerably increased. The destruction of the French vines by the Phylloxera insect having created a great demand for foreign grape-juice to meet the demands on the French wine-market, the Spanish vine-growers in 1882 voted to sacrifice Spanish manufactures to their French rivals in exchange for concessions which would give them advantages over other vine-growing countries. The new commercial treaty caused great disturbances, and even riots, in Catalonia.

§ 292. Two European countries enjoy the unhappy distinction of illustrating the miseries inflicted upon nations industrially weaker when they engage in free competition with those that are stronger.

(1) *Portugal* in 1681 began the development of her woollen manufactures, the Count de Ericeira being Prime Minister and author of this policy. "Our woollen cloths, cloth serges and cloth druggetts," says the old *British Merchantman*, "were prohibited" after 1684; "they set up fabrics for making cloth, and proceeded with very good success, and we might justly apprehend that they would have gone on to erect other fabrics, until at last they had served themselves with every species of woollen goods." The prohibition not extending to all woollen fabrics, but only to those most in use, was repeatedly evaded by making goods that differed from these only in some trifling respect, but bore names invented to suit the Portuguese tariff. At last, in 1703, after the death of Ericeira, Portugal negotiated the Methuen Treaty with England, by which Portuguese wines were admitted into England at lower rates than those of France, and English goods into Portugal at the old rates of duty. The aristocracy, who were large wine-growers, were chiefly interested in the new arrangement. "Their own fabrics," says the *British Merchantman*, "were perfectly ruined, and we exported £100,000 value in the single article of cloths the very year after the treaty. The court was pestered with remonstrances from their manufacturers; . . . . but the thing was passed, the treaty was ratified, and all their looms were ruined." One of the first effects was such a drain of silver from Portugal that "there was left very little for their necessary occasions," and this was followed by a drain of gold. Exchange stood at fifteen per cent. against Portugal, and her export of coin to England rose to £1,500,000 a year. Goods were not paid for in goods, as Free Traders allege.

Her people were reduced to the monotony of a single occupation; the amount of their productive labor was vastly diminished; their power of association and mutual helpfulness was destroyed. The difference between the price of their raw produce and the manufactured goods for which they exchanged them, increased as the workshop was carried away from the neighborhood of farm and vineyard. The aristocracy of landowners found that they had been killing the goose that laid the golden eggs, for though, as there was no occupation but farming, the people were competing for the possession of land, the rents that they were able to pay were much less than if a varied industry had furnished a home market by withdrawing a large part of the people from agriculture. One new industry was created—smuggling. "We do not deny," says Mr. Macgregor in his *Commercial Statistics*, "that there were advantages in having a market for our woollens in Portugal, especially one of which, if not the principal, was the means afforded of sending them afterward, by contraband trade, into Spain." As to her legitimate commerce, Mr. McCullough says that the tonnage of her shipping is about one-thirtieth of what it was, and that her produce is mostly carried in foreign ships. Every year saw a decline of the nation in wealth, civilization, power and prestige. Her people retrograded in intelligence and skill. "It is surprising," says an English traveller, "how ignorant, or, at least, superficially acquainted, the Portuguese are with every kind of handicraft; a carpenter is awkward and clumsy, spoiling every work he attempts, and the way in which the doors and woodwork, even of good houses, are finished, would have suited the rudest ages. Their carriages, of all kinds, from the fidalgo's family coach to the peasant's market cart, their agricultural implements, locks and keys, &c., are ludicrously bad. They seem to disdain improvement, and are so infinitely below par, so strikingly inferior to the rest of Europe, as to form a sort of disgraceful wonder in the middle of the nineteenth century" (Bailly). "The finances," says the *Annuaire de l'Economie Politique* for 1849, "are in the most deplorable condition; the treasury is dry, and all branches of the public service suffer. A carelessness and a mutual apathy reign throughout the government and the nation."

Nor has England gained as much as Portugal has lost; the country is too poor to be a good customer. The Portuguese demand for English goods is now of no importance, and has no effect on the English market. The country is a sucked orange, a thing to be got rid of—"a burden and a curse to England," Mr. Cobden says.

After the defeat of the Church party and its leader Don Miguel, a protective tariff was adopted in 1837, and its rate of duties increased in 1841. It has the merit of being "specific" in its method, so that its rates fall most heavily upon the commoner and cheaper articles. But in a country so demoralized by contraband trade, so stripped of all the elements of industrial wealth, so bereft of skill and enterprise, it can only operate slowly in retrieving the fortunes of Portuguese industry. Still it has made a change. It has turned the balance of trade with England in Portugal's favor, and already "manufactures of woollen and cotton goods, paper and tobacco, employ many persons in Lisbon, and the printing of cotton goods imported from England, has nearly put a stop to the trade in English printed goods" (Dr. Yeates).

§ 293. Turkey, Mr. Cobden thinks, is also "a burden and a curse" to the commercially powerful nation with whom she has long enjoyed free trade. Turkey was once a burden to nobody; was one of the chief commercial nations of the world. "Greece and Asia Minor furnished us with their manufactured products, together with those of India, long after their conquest by the Turks, and up to the period when the industry of Europe reached its development. To-day their manufactures have all but disappeared, and those unhappy countries have nothing but farm products" (Constant). When the power-loom superseded the hand-loom in Western Europe, there was an immense importation of British goods. The muslins, the ginghams and the carpets that for centuries had commanded the markets of the world, that fifty years ago were worn in the backwoods of America, were driven out of their own home markets. "Although," says McCulloch, "our muslins and chintzes be inferior in fineness to those of the East, and our red-dye be inferior in brilliancy, those defects are more than balanced by the greater cheapness of our goods; and from Smyrna to Canton, from Madras to Samarcand, we are everywhere supplanting the native fabrics." Turkish carpets are still unequalled by the Western fabrics, but the latter have driven them out of the market. "Of six hundred looms for muslins in Scutari in 1812, only forty remained in 1831; and of two thousand weaving establishments in Tournovo, there were only two hundred" left.

Under any financial system, short of enforced prohibition of foreign manufactures, these Eastern industries would have had a severe struggle, but would most probably have survived it. Protection might have been the means of importing foreign skill, and perhaps, in spite of English prohibition, the necessary machinery. But the Turkish merchants had all the odds against them. In the absence of a sufficient revenue from customs' duties, and of direct taxation, the native industry of the country was severely taxed. Taxes on trades, taxes on tools, taxes on every sort of raw material, taxes on every kind of home-made fabric, licenses and monopolies, all were laid upon the workman at home, while his competitor from abroad paid the merest trifle in customs' duties, and, by special treaties with France and England, even that was reduced from five to three per cent. *ad valorem*, in consideration of the exemption of Turkish vessels from certain harbor duties. Native exports pay twelve per cent.

For a time there was left to Turkey a lifeless trade in raw silk, cotton and the like. Now even that is gone to countries less burdened with taxation. "Ships carrying goods to Constantinople either return in ballast, or get cargoes at Smyrna, Odessa, &c." Only a few of the ruder manufactures are still carried on; a woman's labor is worth four cents a day; a man's will command as much as fifty cents a week in the seaports.

"The provincial populations, though not devoid of capacity for better things, are at present condemned to wither under a general atmosphere of maladministration and decay. . . . Beggars all, beggars all, marry, good sir; little doing, less likely to be done; trade degenerated into pedlary, enterprise into swindling, banking into usury, policy into intrigue, lands untilled, forests wasted, mineral treasures unexplored, roads, harbors, bridges, every class of public works utterly neglected and falling into ruin, pastoral life with nothing of the Abel about it, agriculture that Cain himself, and metallurgy that his workman-son might have been ashamed of; in public life, universal venality and corruption; in social life, ignorance and bigotry; and in private life, immorality of every kind; not 'something,' but everything 'rotten in the state of' Turkey. Such is the picture" drawn by Dr. Lennep. "We may add that it is hardly an overdrawn one."

See for this and the quotations that follow, the article "Provincial Turkey," in the *London Quarterly Review* for October, 1874.

Yet the fault is not in the country or the people; for the Turks are "as a rule industrious, simple, thrifty, ingenious too, peaceable and orderly;" as free from the grosser and worser forms of vice and crime as any nation under the sun. "That they enjoy a climate than which few are more favorable to labor and produce; that the soil is almost everywhere fertile above, and rich in valuable ores below; that the coast abounds in places of shelter, and the inland with noble rivers, are facts which no one will question. Yet it is no less certain that capital has vanished from the land, that every undertaking, every enterprise, is surely smitten with failure; that the social condition is deteriorating in every respect, the number of the inhabitants diminishing, and that the symptoms precursive of a general bankruptcy, not of means and finances only, but of vitality and of men, become more menacing year by year, almost day by day."

And at the bottom of all the mischief lies the impoverishment of the people through a bad national economy. "Want of capital is the head and front of Turkey's ills throughout her length and breadth at the present day; want of men, the necessary correlative or result of the former, the second." Nothing is left her but agriculture, and such an agriculture! "All up the sides of the green hill" upon which a Turkish governor's palace is perched, "far over the wide Asiatic plain, we see the yet uneffaced traces of irrigation channels, now broken down and dry; while removed from their original places, and strewed at random over the ground here and there, lie the boundary stones that once marked the limits of fields since abandoned to weed and bush. At forty per cent. taxation, and such is the very lowest rate levied by the Stamboulee tithe-gatherers on the Turkish—if the crop be bad, the percentage may amount to something much higher—agriculture is not a paying business; and such luxuries as irrigation, drainage, manure, and improvements of any kind, are out of the question. The landowner, impoverished and in debt, cannot make them; the government has very different uses for the money it takes from them, and will not."

"Another blight overspreads the land as pestilence follows famine. What the tax-gatherer has left is gleaned by the usurer. . . There exists even now no credit-system in Turkey, no country bank, no means of obtaining an advance except by private loans; no investment except in such loans; no limit to the terms, no security on the payment." With the destruction of capital through the paralysis of societary circulation, and the drain of money abroad, the destruction of credit has gone on *pari passu*. There are a few banks in the seaport towns, but as their transactions are chiefly the negotiation of government loans and speculations with foreign or mixed companies, they tend " to draw off the wealth of the Empire, not to husband it; they are not reservoirs, but drains. The peasant, pressed by the claims of the tax-gatherer, the landowner in need of money for improvements, the shopkeeper desirous of outfit, the artisan who would set up or extend his workshops, are one and all driven into the hands of the private lender. . . The unfortunate peasant is thus ground as between an upper and a nether millstone. Three per cent. a month is the ordinary rate of interest; and this, if unpaid, is at the end of the year added to the principal. The day of selling out soon comes; the family emigrates or starves. We have known a single money-lender thus draw to himself the substance of a whole district. Another evil that naturally follows is that capital wherever it exists is certain to be applied almost exclusively to loans of this nature, while for productive investment scarce a farthing can be found. A profit of thirty-six per cent. is sure, particularly with the Asiatics, to be preferred to one of four or five per cent. though more solid and made by honester means, such as mining, agriculture, and the like. Hence, too, every work of public utility is thrown into the hands of foreigners; foreign capitalists construct harbors, work mines, utilize forests, lay down railroads, or at least organize companies which profess to do all these things; while the profits, if any, are shared among foreigners and outside the country. . . Lastly, whatever home-made capital still remains in the territory is unavoidably, by the very universality of small private loans, so broken up and subdivided as to become practically useless for any serious purpose. Of all the sinister influences at work within the empire, none is more directly destructive of its internal prosperity, and, above all, of its agricultural and landed well-being, than this. 'Not a single property, great or small, within this district, but is burdened to my certain knowledge with obligations and liabilities exceeding the value of its possible produce for two generations to come,' said a Turkish provincial governor."

The outside world is continually deceived by a show and pretence of reform, but these go no deeper than the surface. Things are growing worse, not better. "The administration is more corrupt than ever, justice more venal, popular education more neglected, taxation much heavier, and the population at large more impoverished and dwindling than in any preceding epoch. . . . When the mines of Anatolia are worked, the manufactures of Syria encouraged, the dikes of the Tigris valley restored; when the bridges, roads, quays, embankments, canals, reservoirs, caravanseries, all that was the pride and profit of local governments, and is now perishing or has perished with them, are repaired and perfected,—then indeed will there be hope for the government and the governed, for Turkey and her Sultan."

Hand-in hand with the destruction of local centres of industry, with the lowering of the people to the level of a single employment, and with the effacement of the freedom and individuality of character that accompany diversified employment, has gone a parallel political revolution that closely corresponds to the economic one. "From a confederacy of half-independent states, each retaining in the main its own customs, privileges and institutions, guaranteed by a strength to defend them, and by a rough but efficacious popular representation, Turkey has within the last fifty years sunk into an absolute, uncontrolled, centralized despotism, under which every former privilege, institution, custom, popular representation—in a word, every vestige of popular freedom and local autonomy—has been merged and lost in one blind centralized uniformity." "She has sacrificed an empire to a capital." And the decline of military power has followed that of industry. "Whoever lists may now assail the provinces with the safe assurance that the regular troops once overcome no further opposition will remain; the people starved, disheartened, disarmed, and thoroughly alienated at heart from a government that is a mere synonym for fiscal extortion, that takes all and gives nothing, that has forgotten the traditions of its youth, and preferred the office of tax-collector to that of leader, will offer no resistance."

§ 294. The history of American industry may be said to begin with the independence of the nation, or rather with the adoption of the present Constitution. The navigation laws confined the carrying trade of the colonies to English or colonial vessels. In 1672 duties were imposed upon goods carried from one British colony to another, and as the West Indies at that time supplied us with sugar, cotton, tobacco and indigo, took timber, grain, &c., in exchange, the trade thus taxed for the benefit of the English treasury was an extensive one.

During the last century the tendency of the colonies to unite manufactures with their agriculture and save the expense of transportation of the raw produce they sold and the manufactured goods they imported, was sternly repressed by English legislation. They saw, as Franklin wrote from London in 1771 that "every manufacturer in our country makes part of a market for provisions within ourselves, and saves so much money to the country as must otherwise be exported to pay for the manufactures he supplies. Here in England it is well known and understood that wherever a manufacture is established which employs a number of hands, it raises the value of land in the neighboring country all around. It seems, therefore, the interest of our farmers and owners of land to encourage young manufactures in preference to foreign ones."

In 1699 the export of wool and woollens from the colonies, as well as from Ireland, was forbidden. In 1731 an inquiry of the Board of Trade ascertained that the colonies were making linens, woollens, iron-wares, paper, hats and leather, and even exporting hats. The carriage of these, even from one "plantation" or colony to another, was forbidden. In 1750 the preparation of iron, except in its rudest form for export to England, was prohibited; and every slitting or rolling mill, tilt-hammer, forge or steel furnace was declared "a common nuisance." The making of pig iron was allowed, because, the application of coal to its manufacture being as yet not invented, and the American woods furnishing an unlimited supply of charcoal, it was thought good policy to encourage the colonies in this line. The law was very commonly evaded, as the ruins of the old steel furnaces and iron works in out-of-the-way places of New Jersey and other states still show.

> The economical theories which underlay this British policy will be found in a standard work of that period—Gee *On Trade*, (London, 1750). "Our colonies," he says, "are much in the same state that Ireland was in when they," the Irish, "began the woollen manufactory, and, as their numbers increase, will fall upon manufactures for themselves. A little regulation would remove all this out of the way. It is proposed that no weaver have liberty to set up any looms without first registering the name and abode of any journeyman that shall work for him; that all negroes shall be prohibited from weaving either linen or woollen, or combing of wool, or working at any manufacture of iron, further than making it into pig or bar iron; they shall for time to come never erect the manufacture of nails, under the size of a two-shilling nail, horse-nails excepted; that all

slitting-mills and engines for drawing wire or weaving stockings be put down; that also they be prohibited from manufacturing hats, stockings or leather of any kind. . . . If we examine into the circumstances of the inhabitants of our plantations, and our own, it will appear that not one-fourth part of their products redounds to their own profit, for out of all that comes here, they only carry back clothing and other accommodations for their families, all of which is of the merchandise and manufacture of this kingdom. . . . All these advantages we receive by the plantations, besides the mortgages on the planters' estates, and the high interest they pay us, which is very considerable; and therefore very great care ought to be taken that they are not put under too many difficulties, but encouraged to go on cheerfully. . . . The colonies have not commodities and products enough to send us in return for purchasing their necessary clothing, but are under very great difficulties, and therefore any ordinary sort sell with them, and when they have grown out of fashion with us, they are new-fashioned enough there."

This is not irony, as we might have supposed if De Foe had written it, but sober earnest. It represents the unquestioned English opinion of that day. Even our friend Lord Chatham declared in the same spirit that the colonies should not be allowed to manufacture "so much as a hob-nail" for themselves.

§ 295. The legislation to keep the colonies to the work of producing raw materials for English manufacturers, and take in pay a small share of English goods, while through their necessities English capital became more and more the master of their estates, was among the provocations that led to the American war of independence. While the war lasted English goods found but scanty access to American markets, and the people were forced to make for themselves the articles of prime necessity which they had hitherto bought in England. Among the worst hardships of the earlier years of the struggle was the absence of those native industries that would have made the country independent of the foreign market. The return of peace in 1783 brought ruin upon the home manufactures which the war had called into existence. England had an attack of the exportation mania. Every one who had hoarded up a few pounds, even the maid-servants, invested their savings in a "venture" to the new country. The American market was flooded with British wares; they soon sold at far less than the English prices, inflicting severe loss upon these "adventurers." But the blow fell still more heavily upon the workman at home. "Not a hatter, a boot or shoe maker, a saddler, or a brass-founder, could carry on his business, except in the coarsest and most ordinary productions of their various trades, under the pressure of foreign competition... The people had gone to war not for names, but for things, .. to redress their own grievances, to improve their own condition, to throw off the burden of the colonial system.... The arm which struck for independence in the field was palsied in the workshop; the industry which had been burdened in the colonies was crushed in the free states." The Articles of Confederation, adopted during the war, constituted a central government too feeble in its powers to remedy this and other evils. Individual states adopted protective tariffs, but these cut the confederation into parts separated by custom-house frontiers. To remedy this a new and stronger union was demanded,—a government constituted directly by "the people of the United States," and not by a contract between the states, a government in whose hands should be placed the power "to promote the general welfare" by providing for the industrial development of the whole country. The new Constitution went into effect in 1789. "I conceive, sir," says Fisher Ames, a leading member of the Convention that drafted it, "that the present Constitution was dictated by commercial necessity more than by any other cause. The want of an efficient government to secure the manufacturing interests, and to advance our commerce, was long seen and pointed out." The power to regulate both foreign commerce and that between the states was clearly vested in the national government by the new document, and for ever taken away from the states.

§ 296. President Washington was inaugurated in a coat of home-spun cloth, and selected for Secretary of the Treasury Alexander Hamilton, a young man who had already distinguished himself as a man of business, a soldier and a political thinker, and was to prove himself perhaps the very greatest of American statesmen. He had an enormous task before him; the country was burdened with an unjustly contracted and justly hated debt;

its credit destroyed, its people all but bankrupt. But his vigorous administration of the finances brought back prosperity.

The first Congress found its table loaded with petitions from the business men of all the leading cities of the Union from Boston to Charleston; these portrayed the ruin that had been wrought by the competition of the foreign trader, not only upon manufactures but upon all the interests of the country, and with one voice asked the intervention of the national government for its protection. A bill was passed (and signed by the President July 4th 1789) imposing "duties on goods, wares and merchandise imported," this being "necessary," the preamble alleges, "for the payment of the debts of the United States and the encouragement and protection of manufactures." These duties were very low,—too low to afford much protection, even in those days when the cost of transport was so great. So we find Washington reminding the adjourned session of this Congress (Jan. 1790) that "the safety and interest of the people require that they should promote such manufactures as tend to render them independent of others for essential (particularly for military) supplies." A second and much more protective tariff was adopted (August 1790) after Secretary Hamilton had been asked to "report a plan, conformably to the recommendation of the President, for the encouragement and promotion of manufactures." At the next session, October 1791, Hamilton made his famous "Treasury Report" on the subject. It was a masterly statement of the new era upon which industry was entering, through the use of machinery and the division of labor; of the advantages that would be lost to the nation who fell behind in this advance; of the interdependence of all the material interests of the country, and of the relation of a diversified industry to national prosperity. He stated with candor and refuted with force the usual objections to a protective policy. He pointed out seventeen branches of manufacture already established, and some of them even in a position to export their products. He reminded Congress that "when a domestic manufacture has at tained to perfection, and has engaged in the prosecution of it a competent number of persons, it invariably becomes cheaper."

Strangely enough, the production of raw cotton was one of the industries specially protected at this period. South Carolina and Georgia were at this time in a state of industrial prostration. India had secured their European market for rice and indigo, and the price had fallen so low that it was not worth while to export them. They were looking around for some other staple, such as hemp; one of their representatives in Congress said in 1789 : "cotton was likewise in contemplation among them, and if good seed could be procured he hoped might succeed." Raw cotton was taxed 3 cents a pound for their benefit, being 8 or 10 per cent. of its value, and this was continued in the face of Hamilton's protest that it was unwise to put a duty on the raw materials of a manufacture. For years every New England factory—almost every New England family—paid three cents a pound more for West Indian cotton. In 1794 Mr. Jay, in negotiating a treaty with Great Britain, put cotton into the list of articles not to be imported thither in American ships. In 1796 a Wilmington firm petitioned Congress for a repeal of the duty, and was refused because it "would damp the growth of cotton in our own country." In 1794 Eli Whitney, a Yankee living in Georgia, and observing the costly and clumsy way in which the cotton was cleaned from the seeds by hand, invented the cotton-gin, which gradually revolutionized the industry and at once put the Southern States ahead of all competition.

<small>The facts are given in detail in Edward Everett's *Address before the American Institute in* 1831.</small>

§ **297.** The breaking out of the wars that followed the French Revolution furnished a still more effective protection to American industry by interrupting the communication with Europe—the British Orders in Council (1806) having declared the coast of Europe in a state of blockade, and the Berlin and Milan Decrees of Napoleon (1806 and 1807) having retorted with a similar paper blockade of the British Islands. American trading vessels had to run the risk of capture by one of these powers when bound for the dominions of the other. This, with England's claim of the right to search American vessels for English seamen, led to acts of retaliation on the latter power. All British vessels were ordered to leave American ports, and an embargo was laid upon American vessels, forbidding them to sail for England. This was followed by a non-intercourse law in 1808, renewed in 1809. In 1812 war broke out between England and America, and the duties upon all species of foreign merchandise were doubled to meet its expenses, the increase to be in force till a year after its close. But in spite of the impulse given to native industry by the political troubles, it found the United States unprepared. "What did we discover," says Dr. Bushnell, "in our war of 1812, but that we had nothing to equip the war? Having no woollen manufacture, we could not clothe our soldiers; we could not even make a blanket. We had been free traders, buying all such things because we could buy them cheaper; but we now discovered that we might better have been making blankets at double the cost for the last fifty years. The same was true of saltpetre for gunpowder; of guns, and cannons, and swords, and iron and steel out of which to make them. . . . . We began, also, to discover that the very insignificant article of salt, coming short in the supply, was nearly a dead necessity—one of the munitions of war—and that manufacturing it for ourselves at double the cost would have been a true advantage. . . . We very soon discovered in the facts referred to the lowness of our organization, and the very incomplete scope of our industrial equipments. Our products were not various enough to make a complete nation."

The tariff legislation up to this war, and, indeed, till 1824, had the defect of the tariff of 1790; while framed with the best intentions, it was, in fact, inadequate. Its authors had as yet no conception of the enormous power brought to bear for the destruction of our industries and the preservation of the supremacy of British manufactures. It was part of the English programme to keep America in the position of colonial dependence by these new weapons after the political independence of the republic had been acknowledged. A Birmingham manufacturer prophesied on the breaking out of the war that the crops of the United States would be devoured with vermin, because there was not skill enough in America to manufacture a mouse-trap. Others put much the same estimates of us into more polished forms; the chief industrial function they saw in the young republic was its power to purchase English goods. As Lord Lyndhurst said in 1838 : " The United States of America was always considered our own especial market." " The extent and swift, regular progress of the American market for English goods," said Henry (afterwards Lord) Brougham in 1813, " we can easily account for. . . . . America is an immense agricultural country, where land is plentiful and cheap; men and labor, though quickly increasing, are yet still scarce and dear when compared with the boundless regions which they occupy and cultivate. In such a country manufactures do not naturally thrive ; every exertion, if matters be left to themselves, goes into other channels. This people is connected with England by origin, language, manners and institutions; their tastes go along with their convenience, and they come to us, as a matter of course, for the articles they do not make themselves." After noting that they bought about £16,000,000 a year of English cloths, he continues : " But it is not merely in clothing. Go to any house in the Union, from their large and wealthy cities to the most solitary cabin or log-house in the forests—you find in every corner the furniture, tools and ornaments of Staffordshire, of Warwickshire, and of the northern counties of England. . . . . The whole population of the country is made up of customers, who require and who can afford to pay for our goods." But the Orders in Council had made a change. The English system was " forcing manufactures all over America to rival our own. There is not one branch of the many in which we used quietly, and without fear of competition, to supply them, that is not now, to a certain degree, cultivated by themselves; many have wholly taken rise since 1807—all have rapidly sprung up to a formidable maturity."

§ 298. When the war ended there was a considerable portion of the people of the United States engaged in manufactures, and a large amount of capital had been turned in that direction, and could not be diverted into others without great loss to its owners. This fact was not due to any financial legislation, wise or unwise; it grew out of the necessities of the war. New England, the chief commercial quarter of the Union, had seen her merchant marine rotting at her quays month after month and year after year. She had groaned and fretted, but she did not fold her hands in fretting. She went into the new work of home manufactures with all her strength. What would the nation do to support these industries that its act had called into being after destroying her shipping—the nation into whose hands she had given the control of her material interests? English capitalists did not wait for the question to be solved; another mania of exportation seized them; they deluged America as they were deluging the Continent, with the goods that the war had hitherto kept them from exporting. "The frenzy," says Brougham in 1816, "I can call it nothing less after the" South American "experiences of 1806 and 1810, descended to persons in the humblest circumstances, and the furthest removed by their pursuits from commercial cares. . . . . Not only clerks and laborers, but menial servants, engaged the little sum they had been laying up for a provision against old age and sickness." He is speaking of the Continental trade, but he adds: "The peace with America has produced somewhat of a similar effect, though I am very far from placing the vast exports which it occasioned upon the same footing with those to the European market the year before; both because ultimately the Americans will pay, which the exhausted state of the Continent renders very unlikely; and because it was well worth while to incur a loss upon the first exportation, in order, by the glut, to stifle in the cradle those rising manufactures in the United States, which the war had forced into existence, contrary to the natural course of things. . . . . Eighteen millions worth of goods, I believe, were exported to North America in one year, and for a considerable part of this no returns have been received, while still more of it must have been selling at a very scanty profit."

§ 299. The first session of Congress after the war began two months before the date at which the double duties on imports would cease. President Madison in his message called attention to the effect that the war had had upon manufacturing industry; "it has made among us a progress, and exhibited an efficiency which justifies the belief that, with a protection not more than is due to the enterprising citizens whose interests are now at stake, it will become at an early day not only safe against occasional competition from abroad, but a source of domestic wealth, and even of external commerce." Of the numerous petitions which urged the same facts upon Congress, that of the cotton-spinners excited most attention. This industry employed some 100,000 persons, and produced goods of the value of $24,000,000, having increased nine-fold during the war; it consumed American cottons, and thus contributed to the prosperity of the South. For this reason, apparently, it received the support of some Southerners, notably that of John C. Calhoun. After hot discussion, a duty of thirty, twenty-five and twenty per cent. was laid on cottons, descending every two years, and $7.50 a ton on pig iron. The whole tariff was a sort of compromise between protection and free trade; like its predecessors, it even fell short of what its authors expected, and formed—as we have seen—no effectual barrier against excessive and speculative imports. The years when it was in operation were years of distress and embarrassment; the tale of bankruptcies lengthened out day by day; the value of home produce and of all sorts of property declined. The revenue showed a yearly deficit, and the national currency fell off fifty-nine per cent. in three years, indicating a general stagnation in commerce. All interests suffered, notably the farmers, who largely petitioned against duties, and talked as if our government could repeal the English corn laws. The manufactures of earthenware, glass, white and red lead, wholly disappeared; that of iron was at the point of extinction. The manufacturers never ceased to petition Congress to extend to them even a fraction of the protection enjoyed by their English and French rivals.

When Congress met in December 1823, President Monroe for the second time urged the adoption of additional duties upon imported manufactures, and in January a new tariff bill was reported. It proposed higher rates of duty because " what in 1816 was called 'a moderate protecting duty,' would scarcely have been adequate protection against a fair and liberal European competition, but was absolutely nothing against the oppression of wealthy foreign manufacturers, who can afford cargoes of their goods at reduced prices or at no prices, in order to break down a growing rival, and indemnify themselves by fleecing the country afterwards." The chief advocate of the measure was Henry Clay, of Kentucky; its chief opponent Daniel Webster, of Massachusetts. The same antagonism of their views had been brought out in the debate on the amount of the duties to be imposed in 1816. New England had already invested a large amount of money in manufacturing, but not so much as to make that a controlling interest; her vote, which was for Free Trade before the war, was now divided (15 to 23). As a large majority of the South were now opposed to the policy which had called their cotton-growing into existence and had given it the command of the home-market in the years of its weakness, the bill was carried by the votes of the Middle and Western States. For the first time the country had a tariff that was, both in its purpose and in its effects, protective. One marked defect it had; the duties on woollen goods, both in their amount and the manner of their imposition, were far from satisfactory. This manufacture languished while all others throve. A bill to remedy this was passed by the House in 1827, and lost in the Senate, which it reached too late for passage.

§ **300.** In December 1828, the Report of the Secretary of the Treasury, Mr. Rush, called attention to the general prosperity that had followed the adoption of the tariff of 1824, and especially the way in which it had given the country such a measure of industrial dependence, as prevented the European panic of 1826 from seriously affecting American interests; he suggested an increase of some leading duties. At the end of January the tariff of 1828 was reported and passed after a brilliant debate, in which Mr. Webster now took the affirmative side, declaring that New England was now for protection. The South complained that they had reaped none of the advantages of the new system; that they were falling off in wealth rather than advancing—complaints probably due to the growing contrast between the regions blighted by slave labor and those blessed with free industry. With some changes in the method of assessing duties, and a few in their rates, this tariff remained in force till 1832.

"We cannot manufacture, said Senator Hayne, of South Carolina, in 1832, "except as to a few coarse articles; slave labor is utterly incapable of being successfully applied to such an object. Slaves are too improvident; too incapable of that minute, constant, delicate attention and that persevering industry which is essential to the success of manufacturing establishments."

§ 301. How did the country prosper under the new system, as compared with the old? "If I were to select," says Henry Clay in 1831, "any term of seven years since the adoption of the present Constitution, which exhibits a scene of the most widespread dismay and desolation, it would be exactly that term of seven years which immediately preceded the establishment of the tariff of 1824." As to the state of the nation when he spoke: "We behold cultivation extended, the arts flourishing, the face of the country improved, our people fully and profitably employed, . . . a people out of debt; land rising slowly in value, but in a secure and salutary degree; a ready, though not extravagant market for all the surplus products of our industry; . . . our cities expanded and whole villages springing up as if by enchantment; our tonnage, foreign and coastwise, swelling and fully occupied; . . . the currency sound and abundant;

the public debt of two wars nearly redeemed, and, to crown all, the public treasury overflowing—embarrassing Congress not to find subjects of taxation, but to select objects which shall be relieved from impost. If the term of seven years were to be selected of the greatest prosperity which this people have enjoyed since the establishment of their present Constitution, it would be exactly that period of seven years which immediately followed the passage of the tariff of 1824."

The tariff of 1828 imposed a large number of duties for revenue upon articles (tea, coffee, &c.) not produced in the United States, in opposition to the wishes of Clay and the consistent protectionists. In 1832 these were removed or largely reduced, while some of the protective duties were slightly so, partly with a view to reducing the revenue, which was considerably in excess of the needs of the government.

§302. In 1833 the question took a political shape; South Carolina, with the moral support of Virginia, Georgia and Alabama, announced her purpose to resist the enforcement of the national tariff legislation. President Jackson, who had always advocated protection, was now full of the impending danger to the Union; he saw all questions through the one medium, and advised a reconsideration of the tariff in detail and the removal of some of its duties. Henry Clay, being likewise a candidate for the presidency, saw matters in much the same light. He was an honest man at heart, who " would rather be right than be President," but the concealed magnet in the White House often makes the most honest compasses deflect from the north star of principle. He introduced a compromise bill into the Senate, providing for a gradual lowering of duties, by which they were to be reduced to twenty per cent. on the 30th of June 1842. It was only three weeks before the end of the session, but the bill was carried through both houses before the session closed. Till 1842 the process of reduction went on, and the gradual closing of American factories and workshops went with it. The capital of the country, the accumulations of years of protected and prosperous industry, being driven from manufactures, sought a channel for investment in other quarters. The sale of public lands rose in 1836 to $24,877,179, or more than ten times what had been the average rate. There was an enormous expansion of the currency and inflation of prices. Imports increased seventy-five per cent. Speculation ran riot; wild-cat banks grew up as fast as mushrooms. The craziest schemes to become rich without the trouble of earning wealth by hard work, found ready listeners. M. Chevalier, who visited America at this time, says in the account of what he saw in 1835: " Everybody is speculating, and everything has become an object of speculation. The most daring enterprises find encouragement; all projects find subscribers." Places were sold as building lots that lay far beyond the range of settlement for years to come; cities grew up in a night—on paper; sites of houses and streets that lay in pestilential marshes, or on naked precipices of rock, or six feet under water, found eager buyers. No new channels for industrial enterprise were opening; the old were closing; the enterprise that must find an outlet somewhere sought all manner of absurd and hazardous channels. We were to produce all sorts of raw materials that the old world had monopolized; the *morus multicaulis* was to give us cheap silk for the whole world. Then in 1837 came the crash, the banks suspended specie payment, and the country wakened up from a feverish dream to find itself on the point of bankruptcy. The revenue fell off so greatly that the government was obliged to ask loans, first in the home and then in the foreign money market, and met only with rebuff in both, although the loan asked was less than a fourth of its ordinary income. Labor ran begging for employment, and during 1839–1841, the cry was heard far and near, " Give me work, only give me work! Make your own terms; myself and family have nothing to eat!"

By 1840 the country was thoroughly aroused, and elected a protectionist President, after the fiercest political campaign in our history. When Congress met in December of 1841, Gen. Harrison was dead, but his successor, Tyler, recommended an increase of duties in a conciliatory spirit. The tariff of 1842, one of the best and most protective ever enacted, was adopted, and no more threats of secession were heard. The prosperity that free trade was to bring to the South had not been achieved, and the preservation and extension of slavery now absorbed the attention of that section. The new policy bore the old fruits; languishing industries were quickened into life; with the growth of the power to purchase, foreign commerce revived; government reaped a large revenue, and the finances of the country were again in a satisfactory state. The home production of great staples was multiplied, and the prices of many of them fell. A better and more trustworthy currency came into circulation.

Then, in 1846, the policy was changed once more, and that of military aggression upon weaker neighbors at home succeeded that of industrial resistance to more powerful nations abroad. England, after some five centuries of rigid protection, had adopted the policy of free trade, and was preaching it with all her eloquence to the rest of the world. Mr. Robert J. Walker, secretary of the U. S. treasury, was one of her disciples. "*Let them alone*," he told Congress, "is all that is required of man; let all international exchanges of products move as freely in their orbits as the heavenly bodies in their spheres, and their order and harmony will be as perfect, and their results as beneficial, as in every movement under the laws of nature when undisturbed by the errors and interference of man." But even a Democratic Congress had not quite forgotten the past, nor broken so far with the Democratic precedents of 1824–1828. The Dallas tariff of 1846 was still protective. It adopted, indeed, the vicious method of imposing *ad valorem* duties, while those of 1842 had been specific; and it taxed a host of articles that better tariffs, before and since, put into the free list. But it still imposed duties of from 40 to 20 per cent. upon the great staples of manufacture. Had these rates been calculated on the average price of the several articles, and then made specific at that figure, the effect would have been far better. For *ad valorem* duties make the home market far more dependent upon the fluctuations of the foreign market, and in the long run bring it under the power of the trader and the foreign producer. Thus during the years 1846–9 English iron was cheap, selling in New York at $40 a ton, and largely driving the home producer out of the market. One-third of the furnaces and iron-mills of Pennsylvania ceased operations soon after the tariff was enacted, many being sold out by the sheriff; the rest were sorely crippled, and the amount of their production greatly diminished. The iron men met, and in a memorial, prepared by Stephen Colwell, expostulated with Congress, showing that the ruin, which was impending over their industry, would be a costly injury to the whole country. They predicted that if home competition were out of the way, the nation would soon learn that the price of British iron was fixed, not by the cost of production but by the demand made upon that market, and the dependent condition of their customers. Their remonstrances were unheeded; the work of destroying a great industry went on, and its traces may be seen in the old furnaces of the Alleghany ridges. In 1851–4, when home competition was virtually out of the way, iron sold for $80 a ton, whereas native iron had been furnished for $60. When English iron was cheap, the duty was also low, and the native producer was driven from the home market. When it rose in price, the duty rose also, and enhanced its value to a degree that greatly checked its consumption. But this rise gave no security to the home producer to increase his turn-out, or to the capitalist to begin iron-works. Neither could tell how soon a real or an artificial cheapness might destroy his market again. There was no security for the home producer, while the home consumer was fleeced to the uttermost.

The Dallas tariff lasted till 1857, and inflicted injuries upon nearly all our industries, preventing the influx of capital in that direction. To compensate for this we were to have an unlimited foreign market for breadstuffs since England had repealed the corn laws. The more we bought of her, the more we must sell her, as "commodities are paid for with commodities." The commodity with which we chiefly paid was gold. The tariff increased the dependence of the country upon both the buyer and the seller of foreign markets. Its bad effects were alleviated by the discoveries of gold in California, which gave an impulse to all kinds of business. In 1857 Congress reduced the duties by twenty-five per cent. This was not a sudden change of policy, but the crowning of the edifice that had been building for eleven years past. It at once intensified all the unwholesome tendencies in our commercial and industrial life, turned capital once more from production to speculation, and led to a large and varying increase of importations. Another great panic followed through the collapse of unsound enterprises, and carried with it many that were sound. Every one had been buying at any price; every one made haste to sell, and found no customers. Lands in what was then the far West, by whose purchase fortunes were confidently expected, were sold by the county to pay the taxes. The treasury was again depleted, and years came in which it must borrow the means to carry on the government.

In 1860 the Republican party, composed very largely of the old Protectionist party, won its first national victory, and broke, for the third time in sixty years, the Democratic succession of Presidents. In 1861 the war for the Union began, and the Morrill tariff was enacted, and up to the present writing that policy has been persisted in by the nation. Not that that tariff, either in its original form or as subsequently modified, is satisfactory in its application of general principles. It has been made more satisfactory, indeed, by fairer protection to the woollen industry, and by the removal of duties that had been laid upon articles that cannot be produced at home. Another great defect in our financial system was the heavy internal revenue duties levied until after the war,—duties that took away with one hand nearly all that was given with the other.

When the war began American industry was unable to furnish all the materials to arm and equip the national forces. Steel and cloth, and blankets, had to be got from England; and fortunately the seas were open. Long before it closed all these elements of the national defence were produced at home, of as good quality and in quantities large enough to meet any demand. But from the very start to the close of the struggle the North reaped the advantage of the possession of that diversified industry which had perpetuated itself in the face of so many discouragements, and now sprang into vigorous life;—while the merely agricultural South was continually hampered through the absence of manufactures, of the middle class who sustain them, and of the industrial habits which they cultivate.

§ 303. Nine times in one hundred years the American people have changed their financial policy, sometimes carried from Protection toward Free Trade by the influence of specious theories, but as often driven back to the policy of Protection by hard experience. The two periods of longest continuance in any policy is the Protectionist period which followed the establishment of the government (1789–1801), and the Protectionist period in which we now are living. Four times the scaffolding of the tariff has been torn down from the uncompleted edifice of our industrial development, and as often the work has been begun again—if not from the foundation, yet from a point much less advanced than had been reached under the previous protective tariff. This time it seems to be the nation's purpose that the scaffold shall be kept up until the roof is on.

§ 304. It is admitted on all hands that the effect of our present protective tariff has been an extraordinary development of our manufacturing industries, and a rapid advance toward a period when we shall be altogether independent of the rest of the world as regards all the great staples which are capable of economical production on American soil. The census of 1870 showed an increase of more than one hundred and eight per cent. in the value of our manufactures; that of 1880 is expected to show a still greater advance. Between these two censuses came the great Centennial Exhibition, which was to multitudes of the American people a revelation of the growth of our industries in quality and in quantity alike. No part of that vast display excited so much patriotic satisfaction as did the accumulated results of American skill and ingenuity exhibited in Machinery Hall. Prof. Rouleaux of Berlin was at least as well fitted as any of our foreign visitors to pronounce an estimate of the whole exhibit of our industries. He declared it to be one for which Europeans were quite unprepared as regards its abundance and magnificence, and the admirable adaptation of means to ends in all our processes and implements. In his opinion American manufacture has escaped a great mischief in aiming at good quality rather than mere cheapness in its products; and he deplores the fact that Germany has injured herself and lost her hold on the best customers by following the lead of England in this respect. In many lines of manufacture, such as cottons of all the lower grades, American goods take precedence of every other in point of excellence; and in England itself a demand exists for our cottons as the most trustworthy that are to be found.

§ 305. Prof. Rouleaux very justly criticised as unsatisfactory those branches of our manufactures which employ the arts of design. He found clumsy earthenwares, ill-designed and crudely-colored carpets, an excess of allegorical motive in our silver and other ornamental wares, and a general failure to put the finest materials in the world to the most effective use. Those criticisms would hardly be just if repeated now. The year 1876 was a time of new beginnings in the development of those branches of manufacture which demand the application of artistic taste and skill. The sight of what other countries had done in this department was a stimulus to our own efforts, and in the following years the application of art to manufactures advanced with rapid strides. Much is still needed, especially in the general diffusion of a knowledge of the arts of design through our public-school system; but a country which is admitted to have outstripped every other in the quality of its wood-engraving must possess in its own people artistic resources which, if developed, will make it altogether independent of the help of foreign designers.

§ 306. In the development of American ingenuity the protective policy has played a remarkable part. Mr. Mill's suggestion, that the establishment of an old industry among a new people is followed generally by improvements in its methods, is fully confirmed by recent American experiences. In many manufacturing establishments there is a standing offer of rewards for such improvements devised by the workmen. American improvements are not monopolized by our manufacturers. We have no law against their export, such as England maintained for nearly a century, and Mr. McCulloch defended in his *Dictionary of Commerce*. Our models of axes, saws and other tools are reproduced in Birmingham; our improvements in the Bessemer-steel apparatus are copied in the North of England; sewing-machines are made abroad under all our expired and many of our unexpired patents, royalty being paid in the latter case; and so-forth. An English authority laments the fact that nearly every labor-saving invention of recent years is of American origin. The centrifugal apparatus for refining sugar is a notable exception to this rule; but it is the rule. The cost of some of the great staples has been reduced, not only to America, but to the world, by the protective policy, which set American invention to overcome Nature's resistance to our getting them cheaply. And we look for still greater results of this kind in the future.

§ 307. Our tariff is found fault with because it does not make men prudent and virtuous, besides giving them the opportunity to become prosperous. (1) It is said to be responsible for the over-production which has characterized some branches of manufacture. Thus, although we do not produce cotton goods sufficient to supply the national demand, we do produce more than enough of the more homely and substantial sorts; and at times our cotton-factories are forced to diminish their production below their capacity, and to reduce the time and wages of their work-people. The same evil occurs, and more frequently, in Lancashire under Free Trade. The common cause in both countries is a defective judgment as to the capacity of the market, and no legislation can be devised which will obviate the difficulty. There still are plenty of openings for the investment of new capital in manufactures, if our manufacturers will study the lists of imports to find where the home supply is inadequate to the home demand.

§ 308. The depression of 1873 and the following year grew out of an excessive construction of railroads in America, and a consequently feverish stimulation of the iron and steel industries. The great outlays in wages to iron-workers imparted a similar impetus to textile and other manufactures, which continued until the collapse of the Northern Pacific Railroad precipitated a panic far less severe than those of 1837 and 1857, but whose effects were felt for years.

§ 309. (2) Again, in the course of time a duty becomes excessive through a change in the conditions of production, and it is said that the American manufacturer, if the home competition do not prevent this, will raise his price to the highest figure permitted by the tariff, and will make excessive profits by doing this. Whether this be an actual situation or not, it is a conceivable one. There are two remedies for it. One is found in the certainty that excessive profits will increase home competition by leading to a large investment of capital in that particular industry; another may be found in the reduction of the duty to an amount sufficient to compensate the disadvantages, as regards labor, capital, taxation and so forth, under which the American producer lies. The principle of protection justifies no duty of a higher rate than this. In so far as the tariff goes beyond it, it is not protective, but prohibitive.

But it is altogether absurd to abuse the tariff because businessmen will not resist the temptation to take advantage of such a situation as has been supposed. The tariff will produce no higher results than the average morality of the business community. This average is in America at least as high in the manufacturing class as in any other. Dr. Lyon Playfair thinks he finds in the honesty of our manufactures the traces of the old Puritan passion for righteousness. His praise may be deserved, without being true of all our manufacturers. But certainly neither he nor any impartial observer would select any of our protected industries as furnishing comparatively glaring instances of our want of a high moral standard. He would select rather the grain, stock and oil gambling of the trading classes and the management of some of our great railroads.

§ 310. It is charged against our protective system that it has resulted in the destruction of American *commerce*. Objectors of this kind use the word "commerce" in the narrow and conventional sense which has been affixed to it by English writers, and which corresponds to the situation of England. They mean by it the export and import of commodities. The true sense of the word is "the exchange of services or commodities between persons of different industrial functions." In this sense Protection is a great promoter of commerce. It creates variety of industrial function within the nation, and fosters the most rapid and continual interchange of services between persons thus differentiated. It promotes association between members of the same nation by producing variety in their employments; while Free Trade between more and less advanced nations always has resulted in the destruction of asssociation among the people of the less advanced, and in their reduction to a monotony of occupation. There is no vaster commerce in the world than that which takes place between the fifty millions of people who live inside the line drawn by the American tariff, and who are growing in mutual interdependence with every year of its existence.

§ 311. As was said in the tenth chapter, we cannot accept the amount of exports and imports as affording any fair test of the country's prosperity. Such a test could have been devised only in a country which had made itself dependent upon others for supplies of food and raw materials, and for customers for its manufactures. But, even when gauged by this test, America is found to have made no retrogression. The proportion of exports of manufactures to the population was greater in 1880 than in 1860. This export might be much greater if we took the proper steps to increase it. It might be expected, for instance, that the nations of South America would be large customers for own manufactures. We buy of them great amounts of coffee, hides and wool. We can furnish them with many manufactures which they have no ambition to make for themselves, and in some cases not the resources. But our chief trade with that part of the continent is conducted in English ships, which go thither with cargoes of English wares, and come back, by way of New York, with cargoes of South American produce, which they replace by cargoes of American wheat. When we secure direct commercial intercourse with the countries which have few manufactures, we may expect to find foreign markets for our own. At present we have such intercourse only with countries largely engaged in manufacture.

§ 312. It is charged that the Protectionist policy has debarred us from getting our fair share of the carrying trade of the world. But American citizens are free to own and sail ships built in any dockyard of the world. Our laws place such vessels under no disadvantage. We admit ships of every build on equal terms to our ports, and remit many of the charges, such as lighthouse dues, which are charged in the ports of other countries. It is true that by a law passed in Washington's first administration, and continued in force by every party which has been in power since that time, ships of foreign build are not admitted to American registration. They cannot carry the American flag, and our government assumes no responsibility for their safety. But American registration confers no commercial advantages. On the contrary, it brings with it serious disadvantages. The laws for the protection of American seamen impose burdens on the owners of ships in our registration much heavier than are borne by others. Our consulate system collects far heavier fees from them; our systems of State taxation impose, as a rule, much heavier fiscal burdens on them; and in return for these the vessel which has American registry receives no compensatory advantages. The nation does not maintain a decent navy for its protection; it does not exert itself with any remarkable energy in the defence of American interests, property or citizens abroad. In these respects it is much behind England, which is ready to continue registration and efficient protection to any ship which Americans may purchase from British owners.

In fine, we have absolute Free Trade in the matter of merchant marine. It is to this, in great measure, that we owe the decline in American shipbuilding—a decline which began in 1855, six years before the Morrill Tariff was enacted. We are almost the only country which has acted on the *laissez faire* maxim in this matter. Great Britain built up hers by a system of subsidies, at first paid openly, afterward under the cover of payment for carrying the mails. France has a subsidy system more thorough and extensive than any other country of Europe. In America the same method was followed until 1855, when, on recommendation of the Senate Committee of Commerce—Mr. Jefferson Davis was chairman—subsidies were discontinued. Their resumption is demanded now by many of the most influential commercial bodies in America, and is expected from the Congress in session at this writing.

§ 313. Protection corresponds to the purpose of the American people to be a complete and entire nation, at peace with every other in so far as in us lies, desiring no advantage at the expense of any other, wishing for them that fulness of national life which we desire for ourselves, but as independent of their good or ill will as the resources of the national domain will permit us to be. It sometimes is denounced as irreligious and selfish, but only by those who have taken no pains to understand it. There is a religion, *The Saturday Review* says, which became current in England about 1851, made up of "Free Trade and the pleasanter parts of Christianity;" with that religion Protection comes into conflict. But there is nothing in it which is inconsistent with the Golden Rule: "Whatsoever ye would that men should do to you, do ye even so to them."

## CHAPTER THIRTEENTH.

### The Science and Economy of Intelligence and Education.

**§ 314.** In presenting what have been found to be wise methods of national economy, and in attempting the solution of economic problems, it has again and again been pointed out in the foregoing chapters, that the education and the consequent high intelligence of the people is essential to the prosperity of a nation.

We have seen that an *agriculture* that is not directed by scientific knowledge is wasteful in itself, and will at last be unable to meet—much less to outrun—the ever-increasing demand of the people upon its productiveness. Experience also shows that, so long as farming is conducted in an unintelligent way, it will never be anything but a distasteful drudgery, which will drive the best young men of the agricultural class into the cities, and to occupations that employ mind as well as muscle.

We have seen that the notion that *labor* will always leave an ill-rewarded employment for one that is better paid, is disproved by facts. The uneducated farm-hand of Dorsetshire, with his mental horizon no larger than the visible one, shrinks from pushing out into an unknown and untried world to seek his fortune, and puts up with ten shillings a week, when a few shires farther north he might earn a competence. The Flemish *boer* works for a half or a third what he might get a dozen miles to the south, because he has never had the chance to pick up the small amount of French that would fit him to labor in Brabant or Brussels.

We have also seen that improvements in methods and in machinery, by discontinuing the employment of some class of workmen, inflicts great injury upon that class if its average of intelligence be low, and its power of adapting itself to a new set of conditions be slight. And we have also seen that all these improvements make a larger demand upon the workman's intellectual gifts, and can only be carried out to the best advantage where these receive a fair measure of cultivation.

It has also been seen that the condition of the working classes is capable of very great improvement, through the adoption of certain methods of economy—labor-banks, coöperative societies, building societies, and the like—which demand the diffusion of a considerable measure of knowledge if they are to be well supported and wisely managed.

We have seen that the *sanatory condition* of a community is capable of very great improvement only when the conditions of life and health are understood by the people. And upon this, as has been said, depends in large measure the industrial capacity and efficiency of the people. English statists estimate that every death represents one hundred and sixty-six days' illness, during which the sufferer, if a working man, is thrown upon the charity of his friends or of society for his support. The consequent total to be subtracted from the productive and accumulative powers of the people is immense.

We have seen that the protective policy is vindicated by its friends and conceded by its enemies to be a measure of national education, whereby special advantages are given to the home producer until he has learnt the habit of manufacture and acquired skill in its methods. A natural accompaniment of such a policy is an active national effort for the technical training of those who are competent to receive it.

§ 315. These and other considerations like them lead us to see the importance of education as a part of a wise national economy. The small outlay of the national resources that is necessary to train every citizen to the highest rank in industrial efficiency that is possible to him, is well expended in the purchase of a larger gain to all classes. It is one of those wise sacrifices of present for future advantage, which distinguish progressive societies from those that are stagnant.

But a national education can never be a merely industrial education,—can never be even first and chiefly industrial. The industrial state is but one aspect of the national life, and an education that could contemplate only its ends would come far short of the training required to fit the citizen for his place in the body politic. It would also defeat its own ends by leaving the man undisciplined in many duties and in right methods of thought, which very greatly influence his industrial worth. On the other hand, there is especial need to call attention to this part of national education, since the conception of the nation as an industrial state is quite a modern one. Napoleon among the men of practice and Fichte among the thinkers—closely followed by Saint Simon—were the first to recognise its truth. And as in earlier theories of national life, so in earlier methods of education, other things were regarded and this neglected.

§ 316. A National Education, limited in its range indeed, but broad enough to embrace the whole scope of the nation's vocation, was enjoined upon the Jews by the Mosaic legislation. Especially of the moral law it is said: "These words which I command thee this day, shall be in thine heart [i. e., thine understanding, thy thoughts;] and thou shalt press them upon thy children, and shalt talk of them when thou sittest in thine house, and when thou walkest by the way, and when thou liest down, and when thou risest up." The later Jews, at a time when the industrial life of their nation had attained a larger development, required that every father, however wealthy, should teach his son a trade, so as to provide against all contingencies of fortune and enable him to avoid becoming either a pauper or a thief.

In Greece we have two great methods of national education standing in very sharp contrast. The Spartan was a system of military discipline, of stern and unnatural restraint. It was the drill of an armed garrison who gave up their individual tastes, ideas and impulses, and submitted to an all-constraining law. The death of the three hundred at Thermopylæ, " in obedience to the laws," was the crown and the flower of the life of the city, which produced no great men of letters, and indeed few great men of any sort. The Athenian method was a full and free development of human nature, especially on its intellectual and æstletic sides. In Athens, more than in any other land or time, we have the results of the extension of the finest culture of mind to the whole free population of a state. Of formal teaching and learning there was comparatively little, except the memorizing of Homer and other poets in the schools; the new science of mathematics seems to have taken its name from the fact that it was the first branch of knowledge that was not picked up—like reading, writing, grammar, politics, the arts—from one's fellow-citizens, from being at the theatre, or from the daily contemplation of great works of art, the sight of inscriptions, &c.; but needed to be *learned* by direct and formal application. Yet their intellectual education was perfect; no accumulations of knowledge or improvement of methods have enabled any people or class to attain a higher or more balanced cultivation of the mind. But they lacked moral balance and self-restraint, and so became the victims of their own cleverness, as Socrates saw and told them.

If the New Testament teaching be true, both these opposite methods were right and capable of being united, because there is in man a higher or spiritual nature which education is to awaken into life and call forth into activity and vigor; while there is also in man a lower or animal nature, by which he must not be governed, and which must be brought under restraint and discipline.

§ 317. The Roman inherited the Greek method of education, but never gave such prominence to it. The Greek governments were systems of education; Roman education was a branch of the civil service. The great university of Alexandria, the *Mouseion*, was not only cherished by the new rulers, but reproduced in other chief cities, especially by the Athenæum at Rome. In lesser places, what we might call colleges, professional chairs and schools were founded, and considerable zeal displayed for the education of the higher class of citizens. But the learning chiefly cultivated had no relation to the practical life of the times. Much attention, for instance, was given to rhetoric and oratory, although all real use of these had disappeared with the cessation of free popular assemblages.

In the Byzantine Empire this Imperial system was perpetuated down to the capture of Constantinople without the slightest change even in the text-books. Except during the brief period when Julian forbade the Christians to use the old classics, no Christian literature of any sort was admitted to the schools of the Eastern Empire, and the use of the Scriptures in such a place would have been deemed sacrilege.

In the west, Karl the Great sought to trace out and revive the old imperial foundations throughout his empire, and the monastic schools at Fulda, Aachen, St. Gall, and other places, were probably the perpetuation of his efforts. More important still was the *schola palatina*, or court school, which he made an adjunct of his household, and which became a tradition of the royal court of France. It was afterwards transplanted to the new capital, Paris, and it enjoyed the service of many able men, such as John Scotus Erigena, who came over from Ireland, then the land of Christian schools and Christian learning. Karl adopted as the basis of instruction in the higher schools the system or classification of Boethius, in which all learning was divided into the seven liberal arts, of which three (the *trivium*) were taught in the higher classes, and four (the *quadrivium*) in the lower. Hence the phrase "Master of *Arts*." In the lower schools reading, writing, arithmetic and singing were taught. This classification lasted till the revival of classical learning.

Out of the court school, or the ecclesiastical school which succeeded it, grew the University of Paris, the mother and mistress of all European universities, except Bologna and Oxford, whose possession made France in the earlier Middle Ages the Kingdom of the University, as Italy was the Kingdom of the Holy See, and Germany that of the Holy Roman Empire. The rise of the University was so very gradual that the steps can hardly be traced, but at the time when Abælard was drawing tens of thousands of pupils to Paris to hear him expound the scholastic philosophy, and partly perhaps through his great success, the University had taken a distinct shape, which was chiefly changed by the division of the professors into separate "faculties," and the students into "nations," and this formed the model after which others were erected in Bohemia, Germany, Spain and Scotland. These institutions were hardly instruments of popular education. They attracted, indeed, an immense body of students to a few great centres of culture; we read of forty thousand at the University of Oxford. But their object was to form a learned class, not to reach the whole people. He who received it betook himself to a new sort of life; he did not go to the schools to learn what would fit him to fill his place in the class in which he was born, but to leave that class and enter another. It was a training for grown men, not for children. Only monastic schools were open to the latter in the earlier Middle Ages; and when others were established they were chiefly preparatory to the universities, and imparted a highly abstract and artificial training in a very tiresome and inadequate way. They were generally trivial schools in which were taught the arts of grammar, music and arithmetic, i. e., the Latin grammar of Donatus, the psalms and hymns of the Missal and their ordinary tunes, and the elements of computation. The only Latin literature read was the *distichs* of Cato and a Latin version of Æsop's Fables; but in course of time, the Catechism (i. e., the Creed, the Lord's Prayer and the Decalogue) were added. Even with the revival of the study of classic learning, no change was made in these schools. Luther went to school under one of the new Humanists, but read nothing of the new literature until he went to the University.

§ 318. To the Reformation, and especially to Luther, popular education owes a very great impulse. In some sense we may say that it began at that date. The claim put forth that the Bible should become the people's book, and the efforts to circulate the new translations of it, as well as other edifying books, involved, as a correlative, a general effort to make the new literature accessible to the common people by a general diffusion of knowledge. But Luther aimed at diffusing a national education that should be truly such. In his appeals to the German cities, urging them to set up good schools—" not such as have been hereto fore, where a lad learned at his Donatus and his Alexander for twenty or may be thirty years, but never learned them"—he especially pleads for the general study of letters—"good poets and histories,"—and for the formation of city libraries of all sorts of good books as the complement of the school system. He would have the chronicles of their own country hold a prominent place in these collections. He would thus provide not only a competent body of educated men for the service of church and state, but also "a plenty of fine, learned, rational, honorable, well-brought-up citizens," as "the best and costliest possession of a city."

The Calvinistic Reformers laid still greater stress upon knowledge and intelligence, as needful for every true Christian. It was their ideal to see the Bible in the hands of a community competent to understand it. In Switzerland, Germany, Holland and France, they carried out this principle with great thoroughness, but nowhere more completely than in Scotland. Knox and his associates and successors worked for the establishment and endowment of English and Latin schools, and the improvement of the universities, as zealously as for the establishment of the Reformed doctrines. In spite of some temporary defeats, they carried their point, and the Scotch became a far better educated and more intelligent people than their richer neighbors at the other end of the island. In England the Reformation was a measure carried through by the government and the aristocracy; it was not so democratic in its character, and it affected but slightly the economic condition of the people. The agitation for a plan of popular education, to reach and provide for the most numerous class—as the higher and middle classes have been provided for by old foundations and private schools—has hardly been mooted there till within the present century. The first appropriation of money for the purpose was the vote of £100,000 in 1847, and only in our own times has there been adopted a plan of national education large enough to reach the whole people. It has, of course, been opposed, (1) by some few consistent free traders, like Herbert Spencer; (2) by those religionists who regard education as a spiritual function and deny the power of the state to exercise such functions; and (3) by those who object to the existing law, because it takes under government patronage the various Church schools that are already established.

Ireland has had an excellent national school system for a good many years past, whose effects in the dissemination of intelligence forbid us to ascribe the poverty of her people to ignorance. They take rank above the English in this respect.

<blockquote>Our chief authorities for the history of education in the old world are Prof. Franz Hoffmann's *Idea of a University* (translated and published in the *Penn Monthly* for October, 1872); Prof. F. D. Maurice's *Lectures on National Education* (London, 1839), and his *Learning and Working* (London, 1855); and Karl Jürgen's *Luther's Leben* (Leipsic, 1846).</blockquote>

§ 319. American education was begun by the churches, and the higher institutions of learning nearly all originated with the ecclesiastical bodies, as most of them are still under their control. The University of Pennsylvania was, through the influence of Franklin, perhaps the first to arise without formal connection with the churches. The colleges and academies of the New England States, and of districts settled from New England, were chiefly modelled after Harvard and Yale, and drew their teachers from those mother institutions and their daughters. Those of the Middle and many of the Western States may commonly be traced to the educational efforts of the Presbyterian clergy from the north of Ireland and from Scotland. The Puritan and Presbyterian elements have been the chief agencies in our higher educational system, and in both cases the interest and the motive was ecclesiastical. Religion, it would appear, was the only force at work in American society at large that was strong enough to overcome the American passion for money-making, to insist on the excellence of a liberal education, and thus to cherish the love of learning and of science till it grew strong enough to stand alone. Only in our own days have institutions of the same character been endowed in a few places by the state governments.

§ 320. Schools for popular education were very early established in nearly all of the colonies. Especially in Pennsylvania the Society of Friends was most zealous in establishing elementary schools, and in imparting to all within their reach the elements of a good English education. At their schools in this city many who were not of their body received their training, and it is very largely to the influence of the Quaker element thus exerted that the Commonwealth owes the solid sense and practical sagacity of its best and most influential elements. But the system of state education originated in New England, and has only been extended to other parts of the country within the memory of persons now living, and to the South only since the recent war. The progress of the system has been very rapid, and it is now recognised as a universally established principle that the state is responsible for the existence of illiteracy and of the crimes and violences that flow from ignorance. The system is opposed (1) by a very few consistent free traders, like the late Gerrit Smith; and (2) by some religious bodies, which regard education as a spiritual function inhering in the church.

Less can be said for the quality than the quantity of the education given by our public schools. Indeed we cannot too heartily recognise the fact that education is yet in an experimental stage among us, and that beyond the clear duty of teaching a few of the first and plainest elements of learning, everything else is open to question. We have too often forgotten that education is a means merely, a very flexible means to any end that we have in view, and that we must first fix the end by careful reflection and then with equal care adjust the means to the end. Education has been talked of as if there were something magical in the contact of a young mind with a series of school books and of teachers. But the magical results have not been forthcoming.

Especially the notion that education—the imparting of knowledge and the discipline of the intellect—was of itself sufficient to abolish all crime, has received a decided refutation. There is indeed a limited amount of truth in this notion. Crimes of violence, for instance, as Henry Holbeach says, very commonly grow out of the imperfect communication of ideas and feelings between uneducated people. Their heartburnings "are born of imperfect intelligence of each other in dilemmas of conscience or affection, upon which such poor means of utterance as they have are thrown away." Hence we speak of quarrelling persons, if they be reconciled, as coming to an understanding.

There is also in the discipline of the school-room, its required order, cleanliness and self-restraint, a powerful moral training for the young, if the teacher be equal to the task. And even the mere power to read, in the great preponderance of good literature over bad, and the great prominence of the best of books in modern society, is pretty sure to do far more good than evil to its possessors, taken as a whole.

Yet our excellent fellow-citizen, Mr. Joseph R. Chandler, gives it as the result of his fourteen years' devotion to the cause of prison-discipline, "that learning has little or nothing to do with preventing or promoting crime, however it may influence the character of the act. . . . While in the lowest order of crime I may have found more unlettered than lettered criminals, I have found the former more amenable to gentle moral dealing than the latter were." But this generalization is not based upon a comparison of two societies of different degrees of intelligence, or two stages of intelligence of the same society, and is, therefore, hardly justified. Indeed, the fact last alleged in its support, and which Mr. Chandler's authority puts beyond question, points to exactly the opposite conclusion. The educated criminal is more hardened, because his fall has been greater; he "sinned against light," and that light of his intelligence was one of the deterrent forces that might have held him back. The more and the stronger those forces, the greater the fall, and the more hardening its effect upon the character. Conscience, however, until enlightened by intelligence, is a mere spur, and not a true guide in life. It has been, when unenlightened, the source of a great multitude of crimes against humanity. There are, indeed, cases in which education has been so abstractly intellectual, so devoid of all moral drift and tone, that the conscience has been almost suppressed. But education may easily be made, or rather can hardly help being made, very different from that,—can never be truly national, truly in accordance with the very first notion of the state, without being very different.

§ 321. Without discussing in detail the merits and defects of our present systems, we shall seek to discover what idea is rightly conveyed by the term *national education*. This term carries us back to the idea of the state as the institution of rights, and as distinguishable into three departments of national activity,—the jural estate, the culture state and the industrial state. Manifestly the second of these now engrosses attention, whereas we hitherto have been chiefly considering the third. A national education, then, is (1) one that develops in the man the intellectual powers and capacities that fit him to understand the ideas and the truths that are the common possession of his fellow-citizens, and that fits him to act with at least that degree of mental freedom that his nation has attained. (2) It is one that impresses upon him the characteristics of an upright and good citizen, a man of public spirit, and a devoted patriot, and that fits him to exercise such political powers as are intrusted to him by the constitution of his country. (3) It is one that gives him such general instruction, and offers him the opportunity to acquire such special training, as will fit him for his special profession, calling or industry, and will enable him to pursue it in the most effective manner.

§ 322. *Firstly*, education to fit a man for his position in the culture state will have reference to the rank in knowledge, insight and mental power possessed by his own nation. The public schools of China or Japan should not give lessons in German philosophy, or in the English language, or any language but their own. Even the intellectual growth of a nation is chiefly from within, and the attempt to import a foreign culture by wholesale, can only result in crushing out that which is of native growth, and in retarding the normal progress of the people. It will merely root out the native plants, and substitute a *hortus siccus* of dry and dead specimens, without sap or root. For every country possesses a certain average of intelligence, and has attained a certain stage in the great historical march of the human spirit from childish subjection to manly freedom. And as the nature of that march is governed by the historical constitution and course of nature, each country must take the next step forward before it can take any subsequent step,—must start from the position that it now occupies, and build upon the foundation that it has already laid.

> Mr. Palgrave, the English art critic, for instance, expressed his fears that Japanese art will be stopped in its natural course of development, through the imitation of foreign models.

The language and literature of each country are at once the perfect expression of the degree and quality of its culture, and the means of education in conformity with that. The sure foundation of all national education, on its national side, is the study of the native speech, through books that record it in its highest and purest forms. But text-books that give only the result of such studies, and teach nothing of their method, such as spelling books, school dictionaries, grammars, manuals of etymology, and the like, are not educational instruments in any true sense. They impart information, without imparting discipline; they give no impulse, save in a very few cases, to the further pursuit of the same studies, but rather weary and disgust the student. They do not render the service that all rightly directed study of a language through its literature will render, in training the judgment to decide between greater and lesser probabilities, by the problems it presents as to the meaning and connection of words. They give rather a phantasm of knowledge about words, a mass of definitions and statements, than an actual acquaintance with words in their living uses. They are more likely to hide from the student than to declare to him the wonder and beauty of the language, as a work of art at once human and divine, as the result of a great process of education, by which men were led on from the sense perception of things material, to the apprehension of the more real and less tangible verities of life.

The study of another than the native language, especially of a language of the same family but of earlier date, gives a great advantage, in enabling the student to compare and contrast the two, and suggests to him open secrets that would otherwise have escaped him. Hence the great use made of Greek and Latin in the higher education, one of which gives the most perfect illustration of the living force of words, the other of the laws of their government, and both correspond to earlier stages in the world's intellectual development. Both have been subjected to an analysis by great scholars that has extended over centuries, and are therefore provided with an apparatus of study the most complete possible.

But these studies cannot be introduced into our public schools generally, chiefly because their curriculum of study is not protracted to years in which these could be effectively pursued. The best substitute attainable in those schools, is that of our own language in its earlier stages, as presented, let us say, by the great English classics from Chaucer to Milton. That literature is as much the heritage of the American as of the English people; while un-American elements may be traced in all the great writers of the following centuries, those earlier masters are free from them. And they furnish a long series of noble books, which embalm the wisdom and the excellence of lives not less noble. With wise guidance, and not too elaborate an apparatus for their study, the scholar might learn from them at once the method of studying words and their history, and the personal friendship for great authors, which constitutes a large part of the truest culture. But mere volumes of extracts, however excellent for some purposes, will not answer here; they prevent the study of literary works as artistic wholes; they do not ordinarily give a full exhibit of the state of the language at any one era; and they cultivate the habit of dipping into books rather than continuous reading.

There is another language, not national but universal, addressing itself not to the understanding but the heart of man—touching fibres of his human nature too fine to vibrate to ordinary language,—fibres that lie closer to his very self and deeper than his ordinary self. Music should, in the opinion of Plato and Milton, form a part of human education; and the general sense of mankind has assigned it a very large place in the great uplifting process which we call civilization. The hold which it has taken upon the working classes in our own days, especially in England, its power to elevate and refine, to harmonize and humanize, to remind men of the ideal to which all worthy life is ever striving, to cheer them with far-off glimpses of it amid the sordidness of the actual, all confirm this high estimate of the human use and worth of music as an educating force. Whatever danger there may be in an excessive devotion to it, it should be made a subject of universal training, and its introduction into our public schools, though something late, is a most excellent revival of what was once a study practised in every school.

*Mathematical* science, in contrast to language, represents the most general form of intellectual culture; it calls forth and disciplines the reason, the universal intellectual power, which belongs to man as man, and apprehends not probabilities but certain and unquestionable truth. Arithmetic, geometry, algebra, have in modern times held a high place in education. In our schools arithmetic is not taught thoroughly, because after a slight amount of instruction in the pure science, the student's attention is diverted to its application to commercial computations. A more thorough discipline in the analysis of number would be of far more use even in practical life than these rules and methods, which are mostly obsolete in our counting-houses. Geometry, for the same reason that too much heed is given to what is thought practical, is either entirely omitted, or is postponed till after the student has mastered the more difficult subject of algebra.

The *physical sciences* are a means of education only when pursued in such a way as to teach their methods as well as their results. The latter may be imparted as information in very large quantities without the student's having attained any real acquaintance with the facts; he may have got no more than a mass of memorized definitions and statements, and, in spite of

Bacon and all who have followed him, may mistake these for the facts. He may have learnt not a whit of the patience, self-distrust, humility, and loyalty to fact, that characterize the true man of science, the original investigator. His powers of attention, observation and accuracy may have been left dormant under it all.

These objections hold with great force against the branch of physical science most taught in our schools, and the method by which it is taught. From the lowest to the highest schools, and by a series of graded text-books, the attention of the pupil is concentrated upon *geography*, with no result save the overloading the memory with a mass of statements which constitute no real knowledge of the earth's surface. They are true in detail, but the whole is false as professing to be an adequate account of our planet. They are a hindrance, therefore, to real knowledge, as they render the student content with what is a mere phantasm knowledge. He mostly learns them by heart without any realizing sense of their meaning, and a question out of the usual run of questions often displays the vacuity of his mind on the subject.

For this earth-lore it would be well to substitute neighborhood-lore—or the study of those facts that actually fall under the scholar's observation, and their scientific explanation. The student might learn the geology of his native district; its relation to all the large geographical facts, such as the isothermal lines, the continental formations, the sea and the tides; its meteorology especially, its weather-lore; its natural history in all its branches, with incitement to collect specimens for the school museums; its social history and progress from the days of the red man's wigwam to the present time. Such a training would be in the line of the providential purpose which ordinarily connects each single life with a single spot of earth; it would give the mind the sense of a hold upon the world, a definite place and starting-point. It would be more likely, by connecting life with knowledge, to be the first stage in a life devoted to knowledge, than if its youth had been spent in loading the memory with notions, which, however real in the knowledge of the scientist, possess no reality for the scholar.

And to come still more close to the student, he should be taught the elements of practical hygiene in connection with the broader physiological laws that govern health and disease. There are few of us but would live longer and more healthful; for such self-knowledge; it would save men from grave mistakes such as often embitter a lifetime by disease, and would thereby add greatly to the industrial power of the nation.

§ 323. *Secondly*, to fit a man for his place in the jural state, education will implant in his mind the convictions of righteousness, of justice, that underlie the national order and the laws by which it is prescribed and enforced. The state is the organization of the whole people for the purpose of securing justice; this is the common vocation of all states, and except as they recognise it and act on it, they are unworthy of the name and forfeit the rights of nations. The elevation of the individual citizen into the true national consciousness is therefore an education in righteousness, in uprightness,—and the means of restraint upon unrighteousness, prohibitions and punishments, are but secondary political agencies. The state must seek first of all to plant the right seed, and secondarily to root out the tares

This is, thus far, only incidentally attempted in our modern system, through the influence of school discipline, the enforcement of order, and the operation upon the mind of studies that aim at other ends, but do effect something towards this end, by familiarizing the mind with the conception of law as the underlying principle in every sphere of life and observation. And indeed it is by indirect teaching, rather than by the imparting of moral information, that most can be effected. The study of the lives of great and good men may do much; such as those biographies in which Plutarch has preserved for us the life and spirit of the great heroes of the Greek and Roman world. And out of biographies already at hand, a corresponding book might be compiled for the modern period and written with the same " universal sympathy with genius " (Emerson), in the same spirit of genuine enthusiasm and admiration, and convey the same inspiration of enthusiasm to its students. Both in its selection and its method, it should contemplate men in the relation of their lives to the life of the state, showing how their virtues contributed to its strength and its freedom, and even how their vices, faults and weaknesses tended to weaken and enslave it. It should be, like Plutarch's, a book " crammed with life," with " genial facility " of style, the embalming of noble lives. It should stand higher than his, as modern society stands above ancient, in the clearer knowledge that " righteousness is of the essence of the state " (Plato), and in the firmer purpose to educate students into that devotion to it which is the truest and highest form of the national consciousness.

The best text-books for this training are wisely written histories, and of these the finest is the Old Testament history of the Jewish nation, which is especially fitted to exemplify the great principle that is to be here inculcated,—that the divine call laid upon every nation is a call to righteousness. The national literature of that people tells how a family became a tribe, a cluster of tribes, a nation; that the law of righteousness was disclosed to them as the foundation of their national life; that their experiences, both light and dark, disclosed to them the truth that they were a strong, united and living people when they lived by it, but weak, divided and dying when they lost sight of it. Especially the prophets of the nation stand out prominently as the interpreters of the meaning of their nation's history,—as pointing out the moral order, the moral " constitution and course of nature," upon which the nation's life, freedom and prosperity depended. Their function was not specially " the prediction of future events;" some of their books contain no predictions whatever, and those that occur in others for the most part flow naturally from that perception of " the laws that circle under the outer shell and skin of daily life,"—laws at once ethical and social—which they were trained to observe in " the schools of the prophets." Their power of prediction was but the test of the reality of their science of the moral order of society, as of all other science (§ 2).

> The Old Testament has been so overlaid with allegorizing, "edifying," and other unhistorical sorts of commentaries, that its political significance has been obscured. One of the best expositions of its political side is given in Prof. F. D. Maurice's *Prophets and Kings of the Old Testament*, (Am. ed., Boston, 1854). In the same spirit Sir Edward Strachey has treated the prophecies of Isaiah in his *Hebrew Politics in the Times of Sargon and Sennacherib*, (2d ed., London, 1874), and Matthew Arnold has published the last twenty-six chapters of that book as a text-book for schools (*The Great Prophecy of Israel's Restoration*).

The most instructive history of any modern nation will be the one that most closely approaches to that Hebrew method of historiography,—not by any affectation of style or the lifeless repetition of Bible phrases, but by the application of the same principles in the selection of the representative facts, and in its severe and faithful, though friendly, judgments of all national transactions. It will start from essentially the same conception of the nature and the calling of the nation, and will trace the same divine hand "shaping" men's "ends" for purposes that they had not foreseen. It will give a lasting importance, an inexhaustible significance to the transactions of temporal affairs, by connecting them with the eternal principles of right. It will make the student feel that his calling, as a member of a nation, is a lofty and solemn thing, and will awake him not only to the consciousness, but also to the conscience of freedom. It will show him that the privileges and franchises of citizenship are a divine trust, a stewardship, and his abuse of them a crime of a very high nature.

It will not be claimed that our present school histories are written on any such plan as this. They have been, for the most part, modelled more after the Fourth of July oration than the Hebrew prophets. They teach too often the silly vanity of national boastfulness, instead of any mere ethical lesson. As the sense of humor has been developed among us, such teaching and such speech-making have turned our brief but honorable history into a theme of jest and popular merriment, which no longer excites the imagination or rouses patriotic enthusiasm. Our educated classes now seek in other lands the scenes of historic association which they no longer find at home.

§ 324. The mere instruction in righteousness is not in itself sufficient for the formation of a human character according to the standard of our own country. The legal maxim, *Summum jus, summa injuria,* has its truth in this connection; the merely righteous man, the just man whose justice is a hard insisting on all his rights, an exacting of his own, comes short of perfect rightness or righteousness, and is often guilty of acts which the popular conscience pronounces to be simply wrong, though not technically so. This is so because we are, however imperfectly, a Christian nation,—because the national standard of character is derived from the Sermon on the Mount as well as from the Ten Commandments. That Sermon does not set aside the old code; it only complements it by enjoining upon the individual heart and conscience a spirit of meekness, of self-sacrifice, and of forgiveness, which counteracts the spirit of self-assertion and hard legalism, which would bring the law itself into contempt by making it the instrument of men's selfishness and rapacity. The old basis of national order, the stern righteousness that demands "an eye for an eye, and a tooth for a tooth," it leaves untouched; but it guards that order against a peril involved in its own nature as applied to the affairs of imperfect men. And it announces these injunctions, not as applicable to some special class of saintly characters, but as laws of the kingdom of God— of God's government of men.

The New Testament, therefore, either in or out of the public schools, should form an essential part of the education of the young for their places as members of a Christian nation. Its exclusion from those schools, even if it be taught sufficiently elsewhere, may have the effect of sundering its lessons from his practical life, and lead him to suppose that the book is a mere " religious " or churchly text-book, whose precepts of Christian courtesy, forbearance and self-sacrifice, concern but slightly his relations to society at large. The chief objections to its introduction are, we believe, based on misconceptions of its real character, many of which are due to those who have come to be regarded as its especial custodians and interpreters.

Even as a literary work, the English Bible holds such a place as a master-piece that no course of education can be complete if it exclude it. Its phrases have become the proverbs and household words of the people; ignorance of the broad outlines of its history and teachings, even of the letter of some especial parts, consigns a man to social contempt. And it has become entwined with all the other classical literature of the language. Not only Milton, Bunyan and Cowper, but even Shakespeare, Scott and Byron would be in places unintelligible to those who have no acquaintance with it. For this reason, among others, the Hindoos prefer to study English in the missionary schools where it is read, rather than in the government schools from which it is excluded. They also resent its exclusion from the latter as a piece of jealousy similar to that with which they once kept the Vedas from the knowledge of Europeans.

> A Roman Catholic writer, the late Father F. W. Faber, says of the English Bible: "Who will say that the uncommon beauty and marvellous English of the Protestant Bible is not one of the great strongholds of heresy in this country? It lives on the ear like a music that can never be forgotten, like the sound of church-bells, which the convert hardly knows how he can forego. Its felicities often seem to be almost things rather than mere words. It is part of the national mind, the anchor of the national seriousness. Nay, it is worshipped with a positive idolatry, in extenuation of whose grotesque fanaticism its intrinsic beauty pleads availingly with the man of letters and the scholar. The memory of the dead passes into it. The potent traditions of childhood are stereotyped in its verses. The power of all the griefs and trials of a man is hidden beneath its words. It is the representative of his best moments, and all that there has been about him of soft, and gentle, and pure, and penitent, and good, speaks to him for ever out of his English Bible. It is his sacred thing, which doubt has never dimmed and controversy never soiled. It has been to him all along as the silent but intelligible voice of his guardian angel; and in the length and breadth of the land there is not a Protestant with one spark of religiousness about him, whose spiritual biography is not in his Protestant Bible" (Preface to *Life of St. Francis of Assisi*, 1853).

§ 325. *Thirdly*, The state should give in its public schools such general instruction, and should offer in special technical schools such opportunity of special and technical teaching, as will fit its members for their places in the *industrial* state.

How far this should include the training of the members of the learned professions, including teachers in public schools, we will not stop to inquire. We will confine ourselves to the education of the persons engaged in the two productive industries, agriculture and manufacturing.

A scientific agriculture is one of the last attainments of even enlightened and progressive nations. As we have seen, nations that have made rapid advances in all the other arts, lag behind in this, importing food for large numbers of their people from abroad, when they could easily have raised enough and to spare at home. In some cases this is partly the effect of a bad system of land tenure, but in all cases the defective intelligence and the superannuated methods employed in farming are chiefly to blame. Since Liebig's great discoveries in agricultural chemistry, it has become perfectly possible greatly to increase the yield of any given area of soil by scientific methods, and to bring under profitable cultivation the most unpromising lands, wherever the local market for food makes it worth while to employ those methods. But even in such situations as this, the farming class cling to old ways, refuse to employ the same foresight and enterprise as are essential to success in manufacturing, and jest at "book farmers" as a set of enthusiasts. Nor are they so much to blame; their comparatively isolated situation, their distance from the great centres of intelligence, and the imperfections of their daily education by contact with other minds, render them a very conservative class. They cling to old traditions with great tenacity.

Two bad consequences result. (1) A divorce of experience and enterprise. The experimental farming of the country is left to editors, lawyers, clergymen, and the like, who have far less practical knowledge than is needed for the undertaking. Their enterprises very often—but by no means always—are needless failures; *i. e.* they might have been brilliant successes in the hands of men who united a large intelligence with a large experience. (2) The young people, who grow up on the farm, learn to regard agriculture as a soulless, mindless routine of hard work, with no chances of using any higher power than the muscles. They carry their brains to the best market. Some become preachers, others politicians, others professional men, others merchants. All these lines of activity are crowded with men of more or less intelligence and mental power, who began life in a farm-house, and might have been more successful and useful in life had sufficient inducements been offered them to end it there.

The technical education of the farming class should begin in the public schools, and with the earliest years of study. The neighborhood-knowledge proposed above would form a good introduction to it. In country schools that teaching should take this direction. The useful branches of natural history, the nature, history and habits of the domestic animals, and of the cultivated vegetables and the agricultural geology of the district, should be among its themes. The child should be taught at once the rightful respect for his father's mode of life as concerned with the most valuable of human sciences, and also to thirst for a more extensive acquaintance with those sciences, as bearing on that occupation. In a word, the school should be, on this side of its life, the preparation for the agricultural college.

In the college the students should receive at once the liberal culture that will fit them to associate on terms of equality with educated men, and the special scientific and technical training, that will enable them to practise a scientific agriculture. Of course the college should be, at the same time, a farm, sufficient in its extent and its variety of soil and of situation to represent the lands upon which its pupils are to be employed. Study and work should be associated in its management,—each to give direction, dignity and practical worth to the other. The best stock, the most improved instruments, the most thorough methods of tillage, should be exemplified on the farm; and a system of experimental agriculture should be carried on as part of its activities. Above all, the pupils should be impressed with a sense of a vocation, firstly as farmers, and secondly as farmers of education—as therefore in some degree intrusted with the education of their class. And no pains should be spared to impress upon the farming class the importance of such a patronage of the institution, as will make it a power to promote intelligence and enterprise in the community.

Farmers should be incited by state and county fairs, agricultural institutes and associations, and the like, to meet periodically to compare past results and devise better methods for the future. Their occupation gives them leisure enough for the purpose at some seasons of the year. In such meetings thoroughly educated farmers would soon hold a prominent place, and become themselves the educators of others. The influence of the technical school of agriculture would be thus multiplied, and would leaven the whole mass.

> The order of the Grangers, or Patrons of Husbandry, recently organized in this country some years ago, and already very widely extended, promises very excellent results in this direction of mutual education, provided that its constitution be rigidly adhered to, and the undertaking be perseveringly sustained. But mere association will not work immediate wonders, nor change at once the material thus united, and there seems to be danger of the order being used for political purposes by ambitious men, or smothered under the meaningless mummery of a secret association.

A governmental department of agriculture may render great services to the farming class, not only by the collection and acclimatization of foreign plants, seeds and animals, and their distribution at government expense; but also by investigating through consuls, and special agents, the methods of foreign agriculture, and by undertaking investigations and publishing information which private publishers would find too expensive. There are very clear limits to the range of its educational activities, but within those limits there is much that can be done to great advantage.

§ 326. Of hardly less importance is the technical education of the other classes engaged in productive industry. The era of the application of science to manufacturing industry may be said to have begun with Napoleon and the Continental system, when upon the French and German *savans* was imposed the task of discovering substitutes for substances which could no longer be obtained from abroad. Up to that time the arts had taken the lead of the sciences; Watt and Arkwright rather furnished problems for scientific investigation, than acted on the guidance of scientific teaching. But now science began to point out new industrial methods, and suggest improvements of those that were traditional. From the study and the laboratory came forth discoveries that revolutionized the workshop. Every progressive and intelligent nation is emulating every other in their adoption, and changes continually occur in great industries, by which old methods are at once abandoned and new substituted. Workingmen of a low and unintelligent grade have not the power of adaptation needed in those who are thus giving up old traditions and adopting new ways. The onward march of the industrial army will be greatly hindered if its troops have not the drill and the mental equipment that fit them for it. And that equipment is twofold. The man must have received such general training as has developed his judgment and his powers of observation, and must have a large measure of specific knowledge as to the nature of his work, and the materials he deals with.

So rapid are these changes, that there are, for instance, sugar refineries in our own country, full of machinery which is far from being worn out, but which is simply rusting out in idleness, because the discovery of new processes for the extraction of sugar from molasses has rendered it useless. The owners could not afford to go on using it, and will finally sell it as old iron.

§ 327. The complexity of modern manufacturing, even if it were thoroughly unprogressive, makes such technical training highly desirable. Things are attempted in modern industry that would once have been voted impossible, and the people who can do the most of these impossible things takes the industrial lead of all others. The resources of the old workshop were as limited in kind as in extent; its workmen plodded on in a dull routine that demanded little more than a slight cultivation of hand and eye. But a walk through a modern watch factory, will show what a vast number of technical educations have been expended upon the several workmen, and to what thoroughness these have been carried in each case. It is true that training of this sort is chiefly the work of active life, and can never be obtained thoroughly in any other way. But it is also true that very much may be done indirectly to qualify the man for his work; much knowledge may be given him that practice will transform into technical expertness. And above all, by showing him the reason of his work, as well as its method, is he not only qualified to act intelligently in any unforeseen circumstances, or to apply the same principles in any new method, but he is also led to take a deeper interest in his work, and to do it with more diligence, —more love for it.

And all this applies with tenfold force to the foremen of the workshop, the non-commissioned officers of industry. They hold a place to which every workman should be taught to look forward as the end of his labors,—as a place of honor as well as of better remuneration. And they should be men who know the "why" as well as the "how" of every industrial process that goes on under their oversight, for no knowledge short of that will enable them to meet all contingencies.

The great industrial exhibitions, which began with that of London in 1851, have opened a new era in technical education. The Continental nations, taught by the display then made of the great staples of English manufacture, especially metals, turned their attention to the diffusion at home of such technical knowledge as would fit their workmen to produce the more elaborate and costly of these,—those sorts, that is, in which the value is chiefly in the workmanship expended, and not in the raw material, much of the latter being imported from England. The results were visible in the Paris exhibitions of 1855 and 1867, and in the second at London in 1862. Each new comparison of results brought new humiliation to England, and even in 1862 the conclusion was reached that before England courted any new comparisons of this sort, she must do great things for the education of her workmen. But 1867 found her still farther in the rear, and almost every competent judge of the question, who expressed any opinion, united in that of Prof. Tyndall, "that in virtue of the better education provided by Continental nations, England must one day, and that no distant one, find herself outstripped by those nations, both in the arts of peace and war." This opinion, which is widely shared by patriotic Englishmen, will mislead us if we ignore the existence of other elements of England's commercial greatness. English competition has destroyed the muslin manufactures of Dacca, and the carpet manufactures of Turkey, in spite of the superiority of those wares to anything of the same sort that she herself produces. But as intelligence and taste are more and more widely diffused in those who use as well as those who produce, superiority of workmanship becomes every day a larger element of industrial power; and Mr. Scott Russell is not far wrong in saying: "Should the day come when our manufacturers are less skilled, less informed, less able than our rivals, the flood of raw materials to our shores, and the back-current of manufactures to replace them, may take another direction and surge on other shores."

See his *Systematic Technical Education for the English People;* London, 1869.

§ 328. The technical education of the workman is especially required for the production of those articles which require beauty of form, of color, or of design, for their production, and in which the joy of the artist is wedded to the toil of the artisan. Our democratic and industrial age has indeed till recently laid but little stress upon the beauty of its industrial products. It has cared more for use and subtance, and less for beauty and grace. There is no real antithesis between the two; the elegantly shaped earthenware from Greek and Roman kitchens and sculleries, with which we fill our museums and adorn our mantels, served their every-day uses of holding salt, oil, or the like, as well as do the ugly shapeless pieces of delft that now take their places, and they had cost no more for being beautiful. We have not had common things about us made in beautiful shapes because we have not cared to have them,—because our minds have lain dormant as regards the whole matter. But during the last forty years there has been an ever accelerating increase in the appreciation and love of the beautiful, and in the hatred and contempt of the mechanical pretences at beauty that once contented us. Our Democracy is passing out of the Thersites stage into that of Pericles, and all the past history of Democracy bids us expect a grand era of the fine and the industrial arts, which have always lived the grandest life when in alliance with each other, and with freedom and popular government. Especially in our industrial age—whatever may be the future of the fine arts—the manufactures that approach artistic merit and excellence may be expected to make great advances upon anything that the past has seen, and to bring the finest combinations of form and color within the reach of all who can compass even the necessaries of life. For this end the artisan must once more become the artist; for all true art in every nation has been born in workshops which were also studios, while it has been pampered, corrupted and finally destroyed in the palaces of nobles and kings.

The art education of the working classes becomes, therefore, every day of greater industrial importance. In England especially it has made very rapid advances, since the Great Exhibition of 1851 brought to light the general inferiority of English goods—especially glass and earthenware—to those of the Continent in this respect. Art schools, especially night schools for workingmen, were at once established in all the large towns, and instruction in art was begun in public and other schools, and the number of pupils receiving this instruction has increased with great rapidity. In 1866 it was over a hundred thousand. The results were at once visible in the exhibition of 1862 in all articles that called for designing and decorative art, and in those that require in the workman a feeling for form or color, and England's great progress in this direction was confessed by Continental observers, while her decline in some others was very evident. The establishment of the great South Kensington Art-Museum is the last measure in a series which have brought England up from the lowest place but one to one of the very highest among the civilized nations that apply art to manufactures. In Germany the same branch of industrial education has been vigorously pursued throughout our century; and their general artistic training, aided by fine fancy and exquisite taste, has kept the French people also in advance of their insular neighbors. America lags far behind all these countries; with us artistic knowledge and culture of every sort is the privilege of the few, instead of being the birthright of all. We are beaten in that which is the peculiarity of our own country, and perhaps our national vocation—the transformation of such privileges into such birthrights. Hence a large part of our work, though equally costly in material and thorough in workmanship, ranks below the corresponding work of Europe because of this defect. And what work of another sort is done among us is either by workmen or after patterns imported from Europe for the purpose. Nor is this a matter of indifference. A very considerable amount of aptitude for art lies undeveloped in this unpicturesque country and among this practical people, and is chiefly a source of annoyance and torment to the teacher as it finds vent in all sorts of irregular ways, whereas it might be made a delight and a benefit. And were our designers and masters of ornamental art native to the soil, their work would be far better adapted to American tastes, far more a source of pleasure and instruction to the people than that which is produced by foreigners in Europe, or after their naturalization among us. It would be the outgrowth of the national spirit, and would react far more powerfully upon the national mind in producing refinement and elevating thought; just as Rodgers's statuettes have done more for us than Thorwaldsen's Apostles could. A truly national school of art would then become possible to us, for our schools of design would serve to winnow out the really artistic minds from among the common people, and give them a sense of the worth of their vocation in its relation to the national life.

> The perfect adaptation of wares to the national tastes is in itself a measure of protection to the native manufacturer. An English dry goods firm sent out instructions to its agent in China, to pick up well-dressed Chinamen of different classes on the street, and buy their clothes off their backs, and send these at once to England. From these samples it could produce goods of the very sort that the Chinese wanted. In other cases the traditional costumes of European peasants were procured and imitated by English firms, with great success. But in a progressive society where a really cultivated, and at the same time distinctively natural taste exists, and where the change of fashions prevents a dead uniformity and monotony, such an imitation would be impossible.

§ 329. Students of the great building eras of the past, those that produced the temples of classic Greece and the cathedrals of mediæval Europe, will never be equalled until the distinction between the function of the architect and that of his workmen is obliterated by raising the latter more nearly to the level of the former. This is a subject of great importance to a young country like the United States, which is putting hundreds of millions into public and private buildings every year, and expects these to last for centuries. The advance of popular taste, such as it is, has already shown us that nothing is so costly or so wasteful as ugly architecture. A mechanical lifeless copy or half-copy of a Doric temple or an Italian palace, or a still uglier, more barn-like building, may please the people who built it and be not offensive to their neighbors and contemporaries. But the human mind wages ceaseless war on ugliness, detecting it instinctively, becoming more sensitive to it with every advance in culture, and finally abolishing it as an eye-sore and a nuisance. All work that is not the best of its kind comes into collision with this subtle, levelling force, which is stronger than mortar and brick, or stone and cement

The mere spread of culture and taste among our professional architects will only half solve the problem. We have had no real architecture—Mr. Ferguson, the very highest authority, tells us—because our artisans have not been artists also, as all the Greek and mediæval stone-masons were; and we shall only go on wastefully—building in one generation what the next will overthrow—till we get back to that point. This is surely the largest problem in the technical education of the working classes; but, after, all, it is only an extreme case, for the same principle is applicable in every other department. Artistic beauty is the crown and the flower of all the reproductive work of man; and to make the artisan an artist—to add the joy of beauty to the strength of toil, is a problem that meets us on every side of industrial life. Only this will lift the life of the workman out of its sordid wearisomeness, and make it tolerable by making it noble.

§ 330. The industrial education of the people should be contemplated in the common school system, as well as in the special technical schools. The school-room itself should be an education in the feeling for and love of the beautiful. Communities and artists should discern that there is no higher use for the best artistic faculty that the community possesses. And while there should be a general training in drawing for all scholars, there should be a special winnowing process for the selection, with a view to the further training, of those who are especially gifted by nature with the artist's eye and hand.

And the neighborhood knowledge proposed above should, especially in our cities, take in the great local industries, their histories, their growth and their methods, and whatever else is suited to awaken an intelligent interest in the student's mind, and lead him to look on with observant eyes at the work that is going on around him.

But technical schools for the special training of actual workingmen must be the chief dependence in this respect. There is nothing new in the attempt to combine learning and working in the same life. It was once the rule in the history of education, while juvenile education, down to the era of the Reformation, was the exception. The two pursuits are not in each other's way; each may give new zest and interest to the other. Nor need the workingman's studies be confined to branches which will be of direct and practical use in his work. The experiment of the Workingmen's Colleges in England shows that this class are fully able to receive and to appreciate what is, in all essential respects, a liberal education, and that not with the view of leaving their own class to enter what is socially construed as a higher, but to remain in it as its educators and leaders— an ideal depicted by our greatest novelist in her *Felix Holt*.

The general education of the working classes in all those branches of learning which will directly conduce to their industrial efficiency, is the natural complement of that protective policy which has already been advocated. That the nation should take any steps in this direction is very consistently denied by a very few free traders like Prof. Thorold Rogers, but in England common sense has always counted for more than logic, and very large outlays of national funds, as we have seen, have been made with a view to this end. She has gone far beyond our own country, although she has not yet overtaken the consistently protectionist peoples on the Continent, who are, both by restrictions on trade and by the schools of the state, training their people to compete with her. We have clung to the former but neglected the latter, and while there have been great advances made in the character of our manufactures, we must again pronounce the results to be unsatisfactory and insufficient. We can do, we must do, greater things than we have ever attempted.

It is beyond the province and the powers of the present writer to discuss the details of the problem. He knows only what he has had at second hand from friends and from books—especially he would refer for details to Mr. Scott Russell's *Systematic Technical Education of the English People*, and Mr. T. Twining's *Technical Training*, London, 1874.

# INDEX.

*Ad valorem* duties, defined, 231–2. Their effect in 1846–54, 355–6.

Agriculture, Quesnay's view of, 18. Adam Smith's, 19. A fundamental industry, 40, 90–1. Its historic beginnings, 49–50, 69, 197. Its progress, 70–2, 113–4. Intensive and extensive, 71–2, 237. Benefited by the neighborhood of other industries, 40, 46–7, 90–3, 212–7, 223, 235–6, 241–5, 259, 263, 276, 291–3, 305, 311, 320, 327, 342, 352–3. Needs intelligence and education, 83, 365, 385–7. In Germany, 72–3, 88–9, 122, 171–2, 323, 327. In Italy, 48, 73, 90, 121. In England, 58–9, 74–83, 97, 122–3, 124, 129–30, 130–1, 212–4, 259. In Belgium, 57, 72, 87–8, 171, 236, 319–20. In France, 86–7, 97–8, 123, 171, 273. In Switzerland, 58, 89. In Spain, 73. In Russia, 89–90, 124. In Scandinavia, 89, 113, 332. In America, 60, 92–3, 109–113, 172, 215, 239–44, 263, 341–2, 343, 348, 350, 357, 385–7.

*Alcavala*, a Spanish tax, 183.

Alcohol, its use a survival, 66. The heaviest tax on the working class, 131–2. Taxes on it, 183, 184. In India, 314–5. In England, 302.

Alleghenies, their settlement, 111.

Annuities, perpetual, 191–2. Terminable, 192.

Apprentices, limited by Trades' Unions, 135.

Arbitration between capital and labor, 136, 139.

Architecture, true and false, 393–4.

Argyle, Duke of, 108.

Aristocracy, its origin, 32–3. Its decay, 64. Loss of power in England, 282–3.

Aristotle, 14, 15, 32.

Arkwright, 128, 220, 281, 388.

Art in relation to science, 11, 14–15, 23, 24, 267.

Arts, use of gold and silver in, 145. Fine art in Japan, 376. In industrial education, 390–4.

"Arts, the seven liberal," 369.

Ashburton, Lord, 156, 166.

Association, man's progress to and by, 29, 32–6, 40, 49, 50, 70, 142, 143, 154, 197, 216–7, 220–1. Its decline, 217, 223, 301–2, 311–2, 334, 337–8, 341. Earliest forms, 32–3, 73–4, 98, 219. Of labor and capital, 115, 123, 135–6, 138–9, 254. Of workingmen, 25, 133–5, 136–8, 139–40, 202–3.

# 398  INDEX.

Atmosphere, the great storehouse, 43–5.
Babbage, 138.
Balance of trade, mercantile theory of, 16, 209. Say on, 20, 21, 207. Tooke, 23–4, 207. Its relative importance, 151–2, 206–8. Between England and Portugal, 334, 336. Between England and America, 343, 356. (See *Passivity of Money*.)
Bank-notes, first issued at Genoa, 153. Then in England, 153–4, 162–3. Their uses, 154–5, 169–70. "Over-issues," 156, 165, 173, 175. Guarantees, 155–6.
Banks, their rise, 153, 157. Their services, 154–6. Their functions, 158–62. Freedom and safety, 155–6, 170, 175. Their impolicy, 161–2, 164, 166, 173. In Italy, 153, 157–8, 161, 162. In Northern Europe, 153, 157, 158, 162, 171, 171–2. In England, 162–8. In Scotland, 168–70. In France, 170–1. In America, 172–8. (See *Bullion, Cash Credits, Clearing-house, Credit System, Discounts, Money of Account, Panics*.)
"Bank-screw" in England, 166–7.
Banks, land, 171–2.
Banks, people's or labor, 139–40.
Bankruptcy, forced and needless, 167, 173. France in Law's time, 170. In America, 350, 354, 357.
Barter, the first form of trade, 15, 142, 152.
Bastiat, 30, 126, 129, 266.
Baxter, Dudley, 211–2.
Beet sugar, 254, 272–3, 319, 322.
Benedictine monks, 14.
Berkeley, Bishop, 26.
Bible quoted: Old Testament, 35, 36, 49, 68, 73, 119, 202, 221. 367. New Testament, 38, 39, 50, 190, 223, 368. Its place in education, 381–4.
Bill of exchange in antiquity, 152. Reinvented by the Caursins, 152-3. Its nature, 153. Use in the United States, 177.
Biography in education, 380–1.
Black death, 74.
Blanqui, 21, 249, 253.
Bolles, Prof., 26.
Bowen, 193.
Bowring, 312, 326, 328.
Bright, John, 187, 192.
Brougham, Henry, 348–50.
Bullion in the Bank of England, 165–7. In that of France, 171.
Büring, 172.
Burke, 20, 225.
Bushnell, Dr. Horace, 227–8, 231, 347.
Byles, Judge, 31, 309.
Cæsar, 214, 283.
Cairnes, J. E., 25, 63, 149.

INDEX. 399

Capital defined, 115, 307–8. Its growth, 55, 237–8, 260–1. Its fair share, 24–5, 115–6, 124–6. Restrained by boundary lines, 19. Its tyrannous power, 28–9, 200–1, 209, 222–3, 281, 301. Its responsibility, 120–1. Its relation to improved agriculture, 72. Its policy toward labor, 119–20, 132–9. Is benefited by varied industry, 129, 237–8, 307–8. Relative sterility when employed in foreign trade, 205–6. Should legislation change its direction? 260–1. Fertilizes labor, 115, 123, 125–6, 135–6, 151–2, 154–5, 207–8, 274. England's accumulations, 125, 149, 151–2, 168, 209, 212, 281. Ireland's want, 130, 307–9. Drained out of Portugal, 334. And Turkey, 339.

Carpets, Turkish, 336–7, 390.

"Cash credits," in Scotland, 154–5, 169. In America, 204.

Cattle, first form of property, 73–4, 142. Early use as money, 142, 143. Early British, 101, 122. Value in agriculture, 46, 72, 92, 244.

Carey, Henry C., 29, 101, 126, 144, 294.

Carey, Matthew, 29, 173.

Carlyle, Thomas, 321–2.

Caursins, invented bills of exchange, 152.

Celibacy, its effects, 56, 65. In antiquity, 60–1. In America, 65.

Census, British, 62. Irish, 62–3. American of 1870 and 1880, 358.

Centennial Exhibition, 358–9.

Chalmers, Dr. Thomas, 23, 55, 288.

Chase, Salmon P., 176, 193.

Checks on population, 54, 56, 65.

Checks, bank, 160, 163.

Chemistry, 11, 15, 67. Agricultural, 46, 59, 113–4, 385, 386. Industrial, 254–5, 272, 322, 387–8.

Chevalier, 21, 149, 249, 250, 354.

Cicero, 152.

City, its history, 32–3. Becomes the empire, 33. Hated by the Teutons, 33. The closest association, 142. Duties, 52–3.

Civilization, its material progress, 29–30, 37–8, 40. Is normal, not exceptional, 56–7. (See *Differentiation of Function, Division of Labor, Power over Nature, Progress.*)

Clay, Henry, 234, 351, 352–3.

Cleanliness, its promotion by law, 52–3, 67. And temperance, 132.

Clearing-house, anticipated in French fairs, 160. Adopted in Scotland, 160, 169. A bank is one, 159–60. Its operations, 160. Between national banks, 176. National proposed, 177–8.

Climate, changed in England, 71. Commerce between climates, 217.

Clover, its use in farming, 45, 244.

Coal, its origin, 44. A labor-saver, 69. Irish and English, 298. Flemish, 318.

Cobden, 149, 187, 192, 230, 273, 288, 330, 336.

Coins, origin and shapes, 143. Of various substances, 148. Superseded by money of account, 157–8.

Coinage, English, under Sir Isaac Newton, 163.
Colbert, 17, 191, 209, 269-71, 273, 279.
Coleridge, S. T., 27, 28, 38, 79-81, 201, 253.
Colwell, Stephen, 30, 208, 356.
Commerce, definition and origin, 197. True sense of the word, 362. Trader's tax on, 198-9. Neighborhood commerce, 199-200, 201-2, 216-7. Distant, 200-1, 210. On credit, 203-5. Smith and Say's theories of foreign, 205-9. The present English theory, 209-16. In raw materials, 214-6. True and false commerce, 217-8. Protection makes commerce equitable, 245-8. French, 273, 274. English, 281, 282, 284-5. Australian, 296-7. Indian, 311-2, German, 328. Portuguese, 334-5. Turkish, 336-7. American, 342-3, 348, 349-50, 355, 356, 357. (See *Credit System*, *Trader*.)
"Commodities are paid for with commodities," 20, 207-8, 334. "Gold is a commodity like any other," 149-52, 207-8.
Commons enclosed in Italy, 73. In England, 77-8.
Community in land, 74, 75, 90, 98-9.
Competition highly estimated by the English school, 19, 22, 287, 309. Its relation to rent, 22, 93-5, 98-9. Restricted in the land market, 96, 305-7. Limited by custom, 24, 74-5, 98-9, 118-9. Does not always adjust prices, 201, 202. When does it raise wages? 129-30, 236, 303. Attempts to supersede it, 25, 136-8, 202-3. Protection promotes it, 226-7, 233-4, 251-2. England's competition with the world, 213, 274, 281, 296-7, 301, 318, 323, 330, 336-7, 350-1, 356. French, Belgian, German and American competition with England, 213, 233-4, 274, 284-7, 319, 328.
"Constitution and course of nature," 12, 29, 31, 37-8, 230, 376. Illustrated in the history of soil, 41-8. As regards population, 63-7. Of human nature in regard to wages, 119-20, 121. As regards the growth of varied industry, 219-21, 258-9.
Constitution of the United States, 224-5, 265. Industrial motives to its adoption, 344.
"Consumer, protection discriminates against the," 256-7, 289, 327.
Continental currency, 172.
"Continental system" of Napoleon, 254-5, 271-3, 281-2, 318, 323, 387-8.
Contraction practised arbitrarily by banks, 160, 161-2, 176. In England in 1783-1815, and later panics, 164, 165. Necessitated by Peel's Bank Law, 166-7, 168. In Scotland, 170. In the United States, 173, 176, 193. Avoided in France, 171.
Coöperation in production, 25, 136-8, 366. In housekeeping, 141. In trading, 202-3.
Copper in coinage, 148. Cheapened by protection, 261.
Copyhold tenure of land, 74, 77.
Coral islands, 43.
Corners in wheat, 200. (See *Forestalling*.)
"Corn Laws" repealed, 283, 284, 288. Their operation, 330, 350.
Cosmopolitical school founded by Adam Smith, 19-20. Its disciples, 20-26.

Opposed by Fichte, 27. By Coleridge, 27-8. By List, 28-9. By Carey and his school, 29-31. Their view of nationalities, 230-1. Their theory of commerce, 205-218, 228-9. Of the sphere of the state, 223-8, 289. The expediency of protection conceded by their chief authorities, 249-51.

Cotton, its production in America, 215-6, 240, 243, 254, 263-4, 280, 346, 350, 351. In India, 280, 311-2. In Turkey, 337. Manufacture in England, 215-6, 280, 284, 285, 311-2, 346. In India, 240, 255, 280, 311-3, 390. In Germany, 326, 328. In Russia, 330. In Portugal, 336. In Turkey, 336. In America, 263-4, 346, 350. Whitney's cotton-gin, 254, 281, 346.

Credit system, 159. Objectionable, 203-5.

Crime and education, 373-5.

Cromwell, Oliver, 83-4, 106, 277-8.

Culture-state, 38, 375-80.

Custom as an economic force, 24, 74-5, 86-7, 98-9, 118-9, 140.

Customs, in England, 187, 283-4, 290. (See *Duties on Imports.*)

Cutlery manufacture in America, 210-1, 255. In England, 277.

Dangerous classes, 76, 120.

Dearness, artificial, 200. Caused by protection, but only temporary, 233, 248, 251-2, 261. A relative matter, 215-6, 241-2, 257-8, 263.

Death-rate, 61-2, 67, 303.

Degradation, its influence on population, 67-8, 303. Effect of low wages, 119-20. Of English peasantry, 76, 78, 83, 95, 131, 212. Of the Hindoos, 311-2, 314-6. Of the Turks, 337-41.

Demesne lands, 181, 185.

Democracy of our age, 115. Its rise in England, 288-9. Relation to art, 391.

Demonetization of silver, 146-8.

Density of population an advantage, 49-50, 59-61, 68-9, 70, 96, 98, 100, 109, 198. Its natural limits, 63-7. In different countries, 57-8, 61, 87, 89, 98, 320.

Depopulation of the Roman Empire, 60-1, 67-8. Of places in India, 311. Of Ireland, 63, 130, 302-3.

Deposits, Bank; their origin, 159-60, 175. Part of the currency, 160, 165, 175, 176. Amount under bank's control, 161, 164, 165, 165-6, 167, 168, 171, 173. Runs on them, 162. A substitute needed, 161, 162, 203. (See *Discounts, Money of Account.*)

Differentiation of function, the essence of social progress, 37-8, 40, 43, 128, 137, 142, 144, 145, 179-80, 197-8, 203, 216-7, 219-22, 238. (See *Division of Labor, Uniformity.*)

Dilke, Sir Charles, 287-8, 295, 297.

Discounts, Bank, 158, 159, 164, 165-6, 173, 203, 204.

Disraeli, 287, 288, 303.

Distribution, law of, on increased production in agriculture, 96-8, 122-3. Same in regard to labor, 124-6, 127, 122-4, 237-8. English theories of, 21-2, 24, 54, 93-5, 116-7, 119, 133-4, 265. The existing system questioned by Mill and other socialists, 24, 116, 264, 266. Its remediable defects, 135-40, 201-3.

Dividends, taxes on, 183.

✓ Division of labor, a part of social progress, 15, 68, 70, 128, 197, 237, 345. Enabled by capital, 209, 237.

Drainage, natural, of poor lands, 100, 108. Artificial, its uses, 72, 102, 105 106, 109, 110, 322.

Drunkenness, how diminished, 132, 138. (See *Alcohol*.)

Dufferin, Lord, 300, 302, 303, 304, 305, 308, 309.

Duffy, Sir Gavan, 85.

Dühring, Dr. E., 30, 266.

Dunbar, Prof., 26.

Dureau de la Malle, 60.

Duties on imports, and their incidence, 231-5, 248. On raw materials, 239-40, 256, 346. Their object and ultimate effects, 251-2. Remedies for excessive, 361. (See *Ad valorem, Dearness, Protection, Specific, Tariffs*.)

Earthenware, why called delf, 275. Manufacture in Germany, 328.

*Economistes*, school founded by Quesnay, 17-8. Adam Smith's relation to, 19. Divorce science from art, 29. Turgot represents, 18, 271.

*Economist* (London) quoted, 284, 313.

Economy, not always parsimony, 14-5, 119-20, 124, 211-2, 227-8, 235.

*Edinburgh Review*, 124, 186-7.

Education, Malthusian hopes from, 55, 56. Promotes longevity, 67. Promoted by good wages, 120. Diminishes drunkenness, 132. National is threefold, 375. (1) For culture state, 375-6. (2) For jural state, 380-4. (3) For industrial state, in agriculture, 384-7. In the arts, 387-95. State provision for, 180, 224, 229-30, 248-9, 286, 366-7, 373-4, 384-5, 395. Neglect in England, 83, 371-2. Ancient education (Judea, Greece and Rome), 367-8. Mediæval (Eastern Empire, France, Germany and England), 71, 369-70. Modern in Europe, 370-1. In America, 372-5.

Edward III., 276.

Elder, William, 20.

Elizabeth, Queen, 72, 83, 106, 277.

Emerson, 110.

Enclosures, 73, 75, 76, 77, 99.

Equality, natural tendency to, 29, 238, 260, 265-6, 327. Hindrances to, 30, 78, 168, 189, 201-2.

Equilibrium of the industries, the goal of industrial growth, 27, 30, 90-3, 212, 259. Destroyed in England, 78, 80-1, 212, 213-4, 259. Not attained in America, 91, 92-3, 212.

*Evening Post* (New York), quoted, 236-7, 247.

Everett, Edward, 346.

Evictions in Scotland, 85-6.

Exchequer, Notes, 164.
Excises, when first imposed, 185. Enormous growth, 186–7. Recent reductions, 186. Revenue from, 291. (See *Internal Revenue.*)
Exhaustion of the soil, 46, 243–4, 304.
Exhibition of 1851, 389, 391. Of 1855, 389. Of 1862, 389, 391. Of 1867, 389–90. Of 1876, 358–9.
Exports, no test of prosperity, 217, 262, 362. England's most valuable, go to Protectionist countries, 246–7, 296–7. Does protection prevent, 262. Increase and modification through protection, 273, 327, 328.
Factory system invented by Arkwright, 128, 220, 281. Its benefits, 128, 220, 330. Not applicable to agriculture, 81. Calls for technical training, 388–90.
Family, the first form of society, 14, 32, 143, 219, 381. Its surrender of industries, 141. Extinction of old families, 64–5.
Famine, characteristic of thinly-settled regions, 59–60. Hunter's specific against, 60. In antiquity, 61. In Ireland, 59–60, 62–3, 109, 302–4. In India, 312.
Farmer, man's third stage as food-producer, 68, 69. History in England, 74–8. Needs direct protection, 239–40. Benefited by variety of industry 90–3, 214–5, 240–5, 350. Needs special training, 385–7. (See *Agriculture, Grain Trade.*)
Farming the revenue, 189–90, 269.
Fashions worth more than mines to France, 279. Should be national, 392–3.
Fawcett, 131, 238–9.
Ferrara, 30, 126.
Fertility of soil, a great process, 42–6. May be destroyed by exhaustion or denudation, 46–8, 244. Of midland England, 106. Of Ireland, 107, 109, 297. Of Southern Illinois, 112.
Feudal system, an enemy of national unity, 34, 179, 221. Its land tenure, 74–5, 79, 86–7, 97. Its villeinage, 74, 88–9, 122–3. Its tenures and services abolished in England at the Restoration, 77, 79, 186. In Prussia by Stein, 88–9, 122.
Fichte, J. G., 20, 27, 221, 367.
"Fields" of the Mark, 74, 75, 76, 197.
Finance; bad methods of early periods, 17, 180–1, 189–90, 268–9, 271, 276. Moslem finance, 189, 313, 316–7, 337, 339. French policy, 170–1, 191, 269–70, 271. German, 321, 322, 323, 324, 325, 326. English, 162–3, 183, 185–7, 189, 190–1, 191–3, 229–30, 276, 283–4, 291. American, 176–7, 181, 183, 184, 185, 188–9, 193–6, 227–8, 229–30, 248–9, 344–5, 347, 352–3, 354, 357. Canadian, 290–2. East Indian, 313–7.
Falkland, 73. (See *Commons, Enclosures, Mark.*)
Food, a prime necessity, 41–2. Man's progress as its producer, 68, 70–2. In Greece, 115. In ancient Italy, 73, 115. In France, 97–8, 123–4, 273. In England, 58, 59, 71–2, 82, 83, 101–2, 122, 187, 212, 213, 241–2, 259, 277, 302–3. In Ireland, 62–3, 109, 130, 302–3. In Belgium, 87–8, 320. In

America, 92-4, 112, 239, 243-4, 341-2, 348, 356. In India, 312, 314, 315.
Foreign commerce. (See *Commerce, International Exchanges.*)
Forestalling the market, the method, 200-1. As practised in Chicago, 200. In Australia and California, 200, 296.
*Fortnightly Review (London)*, 200, 226-7, 297.
Fourier, 199.
Franklin, Benj., 18, 65, 242-3, 342, 372.
Frederick the Great, 171, 190, 272, 321-2.
Free banking, 155-6. In Scotland, 169. In Rhode Island, 174-5.
Free contract, English faith in, 19, 119, 307. Does not extend to land, 23, 70, 96, 305-7. (See *Competition, Custom, Socialists.*)
Freedom, the nation's aim, 35, 39, 376. It increases with closeness of association, 68, 220-1. Declines with its decline, 221, 306, 341. Industrial freedom, 225-7, 306.
Freeholders, 75.
√ "Free Trade," proposed by the *Economistes*, 18. By Adam Smith and Say, 19, 20, 206, 207-8, 260-1, 272. By Torrens, Ricardo, and Mill, 22-3, 209-10. Opposed by Fichte and List, 27, 28-9. Based on the *Laissez faire* theory of the state's functions, 19, 223-6, 264-7, 287, 289, 309, 355. Injurious between countries of unequal industrial status, 222-3, 301, 310-2, 329-30, 334-5, 336-7. Means mostly the exchange of raw materials for manufactured goods, 212-3, 214-6, 246-7, 263, 280, 291, 303, 311. Removes across the ocean the points where their prices tend to converge, 215-6, 240-1. Means uniformity of occupation in the weaker country, 212-3, 215-6, 217, 235-6, 237, 238, 239-40, 242, 253, 295, 301-2, 303, 309, 311-3, 318, 329-30, 334-5, 337-8. Involves a bad economy of the weaker nation's labor, 129-30, 211-2, 215-6, 235-6, 237, 254, 295, 298, 302, 303, 306, 311, 312, 320, 332, 334-5, 337-8, 344, 354. Involves bad and wasteful farming, 90-3, 214-6, 237, 239-45, 263. Involves an unfavorable balance of trade, 206-8, 258, 260, 329-30, 334-5, 337, 339, 356. Rejected by great statesmen: by Colbert, 269-70. By Napoleon, 271-3, 281-2. By Edward III., 276. By Elizabeth, 277. By Cromwell, 277-8. By Frederick the Great, 321-2. By Joseph II., 322. By Alexander I. and Count Nesselrode, 330. By Gustavus Adolphus (see Häusser's *Period of the Reformation*, p. 455). By Count Ericeira, 334. By Fisher Ames, 344. By Gen. Washington, 344, 345. By Alex. Hamilton, 27, 29, 344, 345. By Thomas Jefferson, 347. By James Madison, 350. By President Monroe, 351. By Henry Clay, 351, 352-3, 353. By Daniel Webster, 352. By John C. Calhoun, 350. By Andrew Jackson, 243, 353. By Gen. Harrison, 354. Rejected by progressive countries: by Greece and Rome, 267-8. By France, 269-75. By England till 1845, 275-81. By the English working classes, 288-9. By the Australian colonies, 294-7. By Belgium, 317-20. By Germany, 320-9. By Russia, 329-31. By Sweden and Denmark, 331-2. By Spain, 332-3. Adopted by England after five centuries of protection, 281-5. The act

of the middle classes, now to be judged by the working classes, 282-9. Adopted by Canada, 290-3. By Prussia temporarily, 323-4. By Russia temporarily, 329-30. By Portugal for one hundred and fifty years, 334-6. By the United States by default of legislation till 1824, 347-51. Again for political reasons in 1833-42, 353-4. Again partially in 1846 and 1857, 355-7. Forced on Ireland in 1801, 301. On India in 1813, 310-3.

Free traders, if consistent, oppose national education, 248-9, 371, 373, 395. And national post-offices, 248. Are too moral to engage in protected manufactures, 247. Generally belong to the servile party in politics, 226, 294. Are liable, by reaction, to become communists, 265-6. Have no faith in the principle of nationality, 230-1. Their ablest men concede the temporary expediency of protection, 249-51. Admit that protection creates no monopoly, 252. Seven of their objections to protection, 256-266. Are, in England, the middle class, 282-3. Are not open to argument, 287, 288. Their conspiracy with Napoleon III., 273. Their defeat in Germany, 324-5. In Belgium, 318. In Russia, 330. In Portugal, 336. Their defeats in the United States, 351, 354-5, 357-8. Their league with the Slave power, 357.

Frontiers, Custom House, inside nations, 17, 322, 323, 324, 332, 333, 344.

Fullarton, *on Currency*, 156, 166.

Funding national debts, 191-2, 193, 229.

Gee, *on Trade*, 342.

Geography in education, 379.

Gladstone, W. E., 96, 183, 187, 192, 273, 283-4, 287, 307.

Goethe, 20, 37, 43, 254.

Gold, why adopted for coinage, and when, 142-3. Its advantages and disadvantages, 144. Probable effects of its demonetization, 27, 145. Its supply, 145. Does not circulate in the East, 148. Its increase in the circulation and the effect on its value, 23, 148-9, 151, 207-8. English legislation about it, 165. (See *Bullion*.) French practice, 171.

Goldsmiths, English, used to act as bankers, 153, 162, 163.

Government, its development through the differentiation of function, 37-8, 179-80. Its function to steer, 36, 225. Its sanatory responsibilities, 50-3. Its growing need of revenue, 180, 229-30. Its earlier methods of getting it, 180-1. Its methods of taxation, 181-90. Its debts, 190-3. Its treasury notes, 193. Its preparation for war in times of peace, 229-9. Its duties to other nationalities, 36, 39, 228-9. Its passivity as regards industry proposed, 18, 19, 223-31, 264-5, 289, 309, 355. That policy contrary to the Constitution, 224-5, 264-5. Its methods of discrimination in favor of home industry, 231-5. (See *Tariff, Duties*.) Its duty to the national domain, 48. Its duties to education, 180, 229-30, 366-7, 373, 395.

Grain trade of Russia, 241, 329-30. Of Sweden, 113, 332. Of Greece and Rome, 267, 268. Of the West with Europe, 92-3, 200, 239-41, 241-2, 263.

Greeley, Horace, 30.

Greenback Party, theory of the, 194.

Greg, W. R., 24, 53, 61, 64, 67.

# INDEX.

Gustavus Adolphus, 331.
Hamilton, Alex., 27, 29, 173, 251-2, 344, 345-6.
Hardware, American, 255.
✓ Harmony of interests, 29-30. Between capital and labor, 119-20, 121, 122, 124, 129, 135-6. Methods to realize it, 135-9. Of agricultural and manufacturing classes, 220, 235-6, 241, 242-5, 263. Of producers and consumers, 215-6, 220, 251-2, 257, 258, 296-7, 327. In true commerce, 197, 220.
Health, duty of the state to promote, 50-3, 180. And education, 366.
✓ Hindrances to natural growth or progress, 28, 30, 118, 127-33, 170, 187, 221-3, 259, 260-1, 263-4.
History, its use in education, 381-3.
Home industry, 16, 40, 211-2, 215, 216-7, 225-6, 235-9, 240-4.
Homer, 121, 368, 391.
Homestead law, 240.
Houses of the working class, 132, 260. In Philadelphia, 238.
Hughes, Thos., 105, 137.
Huguenots driven from France, 17, 271. In Germany, 322. In England, 277, 278-9.
Humboldt, A., 207.
Humboldt, W., 324.
Hume, David, 64, 149-50, 191.
Hunter life, 49, 68, 71.
Hunter, W. W., 60.
Huskisson, 222, 283, 324.
Imagination, its power, 263-4.
Immigration into the United States, 237, 242, 291.
Implements, agricultural, 70-1, 100.
*Impôt progressif*, 189.
Improvements in production, 57, 69, 72, 237, 250, 254-5. In machinery, 127-8, 238, 254-5, 280, 281, 336, 346, 388-9.
Incidence of taxation, 181-3, 185. Of protective duties, 332-5.
Income tax, fairest in theory, 185. Practical objections, 187-9. In England, 185, 187, 189. In America, 188-9.
Individuality the correlate of interdependence and close association, 40, 216-7, 220-1.
" Industrial partnerships" preferable to co-operation, 138-9.
Industrial state, as conceived by Fichte and List, 27, 28-9, 367. Its nature, 38. Its divisions, 40. (See *Equilibrium of the Industries*.) Communists make it everything, Free-traders nothing, 224-5, 264-6. National education regards it, 375, 384-94.
Industry, Quesnay's view of, 18. Adam Smith's, 19. Fichte's, 27. Distinctive character of modern industry, 72, 115, 127-8, 281, 345. As related to money, 150, 151-2, 154-5, 207-9. Obstructed by wrong taxation, 182-3. Its natural growth in variety, 19, 30, 90-1, 219-20, 259.

Inequality of condition, Ricardo accounts for, 22, 93-5, 117, 265. Carey on, 30, 117-8, 265. Promoted by panics, 168, 173. By indirect taxes, 182-3, 189. By free trade, 238, 260, 314, 339-40.
Inflation of prices, 354.
Ingram, Prof., 26.
Inheritances, taxes on, 183.
Instruments, the law of progress as regards, 124-6, 144, 198, 245-6. Money the instrument of association and exchange, 142, 144, 151, 154, 162.
Intensive agriculture, 72, 87, 89, 237.
Interference. (See *Hindrances*.)
Interest on money, 151, 159, 162, 163, 165-6, 169, 172.
Interest, what is a man's, 231, 257-8.
Internal revenue, 183. (See *Excises*.)
International exchanges: Smith and Say's theory, 19, 20, 205-6, 207-9, 260-1. Ricardo and McCulloch's criticism of it, 206-7. The theory of Torrens, Ricardo, and Mills, 22-3, 209-10, 256-9. Some objections to it, 210-6, 256-9. No test of national prosperity, 217, 262, 274, 292, 301, 312, 332.
Inventions, 238, 281, 388, 360.
Iron: use in coinage, 148. Imported into mediæval England from Normandy, 72, 276. Yarranton would import the industry, 278. Its protection, 1771-1834, in England, 280. Prussian and Belgian rivals the English, 285-7, 319, 328. Belgian protection, 318. French, 275. German, 326. In Ireland, 298, 301. In India, 259. In America, 210, 234, 255, 342, 347, 350, 351, 356, 357-8.
Jackson, Andrew, 174, 243, 353.
Jevons, Stanley, 149.
Jural state, its nature, 38. Its development, 179-80. Chief theme of early political philosophers, 267. National education regards, 375, 380-4.
Justice or righteousness of the essence of the state, 34, 36-7, 225, 380-3. Is twofold, 37, 225. Is not all of morality, 383. Justice of war, 228-9, 259. "Justices' justice," 179.
Karl the Great, 369.
*Kathedersocialisten*, school of the, 25, 26.
Kingsley, Chas., 132, 288.
Knox, John, 371.
Kraus, C. J., 88, 323.
Labor, the source of wealth, 16, 18, 19, 41, 114. Its development in method, 49-50, 68-9, 70-2, 100, 115, 121-4, 127-8, 197, 219-20, 237-8. Its growth in power over capital, 74, 97, 124-6, 237-8, 265. It is most abundantly employed and best paid in the neighborhood of varied industry, 129-30, 211-2, 235-9, 294-5, 301, 303, 305, 306, 311-2, 327, 337. "More labor is less efficient in agriculture," 81, 88, 93, 94, 95. (See *Co-operation, Industry, Wages*.)
*Laissez faire*, 270, 364. As a theory, 286, 289, 355.
Land, the alleged monopoly of it, 22, 93, 95-6. Derives its value from labor

expended, 114, 125. The worst is settled first, 99–100. (See *Settlement*.) Much lies idle in England, 59, 82. Very little is farmed scientifically, 58–9, 82. It supports a relatively scanty population, 78, 212, 213, 259. Is owned by a small and diminishing number of persons, 77–8, 82–3. In progressive countries it is owned by a large and increasing number, 72–3, 86–90, 122. Duties of the state toward it, 48, 70, 88, 95–6, 304–7. (See *Agriculture, Farmers, Rent, Soil*.)

Land-banks in Europe, 163, 171–2. In the colonies, 172, 173.

Land-acts of 1870 and 1881, 85.

Landlords in Ireland, 84.

Land-tax, raises rents, 184. Better than taxes on personal property, 185. English, 186. American, 185, 188. East Indian, 313–4.

Land tenure, primitive, was communistic, 24, 73–4, 75, 90, 98–9. Feudal, 74–5, 86–7, 88. In Scotland, 85. The Highlands converted into private estates, 85. Abolished in England at the Restoration, 77, 79, 186. In Prussia by Stein, 88–9, 122. The modern English and its failures, 75–83, 212, 213. Does not account for the poverty of Ireland, 304–5.

Language, and nationality, 34, 376. Two in Belgium, 317, 365. Language in education, 376–7. Of the English Bible, 384.

Large estates in Saxony, 72. "Ruined Italy," 73. Their growth in England and Scotland, 77–83.

Lassalle, 30, 117–8, 266.

Laveleye, E. de, 24, 26, 72.

Lavergne, M. de, 87.

Law, John, 170, 271.

Legal tender, 146–8.

Legislation, its formal beginnings, 33. Its true progress, 35, 38. Industrial, presents nice problems, 225. Its true province, 30, 224–6, 258–9, 264–5. As to health and population, 52–3, 60–1, 180, 249. As to pauperism, 54, 130–1. As to land, 73, 75, 77, 79, 86–7, 88–9, 90, 96, 99, 305–7. As to slavery, 89–90, 122. As to labor, 122–3, 130–1, 133, 136. As to temperance, 132. As to coined money, 146–8. As to banking, 155–6, 157–8, 162–3, 165–7, 169–78. As to revenue and taxation, 180, 181, 190, 229–30, 313–7. As to national debts, 190–3. As to promoting home industry, 210, 213, 223–8, 231–5, 239–40, 247–52, 255–6, 259–61, 264–7. As to hindering it, 221–2, 270–1, 273–5, 289–94, 297–302, 309–12, 323–4, 329–30, 332–7, 341–3, 353–4, 355–7. As to education, 180, 248–9, 366–9, 371–3, 384–5, 387, 390, 392, 395.

Leslie, Cliffe, 26, 78, 81, 117, 129, 130, 236, 319–20.

Levees, 112.

Licenses, 132, 181.

Linen manufacture in Ireland, 130, 298–300. In England, 278, 279. In Belgium, 275, 319. In Germany, 328.

List, Frederick, 28, 323, 325, 326, 328.

Local centres, 311, 314.

# INDEX. 409

Lock-outs, 134, 198.
London, 67, 151, 277, 389.
*London Quarterly Review* on Turkey, 337–41.
*London Review*, 286.
Lotteries, 180.
Ludlow, J. M., 137, 310–1, 314, 315.
Luther, 372.
Macaulay, T. B., 13, 67, 77.
Macgregor, 335.
Machinery, its introduction affects labor, 50, 57, 127–9, 345, 365–6. Has destroyed some local industries, 312, 317, 320, 336–7, 390. England prohibited its export, 281, 312, 317, 330, 337. Its accumulation in England, 281. Invented or improved in America, 238, 281, 346.
Madison, James, 174, 350.
Magistrates, professional the best, 179.
Maine, Sir H. S., 24, 99.
Malthus, Rev. T. R., 21, 22, 24, 25, 53–69, 93, 94, 97, 118.
Man, not to be treated as a thing, 11–12, 119–20, 121–2. His relation to Nature, 29, 41–2, 368.
Manchester, 238–9, 280, 300.
Manor, its constitution, 74, 98–9, 179. Its copy or roll (*rotulus*), 74, 77, 276.
Manufactures, Quesnay's theory of, 18. Adam Smith's, 19. Their natural growth, 219–23, 258–9. Benefit of their neighborhood, 90–2, 128, 129–30, 237–9, 240–7, 262–3. Their destruction in Ireland in the reign of William III., 84. Effects of their absence, 40, 57, 90–3, 214–6, 222–3, 227–8, 235, 292, 305–6, 311–2, 330, 334–5, 336–41. Concentration in England, 212–4, 280–1. Their history in Asia, Europe, and America, 267–364. In relation to education, 387–95. (See *Equilibrium of the Industries, Machinery, Protection.*)
Manure, needed, but wasted, 46, 71, 72, 92, 243, 244, 273, 317.
Mark, the Teutonic, 33–4, 73–4, 197. (See *Manor.*)
Markets, their primitive character, 197. "Buying in the cheapest," 210, 211, 215–6, 257–8, 292. Fostering a home market, 46–7, 224, 226, 241, 242, 243, 244, 245–6, 255, 261, 301, 332. The competitions of the home market, 226–7, 251–2. The trader's power over. (See *Forestalling, Prices.*)
Mathematics in education, 378.
Maurice, F. D., 28, 39, 137, 221, 372, 382.
McCulloch, J. C., 23, 55, 57, 61, 166, 185, 191, 206, 207, 252, 335, 336–7.
"Mercantile School," 16–7, 209.
Metals, precious: their history, 142–52. Their use as money, 143. Our supply, 357. (See *Gold, Silver, Money.*)
Metayer system of land tenure, 90.
Method of economic study, 25, 31, 57.
Middle class in England, 282–4, 287, 288. None in the South, 358.
Military supplies, depend on manufactures, 227–8, 297, 345, 357–8.

Mill, James, 22, 54.

Mill, John Stuart, 24, 25, 31, 51, 54, 55, 56-7, 95, 118, 124, 127, 150, 201-2, 209-10, 249, 250-1, 266, 301, 303.

Milton, John, 377, 378, 384.

Mind, its growth limits that of numbers, 65-6. Mind and muscle, 127-8, 237. (See *Culture State, Education*.)

Mirabeau, 18, 322.

Mohammedan regard for trees, 48. Oppressive as rulers, 61, 67-8. Their bad finance, 189, 313, 316-7, 337-8.

Money, its origin, nature and advantages, 142-4. Coined money, 143, 144-5, 148-9. (See *Gold, Silver, Coinage, Metals Precious*.) Paper money, 149, 152-6. (See *Bill of Exchange, Bank Notes*.) Money of account, 153, 156-62. (See *Banking*.) The instrument of exchange and of association, 143. The relation of its quantity to its purchasing power, 149-52. Its supply at different periods, 16, 148-9, 207. Its plenty stimulates production, and *vice versâ*, 151-2, 154-5, 208-9. Unequal commerce drains a country of its money, 151-2, 206-7, 209, 329-30, 334, 336, 338, 339, 356. Prohibitions on its export, 16, 17, 321. Unprogressive countries sometimes absorb it, 151, 166, 206. English theories about, 22-3, 23-4, 149, 156, 165, 206-9.

Monopolies as a source of revenue, 17-8, 180-1, 183, 271, 313-7, 322. "Monopoly of land," 22, 23, 93, 95-6, 114. In trade, 223, 267-8. In banking, 163, 169, 171, 174-5, 176-7. Protection does not create monopoly, 251-2. Its aim and tendency to destroy actual monopolies, 225-7, 295.

Monroe, President, 351.

Morality of a nation, 34-7, 39, 361-2, 380-3. Christian or individual morality, 383-4. Its relation to celibacy, 56, 61, 65, 110. And to wages, 120, 121. And to education, 374-5.

More, Sir Thomas, 75-6.

Morris, Robert, 172-3.

Mountain districts often settled before the plains, Chap. VI., *passim*.

Murdock, John, 86.

Murphy, J. N., 301-2, 307-9.

Music, a science and an art, 15, 23. In education, 377-8.

Napoleon, 136, 158, 255, 271-3, 281-2, 318, 329, 346, 367, 387-8.

Napoleon III., 273-4.

Nasse, 24, 75, 98-9.

*Nation* (New York) quoted, 91, 178, 264.

Nation: historical origin, 33-4. The modern form of the state, 33. Its true nature, 14, 34. A moral personality, 35-7, 380. Its vocation, 36, 225. (See *Jural State*.) Its progress, 37-8, 40. Its industrial existence, 38, 40. (See *Industrial State*.) Its self-preservation not selfishness, 39. Its right of "eminent domain" over its soil, 48, 70, 95-6. (See *Land, Soil*.) The territory of each is capable of feeding its people, 113, 217. Its unity is strengthened by variety of industry and individual freedom, and *vice versâ*,

40, 216–7, 220–1, 223, 328–9, 341. Is wise to make sacrifices, 248–9, 226, 292. Its war powers and duties, preparations, 227–8, 347, 357–8. Its peculiar financial policy, 229–30. Is ignored by the cosmopolitical school, 19–20, 230–1.

National banks, 176–7.

National debts, 190–3, 229, 344–5, 353.

National economy, 11, 14.

National education, its policy, 365–7, 373–5. Its history, 367–73. Its proper shape and drift, 375–95. Its opponents, 248–9, 371, 373, 395. (See *Education*.)

Nationalist economists; the "mercantile school," 16–7. Bishop Berkeley, 26. Fichte, 27. Coleridge and Maurice, 27–8. List, 28–9. H. C. Carey and his school, 29–31. Horace Bushnell, 231.

Nationalist policy. (See *Protection*.)

Natural advantages of each country, 210, 258–9, 293.

Nature. (See *Man, Wealth, Value*.)

Navigation laws, English, 277–8, 300, 324, 341.

Necker, 171, 191.

Neighborhood of farm and factory benefits agriculture, 46–7, 90–3, 214–6, 239–45, 263, 276, 303. Of different industries raises wages, 129–30, 211–2, 235–9. Of producer and consumer diminishes the trader's profits and his power, 198–201. Neighborhood knowledge, 379–80, 386, 394.

Nesselrode, Count, 330.

New York, 173, 238.

Nickel in coinage, 148.

*North British Review*, 284–5.

Opium in India and China, 206, 310–1, 315–6.

Over-issues. (See *Bank Notes*.)

Over-production, 214–5, 261.

Owen, Robert, 136, 202.

Panics, their nature, 161–2. In England, 163–4, 165, 166–8, 282, 349. In Scotland, 170. In France, 170, 171, 274. In America, 173, 174, 205, 354, 357, 361.

Paper-money, 152–6, 193–4.

Parsimony, not always economy, 14, 119–20, 211, 235. The law of parsimony applies to instruments, 119, 144, 198, 245.

Passivity, governmental, in regard to industry, 18, 19, 21, 22, 30, 210, 212, 223–6, 264–6, 291, 321. In regard to popular misery, 54, 95, 289.

Passivity of money, 22–3, 23–4, 149–52.

Paterson, W., 162, 168.

Patriotism in relation to national economy, 20, 39, 80, 83, 191, 212, 227–8, 288–9, 328–9, 341. Its truest type, 39, 382.

Patterson, R. H., 146, 149, 150, 156.

Paul, 38, 221, 257.

Pauperism, the Malthusian view of, 22–3, 54, 116–7, 265. The true view, 30,

114. In England, 83, 130-1, 212. In Ireland, 303, 304, 308. In Belgium, 88, 236, 320. In America, 238-9.
Pearson, C. H., 101-7.
Peasantry, 78, 80, 82, 82-3, 89.
Peel, Sir Robert, 165-8, 183, 187.
People's banks in Germany, 120, 366.
Personal property taxed, 184-5.
Philadelphia, 111, 172-3, 238-9.
Phosphorus in the human frame, 67.
Physical science in education, 378.
Pilgrimages, sources of pestilence, 67.
Pitt (the elder), 185, 186, 189.
Plants, their geological history, 42-3. Their food, 42, 43-7.
Platinum in Russian coins, 148.
Plato, 14, 36, 378, 381.
Pliny the elder, 73, 121.
Plutarch, 381.
Poorer classes, the statesman's problem, 115. Affected by indirect taxes, 182-3, 189. Buy the dearest, 202. Poorer nation injured by unrestricted trade with a richer, 222-3. (See *Free Trade*.)
Population: its growth the first condition of advance in wealth, 49-51, 70-2, 100, 113-4, 198, 219. Duty of the state to foster that growth, 50-4, 366, 380. Malthusian theory, 21-2, 53-7, 94, 95, 110. Its English critics, 24, 53. Discredited by facts, 57-63. Is the parent of Ricardo's theory of rent, 93. And of the wage-fund theory, 116-7. Population is self-regulative, 63-9. That of England, 58, 61, 62, 64, 101-2. Of Ireland, 58, 59-60, 62-3, 109, 130, 302-3. Of Belgium, 57, 58. Of France, 61, 62, 64, 123. Of America, 62, 64-5.
Post-office, 180, 184, 248.
Poverty. (See *Pauperism*.)
Power over nature, 29, 41, 49, 66, 69. Power to consume, the test of prosperity, 217, 327.
Premiums, 16, 231.
Prices determined by cost of reproduction, 125. Their relation to the supply of money, 22-3, 23-4, 150-3, 207-9. When can the trader fix prices, 200-2, 245, 294, 296-7, 356. Raised temporarily, but ultimately reduced by protective duties, 233-4, 248, 251-6, 280, 327, 345, 346, 355. Of labor. (See *Wages*.)
Primogeniture, right of, 79.
Prison labor, 131. Its effect on the working classes, 131.
Production, Quesnay's theory, 18. Adam Smith's, 19. Its development, 68-9. Promoted by the plenty of money, 151-2, 207-9. And by machinery, 127-8, 281.
Profits: their inequalities, 19. Diminished by waste, 120, 138. Profits of

INDEX. 413

farming, 72, 91, 214–6, 241, 242–7. Of banking, 155, 175. Of the trader, 198–203, 245–6. Of manufacturing, 247, 252.
Progress is normal, 19, 29–30, 34–5, 57, 69, 113–4, 125–6, 265–6. Its industrial goal, 27, 29, 40, 115, 220, 259. Its method. (See *Differentiation of Function*.)
Prohibition of imports, 231, 248, 272, 276, 279, 280, 283, 284, 310, 322, 323, 324, 332, 333. Of exports, 16, 276, 281, 298–9, 312, 317, 322, 324, 330, 337. Of free contract, 96, 305–7.
Proletariat, 61, 73, 115.
Prolongation of life, 67.
Prophets, the Hebrew, 381–2. Isaiah, 73.
Protection is natural resistance to an unnatural status, 212–4, 226–7, 259. Its method, 231–5. It benefits labor, 231–9, 129–30, 211. It benefits agriculture, 90–3, 214–6, 239–45. It makes commerce equitable, 245–8. Is not irreligious and selfish, 364. Its effect on manufactures, 248–56. Seven common objections to it answered, 256–66. It has the sanction of the greatest free traders, 249–51. It is a measure of national defence, 227–9, 345, 347. It is the policy of progressive nations, especially in their youth, 226–7, 273, 275, 294–5, 317, 328. Is a great promoter of commerce, 362. It does not create monopolies, 251–2. It has the sanction of the U. S. Constitution, 224–5, 265, 344. Its history in Europe, 267–80, 300–1, 317–333, 336. In America, 344–364. In Australia, 294–7.
*Prudhommes, Conseils de*, 136.
Publicans, 190.
Purchasing power of money, 22–3, 23–4, 148–52, 217. Of wages, 63, 123, 125, 237.
Rack-rents in Ireland, 84, 99, 304, 305. In England, 76, 78.
Railroads, subsidies, 240. Growth in India, 259.
Rainfall, affected by trees, 47–8, 104–5.
Rapidity of social circulation, 68, 144, 152, 156, 160, 199. How promoted, 150–1, 154, 198, 204–5, 205–6, 260–1, 309. How checked, 182–3, 223, 292–3, 301, 307–8, 311–2, 337–8.
Rate of increase of population, 53, 61–3, 66–7, 94, 303.
Rate of wages, 116, 117, 119, 123–4, 129–30, 133–4, 140.
Raw materials: their export unprofitable, 91, 214–6, 241, 314. Their production protected, 239–40, 256, 346. Progressive countries cease their export, 246, 328. The relation of their price to that of manufactures, 241.
Raw material associations (*Roh-stoff-vereine*), 139–40.
Reciprocity between England and other countries, 312, 324, 330–1. Between Belgium and Holland, 318. Between Austria and Germany, 325.
Reformation, 76–7, 288–9.
Rent, its supposed origin, 22–3, 93–5. Its relation to the whole product, 96–8. In primitive society is customary, not competitive, 24, 74–5, 98–9. In England, 74–5, 76–7, 78. In Ireland, 304–7.
Reproduction: its cost determines prices, 125–6.

"Reproductive consumption," 256.
Responsibility of the capitalist for rate of wages, 120–1. Of governments for the public welfare, 37, 224–5, 264–5. (See *Education, Government.*)
Resumption. (See *Specie Payments.*)
Revenue: growing need of, 179–80. Earlier methods of getting, 180–1, 186, 276. Modern methods. (See *Excises, Customs, Income Tax, Taxation, Land Tax, Tariff.*) Should cover current expenses, 190–1. Revenue tariffs objectionable, 232, 290–1, 347, 350–1, 354, 355–7. Protective tariffs yield a large revenue, 233, 333, 353, 355. How raised in England, 186, 187, 291. In Germany, 325–7. In India, 313–7. In Turkey, 337, 339. In Russia, 90.
Revolutions are abnormal, 34–5, 230. English, 123, 162, 186, 298. French of 1789, 86–7, 171, 271. American, 172, 193, 281, 343.
Ricardo, 22, 23, 24, 25, 93, 114, 118, 191, 206, 207, 209, 273.
Rights, natural in their relation to the state, 34, 36, 223–4. The supposed right of free trade, 223. The imperfectly defined rights of the feudal land tenure, 74–5, 79, 88–9, 306.
Risks, the farmer's, 91, 211–2, 214, 244–5. The trader's, 203–4. The manufacturer's, 215.
Rivers, 47, 48, 100, 105, 112, 113.
Rogers, Thorold, 71–2, 74, 123, 212–3, 223, 251, 252, 395.
Roscher, Prof., 26.
Rossi, 21, 249–50.
Rotation of crops, 46, 72, 74, 92, 243–5, 385.
Rouleaux, Prof., 359.
Sacrifices, national, their wisdom, 201, 226, 248–9, 253, 286, 292, 295, 318, 366.
Sailors, 216, 236, 246, 259.
Saint Simon, 118.
Salt, 240, 315, 347.
*Saturday Review*, 31, 364.
Savage state, 29, 30, 38, 49, 157.
Say, J. B., 20, 21, 205, 207, 249, 272.
Schultze-Delitzsch, 30, 31, 117–8, 139–40, 203, 266.
Science, its nature and stages of development, 11–12, 14–15.
Scott, Sir Walter, 122, 154–5, 170, 384.
Selfishness not chargeable on patriotism, 39. It is short-sighted, 48, 51–2.
Senior, N. W., 23, 24, 53, 56, 78–9, 97, 288.
Serfdom, mediæval, 74, 122. Abolished in Prussia by Stein, 88–9, 122. In Russia, 89–90, 331.
Settlement of the soil: its true law, 99–101. Exemplifications of the law, Chapter VI.
Several. (See *Community.*)
Sheffield, 52, 233–4.
Shepherd life, 49, 68, 71.

INDEX. 415

Shipping, English, 277-8, 324. Prussian, 324. Spanish, 333. American, 347, 349, 363, 364.
Silica in the soil, 45.
Silk production and manufacture in France, 269, 270. In China, 206. In England, 246, 279, 284, 285, 289. In Ireland, 300. In Germany, 328. In Russia, 330-1. In America, 354.
Silver in coinage, 142-52. Demonetization of, 146-8. Absorbed by the East, 148, 166, 206, 313.
Sinking fund, 192.
Slavery, European, 104, 121-2. American, 352, 355, 357.
Small farms, 72, 90.
Smiles, Samuel, 271, 275, 277, 279.
Smith, Adam, 18, 19, 20, 26, 29, 80, 99, 124, 165, 191, 205, 206, 249, 260, 266, 269, 270, 323, 324, 329-30.
Smith, E. Peshine, 30.
Smith, Gerrit, 248, 373.
Smith, Sidney, 186-7.
Smuggling, 184, 232. In Germany, 323. Through Portugal into Spain, 335.
Socialism, 25, 30, 96, 117-9, 136, 199.
Social science, definition, 11-15. Younger than national economy, 14-15, 267. Its history, 15-31.
Society co-extensive with the human race, 13. Human welfare depends on, 13-14. Its general development, 32-4, 36, 38. Its industrial development, 29-30, 38-40, 49-50, 68-9, 70-2, 99-100, 142, 144, 197-8, 216-21.
Soil: man's dependence on it, 41-2. Its history and composition, 42-5. Its exhaustion, 46-8, 92, 243-4, 304. Rarely well cultivated, 58-9, 385. (See *Agriculture, Farming, Land, Settlement.*)
Solomon, 73, 119, 202.
Specie payments, suspended in England, 163, 164. Resumption in England in 1821, 164. Resumption of, in the United States, 194. Suspension in 1837, 354.
Specific duties the best, 231-2, 233. Preferred in England, 284. In Germany, 326-7. In Portugal, 336. (See *Ad valorem.*)
*Spectator* (London), 132, 255, 287, 306, 307, 313.
Speculation and the credit system, 204. In England, 164, 165, 282, 347 l, 349-50. In America, 173, 174, 353-4, 357. In France, 170.
Spencer, Herbert, 24, 37-8, 53, 66, 69, 219, 248, 371.
Stamp duties, 183.
Standard of value, 148-9.
State, the tribe and the city its ancient forms, and the nation its modern, 32-3. Exists *jure divino*, 35-6. Its duty to industry, 30. (See *Government, Nation.*)
Steam, adapted to small establishments, 128-9. Watt's invention, 128, 281. John Fitch's, 216, 281. Steam-power comparable to paper-money 152.

Steel, English, 233–4. American, 256.
Stein, 88, 122.
Steuerverein, 325.
Stowe, Harriet Beecher, 86.
Strikes, 133–4. In Philadelphia, 238.
Subsidies, 240, 364.
Sugar, 284. (See *Beet Sugar*.)
Sully, 269.
Suspension. (See *Specie Payments*.)
Swift, Dean, 183, 299, 302.
Syme, David, 200, 226–7, 295, 296, 297.
Talleyrand, 294.
Tariffs and their methods, 231–5. (See *Ad valorem Duties, Incidence, Specific Duties*.) Tinkering the tariff, 190, 234, 247. "A tariff and internal improvements," 240. Not "sectional" in their purpose, but national, 263–4. Revenue tariffs, 232, 290–1. *French*, of 1664, 269–70. Of 1786, 271. Of 1815-60, 272–3, 282. Of 1861, 273–5. *English*, of the seventeenth century, 278, 279. Of the eighteenth century, 280. Of 1819, 280, 283. Of 1832, 1845–6, 1851, and 1853, 283–4. Of 1861, 284, 285. *Canadian*, 290–1, 313. *Australian*, 294–7. *Irish* of 1699, 299. Of 1783–1801, 300–1. Of 1808, 301. *East Indian* of 1813, 310, 312. Of 1857, 1859, and later, 255, 313. *Belgian*, of 1844, 318. *German* of last century, 322. Of 1813, 323. Of 1818, 324–6. Of 1843–5, 326. Of 1864 and 1879, 329. Of the *Steuerverein*, 325. *Russian* of 1820 and 1822, 330. Of 1830 and 1869, 330–1. *Swedish* of 1824, 332. *Spanish* of 1722, 332. Of 1778, 333. Of 1845 and 1869, 333. *Portuguese* of 1684, 334. Of 1703, 334–5. Of 1837 and 1841, 336. *Turkish*, 337. *American* of 1789 and 1790, 346, 358. Of 1812, 347, 350. Of 1816, 350–1. Of 1824, 347, 351–2. Of 1828, 352–3. Of 1832, 353. Of 1833–42, 353. Of 1842, 355. Of 1846, 355–6. Of 1857, 357. Of 1861–9, 275, 357. Of 1867, 256. Of 1869, 261. Effect of the present protective tariff in the United States, 358, 360.
Taxation the modern source of revenue, 180, 181. Points in its economy, 189–90. Its incidence, 182. Direct and indirect sorts, 181. Indirect taxes objectionable, 181–3, 186–7. Yields most when lightest, 183–4. Direct taxes, 184. Capitation tax, 184–5. Taxes on real and personal property, 185–8. Taxes on income, 185, 186, 187–8. English taxation, 185–7, 189, 229–30, 291. Canadian, 291. East Indian, 313–7. Russian, 90. Spanish, 183, 268, 332. Turkish, 337–9. American, 183–5, 188–9, 195, 196, 229–30, 240.
Tenant-right, 84.
Tennyson, Alfred, 213, 217, 228, 254.
Textile fabrics, once imported by England, 275, 276, 309. Their manufacture begun and protected, 277, 279–80. Their manufacture in France, 270, 285. In India, 309–10, 312, 313. In Belgium, 317, 319. In Germany,

326, 328. In Russia, 330-1. In Denmark, 211, 332. In Portugal, 334, 336. In Turkey, 336-7. In America, 342, 347, 350, 357-8.

Thiers, Adolph, 264.

Thornton, W. T., 24, 117, 125, 133-4, 304.

Thorp, 73, 74.

Tooke, Thomas, 23, 24, 156, 207.

Torrens, Col., 166, 209.

Trade. (See *Commerce, International Exchange.*)

Trader, his function and services, 197-8, 205, 245. His power, 198-9, 201-3, 245-6. His speculations, 199-200.

Trade spirit described by Coleridge, 27, 79-81. Its relation to war, 229-30. And to education, 372.

Trades' unions: their origin, 133, 134-5. Their success, 117, 133-4. Outlawed, 130, 133. An exotic in America, 135.

Transportation, an unproductive and laborious employment, 216, 217, 246, 259, 274. Its cost an unequal tax, 214, 215, 241, 245-6, 341. How to avoid paying it, 245-6, 259, 263.

Treasury notes, 194.

Treaties of commerce: English with France, 270, 271, 273-5, 284. Belgian with Holland, 318-9. Austrian with Germany, 325. German with England, 324. Portuguese with England, 334-5. Turkish with France and England, 337. American with England, 346. With Canada, 293-4.

Trees affect rainfalls, 47-8, 101-2, 105. Their sustenance, 44-5. One obstacle to the settlement of the best soils, 100, 101-2, 104-5, 105-6, 113.

Tribe, grew out of the family and into the city or nation, 32-3, 381. Its communistic land tenure, 73-4, 98-9. Its jural and industrial methods, 68, 179, 219. Its poverty, 59-60, 68, 71, 102, 107, 109, 219.

Turgot, 18, 171, 208, 271.

Twiss, Dr. Travers, on Colbert, 269, 270.

Tyndall, on industrial education, 390.

Ulster, Scotch settlers in, 83.

Uniformity of occupation marks a low industrial status, 37-8, 40, 216-7, 223, 261, 294, 295, 301, 305, 306, 335, 338. Is associated with famine, 59, 60, 302-3, 312.

University, 368, 369-70, 372.

Usurers, 338, 339, 340.

Utility not value, 41, 113-4.

Value, its nature, 41, 126. Values diminish with growth of society, 125-6. Of land, 114, 125. Of gold and silver, 145-9. The trader adds to value rather than to wealth, 198-9, 245.

Varied industry. (See *Farmer, Labor, Differentiation of Function, Protection.*)

Vegetable kingdom feeds man, 42. Its development, 42-3. Its sustenance, 43-5. Vegetables in England, 72, 101, 277. When profitable as a farm crop, 92, 243-5.

Venice, 157-8, 161, 228, 275.
Villeinage in mediæval Europe, 74, 89, 99, 122.
Von Maurer, 24, 95-6.
Wage-fund theory, 22, 24, 116, 133-4.
Wages are labor's share of the joint product of labor and capital, 115-6, 137. English theory of a natural and necessary rate, 21-2, 24, 54, 116-8, 119, 133-4, 265. And of their equality, 19, 118-9. They are highest in the neighborhood of varied industry, 129-30, 235-9, 260. Trades' unions have raised them, 133-4. Attempts to abolish the wages system, 25, 118, 136-8, 264, 265. Or to modify it, 138-9. The wages of women, 140. History of wages in England, 74, 83, 122-3, 124, 128, 129-30, 130-1, 133-5, 136, 137, 138, 211-2, 236, 288. In Ireland, 63, 130, 236, 302-3. In France, 97-8, 123. In America, 124, 128, 138, 235, 236-7, 238-9.
Walker, Prof. F. A., 26.
Walker, Hon. Robert J., 355.
War a "check" on population, 54, 60, 62. War and debts, 190-3. Varied industry a preparation for it, 227-9, 347, 357-8. War is not the worst of national calamities, 192, 226, 228-9.
Warfare, industrial, its methods, 201, 212, 222, 252-3. Instances, 253, 296-7, 301, 347-50, 351.
Washington, George, 344-5.
Waste lands in England, 59, 82.
Water: its value, 41, 69. Its utility, 41, 42, 53. Its circulation in nature, 47-8, 100, 102.
Watt, James, 281, 388.
Wayland, Dr. Francis, 25, 255.
Wealth defined, 41, 49. Its discussion by the economists, 18, 19, 20, 23, 27, 28, 29, 30. The tendency to attain wealth is natural and normal, 29-30, 57, 265-6. The conditions of its growth. (See *Labor*.)
Webster, Daniel, 351, 352.
Wells, Hon. David A., 25, 252.
"Wet prairies," 112.
Whale fishery carried on by co-operation, 138.
Whately, Archbishop, 55.
Wheat, its yield in England, 58-9, 71, 75, 82. Its excessive cultivation in the West, 92-3. (See *Food, Grain Trade*.)
Whitney's cotton gin, 254, 281, 346.
Wilson, James, 313.
Woman, in primitive stage of society, 197. Hours of work in factories, 51. Woman's wages, 124, 337. Woman's work, 140-1.
Wool production in England, 275. In Ireland, 298. In America, 256, 342. In Australia, 294, 295.
Woollens, manufacture of, in England, 276, 277, 279, 280, 348. In Canada, 291. In Australia, 297. In Ireland, 298-9, 301. In France, 269, 275.

In Germany, 328. In Russia, 331. In Portugal, 334, 336. In America, 256, 342, 347, 351, 357-8.

Yarranton, Andrew, 16, 278.

Yeates, Dr., 336.

Yeomanry in England, 76, 77. Its decline, 78. Growth elsewhere, 86.

Young, Arthur, 86, 109, 124, 207.

*Zollverein*, 282, 325-9.

Zumpt, 60.

**THE END.**

# Famous Castlemon Books.

No author of the present day has become a greater favorite with boys than "Harry Castlemon;" every book by him is sure to meet with hearty reception by young readers generally. His naturalness and vivacity lead his readers from page to page with breathless interest, and when one volume is finished the fascinated reader, like Oliver Twist, asks "for more."

N.B.—Any volumes of the sets sold separately.

## By Harry Castlemon.

**GUNBOAT SERIES.** By Harry Castlemon. In box containing the following. 6 vols. 16mo. Cloth, extra, black and gold . . . . . . . . . . . . . . . . $7 50
Frank the Young Naturalist. Illustrated. 16mo. 1 25
Frank in the Woods. Illustrated. 16mo. . . . . 1 25
Frank on the Prairie. Illustrated. 16mo. . . . . 1 25
Frank on a Gunboat. Illustrated. 16mo. . . . . 1 25
Frank before Vicksburg. Illustrated. 16mo. . . 1 25
Frank on the Lower Mississippi. Illustrated. 16mo. . . . . . . . . . . . . . . . . . . . . . . 1 25

**GO AHEAD SERIES.** By Harry Castlemon. In box containing the following. 3 vols. 16mo. Cloth, extra, black and gold . . . . . . . . . . . . . . . . 3 75
Go Ahead; or, The Fisher Boy's Motto. Illustrated. 16mo. . . . . . . . . . . . . . . . . . . . . 1 25
No Moss; or, The Career of a Rolling Stone. Illustrated. 16mo. . . . . . . . . . . . . . . . . . 1 25
Tom Newcombe; or, The Boy of Bad Habits. Illustrated. 16mo. . . . . . . . . . . . . . . . . 1 25

**ROCKY MOUNTAIN SERIES.** By Harry Castlemon. In box containing the following. 3 vols. 16mo. Cloth, extra, black and gold . . . . . . . $3 75

Frank at Don Carlos' Rancho. Illustrated. 16mo. 1 25

Frank among the Rancheros. Illustrated. 16mo. 1 25

Frank in the Mountains. Illustrated. 16mo. . . 1 25

**SPORTSMAN'S CLUB SERIES.** By Harry Castlemon. In box containing the following. 3 vols. 16mo. Cloth, extra, black and gold . . . . . . . . 3 75

The Sportsman's Club in the Saddle. Illustrated. 16mo. Cloth, extra, black and gold . . . . 1 25

The Sportsman's Club Afloat. Illustrated. 16mo. Cloth, extra, black and gold . . . . . . . . . . 1 25

The Sportsman's Club among the Trappers. Illustrated. 16mo. Cloth, extra, black and gold . . 1 25

**FRANK NELSON SERIES.** By Harry Castlemon. In box containing the following. 3 vols. 16mo. Cloth, extra, black and gold . . . . . . . . . . 3 75

Snowed Up; or, The Sportsman's Club in the Mountains. Illustrated. 16mo. . . . . . . . . . . . . . 1 25

Frank Nelson in the Forecastle; or, The Sportsman's Club among the Whalers. Illustrated. 16mo. 1 25

The Boy Traders; or, The Sportsman's Club among the Boers. Illustrated. 16mo. . . . . . . . . . . 1 25

**BOY TRAPPER SERIES.** By Harry Castlemon. In box containing the following. 3 vols. 16mo. Cloth, extra, black and gold . . . . . . . . . . . . 3 75

The Buried Treasure; or, Old Jordan's "Haunt." Illustrated. 16mo. . . . . . . . . . . . . . . . . 1 25

The Boy Trapper; or, How Dave filled the Order. Illustrated. 16mo. . . . . . . . . . . . . . . . . 1 25

The Mail Carrier. Illustrated. 16mo. . . . . . . 1 25

**ROUGHING IT SERIES.** By Harry Castlemon. In box containing the following. 3 vols. Cloth, extra, black and gold . . . . . . . . . . . . . . . . $3 75

George in Camp; or, Life on the Plains. Illustrated. 16mo. . . . . . . . . . . . . . . . . . 1 25

George at the Wheel; or, Life in a Pilot House. Illustrated. 16mo. . . . . . . . . . . . . . . 1 25

George at the Fort; or, Life Among the Soldiers. Illustrated. 16mo. . . . . . . . . . . . . . . 1 25

**ROD AND GUN SERIES.** By Harry Castlemon. In box containing the following. 3 vols. Cloth, extra, black and gold . . . . . . . . . . . . . . . 3 75

Don Gordon's Shooting Box. Illustrated. 16mo. 1 25

Rod and Gun. Illustrated. 16mo. . . . . . . . . 1 25

The Young Wild Fowlers. Illustrated. 16mo. . 1 25

**FOREST AND STREAM SERIES.** By Harry Castlemon. In box containing the following. 3 vols. Cloth extra, black and gold . . . . . . . . . . . . . 3 75

Joe Wayring at Home; or, Story of a Fly Rod. Illustrated. 16mo. . . . . . . . . . . . . . . . . 1 25

Snagged and Sunk; or, The Adventures of a Canvas Canoe. Illustrated. 16mo. . . . . . . . 1 25

Steel Horse; or, The Rambles of a Bicycle. Illustrated. 16mo. . . . . . . . . . . . . . . . . . . 1 25

**OUR FELLOWS**; or, Skirmishes with the Swamp Dragoons. By Harry Castlemon. Illustrated. 16mo. 1 25

# Alger's Renowned Books.

Horatio Alger, Jr., has attained distinction as one of the most popular writers of books for boys, and the following list comprises all of his best books.

## By Horatio Alger, Jr.

**RAGGED DICK SERIES.** By Horatio Alger, Jr. In box containing the following. 6 vols. 16mo. Cloth, extra, black and gold . . . . . . . . . . . . . $7 50

**Ragged Dick**; or, Street Life in New York. Illustrated. 16mo. . . . . . . . . . . . . . . . . . . . . 1 25

**Fame and Fortune**; or, The Progress of Richard Hunter. Illustrated. 16mo. . . . . . . . . . . . . 1 25

**Mark the Match Boy**; or, Richard Hunter's Ward, Illustrated. 16mo. . . . . . . . . . . . . . . . . 1 25

**Rough and Ready**; or, Life among the New York Newsboys. Illustrated. 16mo. . . . . . . . . . . 1 25

**Ben the Luggage Boy**; or, Among the Wharves. Illustrated. 16mo. . . . . . . . . . . . . . . . . 1 25

**Rufus and Rose**; or, The Fortunes of Rough and Ready. Illustrated. 16mo. . . . . . . . . . . . . 1 25

**TATTERED TOM SERIES.** (FIRST SERIES.) By Horatio Alger, Jr. In box containing the following. 4 vols. 16mo. Cloth, extra, black and gold . . . . 5 00

**Tattered Tom**; or, The Story of a Street Arab. Illustrated. 16mo. . . . . . . . . . . . . . . . . . 1 25

**Paul the Peddler**; or, The Adventures of a Young Street Merchant. Illustrated. 16mo. . . . . . . . 1 25

**Phil the Fiddler**; or, The Young Street Musician. Illustrated. 16mo. . . . . . . . . . . . . . . . . 1 25

**Slow and Sure**; or, From the Sidewalk to the Shop. Illustrated. 16mo. . . . . . . . . . . . . . . . 1 25

**TATTERED TOM SERIES.** (Second Series.)
In box containing the following. 4 vols. Cloth,
extra, black and gold . . . . . . . . . . . . . . . $5 00
**Julius**; or, The Street Boy Out West. Illustrated.
16mo. . . . . . . . . . . . . . . . . . . . . . 1 25
**The Young Outlaw**; or, Adrift in the World. Illustrated. 16mo. . . . . . . . . . . . . . . . 1 25
**Sam's Chance and How He Improved It.** Illustrated. 16mo. . . . . . . . . . . . . . . . . 1 25
**The Telegraph Boy.** Illustrated. 16mo. . . . . 1 25

**LUCK AND PLUCK SERIES.** (First Series.)
By Horatio Alger, Jr. In box containing the following.
4 vols. 16mo. Cloth, extra, black and gold . . . . 5 00
**Luck and Pluck**; or, John Oakley's Inheritance.
Illustrated. 16mo. . . . . . . . . . . . . . . . . 1 25
**Sink or Swim**; or, Harry Raymond's Resolve. Illustrated. 16mo. . . . . . . . . . . . . . 1 25
**Strong and Steady**; or, Paddle Your Own Canoe.
Illustrated. 16mo. . . . . . . . . . . . . . . . . 1 25
**Strive and Succeed**; or, The Progress of Walter
Conrad. Illustrated. 16mo. . . . . . . . . . . . 1 25

**LUCK AND PLUCK SERIES.** (Second
Series.) In box containing the following. 4 vols.
16mo. Cloth, extra, black and gold . . . . . . . 5 00
**Try and Trust**; or, The Story of a Bound Boy. Illustrated. 16mo. . . . . . . . . . . . . . . . 1 25
**Bound to Rise**; or, Harry Walton's Motto. Illustrated. 16mo. . . . . . . . . . . . . . . . . 1 25
**Risen from the Ranks**; or, Harry Walton's Success.
Illustrated. 16mo. . . . . . . . . . . . . . . . . 1 25
**Herbert Carter's Legacy**; or, The Inventor's Son.
Illustrated. 16mo. . . . . . . . . . . . . . . . . 1 25

**CAMPAIGN SERIES.** By Horatio Alger, Jr.
In box containing the following. 3 vols. 16mo.
Cloth, extra, black and gold . . . . . . . . . . . 3 75
**Frank's Campaign**; or, The Farm and the Camp.
Illustrated. 16mo. . . . . . . . . . . . . . . . . 1 25
**Paul Prescott's Charge.** Illustrated. 16mo. . . 1 25
**Charlie Codman's Cruise.** Illustrated. 16mo. . . 1 25

**BRAVE AND BOLD SERIES.** By Horatio Alger, Jr. In box containing the following. 4 vols. 16mo. Cloth, extra, black and gold . . . . . . . . $5 00

Brave and Bold; or, The Story of a Factory Boy. Illustrated. 16mo. . . . . . . . . . . . . . . . . 1 25

Jack's Ward; or, The Boy Guardian. Illustrated. 16mo. . . . . . . . . . . . . . . . . . . . . . . . 1 25

Shifting for Himself; or, Gilbert Greyson's Fortunes. Illustrated. 16mo. . . . . . . . . . . . . . . . 1 25

Wait and Hope; or, Ben Bradford's Motto. Illustrated. 16mo. . . . . . . . . . . . . . . . . . 1 25

**PACIFIC SERIES.** By Horatio Alger, Jr. 4 vols. 16mo. Cloth, extra, black and gold . . . . . . . . 5 00

The Young Adventurer; or, Tom's Trip Across the Plains. Illustrated. 16mo. . . . . . . . . . . . 1 25

The Young Miner; or, Tom Nelson in California. Illustrated. 16mo. . . . . . . . . . . . . . . . 1 25

The Young Explorer; or, Among the Sierras. Illustrated. 16mo. . . . . . . . . . . . . . . . . . 1 25

Ben's Nugget; or, A Boy's Search for Fortune. A Story of the Pacific Coast. Illustrated. 16mo. . . . 1 25

**ATLANTIC SERIES.** By Horatio Alger, Jr. 4 vols. 16mo. Cloth, extra, black and gold. . . . . 5 00

The Young Circus Rider; or, The Mystery of Robert Rudd. Illustrated. 16mo. . . . . . . . . . 1 25

Do and Dare; or, A Brave Boy's Fight for Fortune. 16mo. . . . . . . . . . . . . . . . . . . . . . 1 25

Hector's Inheritance; or, Boys of Smith Institute. 16mo. . . . . . . . . . . . . . . . . . . . . . . 1 25

Helping Himself; or, Grant Thornton's Ambition. 16mo. . . . . . . . . . . . . . . . . . . . . . . 1 25

## NEW VOLUMES.

The Store Boy; or, The Fortunes of Ben Barclay. By Horatio Alger, Jr. Illustrated. 16mo. Cloth, extra, black and gold . . . . . . . . . . . . . . . 1 25

Bob Burton; or, The Young Ranchman of the Missouri. By Horatio Alger, Jr. Illustrated. 16mo. Cloth, extra, black and gold . . . . . . . . . . . 1 25

## By C. A. Stephens.

Rare books for boys—bright, breezy, wholesome and instructive; full of adventure and incident, and information upon natural history. They blend instruction with amusement—contain much useful and valuable information upon the habits of animals, and plenty of adventure, fun and jollity.

**CAMPING OUT SERIES.** By C. A. Stephens. In box containing the following. 6 vols. 16mo. Cloth, extra, black and gold . . . . . . . . . . . $7 50

**Camping Out.** As recorded by "Kit." With eight full-page illustrations. 16mo. . . . . . . . . . . 1 25

**Left on Labrador;** or, The Cruise of the Schooner Yacht "Curlew." As recorded by "Wash." With eight full-page illustrations. 16mo. . . . . . . . . 1 25

**Off to the Geysers;** or, The Young Yachters in Iceland. As recorded by "Wade." With eight full-page illustrations. 16mo. . . . . . . . . . . . . 1 25

**Lynx Hunting.** From Notes by the Author of "Camping Out." With eight full-page illustrations. 16mo. . . . . . . . . . . . . . . . . . . 1 25

**Fox Hunting.** As recorded by "Raed." With eight full-page illustrations. 16mo. . . . . . . . . . . 1 25

**On the Amazon;** or, the Cruise of the "Rambler." As recorded by, "Wash." With eight full-page illustrations. 16mo. . . . . . . . . . . . . . . . . 1 25

## By J. T. Trowbridge.

These stories will rank among the best of Mr. Trowbridge's books for the young—and he has written some of the best of our juvenile literature.

**JACK HAZARD SERIES.** By J. T. Trowbridge. In box containing the following. 6 vols. 16mo. Cloth, extra, black and gold . . . . . . . . . . . 7 50

**Jack Hazard and His Fortunes.** With twenty illustrations. 16mo. . . . . . . . . . . . . . . 1 25

**A Chance for Himself;** or, Jack Hazard and his Treasure. With nineteen illustrations. 16mo. . . . 1 25

**Doing His Best.** With twenty illustrations. 16mo. $1 25

**Fast Friends.** With seventeen illustrations. 16mo. 1 25

**The Young Surveyor;** or, Jack on the Prairies. With twenty-one illustrations. 16mo. . . . . . . . . 1 25

**Lawrence's Adventures Among the Ice Cutters,** Glass Makers, Coal Miners, Iron Men and Ship Builders. With twenty-four illustrations. 16mo. . . 1 25

## By Edward S. Ellis.

A New Series of Books for Boys, equal in interest to the "Castlemon" and "Alger" books. His power of description of Indian life and character is equal to the best of Cooper.

**BOY PIONEER SERIES.** By Edward S. Ellis. In box containing the following. 3 vols. Illustrated. Cloth, extra, black and gold . . . . . . . . . . . $3 75

**Ned in the Block House;** or, Life on the Frontier. Illustrated. 16mo. . . . . . . . . . . . . . . . 1 25

**Ned in the Woods.** A Tale of the Early Days in the West. Illustrated. 16mo. . . . . . . . . . . 1 25

**Ned on the River.** Illustrated. 16mo. . . . . . 1 25

**DEERFOOT SERIES.** By Edward S. Ellis. In box containing the following. 3 vols. Illustrated. 16mo. . . . . . . . . . . . . . . . . . . . . 3 75

**Hunters of the Ozark.** Illustrated. 16mo. . . . 1 25

**Camp in the Mountains.** Illustrated. 16mo. . . 1 25

**The Last War Trail.** Illustrated. 16mo. . . . . 1 25

**LOG CABIN SERIES.** By Edward S. Ellis. In box containing the following. 3 vols. Illustrated. 16mo. . . . . . . . . . . . . . . . . . . . . 3 75

**Lost Trail.** Illustrated. 16mo. . . . . . . . . . 1 25

**Camp-Fire and Wigwam.** Illustrated. 16mo. . 1 25

**Footprints in the Forest.** Illustrated. 16mo. . . 1 25

THE

# Fireside Encyclopaedia of Poetry

COLLECTED AND ARRANGED

By HENRY T. COATES.

---

27th edition, enlarged and thoroughly revised, and containing portraits of prominent American poets, with facsimiles of their handwriting.

---

| | |
|---|---|
| Imperial 8vo., cloth, extra, gilt side and edges | $5 00 |
| Half calf, gilt | 7 50 |
| Half morocco, antique, gilt edges | 7 50 |
| Turkey morocco, antique, full gilt edges | 10 00 |
| Tree calf | 12 00 |
| Plush, padded sides, nickel lettering | 14 00 |

The remarkable success that has attended the publication of "The Fireside Encyclopædia of Poetry"—26 editions having been printed—has induced the author to thoroughly revise it, and to make it in every way worthy of the high place it has attained. About one hundred and fifty new poems have been inserted, and the work now contains nearly fourteen hundred poems, representing four hundred and fifty authors, English and American. The work is now illustrated by finely-engraved portraits of many prominent poets, with their signatures and facsimiles of their handwriting.

---

# The Children's Book of Poetry.

Compiled by HENRY T. COATES.

With nearly 200 illustrations. The most complete collection of poetry for children ever published. 4to.

| | |
|---|---|
| Cloth, extra, gilt edges | 3 00 |
| Full Turkey morocco, gilt edges | 7 50 |

# THE HANDSOMEST AND CHEAPEST GIFT BOOKS.

## The "Bells" Series.

The "BELLS" Series has been undertaken by the publishers with a view to issue original illustrated poems of a high character, at a price within the reach of all classes.

Small 4to. Cloth, gilt edges . . . . . . . . . . . . . . . . . $1 50
Ivory surface . . . . . . . . . . . . . . . . . . . . . . . . 1 50
Embossed calf, gilt edges . . . . . . . . . . . . . . . . . . 1 50

### GEMS FROM TENNYSON.

By ALFRED TENNYSON. Elegantly illustrated by Hammatt Billings.

### BEAUTIES OF TENNYSON.

By ALFRED TENNYSON. Elegantly illustrated with twenty engravings, from original drawings by Frederic B. Schell. Beautifully printed on the finest plate paper.

### FROM GREENLAND'S ICY MOUNTAINS.

By BISHOP HEBER. Elegantly illustrated with twenty-two engravings, from original drawings by Frederic B. Schell. Beautifully printed on the finest plate paper.

### LADY CLARE.

By ALFRED TENNYSON. Elegantly illustrated with twenty-two engravings, from original drawings by Alfred Fredericks, F. S. Church, Harry Fenn, F. B. Schell, E. P. Garret and Granville Perkins. Beautifully printed on the finest plate paper.

### THE NIGHT BEFORE CHRISTMAS.

By CLEMENT C. MOORE. Never before has this popular poem—a favorite with both the old and the young—been presented in such a beautiful dress. It is elegantly illustrated with twenty-two engravings, from original drawings by F. B. Schell, W. T. Smedley, A. Fredericks and H. R. Poore.

### BINGEN ON THE RHINE.

By CAROLINE E. NORTON. Elegantly illustrated with twenty-two engravings, from original drawings by W. T. Smedley, F. B. Schell, A. Fredericks, Granville Perkins and E. P. Garrett.

### THE BELLS.

By EDGAR ALLAN POE. Elegantly illustrated with twenty-two engravings, from original drawings by F. O. C. Darley, A. Fredericks, Granville Perkins and others.

### THE DESERTED VILLAGE.

By OLIVER GOLDSMITH. Elegantly illustrated with thirty-five engravings, from drawings by Hammatt Billings.

### THE COTTER'S SATURDAY NIGHT.

By ROBERT BURNS. Elegantly illustrated with fifty engravings, from drawings by Chapman.

# Standard Histories.

**History of England, from the Accession of James the Second.** By Thomas Babington Macaulay. *Standard edition.* With a steel portrait of the author Printed from new electrotype plates from the last English edition. Being by far the most correct edition in the American market. 5 vols., 12mo. Cloth, extra, per set . . . . . . . . . . . $5 00
    Sheep, marbled edges, per set . . . . . . . . . 7 50
    Half Russia (imitation), marbled edges . . . . . 7 50
    Half calf, gilt . . . . . . . . . . . . . . . . . 10 00

**History of the Decline and Fall of the Roman Empire.** By Edward Gibbon. With notes by Rev. H. H. Milman. *Standard edition.* To which is added a complete Index of the work. A new edition from entirely new stereotype plates. With portrait on steel. 5 vols., 12mo. Cloth, extra, per set . . . . . 5 00
    Sheep, marbled edges, per set . . . . . . . . . 7 50
    Half Russia (imitation), marbled edges, . . . . . 7 50
    Half calf, gilt, per set . . . . . . . . . . . . . 10 00

**History of England, from the Invasion of Julius Cæsar to the Abdication of James the Second, 1688.** By David Hume. *Standard edition.* With the author's last corrections and improvements, to which is prefixed a short account of his life, written by himself. With a portrait on steel. A new edition from entirely new stereotype plates. 5 vols., 12mo. Cloth, extra, per set . . . . . . . . . 5 00
    Sheep, marbled edges, per set . . . . . . . . . 7 50
    Half Russia (imitation), marbled edges . . . . . 7 50
    Half calf, gilt . . . . . . . . . . . . . . . . . 10 00

# Miscellaneous.

**A Dictionary of the Bible.** Comprising its Antiquities, Biography, Geography, Natural History and Literature. Edited by William Smith, LL.D. Revised and adapted to the present use of Sunday-school Teachers and Bible Students by Revs. F. N. and M. A. Peloubet. With eight colored maps and 440 engravings on wood. 8vo. Cloth, extra . . . . . . $2 00
    Sheep, marbled edges . . . . . . . . . . . . . 3 00
    Half morocco, gilt top . . . . . . . . . . . . 3 50

**History of the Civil War in America.** By the Comte de Paris. Translated with the approval of the author. With maps faithfully engraved from the originals, and printed in three colors. 8vo.
    Cloth, extra, per vol. . . . . . . . . . . . . . 3 50
    Red cloth, extra, Roxburgh style, uncut edges, per vol. 3 50
    Sheep, library style, per vol. . . . . . . . . . . 4 50
    Half Turkey morocco, per vol. . . . . . . . . . 6 00
Volumes I, II, III and IV now ready, put up in a neat box, or any volume sold separately.

**The Battle of Gettysburg.** By the Comte de Paris. With maps. 8vo. Cloth, extra . . . . . . . . . 1 50

**Comprehensive Biographical Dictionary.** Embracing accounts of the most eminent persons of all ages, nations and professions. By E. A. Thomas. Crown 8vo.
    Cloth, extra, gilt top . . . . . . . . . . . . . 2 50
    Sheep, marbled edges . . . . . . . . . . . . . 3 00
    Half morocco, gilt top . . . . . . . . . . . . . 3 50
    Half Russia, gilt top . . . . . . . . . . . . . 4 50

**The Amateur Photographer.** A manual of photographic manipulations intended especially for beginners and amateurs, with suggestions as to the choice of apparatus and of processes. By Ellerslie Wallace, Jr., M.D. New edition, with two new chapters on paper negatives and microscopic photography. 12mo.
    Limp morocco, sprinkled edges . . . . . . . . . 1 00

www.ingramcontent.com/pod-product-compliance
Lightning Source LLC
Chambersburg PA
CBHW051735300426
44115CB00007B/578